The
Stiff Records
Story

By
Richard Balls

soundcheck books
the stories behind the sounds

First published in Great Britain in 2014
by Soundcheck Books LLP, 88 Northchurch Road, London, N1 3NY.

Copyright © Richard Balls 2014

ISBN: 978-0-9575700-6-1

CIP record for this book is available from the British Library

Book design: Benn Linfield (www.bennlinfield.com)

Cover picture credits: Graham Parker (Pictorial Press Ltd/Alamy),
Shane MacGowan & Cait O'Riordan (Pictorial Press Ltd/Alamy),
Suggs (SuperStock/Alamy), Elvis Costello, Nick Lowe, Wreckless Eric,
Larry Wallis, Ian Dury (Chris Gabrin/Redferns). Badges from Tony Judge's
collection, with permission from Stiff Records.

Printed by: Bell & Bain, Glasgow

For Anne, Katherine and Jessie

Acknowledgements

—

This book has been a labour of love and I've felt privileged to meet and speak with so many of those who made Stiff such an amazing label. Drinks with Shane MacGowan, a train ride with Rat Scabies, lunch in Soho with Ed Tudor Pole, and a wonderful afternoon in the company of Jona Lewie were just some of the highlights. And it's not every day you get the chance to chat with Lene Lovich and Wreckless Eric in your own sitting room.

Former artists and employees, some living abroad, shared their thoughts with me via Skype, phone or email as I attempted to get first-hand accounts from as many people involved with Stiff as possible. So, for kindly giving up their time to speak to me or answer questions, my thanks go to ...

Danny Adler, Gaye Advert, Jane Aire, Bob Andrews, Mark Bedford, Joe "King" Carrasco, Glen Colson, Paul Conroy, Alan Cowderoy, Dick Crippen, Nigel Dick, Barry Farmer, Chris Foreman, Mickey Gallagher, Barbara Gaskin, Greg Geller, Ian Gomm, Clive Gregson, Mike Herbage, Jakko Jakszyk, Brian James, Chaz Jankel, Mickey Jupp, Jona Lewie, Bob Lewis, Lene Lovich, Shane MacGowan, Jenny McKeown, Chris Morton, Marina Muhlfriedel, Andy Murray, Graham Parker, Davey Payne, Henry Priestman, Sonnie Rae, Paul Riley, Fred Rowe, TV Smith, Rat Scabies, Genevieve Schorr, Lesley Shone, Jamie Spencer, Liam Sternberg, Dave Stewart, Nick Stewart, Bruce Thomas, Pete Thomas, Philippa Thomas, Ed Tudor Pole, Sean Tyla, Larry Wallis, Dick Wingate, Wreckless Eric.

I am also indebted to others who have helped out with comments, information, interview assistance and general encouragement. They include: Vicky Ball, Mary Bird, John Blaney, Fran Burgess, Chris Butler, David Cooper, Richard Crouse, Adrian Evans, Stephen Flannery, Pete Gardiner, Steve Gedge, Lasse Karbakk, Edwin Pouncey, Stephen McCathie, Malcolm McGregor, Ian Peel, Peter Purnell, Paul Ronan, Paul Slattery, Tobbe Stuhre, Martin Talbot, Robert Webb.

Phil Godsell at Soundcheck Books has been extremely supportive and a pleasure to work with. His faith in this book has been unwavering and I am indebted to him and his wife Sue.

Very special thanks go to Tony Judge from www.bestiff.co.uk. A long-time collector and a mine of information, he supplied a vast amount of material, including original press cuttings, images and memorabilia, as well as the discography. He was incredibly generous with his time and without him the task would have been much harder.

Finally, I would like to thank my wife Anne, who now knows more than she ever wanted to know about Stiff Records, and also did some invaluable editing in the final stages.

Contents

—

Acknowledgements	vii
Prologue	xi
1. A Present For The Future	1
2. Undertakers To The Industry	28
3. Smash It Up	50
4. Elvis Is King	76
5. Whole Wide World	98
6. Dumping Music On The People ... In Your Town!	121
7. Be Stiff	146
8. Hit Me!	173
9. Nutty Boys	189
10. America Gets Stiff	207
11. Stop The Cavalry	227
12. Wunderbar	243
13. Sign Of The Times	264
14. Boys From The County Hell	280
15. Grey Day	299
Epilogue: Yesterday's Hits Today!	309
Discography	314
The Stiff Tours	330
Notes & Sources	334
Index	337
About The Author	343

Prologue

—

32 Alexander Street, London, W2

*1977. An office in a former house in Bayswater, now home to a small
record label. Inside is a garrulous Dubliner with scruffy hair, a couple
of women hard at work, and a boyish-looking singer called Wreckless
lounging in a chair. The door opens and a bloke comes in carrying
several large cardboard cut-outs of some of the label's exciting new
acts. One cut-out is of a nerdy, pigeon-toed singer with a sneer and a
Fender Jazzmaster.*

"Ah great, they're here. Great," says the Irishman. "Jesus, these are
pretty good. I love the one of Elvis. These look all right." Excitedly he
picks them up and admires them, before grabbing a hammer from a
drawer and climbing on a chair. "Hey Suzanne, would you pass me
a nail? I want to put these up. These are gonna look great up here."
Bemused at this sudden burst of activity, the singer looks on as the
giant shop displays are banged into place. "That's the sort of stupid
thing I'd do," he thinks to himself.

As the hammering goes on, a wild-eyed, intimidating figure bursts
in and looks up at the wall, horrified. "Yeah, we've got the displays,"
says the Irishman. "They're fucking great aren't they? Great."

"What the fuck?" yells the other guy. "What fucking moron did that?"
"Well we've got to put 'em up, Jake, you know?" he replies. "Put 'em
up? Do you want to see Elvis Costello with a fucking nail through his
head? I fucking don't." Jake then storms out of the office, slamming
the door behind him, and disappears along the busy London street.

A storm is brewing. Something is going to blow.

1

A Present For The Future

One word sums up why Stiff Records came into being: frustration. Frustration at the complacency of the UK music industry in the early seventies. Frustration that so many exhilarating groups and ingenious songwriters were being denied the audiences they deserved and were left hauling their gear from one pub to another. And frustration at the corporate major labels of the day, where the music itself had become an irrelevance.

Stiff's creators Dave Robinson and Jake Riviera were music freaks who felt an affinity with music's "square pegs". The whole situation made their blood boil. Record buyers were being shortchanged with substandard, unimaginative product, while self-important record company executives dined out on expense account lunches and dished out increasingly ludicrous advances to their stellar acts – some of whom they would never promote. And in an industry that wanted glitter and light entertainment, the prodigious singer-songwriters Robinson and Riviera spent their evenings being blown away by were seen as nothing more than social misfits who would never get anywhere. In pop's timeline, this was the period BS – Before Stiff. A futurescape where these old lags in musty clothes would be transformed into household names could only have been imagined by the deluded or the insane.

Any number of Irish expressions would have fitted Dave Robinson when he lived in his native Dublin. He'd have been seen as "an awful bleedin' chancer" or, better still, "a cute hoor". Full of chat and with charm to burn, he hadn't simply kissed the Blarney Stone; he'd practically swallowed it. But he wasn't just talk. He could sniff talent from a mile away, he knew how to get things moving and he was always looking ahead, trying to anticipate where things were going next. Throwing in the towel wasn't Dave Robinson; the word "can't" was simply not in his vocabulary.

Watson David Robinson (he opted to use his middle name) grew up in Dublin, on the city's northside. From a young age he sought out any opportunity to get involved in the music scene. A keen photographer, he had worked as a freelancer, taking pictures at gigs, and was among those who captured The Beatles at The Cavern in Liverpool. When a new club called Sound City opened up beneath a slot machine arcade on Dublin's Burgh Quay, he produced posters to help promote it. So, when The Rolling Stones arrived for their first tour of Ireland in January 1965, Robinson was drawn to them like a moth to the flame.

Jagger and co. were in town to play the Adelphi cinema in Middle Abbey Street and had holed themselves up in the Intercontinental Hotel in Ballsbridge (now Jurys). No interviews were to be given to the media – something Robinson and a teen magazine named *Miss* viewed merely as a challenge. As Robinson had recently returned to Dublin from London, where he had got to know the Stones' manager Andrew Loog Oldham, the magazine saw him as its "secret weapon". So, with a journalist and photographer in tow in the hotel lobby he managed to sweet talk the receptionist to put a call through to his contact on the top floor.

Initially, the band's manager stuck to the "no interview" policy. Cannily, however, Robinson had sent ahead a copy of *Miss* in which the reporter had come down firmly on the side of The Beatles, in the great "Beatles vs. Stones" debate of the day. Worse still, the *Miss* reporter had said Jagger couldn't sing. When the Stones heard the offending reporter was in the lobby, they were summoned up and a bad-tempered exchange of views ensued. It stopped short of coming to blows, although it got nasty. Keith Richards was angry at the part of the article where the author claimed the Stones' previous show at the Adelphi had been tame compared to that of The Beatles in November 1963 and he had to be restrained by the others after telling the journalist, "I've got a good mind to give you a bust in the snot". No scoop then, but it was Robinson's contacts and nerve that had got them into the band's inner sanctum. The opportunistic "Dub" had quickly learned the importance of knowing the right people and being in the right place. It was a skill he would exhibit again and again during his colourful career at Stiff.

In the mid-sixties Van Morrison returned to his native Belfast, disillusioned with the manipulative nature of the music business, which he blamed for the breakup of his group Them. As the unsettled troubadour pondered his next move, Robinson befriended him, road-testing his managerial skills for the first time. During this period, "beat groups" were proving a phenomenon on both sides of the Irish border – in the cities, at least.

From the early sixties right through to the end of the decade, bands emerging from this exciting scene were all the rage, sending wide-eyed youngsters into delirium and God-fearing mammies into shock. Groups like Bluesville, The Greenbeats and The Chosen Few turned pubs and other intimate venues "black" (Dublin slang for packed) and served up a live music experience that must have seemed positively dangerous. Back then, the showbands had a well-established hold on the music scene, particularly in towns and rural areas, and the Catholic Church had an iron grip on the people. Beat clubs sprang out of nowhere, like Sound City in Dublin, its sign declaring: "For pretty young people only".

But Robinson really began to launch his reputation when he teamed up with a beat/soul group from Belfast which would make a significant impression in Dublin. The People had emerged from the embers of The Telstars and moved across the Irish Sea to set up in Blackpool for a while, before guitarist Henry McCullough (later in Wings) suggested there was more money to be made in Dublin. Fronted by high-pitched singer Ernie Graham, who would later release a one-off solo record on Stiff, they proved popular in this new wave of clubs. They performed at the opening night of Club A-Go-Go, "Limerick's Exclusive Beat Club" in the summer of 1966. They also featured on the compilation album *Ireland's Greatest Sounds*, released earlier the same year. By the time they relocated to London the following spring, Robinson was no longer managing them, and things got off to a slow start in the capital. But all that changed when they ran into him again and he offered to drum up a couple of gigs. True to his word, he booked them to play The Speakeasy and the UFO Club, a chemically-enhanced late-night hang out, where bands stared out from the stage at people sitting or lying on the floor, tripping out to the drugs, hypnotic light shows and music. The UFO was based in an Irish showband-style ballroom called The Blarney Club beneath a cinema in Tottenham Court Road, which must have made Robinson feel at home.

The People must have needed matchsticks to prop their eyes open as they waited to go on. Agent Tony Howard had come up with the idea of a "milkman's matinee" audition slot at 5am and The People were one of the first acts to fill it. But the arrangements hadn't been made clear to Robinson and he was put out when he heard. He bowled up at 11pm "all anxious and speedy," recalled Joe Boyd, one of the club's co-founders. "He thought the starting time on the contract must be a misprint: they were outside in the van and ready to go on straight away. I explained the deal to him and his face fell. He asked for the £5 fee in advance and I said they had to play first. I did agree to his last request: that someone bang on the side of their van at 4.30am as an alarm call. They had no money in the intervening period to do anything but sleep." [1]

In the event, the timing of the show could not have been better. The People ended up going on after Procol Harum, whose "A Whiter Shade Of Pale" had been released that day (12 May 1967). More significantly still, one of the industry's most influential movers and shakers was in the audience. Mike Jeffery, along with former Animals bassist Chas Chandler, managed The Jimi Hendrix Experience, and had just signed up Soft Machine. Boyd says Jeffery, who stood out like a sore thumb dressed in a shirt and tie, might have left before the end if he hadn't tipped him off that an Irish blues band was due on at 5am. His decision to stay was a turning point for The People, and Robinson couldn't believe their Irish luck.

"Because we'd had such a good night, I gave their manager [Robinson] two crisp £5 notes," remembered Joe Boyd. "A few minutes later he sought me out again. 'Look Joe, can you give me a hand? There's some nutter in the dressing room upsetting the lads. He says he manages Jimi Hendrix and he wants them to open for him on a tour to America. Will you help me get rid of the guy?' When I told him that Jeffery actually did manage Hendrix, he looked at me for a second, then dashed back to the tiny dressing room." [1]

For Jeffery, there was an added incentive for signing The People – their passports. He needed a band to support Hendrix on dates in America and, because they were Irish, they fell outside the Musicians' Union exchange programme. This meant he wouldn't have to find US musicians to play an equal number of shows in Britain to get the required permits. He snapped up the band and someone – reportedly Jeffery's wife – came up with the new name of Eire Apparent. When it was suggested they get a personal manager, the group opted for Robinson.

So, by November 1967, a band that a few months earlier had been kipping in a van found themselves on a two-month UK package tour featuring Hendrix, The Move, Pink Floyd, The Nice, Amen Corner and Outer Limits. The following year they toured North America with The Animals and then with Hendrix and Soft Machine, and Hendrix also produced their album *Sunrise*. Still only in his 20s, Robinson became part of Hendrix's inner circle, sharing flats in London with both him and bass player Noel Redding, road managing the band and touring extensively with them before the guitarist's death in 1970. In a surviving photograph taken in a studio or rehearsal space, a frizzy-haired Robinson, in a cheesecloth shirt and black waistcoat, can be seen standing behind Hendrix as he sits and plays. These were heady times and the cocky Dubliner made sure he was in the thick of it.

As well as being persuasive and well connected in the business, Robinson was also ambitious, and by the tail end of 1969 he was ready to move up a level. For all manner of reasons, the management agency he helped to launch was to leave an indelible mark. At the time, the Bryan Morrison Agency was one of the most successful music publishers and booking agents around and Eire Apparent were on its books. As a result, Robinson was a regular visitor to its offices and the secretary there caught his eye. His charm and way with words won her over and he was soon making nocturnal calls to the house she shared in Barnes, climbing in through her bedroom window.

Dorothy Burn-Forti had at one time done some modelling and was married to the actor Jonathan Burn-Forti who had done television work and featured in the musical *Hair*. By now the couple had separated and "Dot" was living in the house of John Eichler, his wife Sue and daughter Sara. Eichler, rather like Elvis Costello some years later, worked for a cosmetics firm, but dreamt of being in the music business. The arrival of Robinson, emboldened by his days on the road with Hendrix, only whetted his appetite. And when Dot was faced with redundancy because of changes at the agency, she, Eichler and Robinson began plotting their own management venture – Famepushers.

At the outset, the only acts on its roster were former Eire Apparent vocalist Ernie Graham and Help Yourself, a group formed by musicians Malcolm Morley and Richard Treece. But when the company secured some financial backing, Robinson seized the initiative taking out an advertisement in the classifieds of *Melody Maker*. "Young Progressive Management Company require Young Songwriting Group with own equipment." The response was overwhelming. More than 80 cassette tapes hit the doormat, including one from a curiously named group from Tunbridge Wells – Brinsley Schwarz. Although the label was not even a glint in Robinson's eye, a crucial Stiff connection was about to be made.

The group had originally been named Kippington Lodge, after the family home (in Kent) of band member Brinsley Schwarz. One of their first managers, John Schofield, had been in a relationship with actress Hattie Jacques, who is said to have occasionally made bacon sandwiches for them when they visited his home. Singles were released on EMI, but their pop songs and line in frilly shirts failed to get them noticed. The scene was frankly awash with bands like them and they needed the help of someone with business knowhow and managerial nous. Replying to Famepushers' small ad was a no-brainer.

Brinsley Schwarz may have looked like the embodiment of the *Old Grey Whistle Test*, with their beards and lumberjack shirts, but from Robinson's perspective they had a number of things going for them. For starters, they had a van and their own equipment, which saved Famepushers from forking out money to set them up. Their wheels and gear also meant he could start touting for bookings from the off and begin spreading the word through the growing live scene.

But Robinson had spotted the most important asset of all – a songwriter, in the shape of one Nicholas Drain Lowe. However, "It was very difficult to get the band off the ground, to get a good record deal, the album publicised and so on," he said. "I remember offering people the band for nothing … I even offered to pay them money, but they'd just say 'Brinsley Schwarz? Bollocks!'" [3]

Desperate times called for desperate measures and Robinson's response epitomised the bullish attitude and determination to get noticed at any cost, for which Stiff would become famous. A publicity stunt was needed – something that no one would be able to ignore. "I'd written this number called 'Ballad Of A Has Been Beauty Queen' and they were going to get all these old beauty queens at the Festival Hall for some complicated extravaganza," said Lowe. "Then someone came up with the idea of getting a gig in America and flying all the press over for it. It was psychologically good, because nobody's going to be impressed with a new band at The Speakeasy, but they would be with a weekend in America." [4]

Robinson didn't just land them any American show. Incredibly, he booked them as support to Van Morrison and Quicksilver Messenger Service at the Fillmore East on New York's Second Avenue. The high profile shows would take place on 3 and 4 April 1970 – with two houses per night – and scores of rock scribblers would be flown over and given the freeloading weekend of a lifetime. Brinsley Schwarz would be paid at union rates of $77 per hour for their warm-up slots at the prestigious venue.

So, how had Robinson managed to bag such a deal for his relative unknowns? "Robbo was hassling Bill Graham and Graham said, 'Hey listen. The next time you're in town, come and see me and maybe we'll do something'," says Jakko Jakszyk (real name Michael Lee Curran), who signed to Stiff in the early eighties. "And Dave got the next plane out and just turned up on his doorstep, and Bill Graham was so freaked out that somebody would do that, he gave them a gig!"

From the outset, Operation Brinsley was beset with problems. Arthur Lee's Love had been due to play in the UK as the other element of the exchange insisted on by the Musicians' Union agreement. But when they pulled out, the Brinsleys were refused their US paperwork and Lowe's minor conviction for possession of cannabis only made things more difficult. But Robinson was nothing if not resourceful. He decided that keyboard player Bob Andrews, Lowe, and Schwarz should fly into Toronto and put in for visas when they got there. Drummer Billy Rankin had American citizenship, so he could fly straight there and wait for the others. Robinson's powers of persuasion were put to the test, but after a few days visas were granted, only for an airport strike to leave them stranded. A small plane had to be hired to get them out and the super-strong joints they were handed as they stepped into the awaiting limousines at an airstrip in Queens must have seemed like the most welcome ever. They sat back getting stoned while the driver tore through the Manhattan traffic. They got to the Fillmore with just 30 minutes to spare.

The press had suffered a similar experience – completing what seemed like a comedy of errors. Their flight from London had been delayed by hours, and when they finally made it into the air they had been diverted to Ireland. When they landed several hours later, vast quantities of drink and drugs had been consumed and they slumped into their seats the worse for wear. At one point, Bill Graham was spitting feathers and had threatened to dump Brinsley Schwarz off the bill and Robinson had to go nose-to-nose with the formidable promoter until he agreed to let them play, delaying the start of the first show so the journalists would actually get to see them.

Predictably, the band were slaughtered by the media and the whole sorry saga became a PR fiasco against which all others would be measured. Robinson, a keen gambler, had, in effect, played roulette with the band's future. By putting the name Brinsley Schwarz up in lights in New York City and foretelling of a musical second coming, the group had to be right on the money come the time. They weren't and the scale of the fanfare heralding their arrival made their fall all the greater.

"It was an attitude we all got," said Robinson. "We got fed up with the idea. You'd go along with what people think you should do, something special, something unusual, and then they'd turn on you. A lot of those people didn't even see the gig who wrote those bad comments. They didn't get in because everything was delayed. The plane was delayed and crash-landed at Shannon Airport, so by the time people got there, 'A' they were drunk and 'B' they didn't want to go to a gig, they wanted to go to a hotel. They treated it like a jolly rather than paying attention and seeing what the band were like." [2]

Some good came of the Fillmore East debacle. A record deal for the USA was negotiated with Capitol Records and Robinson managed to get some publishing money, which was used to pay off creditors in New York. Some gigs were also booked on the back of it and, rather than being deflated by the experience, he was spurred on, determined to turn it to his and the band's advantage. Such ebullience and dogged determination would come to define his Stiff tenure.

"It was a huge success," he said philosophically. "Here was a little band from Tunbridge Wells that was going nowhere. They say any publicity is good publicity, that's not always strictly true, but we did a lot of things off the back of that. And eventually the attitude of turning your back a little bit on the major record companies caused us to start the pubs and that whole thing going. It had an effect." [2]

Robinson may have lost face, but he still had more front than Brighton and he put this to use with immediate effect. After a showdown with business consultant Edward Molton, who he discovered was operating under a false name, he had pulled out of Famepushers and taken what money there was with him. It was decided that the Brinsleys would move lock, stock and barrel and live under one roof; families, dogs and all. Their ever-resourceful manager got roadie Malcolm Addison on the case who identified a large property with a garage for £40 a week, a rent they could afford with their regular gigs.

Much of their time in the first year after the Fillmore East debacle was spent rehearsing and hanging out with their manager's other charges Ernie Graham and Help Yourself. In 1971, in an early indication of Robinson's interest in package tours, he put all three out on the road together under the banner of the Down Home Rhythm Kings (Famepushers had now been replaced by Down Home Ltd). In the same year, the Brinsleys and Help Yourself also backed Graham on his self-titled solo album, and appeared on the bill at the second Glastonbury Fayre festival, alongside David Bowie, Traffic and Hawkwind.

What hadn't killed them had made them stronger, and Brinsley Schwarz were to emerge from their new headquarters with renewed vigour. Rhythm guitarist Ian Gomm had been recruited with the aim of filling out the group's sound on stage, and in awe of The Band's eponymous second album and unapologetically raw, bluesy songs, they abandoned their post-psychedelic pop leanings in favour of a more rootsy sound. Brinsley Schwarz began writing and playing infectious new songs such as "Country Girl", a regular crowd pleaser.

Robinson was never off-duty, his mind constantly whirring. When he caught an American three-piece outfit, Eggs Over Easy, at the Marquee in Wardour Street, he saw a golden opportunity. Blown away by their musicianship and bright and breezy style, he made a beeline for the dressing room after the show. They reminded him of the country rock group Clover, he said. And, in true Robinson style, he invited them there and then to drive out to Northwood, North West London, where the Brinsleys communal home was situated.

"The penny just dropped, it was one of those things," said Robinson. "Bands in those days did very long, prog rock because that's what was required to be able to play the universities and everyone was smoking an awful lot of dope, so their music was a bit boring and long. Here was a band playing three-minute numbers, some of them covers, but with a certain kind of attitude which I had thought all along was how it should be. So here was somebody who could demonstrate that it was a worker, that it sounded great." [2]

Pub rock would become as British as a pork pie and a pint of ale, but much of the music was inspired by groups from the other side of the

Atlantic such as The Band and Little Feat. Indeed, Eggs Over Easy was the US band that laid its foundations here. They had been sharing a house in Kentish Town and wandered into a nearby local, The Tally Ho, which had a jazz-only policy. To get the gig, they pretended to the landlord they played jazz, but he didn't mind when they began drawing large crowds. Among those who got wind of this accomplished American group playing a mixture of their own material and covers were musicians like Lowe, Graham Parker, and an unknown singer called Declan MacManus, later to become Elvis Costello. So knocked out was former Tally Ho jazz player Barry Richardson that he formed Bees Make Honey, who would also end up getting a residency at the pub.

Rather than trying to book the Brinsleys into ever bigger and better known venues, Robinson wanted to do something much more rewarding and, ultimately, more powerful. He wanted to create a buzz. The laid-back, good time music played by Eggs Over Easy, Brinsley Schwarz, Bees Make Honey, and other acts was perfect to drink to. Also, with the audiences practically standing on top of the groups, there was an intensity that was noticeably lacking in the university halls and other big venues. In turn, the bands fed off the excitement of these beery, smoke-filled rooms. They played out of their skins, sweat dripping down their faces.

The UK charts must have seemed a world away for pub rock bands as they unloaded their gear from vans outside The Nashville Rooms in Kensington, The Greyhound in Fulham, and The Red Cow on Hammersmith Road. But not Robinson. He knew this was just the kind of scene in which the Brinsleys and others could thrive. The more pubs that could be persuaded to join the network of pulsating live music instead of soporific jazz evenings, the more options there would be for the groups. What Robinson couldn't have known then was that he was helping lay the ground for a revolutionary record label and a counterculture that would challenge the status quo.

From 1971 to 1973, the Brinsleys pounded the pub circuit and built a loyal following. But financially they had little to show for their efforts, the day-to-day running of the band accounting for most of the money they earned. The lease was almost up on the house in Northwood and frustration was setting in.

Momentarily, a light appeared on the horizon. The band were booked to play a benefit gig at the Hard Rock Café in London, with Wings on the same bill. This led to an invitation to join Paul McCartney and his group as the support on a national tour. There was a *caveat*, however, and

Robinson wasn't happy about it. Wings' manager Vince Romeo said the Brinsleys would have to pay for the privilege and, although the publicity could be worth its weight in gold, Robinson was adamant they couldn't afford it. He would have to pull a string and he knew just where. Wings' then guitarist Henry McCullough had been in Eire Apparent back in the days when Robinson managed them. Not only did the Irishman's persuasiveness get them out of having to pay, Romeo also agreed to give them £125 per night and they could travel on McCartney's tour bus. Even better from a financial perspective, the tour schedule meant they could fit in some of their previously arranged gigs, going on at 7.30pm for their support slot and then heading off for their own headline shows.

But things were unravelling and the band's relationship with their manager was becoming fractious. Robinson was driven and was frustrated at what he saw as a lackadaisical approach on their part. Warming up audiences for Wings was a gilt-edged opportunity and Nick Lowe wandering on stage halfway through the set at the Liverpool Empire because he'd gone for a drink sent out entirely the wrong message. It was now clear to Robinson that as well as being able to write their own songs and cut it on stage, bands under his control would also need to share his ambition. Robinson said:

I was frustrated, not at the lack of success, but at the lack of work. They could have worked harder and as a result they would have got further. That was my attitude and there was no point me killing myself if they weren't going to. I'd spent four years being at every gig, getting up and being in the office every day trying to move the thing forward. There comes a point when you think, you know, if you're into it, let's do it; if you're not into it ... the Wings tour was where I realised that Paul McCartney, who didn't need to, was still working very hard, and at sound checks trying to polish the music, trying to get it to be better, and my lot were in the pub. [2]

Bob Andrews says: "I think Dave left at the Liverpool gig when Nick failed to turn up for the set and I played bass. Funnily enough, someone sent me a bootleg of that concert, and it was, 'Well we can't seem to find the bass player. Anyway, here we are, Bob's going to play bass,' and then Mr Lowe sheepishly comes on halfway through the set. I think that was the night Dave said, 'I'm not going to be doing this anymore with you guys'. We were all down the pub, probably, but some of us had watches!"

The tour ended at Newcastle Odeon on 10 July 1973 and, incredibly, the pub rockers had been offered a US tour with Elton John starting on 15 August, but they had passed it up. Most bands and their managers would have bitten John's arm off, especially given his increasing profile at the time. Instead, it seems they sat agonising over the pros and cons of this offer, before deciding to turn it down. The Sutherland Brothers went instead and went on to become successful. Andrews recalled the group not wanting to play to Elton John's audience and Rankin felt they were a bit too philosophical for their own good. But Schwarz himself has said it was on Robinson's advice they decided against it.

Whatever the reasoning for the decision not to tour with "Rocket Man", as he enjoyed the most critically acclaimed period of his career, Robinson and the group he had spent four years managing parted company. By the time viewers of the *Old Grey Whistle Test* tuned in to see Brinsley Schwarz, complete with Nick Lowe's short haircut and protruding ears, performing "Surrender To The Rhythm" that autumn, their long-time Irish mentor was gone.

Chance connections and friendships litter the road to Stiff, moments in time without which it would probably never have happened. Entering the story is Charlie Gillett. A presenter on BBC Radio London, he not only lived and breathed popular music, but had an encyclopedic knowledge of it. The living room of his home in Clapham, South London, was ceiling to floor with records on all sides, and boxes of tapes, CDs and other pop paraphernalia covered much of the floor space. A man of eclectic tastes, he always kept his ear to the ground and he was respected as one of pub rock's most ardent ambassadors.

Honky Tonk was a 45-minute show broadcast every Sunday morning and anyone wanting the lowdown on the London music scene, particularly anything out of the ordinary, knew to listen in. Gillett would play records, interview people and highlight forthcoming gigs around the capital. Musicians already on the circuit, and those looking to join bands, were among those who regularly tuned in. Aside from presenting his radio show, Charlie and a dentist friend of his, Gordon Nelki, had been toying with the idea of establishing their own record label. The duo had recently returned to the UK from Louisiana in an almost evangelical mood about Cajun records, which they had picked up. Unable to find a taker for the New Orleans compilation they had envisaged, they discussed putting it out themselves. But a sequence of events that led to the very roots of Stiff diverted them.

In November 1972, a Bohemian group who looked like they were on day release from an institution wandered into the fashionable West End joint The Speakeasy, the favoured haunt of rock glitterati. Inside, Leo Sayer was rehearsing. The band asked if they could play and were given a gig for £15. The date they were given could not have been better. Keith Moon and Pete Townshend were both in the club that night, as were two other lesser-known faces who the singer later recalled were "looning about" – Dave Robinson and Nick Lowe. The group on stage was Ian Dury's Kilburn And The High Roads. Dave Robinson had been left gobsmacked, not only by the band's bizarre look, but also their extraordinary set, which somehow fused reggae, calypso and rock 'n' roll, with Tommy Cooper-esque theatrics.

During the interval, he banged on the dressing room door and implored the singer to get involved in the pub circuit. Although it was not a scene they were particularly enamoured with, the Kilburns needed the dough and decided to give it a whirl. Robinson hooked them up with Martyn Smith from Iron Horse, a booking agency for major pubs, and a date at The Tally Ho was set. Things got off to a slow start, but built gradually, and they began regularly playing The Kensington, The Cock and other pubs on the beery merry-go-round Robinson had cranked into life.

It was spring 1973 and Robinson was still managing Brinsley Schwarz and trying to spread the word about what was happening in the back rooms of London boozers. Pub rock was, by and large, esoteric, certainly to those who found out about music via the BBC radio stations. So, Robinson phoned Gillett and said he liked what he was playing on his radio show, and arranged to call round and see him. As it happened, the voice of *Honky Tonk* had already been alerted to the strange and mysterious ways of the Kilburns. Steve Nugent was an American student living in London who had written a piece about the group for *Let It Rock* magazine and had clearly spoken with Dury. The group would, he wrote, "like to have their own villain to look after their interests". Nugent, who had effectively placed an advertisement for someone to manage the band, had got in touch with Gillett and recommended them to him. Gillett didn't follow up this tip-off, but when Robinson paid a visit, he became curious.

Gillett said:

What he was doing was going to places where somebody might have jazz on a Saturday evening or a Sunday lunchtime and saying, "You've got nothing happening here Tuesday nights, let me bring a band in here. I take any money on the door, you get increased bar takings and we're both happy". So, mainly he wanted me as a DJ with my own radio show to be mentioning these gigs. That was the purpose of the visit really. But in passing he said, there's a band who I think you should go and see. I think you'll really like them. Even then I didn't go straight away, but the two of them were both saying the same thing and eventually I went to see Kilburn And The High Roads playing at The Tally Ho in Kentish Town. [6]

Gillett responded with wonder and disbelief in equal measure. Here was a group who looked like "they just met at a bus stop", representing an unusually wide age range, and with a singer and drummer who were both disabled. Their choice of covers was nothing short of bizarre: "Tallahassee Lassie" by Freddy Cannon; "The Walk" by Jimmy McCracklin; "Twenty Tiny Fingers" by Alma Cogan. The saxophone player, who had wild, staring eyes, would suddenly go off on an Albert Ayler-style free jazz solo, leaving Gillett – and probably his bandmates – unsure of what was going to happen next. As for Dury, he cut a disturbing, almost villainous figure and some of his material was decidedly near the knuckle. "The singer was saying all sorts of vaguely scurrilous things between the songs and the lyrics … 'I'll have you down behind the bike shed' and 'when I was 16 I wore a black drape jacket, sideboards to my chin'," recalled Gillett. [6]

Immediately he urged his *Honky Tonk* listeners to go and see this crazed musical phenomenon and, after seeing them for the third or fourth time, Dury took him aback by asking him to manage them. Despite being complete novices in this side of the business, he and Nelki agreed to take them on, with Robinson lending a helping hand.

But while they were getting to grips with the vagaries of management, Robinson had his own project on the go. After his split from Brinsley Schwarz he had moved into The Hope & Anchor, a large traditional pub in Islington, North London, run by an acquaintance, Fred Grainger. The cellar had a small space where Grainger had initially put on jazz, folk and blues and then bands from the emerging pub scene. In the summer of 1974, it hosted a pub rock festival, organised by Robinson.

Both the landlord and Robinson could see the benefit of having not only a venue downstairs, but a small studio upstairs in what had been a function room. The landlord ripped out the glass surrounding the room and replaced it with a brick wall, and Robinson went off in search of some equipment. Ever the wheeler-dealer, he discovered Decca Studios was throwing out valve desks that had been used to record The Rolling Stones among others, and picked these up cheaply, along with equipment used by The Beatles at Abbey Road. After a year of hammering, welding and cursing, Robinson had proudly put together his own eight-track recording studio. What was laid down on the machines there over the next couple of years was, in effect, the foundations of Stiff Records and what would become known as the "new wave".

Just as Grainger had envisioned, the Hope & Anchor had become a hotbed of activity and a place for people to crash. And it was here that one of the tightest and most exciting groups of the period was assembled. Drummer Steve Goulding and bassist Andrew Bodnar joined forces with Brinsley Schwarz and Bob Andrews from the Brinsleys and guitarist Martin Belmont, who was living at the Hope and co-running the bar. The result was Bontemps Roulez, a band that played the kind of energetic rhythm and blues that Robinson craved and, propitiously, Robinson had been introduced to unknown singer songwriter Graham Parker, who was desperate to form his own band.

An angular 24-year-old, he was working as a petrol pump attendant in Surrey and barely knew about the pub rock scene, never mind being part of it. As a live performer, he was pretty green when compared to Dury, Lowe, Costello and others who'd been traipsing around the circuit for years, but he had no shortage of confidence; quite the reverse. Utterly convinced by the quality of his songs, he believed it was a question of when – and not if – he would be discovered.

Although not part of any scene, pub rock or otherwise, and living in the suburbs, Parker had been to see the Naughty Rhythms Tour in 1975 (the brainchild of Jake Riviera, more of this anon) and had been captivated. The sight and sound of sharp looking bands with short hair, giving off the energy and feel of soul and R&B, confirmed he was on the right track. It was when the strains of Motown, Van Morrison and The Rolling Stones emanated from the radio that Graham Parker got goose bumps. Longhaired musicians who were into prog were no use to him. What he needed were the kind of players he had seen in

Dr. Feelgood and Chilli Willi on the Naughty Rhythms tour the year previously, and it was through the latter's slide guitarist Noel Brown that he got the break he wanted.

Brown answered an advert Parker had placed in the *Melody Maker* and then introduced him to another ex-Chilli, Paul "Bassman" Riley. The three began jamming together and there was no doubt in their minds that his songs were strong. Instinctively, however, Riley knew it would take someone with real vision to see how to play this wild card.

"Paul Riley introduced me to Dave Robinson," remembers Parker. "He said, 'You've got to meet this guy, he manages Brinsley Schwarz', whose name I'd seen in the paper in the gig guide. So, he heard my stuff and I think the lights went off. It was like, 'This guy is not part of the pub rock scene or anything'. All those bands had broken up, like Ducks Deluxe, Ian Dury could play to a half-filled pub. Nick Lowe was in remission or something, there was no career. All I knew about Nick Lowe when Dave said, 'He's going to be your producer', was that he had made a record called "We Love You Bay City Rollers" under the name The Tartan Horde. So, I thought he was a bad novelty writer.

"But then Dave said he [Lowe] was in Brinsley Schwarz. Okay, I don't know about them ever, but I know Brinsley is a fucking good guitarist because we'd rehearsed and I thought I'd never played with anybody this good and they understood what I was doing. I was in the suburbs where people were still into Uriah Heep. Don't get me wrong, I was a hippie a year before I got a record deal and I was into King Crimson and the Floyd. But I knew there was something else and that's how I started to formulate my songs using soul, the Stones and all those influences. So this is all going on, I meet Dave Robinson, the lights go off, he thinks I might be the new Bob Dylan or something. He starts recording me in the Hope & Anchor."

The results were incredible. From the moment he heard the tapes, Robinson knew Parker was hot property and jumped into action. He took a handful of demos by various artists produced in the small studio to Charlie Gillett and, for him, only one song stood out – "Between You And Me" by Graham Parker. When he played it on his show the following week, Phonogram A&R man Nigel Grainge called him up and said he wanted to sign him. With a deal in the bag for his prized new asset, Robinson then showed that not only could he spot a talented songwriter and performer, but he could bring them together with the right musicians. Wheedling away at the Hope &

Anchor, he choreographed one of rock's most pulsating groups ever, uniting Andrews, Bodnar, Goulding and Belmont as his new backing band. Graham Parker & The Rumour was born.

"Suddenly, where it normally takes forever, within the period of a week there was an offer from Phonogram Records to sign Graham Parker to a record deal," said Robinson. "He had a kind of vision in his own mind about how it was going to be and I think we fitted that vision. He thought it would be this easy. He believed he was so good he would be discovered quickly and, as it turns out, he was." [7]

Parker's take on it is: "I just had this confidence and this complete bullshit front that I was the man and that was what I needed. I had to do that because otherwise I'd be, not a shy person pathologically, but it's very hard to stick yourself out there. I had no experience, I had never played in bands. People say, 'Oh, you were in lots of pub bands'. No, I wasn't … Dave got hold of me and took me away from Paul Bassman and organised this band around me. He saw that band. He knew them all, he'd worked with them, he'd managed them, whatever. He knew Steve and Andrew, these really young guys who could play reggae, they could play soul. They'd hardly done any gigs. They had Bontemps Roulez, which I'm not sure did any gigs. But they were obviously ace and they could play my stuff."

The successful outcome of Graham Parker's sessions at the Hope & Anchor did, however, end his new manager's time there. Fred Grainger had reportedly been kept out of the studio when Parker was recording and assured by Robinson he was simply trying things out with a few people and nothing of note was occurring. When Nick Lowe let slip what was really happening and that Parker had a deal, Grainger was livid and a bust up followed. Robinson moved out and the studio was dismantled and sold off. As for the recordings made at the pub during Robinson's tenure, Grainger approached Jonathan King at UK Records, but Robinson is said to have been opposed to any such deal.

To say there were undiscovered gems contained in those reels of tape would be an understatement. The recordings may have been basic, but one singer's thought-provoking lyrics and a voice that could kill a room stone dead made him stand out. An utterly captivating performer, Elvis Costello would very soon breathe life into Stiff Records and, unintentionally, cast a shadow over the career of Graham Parker in the same moment.

In 1974, Costello was still Declan MacManus, the singer in Flip City, a country tinged, five-piece outfit that had embraced London's happening pub circuit. He cut a slight and rather earnest figure, with his thin-rimmed glasses and dark, neck-length hair. At a time when the preening peacocks of glam rock were strutting their sequined stuff, his stage wear was dungarees or turned up jeans and a check shirt – more *The Waltons* than *Top Of The Pops*.

MacManus had taken his first hesitant steps as a performer with Rusty, a Merseyside folk group that had begun as a three-piece and downsized to a duo. They wore their musical hearts on their sleeves, playing covers like "Dance Dance Dance" by Neil Young and "I've Been Working" by Van Morrison, as well as airing their own compositions. But other records in Costello's diverse vinyl collection signalled a pull towards the more esoteric lyricists emerging from America: Jesse Winchester, Randy Newman, Hoagy Carmichael, Loudon Wainwright and David Ackles.

One of Rusty's dates in the capital in 1972 was supporting Ralph McTell, Bridget St John and Swan Arcade at the Troubadour in South Kensington. Making the most of their weekend trip, they took in an all-night show by American underground figure Lou Reed and also Brinsley Schwarz, whose third album *Silver Pistol* had just been released. It was a defining moment for the young musician and his obsession with that record was demonstrated when four tracks from it and eight in total by the Brinsleys featured in Rusty's last ever show. MacManus became a regular face at their gigs and even went on to roadie for them. Naturally, Nick Lowe carried a certain cachet for the young musician. So, when he got chatting to him over a pint in The Grapes, a pub in Liverpool across the road from The Cavern Club, where Brinsley Schwarz were playing that night, the reverberations were to be long-lasting.

"When we've worked together, it's been 'I can't see what's so difficult about it, it's just four chords' – and he'd bang them out. He always had that attitude – it was quite a revelation to me," said Costello. [8]

By the time he popped up in London in Flip City, country was firmly on the MacManus agenda. Like so many, he had heard and fallen in love with The Byrds' landmark album *Sweetheart Of The Rodeo* and tracing its musical genealogy had signposted him to Gram Parsons and then to George Jones and Merle Haggard. He was immersing himself in Americana and the band made no secret of the template they were trying to follow. They even moved into a house together, hoping to emulate the Brinsleys' communal living arrangements and The Band's world famous homestead, The Big Pink. For the young musician making increasingly frequent trips from Liverpool to London, the genuine soul and good-time vibe of the Brinsleys and other protagonists of pub rock was contagious. Somehow it vindicated the discomfort he felt at the bands that were enjoying success at the time. "In London I discovered all the music I liked secretly, that I'd been hiding from my friends – that was what was great fun in a bar: Lee Dorsey songs! Suddenly it was all right to like it: that was when I saw the light," said Costello. [8]

Flip City made their first recordings at the BBC's Maida Vale Studios in the summer of 1974. But it was in Dave Robinson's studio that Parker and so many others put their stake in the ground, where two subsequent sessions were done in 1975. "I booked them at the Hope & Anchor and recorded, I think, 26 tracks with him personally singing," said Robinson. [14] "So, all those early songs we recorded at the Hope & Anchor three years earlier. I found the tapes and gave them to Elvis after he made his third album." [8]

So, by 1975, when he moved his stuff out of the Hope & Anchor, Robinson had already made fateful connections with Nick Lowe, Ian Dury and Elvis Costello, all three of whom would loom large in his life in ways he could not possibly have foreseen. He had also crossed paths with another figure who was to play a far greater role in his life.

Jake Riviera was a force of nature, a human tornado you only ever wanted to be on one side – yours. A frenzied ball of energy, fuelled by an intoxicating mix of adrenalin, cider and pills, only the very foolish or naive would attempt to stand in his path. Like Robinson, he was fervent and hugely knowledgeable about music and had his ear to the ground, alert to new groups and scenes bubbling away under the surface. Whenever he left the country he came back with cases stuffed with records that were unavailable in the UK. He was increasingly angry at the inertia of an industry which was stifling the real talent and therefore depriving it of the audience it deserved. Unluckily for those who crossed him or got in his way, he could explode into fury or violence at the drop of a hat. Even in a scene full of volatile characters, Riviera had a fearsome reputation.

Born Andrew John Jakeman in Edgware, Middlesex, he got into music early, eagerly embracing the beat scene of the early sixties. A natural salesman, he was interested in advertising and for a time worked as a messenger for the famous Mather & Crowther agency. By 1967, he was living in France and spent two years there productively, learning the language, becoming a connoisseur of food and wine, and making valuable contacts in Paris. He also worked as road manager and translator for Les Variations, a rock band that sang in English and would go on to become the first French group to tour America and sign with a US label.

Riviera's C.V. became even more varied on his return to the UK. He worked behind the counter at the Record & Tape Exchange in Notting Hill Gate, West London, drove a van for *Time Out* magazine, and sold candles from a stall on Kensington Market. And when pub rock began to catch light, he was a moth to the flame, drawn to The Tally Ho, The Kensington, The Nashville and other music joints.

As a roadie, he worked for Darryl Way's Wolf, formed in 1972 by one of the founders of Curved Air. But soon he was also shifting gear for one of the bands playing in the pubs he frequented. One night at The Kensington, Riviera spotted their PA was faulty and provided them with a spare he had in his van. Unfortunately, word got back to Way's management that their equipment had been loaned out without permission and Riviera hadn't even charged them for the hire. He was sacked. When he told the Brinsleys he was jobless, they suggested he talk to Martin Stone from Chilli Willi & The Red Hot Peppers, who were then without a roadie.

Chilli's roots had been in the folk/rock duo of guitarist Martin Stone and Philip Lithman, both of whom had been members of Junior's Blues Band. In the late sixties, Lithman relocated to San Francisco while Stone remained in England, playing with blues band Savoy Brown and the psychedelic rock outfit Mighty Baby. When Lithman returned in 1972, they took up where they had left off and decided to make an album. Needing session musicians to give them a fuller sound on the record they had in mind, they put out feelers on the pub circuit where they had secured a few bookings. Surprise, surprise, who should be recruited from the incestuous London scene but Nick Lowe, Bob Andrews and Billy Rankin from Brinsley Schwarz. Backing vocals were also provided by Jo Ann Kelly, one of the only female acts on the boozy, blokey circuit. The Women Of Pub Rock would surely be a contender for the world's shortest book!

The resulting record *Kings Of The Robot Rhythm,* released by Revelation Records, was a home-on-the-range bluegrass affair, awash with fiddle, banjo, fingerpicked guitar and vocal harmonies. Although it was not the music contained in its twelve tracks that were noteworthy from a Stiff perspective, but the eye-catching sleeve. The cartoon image on a washed out sleeve of a 1930s girl on a tropical island, evocative of Disney's earliest animations, had been drawn by a designer who went by the name of Barney Bubbles.

An intensely creative individual, although sensitive to the point of vulnerability, Colin Fulcher, A.K.A. Barney Bubbles, had been at the vanguard of the underground scene for several years and knew Robinson. In 1969 he moved into a three-storey building at 307 Portobello Road in the happening Notting Hill district, and established his own agency, Teenburger Designs. When he hooked up with the rather shady entrepreneurial double act of Edward Molton and Stephen Warwick, who had helped Robinson establish Famepushers, it became part of Motherburger. It was one of Bubbles' designs that ended up being the gatefold sleeve for the eponymous Brinsley Schwarz album, released in April 1970. An American Indian on a horse staring across the plains at an alien planet, the brightly coloured, captivating painting had been rejected by Fontana and was spotted by Robinson propped up against a wall.

Just as Martin Stone had pointed Riviera towards Chilli Willi, so the guitarist had signposted Bubbles towards the nascent independent label, Revelation, where he was installed as house designer. Revelation, however, had financial problems. That summer it had released *Glastonbury Fayre*, a highly ambitious triple album containing live tracks from the second year of the festival (Brinsley Schwarz, The Pink Fairies, Help Yourself and Mighty Baby were all on the bill) and other donated material. A live recording of "Dark Star" by The Grateful Dead filled one entire side on Revelation's inaugural album. In design terms, it was a masterpiece. One side of the cover folded out into a giant poster of the pyramid stage illuminated at night. Another had a black and white daytime crowd shot. Detailed booklets and a cut-out pyramid were among the other features of the elaborate package.

When Riviera walked into the label's offices he saw Bubbles painstakingly assembling each album and began helping him to fold them up. The 15,000 copies it eventually sold couldn't save Revelation from going under, but it was enough to whet Riviera's appetite and he learned from the experience.

Shortly after the release of *Kings Of The Robot Rhythm,* a new band line-up was put together with a view to promoting the record. Stone and Lithman were joined by Paul Bailey on banjo and Paul Riley on bass and after a bit of rehearsing, they supported Hawkwind at The Roundhouse. At Riley's suggestion, it was decided that another Red Hot Pepper was needed to give things a kick, and so entered a lanky, longhaired drummer named Pete Thomas. Still in his teens, Thomas was at that time working with a songwriter named Robin Scott, who had previously played with Stone, and also drummed for a group called Ocean.

"I was so junior, I was just 19," says Thomas. "If you liked the Burrito Brothers and Commander Cody and Little Feat, and Paul Butterfield in England, you would come and see Chilli Willi. It was like The Beatles did with American music, we were just rehashing it. So, I learned about all those American bands and that's when I developed my love for that stuff."

At the time, the band were being managed by John Coleman. However, Riviera gradually took on more responsibility for the organisation of the band and his burning ambition and drive was there for all to see. The gigs that were needed to recoup the outlay for the new PA were coming in, but as with Robinson and Brinsley Schwarz, Riviera felt Chilli Willi needed to start looking a bit livelier. Through his girlfriend of the time, Sue Barber, he arranged for them to rehearse at a farm in the remote Cornish village of Camelford. When a row between band members ensued during their stay, they were left open mouthed as they witnessed one of his volcanic eruptions. But as discomfiting as his comments may have been, one thing was obvious: Riviera would make one hell of a manager. So, when Riviera then got Barber, who worked at Revelation as a booking agent, to concentrate on Chilli Willi over and above its other acts, no one needed any further convincing. Stone recalled:

One night we were leaving Southampton and a police car overtakes us. Jake throws a beer can bouncing off the police car's roof and the cops carry on as if nothing has happened. I say, "Jacko, do you wanna be promoted to manager?" It was then that we started doing good. [9]

Pete Thomas says: "Jake was really businesslike. We did over 270 shows in one year with Chilli Willi; all the universities, all the clubs. It was just every day you'd get picked up, you'd drive somewhere, stay in some place. It worked. We got through a few roadies and things, but it's what you're supposed to be doing."

Riviera didn't see Chilli Willi as merely a good-time pub band. He wanted them to be big, and to realise that ambition they needed a plan. Chris Fenwick, then manager of Dr. Feelgood, similarly wanted to get his rocket-propelled R&B group, who were reluctant to stray too far from their native Canvey Island, to make the step up from provincial pub rockers to household names. To move forward, they looked to the past. Package tours were a tried and tested formula and had helped break the biggest acts of the sixties, courtesy of impresario Larry Parnes. The Tamla Motown Revue in March and April 1965 heralded the label's invasion of the UK, giving ecstatic British audiences a chance to see the likes of The Supremes, Smokey Robinson & The Miracles, Stevie Wonder and Martha Reeves & The Vandellas appearing on the same bargain bill. What Robinson had done four years earlier for Brinsley Schwarz when he sent them out as part of the Down Home Rhythm Kings tour, Riviera was about to do for Chilli Willi.

They were to head out on the road with the Feelgoods, who were attracting a reputation as a red hot live band, and Kokomo, a ten-strong collective whose funky, infectious style left many who saw them speechless, and who had been signed by the American label CBS. The idea was to emancipate the three acts from the confines of the cliquey London pub scene and present them to the nation. But Riviera knew that piling a load of musicians into a bus and dragging them around universities and halls wouldn't be enough. An added ingredient was needed to make people sit up and take notice and what better than to tap into the bawdy British sense of humour? It would be called The Naughty Rhythms Tour.

"There are lots of managers who are like practical enablers, you know, they'll do what the artists want and they'll do the deals," says Thomas. "But Jake was like an advertising guy and he just had this great imagination and when anything came up, a new record or a new band or anything, he'd have a vision. Then you had Barney Bubbles who gave the whole thing an image and we were spoilt because, ever since, I've never run into anything as dynamic or imaginative as that. Most have managers that are practical and some are nicer than others, but they are not ideas people and I've never really run into anyone else like Jake."

Riviera had a razor-sharp wit and could pump out gags and one-liners with machine gun velocity. This, combined with Bubbles' stimulating pop art and visual sense of fun, created the perfect hype. A lady coming out of a banana above the words Naughty Rhythms made up the black and white tour logo created by Bubbles, giving it an easily identifiable brand and a hint of something salacious. Advertisements in the music press and concert posters were suitably gung-ho. "Watch out! First time ever! Non-stop real music coming your way at 100 miles an hour!"

This impudent, in-your-face approach had already been road-tested for Chilli Willi's wittily named album of the previous year, *Bongos Over Balham*. Released on Mooncrest, a subsidiary of Charisma, the surreal sleeve was striking. But it was the ink from the accompanying press adverts that would eventually show up on the Stiff blotter. In them was Vinyl Mogul a pig chewing on a cheroot, with the record sleeve above him being held up by something that had punched its way through the paper. Riviera being Riviera, there was not one ad, but three versions featuring a shop dummy's hand holding a cigarette, a pig's trotter and a dildo. The ad read: "Chilli Willi & The Red Hot Peppers is not a frozen food. It's a band. And their first real album *Bongos Over Balham* is available now on Mooncrest Records. Buy it. It'll look good in your fridge." Such a down-to-earth attitude couldn't have been in more contrast to the self-importance and earnestness of the rock giants who bestrode the earth in 1975. Popular music was suffering a mid-life crisis and wasn't yet ready to lighten up. Riviera and Bubbles were ahead of the game.

The Naughty Rhythms Tour kicked off at Bristol University on 11 January 1975 and wound up at North London Polytechnic on 28 February. As with the Stiff tours that would follow, the bill was rotated each night, and each act had an album to promote. Dr. Feelgood had released *Down By The Jetty* and Kokomo had issued its first, eponymously titled album. The tour had plenty of financial backing and most of the money was put up by Andrew Lauder, boss of United Artists (the Feelgood's label), Tony Stratton-Smith, owner of Charisma, and Steve O'Rourke, manager of Pink Floyd, who had signed Kokomo to CBS.

One of Riviera's close acquaintances at the time was publicist Glen Colson. Although he had worked for prog pioneers Van der Graaf Generator and Genesis at Charisma, he preferred to spend his evenings in the less glamorous company of pub rock bands. He believed Charisma should have been realising the potential of acts like Ian Dury, Dr. Feelgood and Chilli Willi, but found its owner "a bit of a snob musically", who didn't want acts who were treading the sticky floors of pubs tramping into his prestigious label. Like Riviera, Colson was a straight-talker and the two had become firm friends after they got chatting in The Kensington one night. At the time of the Naughty Rhythms Tour, he was working for Pink Floyd manager Steve O'Rourke and helping to manage Kokomo.

"They were exciting, so when we went on the road, Kokomo were like the kings," says Colson. "They thought they were going to be topping the bill and they were going to blow everybody away. But it was Dr. Feelgood that blew everybody away and Kokomo ended up being a bit demoralised because Dr. Feelgood, this dodgy old band that were playing Johnny Kidd & The Pirates' numbers, had blown them off stage because they were magic. Poor old Chilli Willi also got blown away a bit. They were so demoralised, after that it was all over for them, which is a great shame because they were sort of our pet band."

Despite Riviera's bolshie manner, Colson found him quite urbane: "We'd go out eating and he introduced me to avocados and strawberries and wine. He was one of the only people in my life I've ever met who spoke French. Jake had been in France being a tour manager for French bands and he had a lot of posters from the Moulin Rouge and stuff like that. So, he was quite cultured and I'm pretty sure he was a grammar school boy."

By the spring of 1975, the pub rock train had hit the buffers, leaving its passengers to disembark and re-assess. For all its highs and the genuine sense of revolution felt by those who had embraced its "back to the music" crusade, commercially it had barely left a pinprick. Ace's single "How Long", which had reached the dizzy heights of No.20 in the UK chart in the autumn of 1974, was the only hit chalked up by the pub rock *cognoscenti*.

Chilli Willi folded in the wake of the Naughty Rhythms tour, with Pete Thomas relocating to the US to play with country singer John Stewart, who wrote The Monkees' hit *Daydream Believer*. No great surprise seeing as Riviera had announced they had split up before the tour was over. Although there had been some suggestion he might manage Brinsley Schwarz, last orders were finally called when they played The Marquee on 18 March. By the summer Ducks Deluxe had also called it a day. Kilburn And The High Roads, certainly as the theatrical and gloriously shambolic band so many had come to know, was also effectively over.

Riviera saw which way the wind was blowing and threw his lot in with Dr. Feelgood. No sooner had the members of Chilli Willi had time to digest what had happened to them than Riviera was working with Chris Fenwick and tour managing the band that had blown audiences away on the Naughty Rhythms Tour.

Many of the pub rock bands could deliver a storming night's entertainment, but Fenwick's charges carried a real threat. Their songs and the shapes they threw on stage had a jagged edge, more akin to some of the bands emerging from New York, but which English audiences had yet to fully experience. So, when impressionable young musicians like Joe Strummer experienced their live act, the future seemed to open up right there and then. A line had been drawn in the sand and not just on Canvey Island.

The four Essex lads with a battered van had gone from 0 to 60 in five seconds. The second album *Malpractice* reached No. 17 in the UK album chart in November 1975 attracting the attention of a number of record companies. Robert Plant had even offered to sign them to Led Zeppelin's own Swansong label. But the lure of CBS proved too great for Fenwick, whose next strategic move was to break the Feelgoods in America. With pens having been put to paper, the band was invited to perform at its new label's legendary annual convention in San Diego. For Riviera, it would be his first flight across the Atlantic. And for the whole party, it would be an initiation into industry excess. Twenty hookers were flown in for the occasion and when guests entered their hotel rooms, they found a sign saying they could enjoy "Total unlimited credit".

But guitarist Wilko Johnson was decidedly uneasy about the whole corporate world into which they were being inducted and a schism was emerging between him and the other three members of the group. Riviera and Fenwick's relationship was a precarious one. "Chris Fenwick was continually trying to paper over the cracks in their friendship," wrote journalist Cal Worthington, "but the matter came to a head when the Figure [the drummer nicknamed The Big

Figure] took a swing at Jake after Wilko discovered that his wah-wah pedal, through some oversight, had not been packed with the rest of the gear." [10]

Things were patched up, but the Feelgoods weren't living up to their name. While singer Lee Brilleaux, bassist Johnny Sparks and The Big Figure spent their time boozing, Wilko became more withdrawn. He retreated to the sanctuary of his hotel room where he sat on the bed, writing songs and getting off his head on speed. The mood within the camp didn't lighten any when the Feelgoods returned to the US six weeks later to play The Bottom Line in New York among other venues. Within a few months, its agitated axeman had left the group.

However, it was during this time, and a subsequent trip to America with the group, that Riviera began harbouring thoughts of creating his own record label. With the American sun on his back and Jonathan Richman's "Roadrunner" constantly replaying in his head, he made his presence known around nightclubs, record company ligs and private parties. He couldn't help but be impressed by the small independent labels operating there and the mushrooming underground punk scene. If Richman was in love with Massachusetts, Riviera had fallen for California.

By the time Dr. Feelgood's tour had ended, Riviera had already decided on his next move as he told Allan Jones in the 6 August 1977 edition of *Melody Maker*:

> We were travelling through Louisiana, in and out of all these one-eyed towns and even there you could find all these thrift shops stocked with all these singles on obscure labels. There's always been that kind of tradition in America. There have been some attempts to do it here, but none of them really worked. I just thought it would be a real gas to start a label.
>
> We were just sitting in this station wagon. And there isn't really a lot to occupy your mind after you've seen the first mile of swamps and you've seen your first three alligators. By the time we finished the tour I'd thought of the name, designed the logo. Everything. [29]

It was game on …

2

Undertakers To The Industry

1976 was, according to a report by the New Economics Foundation published in 2004, the year in which the British people were at their happiest. Kids in parkas roamed school playgrounds, space hoppers were an affordable means of transport and Tom Baker was Doctor Who. The economic picture was bleak though, with inflation at 17% and rising unemployment. An iron-fisted blonde was ominously pointing her handbag in the direction of No.10 Downing Street. For most youngsters growing up in what felt more like Grey Britain than Great Britain, the lives of the rock stars whose images adorned their bedroom walls seemed as remote as any hopes of a future job.

Rock's biggest acts were living like royalty. The Beatles, The Rolling Stones and The Who might have put Britain on the map, but they were long gone, living instead as tax exiles in America and other foreign climes, due to the top rate of income tax payable in Britain standing at an eye-watering 98%. As supergroups like Pink Floyd, Genesis and Yes demanded ever grander venues when they did deign to visit these shores, so the gap between them and those buying their records had become a yawning chasm. For budding musicians with ambitions of emulating them, stardom must have seemed a galaxy away. Abba had the Top Ten in a sequined vice-like grip on the UK chart. Radio 1 DJs, who appeared on *Top Of The Pops* flanked by teenage girls, had acquired almost God-like status and the flagship BBC show they presented had descended into farce.

In his rented quarters at 48 Queensgate Terrace in South Kensington, Jake Riviera was exasperated. The flat was around the corner from the Royal Albert Hall, but the odds of Nick Lowe ever playing there seemed longer than ever. Riviera had become a close friend as well as manager to the talented singer-songwriter. They'd met at the Wardour Street's Marquee Club and from the outset it was clear they had much in common. Each had an insatiable appetite for music and, as Riviera had a happy knack of acquiring vinyl few others had heard, new sounds were never in short supply.

Fuelled by booze and other stimulants, they hit clubs and venues in and around Soho and the additional buzz they got from playing pranks and winding people up only cemented their reputation as an on-the-town double act. When Brinsley Schwarz dispersed, Lowe had initially decamped to his sister's. But when this domestic arrangement didn't work out, Riviera said he could sleep on his sofa. Weeks turned into months and he ended up living in the four-storey terrace, which in time would become home for a colourful array of artists.

Recalling the coming together of this heady partnership, Brinsley's guitarist Ian Gomm says: "When Brinsley Schwarz split up, that's when Jake Riviera popped his head up and seemed to be there; Nick took to him immediately. That's the first time cocaine started to appear and I wasn't really like that. I'm more of a pint of bitter man, you know. We used to watch him [Lowe] going manic. The plan was that because Nick and me were writing all the songs at the end of the Brinsleys – like 'Cruel To Be Kind' – we wanted to turn United Artists in Mortimer Street into the Brill Building.

"Nick and I had a meeting with the top dog, Martin Davies, and he said, 'Well, if you want to get anywhere in this business you're going to have to wear out a lot of shoe leather.' We were like, 'What? Shoe leather? We want to write songs in a room.' He was talking about Tin Pan Alley and going round hawking your songs. We thought, this isn't going to work. Nick went off with Jake to Stiff Records and Jake wanted to manage me as well. But I said no and he's never forgiven me for that. I didn't like him and didn't trust him. If it was Dave, yes, but Jake I didn't really know that well. And he still hates me to this day, I know he does."

Lowe had been dropped by United Artists, by coincidence Dr. Feelgood's UK label, and, via his contacts, Riviera identified a couple of record companies that might be interested in signing him. Jet was a major player that included the Electric Light Orchestra on its roster, while Beserkley was a much smaller operation based in San Francisco, whose initial run of singles had all failed to chart. But one of them – "Roadrunner" by Jonathan Richman & The Modern Lovers – blew Riviera away when he heard it and it was the edgier Californian label he favoured. When Dr. Feelgood flew to the States for a second string of dates, Lowe was their road manager, and during the trip Riviera took the opportunity to meet Matthew "King" Kaufman, owner and chief producer at Beserkley.

Formed in 1973, it had initially released only 45s. None of them charted, but in 1975 singles by The Rubinoos, Earthquake, Jonathan Richman and Greg Kihn had been resurrected on a compilation entitled *Beserkley Chartbusters Volume 1*. "Home Of The Hits" the front cover declared, indicating some self-deprecation on the part of the label. Recalling Beserkley's inception, Kihn recalled:

> It is an interesting story because the label was formed by Matthew Kaufman, who was in the band Earthquake. They had been dropped from A&M Records after two albums. At the same time, I had been dropped from my development deal at A&M. Warner Bros had just dropped Jonathan Richman And The Modern Lovers. We were all sitting around commiserating and we said, "Screw it, let's just make our own label." [11]

After rummaging around in record stores and observing how Beserkley and other independents there operated, while on tour with the Feelgoods, Riviera had come to the same conclusion.

Riviera found out that Matthew Kaufman, who ran the Beserkley and Home Of The Hits labels, had deleted Jonathan Richman's album *The Modern Lovers* to pave the way for a solo Jonathan Richman record scheduled for the autumn. Riviera was keen to pick up the album for release in the UK and he and Lee Brilleaux headed to The Troubadour to broker a deal with Kaufman as Riviera explained to *Sounds'* Chas de Whalley in August 1976:

> I told him I was certain there is a market for *The Modern Lovers* in Britain and I think we were close to an agreement. But we all got very drunk indeed and had a fight with Stevie Wonder's manager. I know me and Matthew shook hands, but I think both of us were in too much of a daze to remember what sort of a deal we made. But, as soon as he's back in his office in San Francisco, I'm going to give him a ring and see what's happening. [8]

Hell bent on getting Lowe a deal, Riviera had considered having an EP released – not as Nick Lowe, but as Spick Ace & The Blue Sharks. He had thought of Skydog, the underground label launched in 1972 by Paris's enigmatic punk pied piper Marc Zermati. In the end though, contractual problems prevented Lowe from joining a roll-call of early releases that included Jimi Hendrix, The Velvet Underground and The Flamin' Groovies. Despite a highly listenable vocal style and a canny knack of writing great pop songs, Lowe seemed destined not to get picked up following his departure from United Artists. He had the "pure pop", but for the moment, it wasn't reaching the "now people".

Paradoxically, it was in their own flat at Queensgate Terrace, not a record company office, where a solution was found. One of Riviera's flatmates was Irene Campbell and when her boyfriend turned up, it was none other than Dave Robinson. Like Riviera, he was dismayed at the total lack of interest shown by record companies in what he saw as exciting acts. Riviera recollected: "I was managing Nick Lowe and he didn't have a record deal, and I thought I could do a better job on my own. And then Dave Robinson was going out with my flatmate and he was managing Graham Parker, and he said, 'Well, why don't we do it?'" [12]

Robinson explained:

> It was Jake that had the idea for an independent record label. At the time I was managing Graham Parker, Ian Dury and various other people and getting frustrated trying to deal with the major record companies and thinking maybe I should start some kind of label. Then Jake came back from America, having looked at a lot of indie record labels over there, and also I had a lot of tapes from the Hope & Anchor and earlier managing situations with all those kinds of bands from the dreadfully named "pub rock" scene. I had a lot of ideas to sign and everything. I was going to blend into a record company/management company.
>
> So, our two ideas came together. I was very frustrated at being a manager in those days. The majors were very pedantic, like they are now; they are always convinced they are running the record business. So, if you wanted a special marketing deal, or to do something off the beaten track, they didn't want to do it, because it was going to cost money. [5]

Parker vividly remembers being in a van going to and from gigs with The Rumour and listening to Robinson expounding on his idea of forming his own label. Robinson had signed Parker to Phonogram only to discover how conservative and unimaginative it was. In an attempt to build on the success of *Howlin' Wind* and *Heat Treatment*, he had the idea of releasing an EP in Beatles or Rolling Stones-style with a cover version on it. Parker flicked through his record collection to find "Hold Back The Night" by Philadelphia soul band The Trammps. He played it to The Rumour, who learned it, and it was decided to release it as part of an EP.

To Phonogram's irritation, Robinson insisted that not only should the record come in a picture sleeve, but be pressed up on pink vinyl. The label was reluctant to agree to such additional costs and feared that other artists would start demanding such luxuries. "It'll ruin the business," they told him. But despite its reservations, Phonogram produced the "Pink Parker" EP. Robinson's imaginative approach was rewarded with a No. 24 hit. But the intransigence he'd met with at the label convinced him that the easiest solution would be to set up his own.

Recalls Parker: "I remember Dave in the back of the bus saying, 'Yeah, we'll start a label, we'll instantly delete records' – and everyone laughed – 'and we'll do some records with The Rumour'. He said, 'Come along to the Hope & Anchor and see this band Flip City, he's a great songwriter this guy'. And there were about ten people there and I thought, 'It sounds like lame country rock, it sounds like the Brinsley Schwarz band'. I didn't get it, didn't get what the Brinsleys' music was because they gave me some albums and I was like, 'Why am I being called pub rock?' I didn't get any of it. But Dave had this idea.

"Then I met Jake, who tour managed us in America, and he was the same. He had these ideas about destroying the system. So there were these two guys talking about destroying everything by making coloured records and deleting them and having these slogans. I was once in a cab with Dave going into New York City and he saw some rotten old sign on a building and he nicked it and it became one of the Stiff slogans. He was like that, he was cherry-picking things all the time, and I thought, 'This is going to go nowhere. All these acts are losers, they can't get anywhere. Maybe they're all talented, but there's no market. I'm the one, pal, forget it'. But he wouldn't. He was determined to do the Stiff Records thing and somehow they came up with the name Stiff."

Robinson said that Stiff was to be a "conduit for people who could not find the music business any other way. My theory was that there's an Elvis Presley out there, but he's working in a factory in Coventry and he doesn't know how to get in touch with me. The best artists are out there, but they don't know how to connect with the music business because it doesn't tell you how. If you go to a couple of majors, they'll put you off for life." [5]

The cash to start up Stiff Records came from Dr. Feelgood's harmonica-wielding frontman Lee Brilleaux – or at least some of it. When Riviera told him about the new label he was planning, Brilleaux asked him how much he needed. Riviera told him about £400 would get it going, whereby Brilleaux whipped out his chequebook and wrote him a cheque.

However, as reported in *Melody Maker,* Stiff's other sponsors were Wilko Johnson, Nick Lowe and photographer Keith Morris, and Riviera had "sold a lot of things" to raise the rest of the money. A list of shareholders in the company submitted in 1977 reveals Lowe, Brilleaux, Chris Fenwick (not Wilko) and Morris as having one share each.

Robinson has since dismissed the £400 from Lee Brilleaux story as a myth and said the money instead came from the management company he and Riviera had set up:

> Stiff wouldn't have happened at all if I hadn't had an artist management company. I managed Graham Parker and various other people, so the income from that is what launched Stiff. This idea that the Feelgoods rolled up with all the money ... the money actually came from a company called Advancedale, which was my management company. That £400 happened, but we never cashed it [Advancedale] that's what kept us going, paid the phones, paid the office. [2]

Graham Parker supports this version of events: "Even Dave has said, 'That thing about the Dr. Feelgood cheque, I don't think we cashed it, we hung it on the wall. I was getting money from people I was managing'". Who was he managing? "Me. I had Ellis Clan, that was my company. Dave had Advancedale and he was getting money from me into Advancedale. He shared a bank account with me.

"It was a lovely legend, but to Jake and Dave, I was the most successful thing on two legs for that brief period until Stiff did take off. Dave was looking for an act like me forever and he found me. Then he had a bit of breathing space to do what he'd always wanted to do, which was to have a completely mad record label that broke the rules and did as much as possible to damage the major labels. In the same way that Joe Meek put out records that he had made in his toilet and his flat and the record labels were going, 'This guy's having No. 1s and he's using a stick with a ball as a bass drum for "Have I The Right"', which was a huge hit record."

The formation of the company the label would trade under was typically Stiff. Rather than start a company from scratch, it was easier to pick an existing one off the shelf. Which is why, on 1 July 1976, Robinson and Riviera became the proud owners of "haulage and transport contractor" Elcotgrange Limited. The business was incorporated on 20 July with a registered office at 557 Finchley Road, Hampstead, North London. Then, at an extraordinary general meeting on the same day, a resolution was passed that the clause stating the purpose of the company be deleted and replaced with a very different one. Elcotgrange would manufacture and sell records and publish music, and operate as "managers, promoters, agents, proprietors of all types of business allied to the entertainment industry". In a nod to its forward-thinking directors, it would also carry on the business of "motion picture exhibitors and distributors".

The company's share capital was increased from £100 to £100,000 through the creation of 99,900 shares of £1 each. Riviera and Robinson, the two directors, were listed as artistes managers, and directors of Advancedale Ltd. Riviera gave his address as 48 Queensgate Terrace, SW7, while beside Robinson's name was written 32 Alexander Street, London W2, a nondescript property that was about to become legendary in pop history.

A row of terraced houses off Westbourne Park Road in Bayswater, Alexander Street is a stone's throw from fashionable Notting Hill and a short tube ride into the centre of London. Today it is an exclusive district, where in 2013 the average price of its 94 properties was estimated at more than £1.5 million. Stiff fans who make a pilgrimage to No. 32 will find it made up of luxurious maisonettes: the two-bedroom garden flat that once housed the label was advertised for rent in September 2012 at £3,142 a month. However, back in 1976, the area was not so well-heeled and No. 32 was next door to The Durham Castle, a pub run by Charrington Brewery.

It was indirectly through Ian Dury that Stiff came to be based there. When things for the Kilburns began to go as flat as the beer in some of the pubs they played in, their manager Dave Robinson decided he could take them no further. Dury could be unpleasant to deal with and the Irishman was glad to make him someone else's problem. So in February 1976, he took Dury to two people who might be interested in managing him and his weird troupe.

Andrew King and Peter Jenner were polar opposites of Riviera and Robinson. They had attended the same grammar school and kept up their close friendship after graduating from university. Attracted to the psychedelic lights and sounds of underground clubs like the UFO, and using inherited money, they had decided to go into management. They began with emerging group Pink Floyd and, along with group founder members Syd Barrett, Nick Mason, Roger Waters and Richard Wright, set up Blackhill Enterprises in 1966.

King and his wife Wendy moved into 32 Alexander Street after getting married. The couple lived on the first floor, while Wendy ran a textile design business from the main room on the ground floor, which had a large window facing out on to the street. Her printing machinery was set up in the basement. After they moved to a different property, the upper floor became Blackhill's office and the ground floor was rented out. Tenants included promoter John Curd and the Wasted Talent agency run by Ian Flooks. At some point Roger Waters lived at No. 32, and Marc Bolan, who was on Blackhill's books, met Barrett's former girlfriend and his future wife June Child while she was working there as a secretary, further cementing it as a rock landmark.

Dury saw the Blackhill duo as hippies still living out the sixties dream and figured they wouldn't get his visceral lyrics and surreal brand of rock 'n' roll. He was wrong, as King explains:

> When Ian came to us, we became his publishers and the first thing I remember is reading the lyrics to "Nervous Piss". He brought a bunch of lyrics typed up and quite honestly, as soon as I read them, I was absolutely determined to sign him as a songwriter. I remember sitting at this table in a great big room at Alexander Street and reading those lyrics. I have always warmed to writers who have really good lyrics. Syd Barrett of the Floyd wrote very good lyrics and so did Ian, so I instantly wanted to do it. [6]

Robinson was delighted. In return for handing over Ian's management to Blackhill, he got a year's free rent of the ground floor and use of the telephones. He moved in and when the idea of Stiff was mooted, it was the most obvious and economically viable place to set up shop. A couple of desks, three chairs, four telephones and a couple of filing cabinets were installed, and a secretary recruited to man the fort. Amid one of the hottest British summers on record, Stiff set out to turn up the heat on the majors.

But what kind of roster was this embryonic label planning to put together? When a journalist from *Sounds* stumbled on a Stiff business meeting at the West End offices of United Artists, Riviera let him in on its manifesto. "We're calling it 'Stiff Records': the most flexible label in the world' and the policy will be very simple indeed," he said. "Basically speaking, we want to put out singles that are two and half minutes long and have got two and a half chords in them. It'll all be very esoteric."

Stiff would also be living up to its name by exhuming material by deceased pub rock bands, from tracks by Chilli Willi & The Red Hot Peppers and Eggs Over Easy to tapes Paul McCartney made of Brinsley Schwarz when they were on the Wings tour of 1973. It would also provide the launch pad for new compositions by one of its own investors and Riviera's partner in crime, Nick Lowe.

Asked by *Sounds* if Stiff could really achieve commercial success with "obsolete bar bands", Riviera replied: "There's a much larger market than you think, especially as we're hoping to be distributed through the specialist shops like Bizarre Records or Rock On. But Nick's songs are very good indeed, and if 'Truth Drug' gets the reviews and the airplay it deserves, Stiff will start straight off with a hit."

───

Three major guitar chords (D, A, E), thundering drums, and the opening line about cutting off a right arm. This was far from your average lyrical opener and clearly not yet another entry into pop's logbook of love. Then again, this was not your average record label. "So It Goes" by Nick Lowe had the undeniable privilege of becoming the first ever Stiff record. Released on 14 August 1976, it had been recorded as a publisher's demo for the exorbitant sum of £45. Steve Goulding of The Rumour sat in on drums, while Lowe played everything else.

"So It Goes" and its B-side "Heart Of The City" were performed and recorded with an economy that constituted a musical ram-raid. Set against an uncluttered backdrop that allowed Lowe's clear vocals and fifties rock 'n' roll guitar to ring out, Lowe's songs had the kind of sound and feel that might have resulted had Phil Spector produced Jonathan Richman's pulsating "Roadrunner".

"So It Goes" came in a plain black sleeve bearing the bubble-lettered Stiff logo. The record itself was stamped with the humour that would come to define the label. "Earthlings Awake" was scratched around the inner groove of the A-side, while "Three Chord Trick Yeh" was etched onto the flip. These hidden messages were the work of cutter Porky Peckham – real name George Peckham – and a feature that fans would eagerly look out for on future releases.

The single's catalogue number was BUY 1, heralding a Stiff trademark that would make not just its music, but its overall design and packaging, collectible. Stiff would go on to produce stunning picture sleeves and brightly coloured vinyl, thus helping to give the British pop single the kiss of life. But for its first foray into the world of 45s, the cover reflected the wonderful simplicity of the record inside.

BUY 1 got the buy-in of influential critics. On 14 August 1976, Caroline Coon of *Melody Maker* made it her record of the week:

"'It's a sound which is happening now,' Nick told me, seriously. 'Clever words over a simple rhythm.' True. 'Basically, I'll do anything. I can write in any style. Peters and Lee, for instance. But all my friends have turned into punks overnight and I'm a great bandwagon climber.' A gent with a sense of humour."

Labels like Stiff were breaking new ground in the UK and were needed to "bridge the gap between the pub no-man's land and the increasingly impersonal, monolithic record companies", wrote Coon. *Sounds* named it Star Single of the week and heralded "Heart Of The City" an "A1 smash"

The signs were encouraging. Music writers were interested in this brave new label and largely impressed with its first shot across the corporate bows. The postbag at Alexander Street contained plenty of mail orders for the record. Phone orders from small record shops stocking the single also led to its initial pressing of 2,000 being increased to 3,000. For all its raw immediacy and Riviera's unshakable faith in Lowe and his songs, "So It Goes" failed to trouble the charts. Stiff's first record had lived up to its name. However, selling many of their records mail order meant a better margin, as they weren't cutting in wholesalers or retailers.

While Stiff was attracting a lot of media interest, it was far from the only independent in town. Chiswick Records had been established by Roger Armstrong and Ted Carroll the previous year. Carroll had managed Thin Lizzy and owned a record stall in Soho Market called

Rock On, while Armstrong was his assistant manager. They were compelled to release rather than just sell records after going to see the 101ers (Joe Strummer's first band) and the Count Bishops: high-tempo R&B groups with attitude to burn. Their first release was the Count Bishops' "Speedball" EP, released in November 1975, showing that it was alive to punk while others were looking the other way. Johnny Moped, Kirsty MacColl's first group The Drug Addix and The Radiators From Space, featuring Pogues guitarist Philip Chevron, were among those who were set on their path by Chiswick.

It was the single and not the long player that was at the core of this new breed of record companies. By 1967, albums had began outselling singles in the UK and US for the first time and by the end of the decade, albums accounted for more than 80% of all records sold. Stiff was to be an antidote to the eleven-minute song, the grandiose concept album and music's love-in with corporate business. It would be a singles label, with songs of the "over-and-out" variety, and if it was to mould itself on any of the major labels, it was Motown. Like Berry Gordy, founder of the Detroit label, Riviera and Robinson had an unshakable belief that they could sniff out a hit better than anyone. Although Stiff's eclectic roster would reflect the catholic tastes of its owners, it would be a pop label that in several ways would follow the Motown template.

A small photographic studio at the back of Motown's first home at 2648 West Grand Boulevard in Detroit, Michigan, was converted into a two-track facility which would become the legendary Hitsville USA's Studio A. Affectionately known as The Snakepit, this modest basement was where the label's in-house musicians The Funk Brothers laid down the legendary Motown sound and its golden era was captured on tape. Stiff too had an in-house studio of sorts, although the cramped space wasn't at Alexander Street.

Pathway had emerged from the embers of "Fire", the Crazy World Of Arthur Brown's smouldering hit, which blazed away at the No. 1 spot of the UK chart in August 1968. Mike Finesilver and Peter Ker had co-write credits to the song (along with Brown and Vincent Crane) and with the royalties they set up a studio in 2a Grosvenor Avenue, in Islington. Dave Robinson had first used it when he burned out one of the heads on his tape machine at the nearby Hope & Anchor, making it an obvious choice for the label's first recording session. Accessed via an alleyway between an end-terrace house and a garage, it was a cramped space that perfectly encapsulated Stiff's DIY spirit.

Barry Farmer, credited as Bazza on Stiff releases, was one of Pathway's first engineers and his memories are still vivid: "It was a genuine shit-hole. You'd be confronted by the smell. It had a problem with damp and it smelled like an autumn woodland or an old toilet. It would cling to your clothes. Two days later you would still smell Pathway. Nick Lowe and I had a long discussion about it once. A few years ago I was getting out some old meters I still had kicking around and hadn't done anything with, and they were in a box that was sealed up. I opened the box and smelled Pathway Studio."

The studio's owners had first approached another engineer and asked him to put together a mixing desk. When the quote that came back was well beyond their budget, they called Farmer. He spent six months in the spare bedroom of his flat, building a desk taken from a design drawn up by Dave Robinson and published in Studio Sounds. "It was eight-track on one inch, which was probably a bit old school, so it was quite good quality," says Farmer. "In fact, the actual quality of the studio was surprisingly high."

In 1976, Pathway could be booked at a rate of £8 an hour and "So It Goes" and "Heart Of The City" were hammered out in just three hours, with Lowe and Riviera producing. Photographs from the time show just how confined Stiff's favourite studio was. "You came in through the porch and there were very steep stairs going up the right and most people fell up them, rather than down them," describes Farmer. "Then you went through a very homemade acoustic door and into the studio. I can't remember the exact dimensions, but it was very small. One of the conditions when we were building the desk was that it actually had to fit. They had to have sixteen channels, but we had to squeeze it down. It was only about six feet wide and probably about five feet deep. You could certainly stretch out your arms from one end to the other.

"Underneath the stairs in the studio there was a space and the bass went there, you could get maybe a keyboard amp or something next to it. The drums had a recess behind the door coming in. It was extremely tight: you were definitely climbing over things to get around."

Stiff's initial game plan was to sign artists on one-off deals with the aim of generating enough money from one paying for the next.

Cashflow was limited as a result and the day-to-day operation was hand-to-mouth. Invaluable to Stiff in the early days was Riviera's friendship with Andrew Lauder. Still in his twenties, the passionate music fan and vinyl connoisseur had worked his way up in the business and had been put in charge of the UK division of American label United Artists. Dr. Feelgood's debut album *Down By The Jetty*, which was as gritty as the shores of Canvey itself, had been released by UA in 1975. Brinsley Schwarz and Nick Lowe had also been on its books, so Riviera had become a regular and conspicuous caller at its offices ahead of Stiff's launch.

UA had a pressing and distribution deal with EMI (who would acquire UA in 1979). The records were pressed at its massive plant in Hayes, Middlesex, and when Stiff wanted a batch of records, UA put the request through. EMI then invoiced UA who in turn, billed Stiff. "So, as they're a large company, by the time they've put their invoices through, I've sold the records and can afford to pay them," Riviera explained. [14]

Once the records were ready for collection, Riviera drove over to UA's London office near Warren Street tube station, or the EMI factory at Hayes. He then put them in the boot of his car, drove them round to the record stores or mailed them off to those who had sent postal orders. While Chiswick got its records out via President Records and Charlie Gillett's Oval used Virgin, Stiff didn't have a formal distribution arrangement. Riviera told *Melody Maker* he was using Bizarre Distribution, which had shifted 1,200 singles by Eddie & The Hot Rods on behalf of Island. He said an "alternative distribution network" was being set up and in just five days 1,200 copies of "So It Goes" had been sold. "W.H. Smith and Boots don't want to know about Stiff Records, and Stiff doesn't really want to know about them, so that's fine," said Riviera. "They ain't gonna break anything new, but Virgin are, and they're a large chain and they take the records." [14]

It's clear that although Stiff had two owners, Riviera was the one getting its name out there. He was being quoted in the music papers and loudly championing his pal Lowe and the record they had produced. The gobby, rent-a-quote label chief with the hip name was a music writer's dream. Get him going over a drink and he was guaranteed to deliver some great one-liners. Riviera, like Stiff, made good copy. And in 1976, good copy could sell a lot of papers.

Riviera also fulfilled a role behind the scenes: that of press officer "Vinyl Mogul". Resurrecting the *nom de guerre* he invented in his

Chilli Willi days, he used it as a sign-off for press releases and letters. Mogul announced:

You are holding the first release from Stiff Records a new independent record company dedicated to releasing limited edition collectors recordings and other smashes. Stiff favours sound over technique and feeling over style. Besides being our first release, this is the first solo single from Nick Lowe. Nick was bass player/singer/song provider for some seven albums with the critically acclaimed Brinsley Schwarz. Since leaving the group he has produced the debut album of Graham Parker & The Rumour, and written songs for Dr. Feelgood, the Kursaal Fliers [sic] and Dave Edmunds. The Stiff titles are "So It Goes" and "Heart Of The City". Both are under three minutes, use less than three musicians and less than three chords. We can't tell you any more than this because the best critic for yourself is yourself. Listen to it.

A handwritten advert for "So It Goes" placed in the *NME* and *Melody Maker* was also classic Stiff. "Sometimes In Life You've Got To Make A Decision" it read above a picture of Nick Lowe and another of a gaudy medallion, bearing the inscription "Major Record Company Hype Victim". From the label of three chords, this was a send-up of grandiose rock bands with three-storey keyboards. Nick Lowe's comparatively "nifty" songs could be bought direct from 32 Alexander Street for 65p, including p&p, or from hip record stores. "This offer is not open to medallion purchasers or men who wear make-up," it advised. As for the medallion offer, it read: "This fabulous limited edition medallion struck on finest recycled vinyl & plated in Rio is available to progressive rock fans who have the complete 'works' of ELP, Yes & Genesis etc. Just send in all the sleeve artwork (not your precious records) together with a cheque or PO for only £99.99 to Stiff Records."

While Riviera was talking to Geoff Brown for *Sounds,* the phone rang and an order for another 500 came in. That meant another 1,000 were needed, taking the total pressed by EMI to 3,000. Stiff would have liked to have pressed more than a 1,000 at a time, but it needed to sell the first batch before committing to further costs. Riviera said his dealings with major record companies in the past "taught me to read small print and to trust my own judgement rather than some 40-year-old expense account person who supposedly has vast experience of the business but only seems to me to have vast experience of handling credit cards in posh restaurants".

Stiff's anti-commercial style of promotion and tongue-in-cheek humour not only grabbed the attention, but gave it a distinctive brand. If people found its press releases, mail order forms, music press advertisements and records fun, Stiff might get their "buy-in". Get people looking out for the label itself, then if they didn't like one single, they might get to hear about the next and buy that. Better still, collectors might want them all. And Britain was the home of the collector.

David Hepworth, the journalist and former editor of *Smash Hits*, commented:

> I was working in the biggest record shop in Britain and so I was obsessed with not just the sound of records, but also what records were, what they were as artefacts. I was obsessed with record culture. And suddenly, with the arrival of Stiff, you had a record label that seemed as much motivated by record culture as it was motivated by the desire to make money, make people famous, expose artists you hadn't heard of. So they were a genuinely exciting, intriguing, constantly unfolding story. You knew what all the releases were, and you collected all the releases, and you poured over the covers and their messages tapped into the same rich vein of humour that you shared. [15]

Stiff's second single was not supplied by a pub rock survivor, but a psychedelic veteran. The Pink Fairies were a speed-fuelled group formed out of The Deviants in 1969. In 1976 they re-formed, this time fronted by Larry Wallis. The wild-eyed, shock-haired vocalist had served time with Shagrat, UFO, the prototype Motörhead, Blodwyn Pig and Mick Farren & The Deviants, and still lived to tell the tale. Riviera's involvement at Stiff meant he wanted in.

Wallis says: "In those good old days, record company receptions were happening all the time, and going to them was 'going ligging'. I seem to remember a whole busload of us bombing down to Luton or some such to see the Feelgoods, and I can only say that I dug Jacko [Jake] from the word go. I absolutely wanted to be involved in anything this dynamic, amusing, great dresser had to offer. I did think, and still do, that Jake was, and is, the business."

If "Heart Of The City" had been an exhilarating drive through the streets, "Between The Lines" (BUY 2) was a high-speed chase, a head-on collision between the rowdier elements of pub rock and the incendiary force of Motörhead. "Spoiling For A Fight", the B-side, was a less frenzied affair, but also implored the listener to crank up the volume. "Between The Lines" had the privilege of having Stiff's first picture sleeve. Designed by Edward Barker, a long-time friend of the Pink Fairies and The Deviants, it featured a pig with a spliff sitting in the path of an oncoming train. The single came courtesy of "Bacon Records", with the A-side produced by "everyone" and the flip by "no one". Stiff ordered 2,000 copies be pressed up.

Riviera and Robinson's plan was to release a string of "one-off" singles and this was the first of them, although Wallis would stay on as a performer and producer. Stiff simply couldn't afford the kind of hefty advances so readily paid out by the major labels and nor did it want its hands tied by lengthy recording contracts. By offering one-off deals, it would give a leg-up to talented artists that wouldn't get a look-in anywhere else.

London's music scene was an incestuous one and a familiar face from the pub rock scene would provide its third single. Riviera knew Robin Scott from his days with Chilli Willi, and by the time Stiff had come into being, Scott was combining his own musical pursuits with the management of Roogalator, an R&B band with an amorphous line-up led by Danny Adler, a singer, guitarist and writer born in 1949 in Cincinnati, Ohio, who began playing music from an early age. He gigged on the local circuit with inspirational players like Bootsy Collins, later of Funkadelic, while still in high school. His professional career began with Amos Milburn's band and the list of artists he went on to play with reads like a Who's Who of American blues: John Lee Hooker; T-Bone Walker; Chuck Berry; Solomon Burke, Memphis Slim, to name a few.

Adler arrived in London in the early seventies to discover a vibrant live music scene and formed the first incarnation of Roogalator, named after the 1966 co-production by Bobby Jameson and Frank Zappa, "Gotta Find My Roogalator". On a Sunday evening in November 1972, the group played its first show at The Marquee. However, its line-up proved more fluid than the Thames and Adler threw in his lot with Smooth Loser which, for a spell featured future Kilburn's drummer Malcolm Mortimore and bassist Georgi Dionisiev. He experimented with all kinds of other styles around Europe before he headed back to London and Roogalator revved back into life. Drummer Bobby Irwin, who would later play with Lene Lovich and Nick Lowe, and Chilli Willi bassist Paul Riley were among those who went in and out, before keyboardist Nick Plytas, drummer Justin Hildreth, and bassist Julian Scott, Robin's brother, eventually collected around Adler's clipped guitar licks and bluesy vocals.

Roogalator built up a formidable reputation on the live circuit at the tail-end of 1975. Wilko Johnson was a huge fan of the band and the *NME*'s acclaimed writer Nick Kent was so blown away by their pulsating live sound he evangelised on their behalf, determined Adler's fame should extend beyond the beer-soaked floorboards of the pub rock scene. "A more satisfying musical climax with ... Roogalator" purred the headline over his review on 20 December 1975. A record deal, however, was still proving elusive. "It was really infuriating because these A&R men would come to see us and they'd say, 'God, I love the band, but how would we market you?'" says Adler. "I remember at one point Chas Chandler came backstage at Dingwalls and said, 'I can make you the next Jimi Hendrix.' And I said, 'I don't want to be fucking Jimi Hendrix. I'm Danny Adler', and he looked at me like I was insane and just walked away."

Roogalator had also attracted the attention of Radio One DJ John Peel. On 13 May 1976, the group recorded their first session for him and the four songs they played included "All Aboard" and "Cincinnati Fatback". It was these that Scott licensed Stiff to release as a one-off single.

"It was bootlegged from a BBC session at Maida Vale," says Adler. "We had the mix and we had to go in and overdub because on the original session I did a blurb like, 'Thanks for listening to the John Peel Show' or something like that, which was very Yank, American sounding, but at the same time they thought it was cute because it was unusual. It wasn't yet considered as sleazy as it really was. So, I had to go in and record over that talk-over and we changed the monologue, remixed it and there it was."

Stiff's inherent sense of mischief was evident in the glossy picture cover of BUY 3. A pastiche of *With The Beatles*, Edward Barker's sleeve was designed to attract attention and EMI reportedly objected to the use of the Emitex advert and trademark. Released as a 33⅓rpm, "All Aboard With The Roogalator" could be listened to in "mono-enhanced STEREO" ("That Gusha Gusha Sound"). The Beatles parody was "cooked up" between Danny and Robin Scott. "We wanted to be seen as something kind of different," says Adler. "I've always loved everything The Beatles did and there was that atmospheric thing that to me, as an American who ended up in England, a lot of that stuff like "A Hard Day's Night" and that black and white sleeve reminds me of that Angry Young Men film period."

He adds: "At that time, I did something really stupid. I was invited to an awards dinner because Roogalator was in the running in the pub rock category and at that point I was very intense and very hard core. So, there's McCartney sitting right opposite me smiling at me and I just glared at him because I just thought, 'You bastard. You broke up The Beatles and now you're doing all this muzak.' So, I didn't go and shake his hand which I really regret now. But I think that at that point we gave him a copy of the thing and he wasn't too pleased."

Disappointingly, sales failed to match the enthusiasm of its high-profile supporters and the single was deleted. Blistering live shows continued, with the group even headlining over The Clash and The Vibrators at Fulham Town Hall. But it was right place, wrong time for Roogalator.

"We had an agency deal with Graham Morris, so we had so much work," Adler recalls. "We were gigging all the time, we travelled about 1,500 miles a week, but we couldn't get a record deal or a big grown-up deal. So, in the end, we put the first Roogalator album out in '77 and then the band started to splinter. Nick Plytas left in late '77, we carried on as a three-piece through most of '78, and I had just been touring and recording non-stop since '75. So, at that point I just had to take some time off and then when I came back I was writing whole new batches of songs. And actually Riviera and Nick Lowe said, 'Don't go back out as Roogalator. Go back out as Danny Adler', which may have been a mistake actually."

—

Riviera's talk of Stiff raiding the vaults of pub rock acts like Brinsley Schwarz and Eggs Over Easy had not, as yet, resulted in any releases. But one of the best-known stalwarts of that scene was to supply Stiff's fourth one-off single. Sean Tyla was, in his own words "a well-educated oik who didn't suffer fools" and spoke his own mind. In 1972, he had formed the pub rock phenomenon Ducks Deluxe and a year later, amid a flurry of interest from record companies, they were picked up by RCA. They graduated from London pubs to well-paid gigs at universities throughout the UK and toured Europe. But their big-time label didn't equate to big-time success and by 1975 the Ducks, as they were affectionately known, had disbanded.

Tyla bumped into Dave Robinson one afternoon when he dropped in at the Hope & Anchor. He'd headed over to Islington to see his former band mate, guitarist Martin Belmont, who was renting a room there and working in the downstairs bar. Tyla and Robinson knew each of old and Robinson had lent the Ducks' road crew a hand when the band played its penultimate show amid high drama. The Ducks had been paid $5,000 to replace Caravan at the Villerupt Festival in North Eastern France. About 25,000 people were in the open-air stadium to see the event, headlined by Van der Graaf Generator, but as the Ducks had begun playing, it was announced that a bomb may have been placed under the stage and the stadium emptied. The Ducks never got to go back on, but Robinson had worked out they'd earned $250 a minute for their short-lived set!

Over a pint of Guinness in the Islington pub, Tyla told Robinson what he'd been doing over the past few months and how he wanted to form a new group, Tyla Gang. Knowing Tyla to be an outspoken individual Robinson laid down an ultimatum: "I'll manage you on one condition," said Robinson. "And what is that?" enquired Tyla. "That you keep your bloody mouth shut! You don't speak to or do deals with anyone without my say so. Just write the songs, play the fuckin' music and shut the fuck up. That's the deal – take it or leave it." Tyla took it. [16]

"It wasn't really an offer, more an instruction!" he says. "Dave wanted a worker drone who obeyed without question. I definitely wasn't that, but I went along for a while because I was so broke."

The two of them went up to the demo studio Robinson had put together and Tyla played him some half-written songs on an acoustic guitar. Robinson instantly picked up on one called "Amsterdam Dog" and insisted he get a rough version of it on tape then and there. He then suggested Tyla come back the next day and record it with a new pub rock supergroup he was excitedly assembling, featuring Martin Belmont, Brinsley Schwarz, Bob Andrews, Steve Goulding and Andrew Bodnar.

Tyla was delighted with the outcome, as was his new boss. But Robinson now saw him as the ideal front man for his pet project – a vision not shared by Tyla at the time. He wanted to swap his pub rock image for something far more threatening, he told Robinson on the phone. "You're off again!" fumed Robinson. "I told you to keep your bloody mouth shut! Why?" "I want to get into some music with attitude," replied Tyla. "I don't think this is Brinsley or Bob's bag and I know it isn't Martin's – that's for sure!" Robinson's cage had been rattled now. "I don't agree with you. Will you never listen? We keep the whole thing commercial. You're a great writer, but you're an idiot when it comes to strategy. Fuck the heavy rock thing, nobody's signing that shite. They want their artistes on *Top Of The Pops*." Tyla was adamant this wasn't the direction he intended to take and they'd have to agree to disagree. "I knew this was a mistake," fumed Robinson. "Give me a call when you're still broke and pissing in the wind in six months' time." [8]

By the time they next saw each other, Robinson had allied Graham Parker with the group he'd pulled together at the pub which was now known as The Rumour. "He [Robinson] felt he could get us a deal," says Tyla. "He didn't have a shilling at that time and I doubted his bravado would come to much. Clearly, I underestimated him, and Graham Parker benefited from a similar offer."

Tyla meanwhile had formed his own band, Tyla Gang, got himself a publishing deal and signed to Stiff. Andrew Lauder, who headed up the UK division of the American label United Artists, had taken him round to Lowe and Riviera's flat in Queensgate Terrace, and it was with them he agreed a deal, which included a single and an album. "I knew Jake from Chilli Willis days," says Tyla, "and always liked him. He got on with stuff and could smell bullshit a mile away. We were kindred spirits."

"Styrofoam", the offbeat song that would appear on the A-side of Tyla Gang's single (BUY 4), certainly took him away from the safer pub rock sound of Ducks Deluxe. Written by Darrell DeVore, the keyboardist from sixties US band The Charlatans, it had come into the United Artists office as a demo and Andrew Lauder had handed it to Tyla. "Brain damage volume required" advised the label. Stiff had that right, even if a pressing error meant the title was obscured and had to be rubber-stamped. "Texas Chainsaw Massacre Boogie", the B-side, reminiscent of early ZZ Top, was penned by Tyla. It sounded like it had come right out of the mist-covered swamps of the Bayou.

The unique Stiff brand humour was ever present. "Artistic Breakthrough Double 'B' Side" declared a message hand-stamped in red ink on the record's plain white sleeve. "This Record Certified Gold On Leaving The Studio". "Basher [Lowe] looked quite bemused when the first strains of 'Texas Chainsaw Massacre Boogie' came through, but Jake was grinning like a Cheshire cat!" Tyla recalls of the moment he played the tape to them in their flat. "'Styrofoam' was another piece of complete madness. He [Riviera] loved the whole thing. It was just zany enough for him and he went for it."

Tyla was among those who witnessed first-hand the growth of Stiff and, like others who dropped in at Alexander Street, he usually ended up being given something to do. He and Lowe sat rubber-stamping sleeves for "Heart Of The City" and "Styrofoam".

"I lived in Kent and was broke, so I would only get up to the office now and then and it was growing like a mushroom," he said. It was when he visited the label's HQ and Dave Robinson walked in that Tyla realised – to his horror – that he was Riviera's partner at Stiff! Robinson, on seeing him, announced he had a claim on his management that he intended to fulfil. And although Lowe mounted a "half-protest" on his behalf, Riviera ceded to his partner. "I was gutted to tell you the truth," confessed Tyla. "I felt Jake had what it took to get me to where I wanted to go. If Elvis hadn't come on the scene, it might have been different."

Robinson wanted Tyla Gang to put together an album and as The Damned had recorded theirs at blistering speed at Pathway, they were expected to follow suit. They were sent to Rockfield to record six new tracks and remix those they had already done. "When Dave started managing me, he asked us to make an album in four days," says Tyla. "It didn't work. He then told me to fire the band, sell our van and all the gear. I had to start all over again and … I did."

By the time Tyla and Stiff had gone their separate ways, another veteran of pub rock had arrived and supplied the label's fifth record. Harmonica-wielding Lew Lewis was part of the vibrant Canvey Island scene and had been pointed in the direction of Alexander Street by one of Stiff's original backers, Lee Brilleaux. Lewis had been a member of Eddie & The Hot Rods and it was his breathtaking blues harp playing that had helped make the band's debut on Island, "Writing On The Wall", such a blistering one.

When the Rods had accelerated towards the harmonica-free zone of punk, Lewis left to continue with his beloved blues. "Boogie On

The Street" (BUY 5) by Lew Lewis & His Band was a quick and dirty helping of 12-bar blues recorded on two Revox tape recorders, which showcased the harmonica playing that had made him a local hero on Canvey. The musicians backing him on his first Stiff outing were given pseudonyms on the back of the sleeve. But as Lee Green, Johnny Ocean and The Sheik Of Araby appeared courtesy of United Artists, there would have been no prizes for anyone unmasking them as members of Dr. Feelgood. Copies of the single recorded in glorious "non-stereo" were sold at gigs and via mail order and in sufficient numbers for UA to give him a deal. He quickly went on to form a new group called Lew Lewis Reformer and recorded his best-loved song "Lucky Seven", which Dr. Feelgood covered on *Sneakin' Suspicion*.

Stiff's first five records may only have registered on the radar of the kind of avid music fan who read *NME* or *Sounds,* listened to John Peel and bought records via mail order. But Riviera and Robinson had kept to their word. They had released records by artists they fervently believed in and given them the chance to reach beyond the geographic and commercial confines of pub rock. Stiff had also shown there was an alternative to the customary practices of the established record companies, whose inflexibility smothered creativity and imagination, and that records could be entertaining too. Most importantly of all, at a time in Britain when alternative music was about to explode, Stiff had created a buzz of interest around its artists – and itself.

3

Smash It Up

A wild-eyed bloke was sat astride a bin outside 32 Alexander Street, dementedly using rolled-up posters as drum sticks. In denim jacket, jeans and laced up boots, he looked like the footballer Denis Law gone mad. On one side was a leather-jacketed air guitarist blessed with the wasted good looks of Keith Richards: on the other, a guy in a sailor's tunic with an impudent face. Completing the line of misfits was a figure whose skin was so pallid against his dark, slicked back hair and shades he looked like he'd just emerged from a coffin. If Stiff were the "Undertakers To The Industry", he looked like he'd already been embalmed.

Such larking about, as was captured on 10 March 1977 by photographer Ian Dickson, was par for the course for The Damned. But although their vamped-up image and zany antics made them the class clowns of punk, they'd stuck a safety pin into the Sex Pistols' hopes of being the first punk band to release a record. A rivalry and distrust had grown up between the two camps and while Malcolm McLaren's snarling charges grabbed the headlines, it was Riviera's incorrigible pranksters who secured that honour and ensured Stiff Records a coup. The presence of such a group on Stiff bestowed genuine kudos on a label that up to that point had been mainly trying to exhume the deceased careers of pub rockers.

"I don't know how much rivalry there was between Jake and Malcolm," says Rat Scabies, the group's tumultuous drummer, "but I'm sure there must have been some. Malcolm always saw The Damned as a threat to the Pistols. As to who fired the first shot, I don't know. But I think beating the other bands to the punch was just the way Jake did things. Stiff was all about being fast and showing the rest of the industry up for the meandering dinosaur it was. So, I don't think the 'New Rose' release was done to specifically fuck over Malcolm, but was also aimed at the rest of the business."

Punk had violently spewed forth from the same London boozers that hosted pub rock and it seemed as English as fish and chips. But it was to the US that its real roots could be traced. Bands like The Stooges, New York Dolls and the MC5 had begun writing the template for punk in the early 1970s, and it was with records by bands like these that Riviera filled his suitcase on his first trips across the Atlantic. He was a first-hand witness to punk's volcanic eruption through the sleazy, hole-in-the-wall clubs in New York and LA that he frequented in late 1975 and early 1976.

So, when he and Dave Robinson incorporated the company that would run Stiff – just two weeks after The Ramones made their UK debut and The Damned played their first real gig on a double bill with The Sex Pistols – their timing was impeccable. Spending their evenings watching live bands and able to sign acts on one-off deals, they exemplified the DIY ethos of punk. The major labels would hold weeks of meetings before signing an act flagged up by their A&R departments, but Stiff could take a decision in the blink of an eye. Punk required labels to seize the moment and few could seize that moment quicker than Stiff.

Roger Armstrong of Chiswick admitted they missed out on The Damned.

> We'd gone to see them early, one of the first Nashville gigs. Jake and Ted and me were all standing at the back after it finished, and we all looked at each other and said, "That was great, somebody's got to sign them". It was terrible, but it was great. I went on holiday shortly after that and when I came back I found that Jake had snapped The Damned up and was putting them in to do an album. [17]

Guitarist Brian James had played in Brighton garage band Bastard in 1974 before joining proto-punk band London SS, whose sprawling membership read like a Who's Who of punk. The collective had been started by art student and future Clash guitarist Mick Jones, and maths graduate Tony James. Chrissie Hynde had been part of an early incarnation of Devo in her native Ohio, and was among those who came and went at the time when bands were being formed and dissolved almost overnight. Another was drummer Chris Millar, christened Rat Scabies when a rat ran across the rehearsal room floor just as he was telling his band-mates he had "the scabies".

Bernie Rhodes and Malcolm McLaren, managers of The Clash and the Sex Pistols respectively, were competing matchmakers in punk's early days. McLaren, in particular, was keen to pull together groups that wouldn't threaten his pet project, but further stir up the boiling sea of punk. Hynde had found herself in demand as they cast around for characters who would look and act the part. Mick Jones invited her to join an outfit managed by Rhodes to be named School Girls Underwear. Then McLaren approached her to join Scabies, a gravedigger from Hemel Hempstead called Dave Letts, alias Dave Vanian, and guitarist Ray Burns, who once cleaned the toilets at Fairfield Hall in Croydon and had played with Johnny Moped. Hynde was reportedly to dress as a boy and carry a cane.

"Malcolm came in and put us in rehearsal for two days and then came down with Helen [Mininberg] and [Johnny] Rotten and all those people! and they sat down watching us, laughing, and told us to fuck off," said Burns. "No commercial possibilities. Malcolm was good to us: he gave us money and talked sense. Chrissie left: we started playing ourselves. Brian and Rat had met Vanian at The Nashville – they thought he looked good. The name 'The Damned' was Brian's idea. We were damned really: everything that could go wrong did." [17]

Sid Vicious had been invited to audition as the band's front man, but he never showed up. "We were expecting Sid to come down with us," says Scabies, "and I can't remember what happened. But somebody messaged me a few weeks ago saying they had got a diary of Sid's and the reason he didn't go was he didn't know where it was, and he was waiting on a phone call to get the address. I don't know who was supposed to do it. I think Dave [Vanian] would have ended up somewhere because Malcolm had earmarked him for greatness and he was outstanding. The first time I met him he was just in a donkey jacket, but he stood out in any room he walked into; you always noticed him – huge charisma."

Managed by Andy Czezowski, Vivienne Westwood's accountant at Sex on the Kings Road, the band rehearsed in a church hall in Lisson Grove for a few weeks. They played a low-key gig at a free festival in Croydon, before making their first official appearance at the 100 Club on London's Oxford Street on Tuesday 6 July 1976. But it was their fifth booking in a bull ring in South-West France that resulted in a deal with Stiff. The first European Punk Rock Festival was organised by French underground music figure Marc Zermati and was held in Mont-de-Marsan. The line-up featured bands from Britain, France, Switzerland and the USA, with Eddie & The Hot Rods topping the bill. The Sex Pistols had been banned after an incident involving Sid Vicious and Nick Kent at the 100 Club and The Clash had pulled out in support. The Damned had no such qualms.

When the four speed freaks climbed aboard the coach, however, it was filled not with punks, but pub rockers – most of whom were signed to Stiff. The Pink Fairies, Tyla Gang and Roogalator were all involved, as well as a one-off group consisting of Richard Hell (ex-Television and Heartbreakers), Nick Lowe and Tim Roper (ex-Ducks Deluxe), billed on the posters as Mirrors. The Damned hadn't appeared on the posters for the embryonic festival as they'd managed to force their way on to the bill after lobbying Riviera. He had been impressed by their riotous set at The Nashville which had got them banned from the pub. And by the time they returned from France, The Damned had a record deal and Ray Burns a new name.

Larry Wallis remembers: "The Dimmed [*sic*] were doing everything to live up to the new Anarchistic Movement, by generally being annoyingly nuts. Because of the rules concerning coach drivers, our chap had to stop overnight at a nice little town called Tours. Us old guard stayed in one hotel, the maniacs in another. On the first morning, Ray thought it a jolly nutty thing to do to smear a fried egg into his hair. Ooh, whacky huh? It stayed there for the entire trip, congealing and smelly, and of course we had to stop at Tours on the way home.

"On the morning of our departure from Tours, Ray boarded the bus with egg still in place. 'Hold up', I said, 'here comes Captain Sensible', and the name stuck. Years later, in Dingwalls Dance Hall, which our nurse Boss was now managing, the Cap'n told me he hated me for years for that name, but he'd changed his mind because it gave him a career. I read recently that he has 'about faced' and decided I didn't give him that moniker. Oh well."

Brian James recalls their introduction to Riviera and Europe's very un-punk festival: "The first time we met Jake and had anything to do with Stiff Records was at Victoria Bus Station where the coach was to take us down to the South of France. We met this guy, who had a bit of a quiff, and not only was his name Jake Riviera, he had that French new wave look from the sixties about him; drainpipes, smart striped jacket, and he looked pretty cool. It was like, 'Who is this guy?' And you get talking to him and it's like, 'I've recently got a demo cassette of this band The Heartbreakers, with Johnny Thunders and Richard Hell, the first time they'd recorded anything and which had never come out, do you want to borrow it and listen to it?' It's like, 'What the fuck? Who is this guy?'

"And he told us he had just started up a record label and by the time we got back from doing the Mont-de-Marsan, he was offering us a one-off singles deal. We discussed which song, and he said he liked 'New Rose' and I was cool with that, fine. Captain wanted to do another song, 'I Fall', but he was outvoted totally. So we went with 'New Rose' and we thought, well let's do something that will get up people's noses on the B-side, especially old Beatles fans. Let's stick 'Help' on the B-side, which we'd recently done because the *NME* journalist Nick Kent had just given me a copy of the first Ramones album that he'd just brought back from New York. He said, 'It's great, have a listen to this.'"

"Jake and Nick were the only ones from the past generation, the pub rockers, that made any effort to hang out with us," James also recalls. "We were at the back of the bus, messing around, having fun, getting drunk, fooling about. Rat famously ripped off Nick's Eddie Cochran T-shirt, which was a real shame because Eddie Cochran was great, but he did it as a kind of a thing and Nick was almost in tears because he loved that T-shirt. It was just really boring and I was really surprised at how boring these other people were. They were almost a bunch of oldies, looking at us and tut-tutting at these terrible youngsters at the back. It's not like we were that much younger than them and it was like, 'For fuck's sake, what's the matter with you, you fucking geezers?'"

There may not have been much punk on stage, but there was plenty off it. The Damned – out of their heads on booze and speed – careered around the hotel and climbed out of windows until an exasperated concierge called the police. With barely any sleep behind them, they took to the stage at midday and thrashed through a chaotic set. "I'm no superstar, I'm not dead yet", read the back of Dave's T-shirt, which was also adorned with a skull and dripping blood. The festival was an unmitigated disaster, with estimates of only about 2,000 people said to have been in the vast stadium. James saw a deflated Marc Zermati sitting with his head in his hands. But as a result of their appearance in the ring, The Damned waved the red flag at Stiff's raging bull.

By the following month, they'd split from Czezowski and punk promoter Ron Watts had taken over as manager. Dave Vanian hung up his grave-digger's shovel and The Damned returned to the 100 Club for their second performance there. Three weeks later they were back again for the two day 100 Club Punk Festival, at which The Sex Pistols were headlining the opening night and The Damned the second.

That there was a rivalry between the two bands spawned at almost the same time and with sharp-witted, pushy managers was no surprise. But thoughts of it being nothing more than a healthy one were suddenly and violently banished as Vanian and co. brought the festival to an end. Eardrums were being perforated with a cover of The Stooges' "1970" when people standing close to the front of the stage were suddenly showered with fragments of glass and some splinters got into a young girl's eye. A pint glass, believed to have been hurled at the stage by Sid Vicious, had struck a pillar. Police were called and arrested Vicious and *NME* reporter Caroline Coon, who believed punks standing at the back of the room had been responsible. As a result, the 100 Club joined the growing list of venues to ban punk groups.

The battle to sign The Sex Pistols was finally won by EMI on 8 October. Polydor had made plans to record "Anarchy In The UK" as the group's first single, but to Stiff's benefit, the band weren't happy with their initial studio sessions with Dave Goodman and recorded some more tracks with Mike Thorne from EMI. Still not satisfied with the results, Chris Thomas, who had mixed Pink Floyd's *Dark Side Of The Moon*, was brought in to oversee things and he envisioned the apocalyptic screams and landslide of guitars that would change things forever. However, while "Anarchy" would be punk's most iconic single, it would not be its first, because while the Pistols dithered, Stiff acted.

The release of "New Rose" on 22 October 1976 gave Riviera bragging rights over McLaren: "Anarchy In the UK" would not hit the shops until 26 November. But if Stiff wanted to bloody some noses, it was those of the major labels. "Young Hot Loud And Stiff" proclaimed a poster for the single, which was "Now available even from the dumbest dealer". "New Rose" was recorded at Pathway – the musical equivalent of assault and battery. You could almost see the hippies diving for cover as The Damned unleashed a terrifying avalanche of noise. A frenzied cover of The Beatles' "Help" on the B-side only promised to further enrage the old guard.

Played at an electrifying pace, "New Rose" sounded like an impassioned paean to a new girlfriend. But James' pounding anthem wasn't inspired by the arrival of a new woman on the scene, but punk. "People say, 'Is it a love song about this girl?' and I say, 'No, it definitely wasn't,' he says. "That I know for sure, because I hadn't just got in a relationship with someone. I wasn't writing some fucking love song about somebody and it wasn't pretend, like I was playing a role. I think what it was really about was the emerging punk scene, I really do. I think that was the impetus for the lyric.

"When I was in Brussels, with my band Bastard, I had that riff in my head and I would play it with my mate Nobby, who was the drummer. I just didn't know what to do with it. We would play it, but it didn't sound right. It didn't sound like what I had in my head. Then when I started playing with Rat, we started messing with things and writing songs, and for some reason that riff just came out. It was a natural thing and when I started playing it with Rat it suddenly made sense. So the next day, or something, I was playing it in a rehearsal situation and messing about with my guitar, and suddenly I had the opening, I knew I wanted it to start with drums, I had the whole thing, it just worked."

Sounds' Newsdesk column trumpeted the arrival of the "first punx on wax" three days before its release. The first 2,000 copies of the single had a picture sleeve featuring a photograph and came with a free poster. The Damned were going to be the "first new wave band to play a major London venue" when they and Sean Tyla supported Graham Parker & The Rumour at Victoria Palace on 26 October. "The group are currently revamping their stage act and will be including a new song called 'Anarchy Courtesy of EMI'," reported *Sounds*.

An accompanying video for "New Rose", was shot during a gig at the Hope & Anchor in December, the video was rough and ready, but not all record labels foresaw the potential of video in 1976 – Stiff did. Scabies comments: "There were quite a few people who saw videos as the emerging market and I remember Jake saying, 'A guy's going to do it for a grand'. We were like, 'That's a lot'. If I remember, that was kind of the deal and there were two versions of it. One of which was blurred and the other which was focused."

The buzz created by the record caught Alexander Street by surprise. It also exposed the limitations of its hand-to-mouth distribution methods and not for the first time. Around 4,000 copies were sold via mail order and, as demand increased, Stiff knew it needed help. "We can easily sell 5,000 EPs in advance, yet only have sufficient funds to place an initial pressing order of 2,000," Riviera admitted in the *NME* on 6 November. Robinson said of the major labels: "They're not sure what we're up to and how we can keep selling thousands of records by people they've never heard of or that they wouldn't want to record."

Rat Scabies recalls: "The only time he [Riviera] really fucked up was with 'New Rose' because it had sold a lot more than they expected it to. Stiff couldn't do it quickly enough. You could only make a minimum of 2,000 records back then, that's the smallest run you could do. And they knew that if they kept the costs down on making all the records, then they would only need to sell 2,000 records to get their money back and maybe make a bit on top. With 'New Rose', they just didn't realise it was going to take off. He [Riviera] got it turned around within a week and I think United Artists were doing the distribution for it. We actually got in the charts, some real low number like 65 or something, and I remember being absolutely fucking astounded. But if they'd have been in place with UA when it came out, we might have actually got even higher."

Further light was shed on how many records Stiff was actually selling when Dave Robinson gave an interview to the *International Times*. "Nick Lowe – I think we're pretty close to 10,000," he said. "Pink Fairies – we've done about 4,000. Roogalator have done about 3,000, which is what we've pressed, so we're pretty much out of stock on that. That's a different deal to the others. Basically we said we'd do 3,000 of that which we did. That was it, a kind of one-off thing. Tyla's done about 3,500 maybe 4,000. Lew Lewis has done about 5,000." This was pretty good going for a newly-established label distributing via the postal system and a network of independent record shops. But if it was to give the major labels a proper run for their money, it was going to need some help.

Riviera's mate Andrew Lauder at United Artists was helping Stiff distribute its records, but Stiff needed a longer-term deal with a major player if it was to extend its audience beyond those avid enough to pay postage and packing for their treasured vinyl. Its owners would have seen going to the larger companies and asking for help as a sell-out; an admission that, for all their bravado, they needed backup from the very labels they wanted to take on. Which is why there was probably only one record company which would have the independence of mind to take a gamble on Stiff, and with whom Stiff would have been comfortable sharing a bed. Island Records.

Under the deal, Island was licensed to press and distribute Stiff product and the first record scheduled to be released in this way was to be The Damned's debut album *Damned Damned Damned,* reported *Sounds*. A three-track single containing two more tracks not on the LP would be released on 18 February 1977, entitled "Neat Neat Neat". Riviera, characteristically tongue-in-cheek, said of the partnership: "I am extremely pleased with this arrangement as it allows Stiff to infiltrate the upper echelons of the record industry and still have the autonomy to double-cross unsuspecting musicians." Tim Clark of Island added: "This deal has required considerable Dutch courage on our part. I only hope it works."

Stiff had put out singles by two more acts by the time the Island deal was publicly announced. One of them was Richard Myers, A.K.A. Richard Hell, a musician from the vanguard of the US punk scene. Hell and his school friend Tom Miller (later Tom Verlaine), both of whom were interested in music and poetry, had started their first band Neon Boys in New York in 1972, along with Billy Ficca on drums. By the close of 1973 they had been joined by guitarist Richard Lloyd and established a new art-punk group, Television. However, it was while playing with the Heartbreakers that the junk-ravaged Hell was spotted by the magpie eyes of Jake Riviera.

Hell and ex-New York Dolls Johnny Thunders and Jerry Nolan made their public debut supporting Wayne County at New York's notorious drag club 82 on 30 April 1975. Riviera had stayed in the US after completing a tour with Dr. Feelgood and was in the audience to witness the band's first performance. So, when Hell upped and left, taking songs like "(I Belong To The) Blank Generation" with him, Riviera wanted in on the action. He moved so quickly the "Blank Generation" EP became BUY 7 before the Voidoids had even played their first gig. The first side was occupied by "(If I Could Live With You In) Another World", while the title track was coupled with "You Gotta Lose" on the flip. All three were co-produced by Hell and Craig Leon, who helped launch the careers of The Ramones, Talking Heads and Blondie.

An ultra-cool, bare-chested Hell posed suggestively on the cover, with the top of his jeans undone. The stylish, black and white picture was taken by his former girlfriend and renowned CBGBs photographer Roberta Bayley, as was the one on the rear of Hell with Voidoids Marc Bell, Ivan Julian and Robert Quine. If he looked wasted, he was. When Legs McNeil, co-founder of *Punk* magazine, called round to Hell's apartment on East 12th Street in New York to take pictures for a photo comic, he was shocked when he stopped to shoot up heroin in front of him. Skinny, with sallow skin, spiked up hair and vacant eyes, he was the American Sid Vicious: except he would somehow survive it all.

His spasming songs were suffused in poetry and even his spiky hair was in part inspired by the French 19th century poet Arthur Rimbaud, who was such an influence on the first woman of punk, Patti Smith. The ripped clothes look he was pioneering at the time of his brief stint with Stiff, came from "dressing off stage the same as on, and wearing T-shirts 'til they'd have holes in them, and pinning them back together and then exaggerating the whole thing," he said. "But it was Malcolm who took it to extremes". [18]

Like "New Rose", "Blank Generation" was an underground hit only and Richard Hell & The Voidoids' album of the same name was released on Sire the following year. But Stiff had shown it had its ear to the ground far beyond the London pub circuit.

The day after "Anarchy In The UK" finally hit record shops, *Sounds* carried an interview with The Damned which had been set up and conducted in true Stiff style. Reporter Giovanni Dadomo was told to get himself to Pathway Studio. Once there, he had to scramble across the roof of a transit van parked across the entrance, before he could get to the tiny studio. His interview subjects then adjourned to a nearby pub.

The Damned were supposed to have been on the road with The Flamin' Groovies, although this had lasted just two days, with their hosts claiming they were the worst band they'd ever played with. However, the next tour The Damned were booted off was much bigger news altogether. The Anarchy Tour was the brainchild of Malcolm McLaren and was due to kick off just a few days after the release of "Anarchy In The UK" on EMI. As well as being a launch pad for the Sex Pistols, it was to see a celebration of the best punk acts from both sides of the Atlantic. The Sex Pistols, The Damned and The Vibrators were to be joined by The Ramones, one of the US bands that had kicked open the doors through which their tailgating British counterparts had swaggered.

McLaren's dream ticket, however, began descending into nightmare before it had even started. The Vibrators pulled out, prompting a decision to draft in The Clash who, finding themselves without a drummer only days before the tour began, recruited Rob Harper via a music paper advert. The Ramones had also refused to join the punk parade and McLaren had replaced them with the untouchables of the American scene, Johnny Thunders & The Heartbreakers, a band that would pretty much join any tour that would have it.

On 1 December 1976, as bands assembled for rehearsals at the former Roxy cinema in Harlesden, North West London, a limousine arrived to ferry the Sex Pistols to the London Weekend Television Studios. Queen had pulled an appearance on the Today programme at the last minute and EMI's new charges had been offered the primetime slot earlier that day in a deal brokered by EMI publicist Eric Hall. The presenter Bill Grundy might have been consigned to obscurity had it not been for what unfolded in his interview with the Pistols and their entourage. The 53-year-old host was in provocative mood, goading the young anarchists about their £40,000 deal with a corporate record company. When Johnny Rotten was audibly heard to say the word "shit", Grundy seized on the opportunity and refused to let go, provoking them into a barrage of swearing. Thames Television's phone lines were jammed with outraged viewers and the Sex Pistols made national headline news. The *Daily Mirror* ran its now legendary headline "The Filth And The Fury" and published the interview in all its glory.

Back at the Roxy, The Damned were eye-witnesses to the fallout from the infamous episode. "They looked utterly miserable," said Sensible of the returning Pistols. "After the show, McLaren tore into them. He was convinced they'd blown it. He was appalled. 'You fucking idiots, you've ruined everything. We're finished.' He was apparently in tears. He thought it was all over. The vibe was bad for the rest of the day." [19]

The Grundy debacle produced not so much ripples as tidal waves. The media was united in its moral indignation. EMI shareholders were livid and staff at its plant in Hayes refused to handle the single. The BBC banned it. A press conference was convened at which EMI's managing director Leslie Hill reassured reporters the label was sticking with the Sex Pistols. But that didn't stop promoters on the eve of the tour calling McLaren's company Glitterbest to cancel dates. A sit-in protest by students at the University of East Anglia in Norwich hadn't saved the opening night, so the curtain raiser was set for the King's Hall in Derby.

However, The Damned weren't on the tour bus when it left. Said Sensible: "We were signed to Stiff – if the latest Costello record didn't sell, the next Ian Dury record didn't get made. There was no money. So we had to stay in bed-and-breakfast places and travel in a transit van." [19]

What followed was one of the most ludicrous scenes ever – quite a claim where punk was concerned. The local council had no objection to the other bands playing, but the Pistols would have to play in private to its leisure committee and meet its approval before they could set foot on stage. They refused, the gig was cancelled and the bus drove on. While The Clash and the Heartbreakers had showed solidarity with punk's pariahs, The Damned's road manager Rich Rogers had said that as their act was not offensive, they would have been happy to audition in front of a jury of councillors. So, Stiff's punk ambassadors were unceremoniously thrown off the tour without having played a single note.

While McLaren's travelling circus rolled on, the relationship between him and the group becoming ever more distrustful, Stiff's hopes for The Damned were bigger than ever. Punk was high on the media agenda and the label was keen to take full advantage. "Neat Neat Neat", the follow-up to "New Rose", would be the first record to benefit from the newly-acquired deal with Island. The group's debut album *Damned Damned Damned* would meanwhile lay claim to being the first British punk album. Both were released on 18 February 1977, long before the Sex Pistols' *Never Mind The Bollocks,* which did not become available on Virgin until 27 October the same year.

The terrier-like Riviera had the bit between his teeth and The Damned would laud yet another victory over their arch rivals by becoming the first British punk band to tour the US. Stiff had big ambitions for a small label only just graduating from mail order, and just as things on the music scene were moving at a lightning pace, here was a label that could keep up with the times.

Another single, "Silver Shirt" by Plummet Airlines, had followed on the heels of Richard Hell's zeitgeist-capturing "Blank Generation". Stiff had called on Sean Tyla to produce the five-piece group, which included bassist Darryl Hunt who would go on to join The Pogues. In keeping with the group's name, the record was a commercial disaster. But the subsequent BUY 9 never even made it as far as the shops. Motörhead's "Leavin' Here", a cover of a Holland Dozier Holland song, backed with "White Line Fever", wasn't issued and only became available when Stiff released BUY 1 to10 as a collectible box-set, following their deletion.

The cover for the Plummet Airlines single had been a black and white affair bearing the band's name bursting from it in 3D. But while the sleeve and the group would soon be forgotten, the newly arrived designer who had drawn it wouldn't. Barney Bubbles had been living in Ireland for a year following the break-up of a long-term relationship. He had been spending his time reading books, raising chickens and broadening his understanding of Art History, finding out what happened between Impressionism and Pop Art.

It was on a brief trip back to England that he met up with Riviera and heard all about the new label he had formed. Riviera realised that Bubbles' rural retreat had made him oblivious to the earth-shattering developments on the English music scene, so he took him to see The Damned at The Roxy. The effect it had on the artist was profound. He moved back to London and began putting his newly acquired knowledge of different art styles into practice at Stiff.

The company still didn't have its own in-house art department and designers Chris Morton and Bubbles worked on a freelance basis. Morton had begun studying at Norwich College of Art and he was travelling up and down to London from there to work for Stiff. He had just produced his own punk sleeve when the intriguing figure of Bubbles arrived at the label to serve up his.

"The first picture sleeve I did was Richard Hell & The Voidoids' 'Blank Generation', which I'm still very proud of," says Morton. "Peter Frame helped with that because he did the artwork for me and took it to the printer because I had to hitch-hike back to Norwich. I used to come down for three days at a time, and take some work home with me and then come back again. I was based in Norwich for at least the first six months. Barney was hardly ever there. He would do stuff, but if he did, he would do it in his own studio."

For years, the single had been the poor relation of the album, but Stiff was alive to the potential of this neglected format, particularly with the youth market. Pocket money could buy a 45 and if a song really took off, sales could run into hundreds and thousands. But young record buyers wanted the packaging to be as engaging as the music it contained.

"We reinvented the single bag," says Morton. "There hadn't been proper picture bags since the mid-sixties when it was for EPs. But even then, it was for bands like the Stones or Yardbirds or quite a big budget thing. You had a generic record company single bag with a big hole in the middle so you could see the label, and the label wouldn't be special either. For us, it was more jumping at an opportunity to make ourselves be noticed."

For the cover of "Neat Neat Neat", Bubbles ran large, stark lettering above a black and white photograph by Chris Gabrin of the band wearing paper bags with eye slits over their heads. The cover was on laminated card and featured the Island logo for the first time on a Stiff product. Mastered by George Peckham, the matrix on the A-side confirmed it as "A Porky Prime Cut", while etched into the B-side was "This Is Your Captain Speaking".

"Neat Neat Neat" and the album from which it was taken were recorded in the tried and tested fashion at Pathway, with Nick Lowe behind its poky desk. However, these two records represented a new and clearly defined chapter for Stiff. Pressed by Island, the artwork looked sharper and more professional and gave Stiff a sure-fire guarantee they would stand out in the crowded racks of record stores. And for a label that had made its mark with one-off singles and EPs, the release of a full-length album was a significant departure. Stiff was becoming a more serious operation and serving notice to the established record companies that it intended to stick around.

Brian James' white-knuckle ride, the sheer speed and energy of which so perfectly epitomised punk, 'Neat, Neat, Neat' clocked in at just over two and a half minutes. The lyrics were virtually lost amid the hailstorm of noise. Scabies' clattering drums and cymbals and Sensible's pumping bass provided a frenetic rhythm. It was the guitarist's brilliantly conceived riff and searing solos, however, that remained scored into the memory, long after the cacophony subsided. It was a perfect storm. On the reverse side, Scabies' "Stab Your Back" came in at just under a minute, and "Singalonga Scabies" was basically the same song minus the lyrics.

The twelve tracks on the album were recorded with the usual efficiency and what resulted was one of punk's standout albums. "Fan Club", a renamed version of "1970" from The Stooges' *Fun House* album, was the only non-original included, a homage to the band that, along with the MC5 and the New York Dolls, had had such an impact on James. With the exception of "Stab Your Back", the rest were written by the guitarist.

Studio engineer Bazza remembers the sessions well and says that despite the group's reputation for mayhem, they were no bother in the studio: "They came in, got set up fairly quickly and they dressed the part, but they were actually quite well behaved lads. I think Nick had a certain quiet authority; he didn't have to go around like a schoolmaster. I think he'd tell a lot of them, 'We're going to make this, it's going to cost a couple of hundred quid and we're going to put it out as a record. So, don't bugger about and we'll get it done'. I don't remember any particular daftness with them.

"One of the things you didn't realise was going on, but was very much part of his skill, was he kept them working well at getting on with the job in hand, without shoving their noses in it, and he got tremendous output. I don't remember any particular heavy hand or, 'It's got to sound like this' or 'It's got to sound like that'. It was things like, 'Carry on what you're doing', and, 'We'll have a bit more of that', and, 'That's nice, great, thank you very much'. What I do remember with The Damned was they were surprisingly well behaved young gentlemen until we had a film crew in and they just switched on and it was The Damned for an hour or so. Then the cameras and lights went away and they were back to being, 'All right, let's get on with it'."

When photographer Peter Gravelle arranged a session with the band, it was not with the intention of producing shots for their album cover. James was going out with Judy Nylon at the time and her best friend Patti Palladin was married to Gravelle. However, the slapstick antics which left the band and the studio dripping with whipped cream were pre-planned. "They concocted this little surprise for us to happen during the photo session," recalls James. "So, out comes the whipped cream and they started getting into this stuff and chucking it. Judy in particular, because I was going out with her. She had a ball, she loved it, although she didn't get me that much. When Barney Bubbles saw the contact sheet he said, 'That's the album cover. That has got to be the album cover.' And we couldn't agree with him more. It was just too bizarre – no one had ever done that."

The first 2,000 copies of *Damned Damned Damned* also featured something that would have been anathema to any other record label. A picture of Island Records act Eddie & The Hot Rods appeared on the back cover with an artificial sticker apologising "for any convenience caused". Riviera was testing Island's sense of fun and also knew that by creating a deliberate mistake, copies from this limited run would be highly sought-after. By engaging in humorous but shrewd stunts like this, Stiff was doing something unique in the industry: it was building a fan club of the label itself.

Many of those who signed to the label also saw the passion Riviera and Robinson had for music and knew they were championing bands they genuinely liked. The Damned's affinity with Riviera was a case in point. "I thought he was great. He was fucking brilliantly horrible," recalls Scabies. "He was funny, but the thing with Jake was he knew who the MC5 and The Stooges were and you talked to him about music. He loved music and he knew good music from bad and that was what set him apart from everyone else that we kind of met. Actually, saying that, that's a little bit unfair on Roger Armstrong and Ted Carroll, because they were good on music as well. But there was something about Jake, he had much more fire in his veins.

"What Ace and Roger and Ted were doing was kind of sedate by comparison and they were kind of doing it for bands they loved, whereas Jake was determined to overturn the industry and to be noticed. So, that was where he was coming from and he was a much more exciting prospect. When he wanted to do it, he sat us down, and he'd say, 'Listen, don't fuck about with this lot. You come with me and I'll fucking make you happen'. And he was always, 'I will. I'm gonna do this. That's what's gonna happen', and it did. But at the same time, he always let me doss on his couch, he'd buy you a pint, you could talk to him about music, you could go and hang out. So, in a funny way he was a bit like a sort of big brother. He was somebody who was a bit older with a little more experience than we had, so it was quite easy to be confident in him."

Brian James says Stiff's anti-corporate image and the rapport they had with Riviera had inspired them to sign with the label and agree to record an album. "I think we recorded 'New Rose' and 'Help' before we even signed the contract, which was totally ridiculous because you're not meant to do that," he says. "But we were just impressed with Stiff. We liked their whole thing, like working out of the shop front. At that time, there were people sniffing around like Polydor and CBS, these people in suits coming down and looking at you, like you were some kind of product. Not so much Dave, who was a bit more like a businessman and a little bit more distant. But Jake was almost like a fifth member of the band.

"It was not long after 'New Rose' was released, he [Riviera] came to us and said, 'I'd like to be your manager and also I'd like you to do an album for Stiff'. We liked the guy so we thought, 'Fuck it, yeah'. I mean, what else were we going to do? Say no to this guy and bum about and sign to some fucking awful record label that might as well be selling sliced bread?"

Jake would make his menacing presence felt on his frequent visits to the offices of United Artists. Before the label had begun distributing for Stiff, industry practice was to press singles in standard slip sleeves bearing the company's logo. Only albums had customised sleeves. Fran Burgess was in charge of product manufacturing for UA at the time, an area bound by rules and procedures. "If ever the rules of oughts and shoulds were challenged," she said "it was by Jake." [20]

She recalled one occasion when she explained to Riviera that he couldn't have the picture bag he wanted: "Who says?" asks Jake. "It's the rule." "So what'll happen?" "John T (the production manager) won't like it," was my feeble reply. Even I knew that wasn't a good enough answer for a client. Jake was the first to have 'proper' sleeves for singles."

Riviera was forever casting his eyes around to see where he could take advantage of a situation and he realised he could save a few quid for Stiff by sneaking its mail into the UA post tray. On one visit, in order to pay for a Damned photo session, the Fagin-like figure pilfered records for his charges to sell on to the shop owned by Roger Armstrong from Chiswick.

"I remember when we did the photo shoot with Chris Gabrin, we didn't have any money and he took us to see Andrew Lauder," Scabies remembers. "When Andrew nipped out of the office, he [Jake] just went through his album cases and gave us about ten albums each and said, 'Right, go and flog these to Roger down at Rock On, and that will give you enough to get over the photo session'. And he would take all of the mail-outs, because Stiff was pretty much a mail-order company; there wasn't that much distribution going on. I mean distribution then was very bitty anyway. There wasn't really a network of alternative record shops. There was some, but you had to deal with a lot of different people, so he used to take all the post-out stuff with him when he went to United Artists and he'd walk through the offices saying hello to everybody and as he was talking to them, he'd just put a handful of records in their out tray so he didn't have to pick up the postage. It was all very hand-to-mouth. I don't think anybody really knew how broke they were. All this about they started on two hundred quid … yeah they did, but the rest of it was blag and bluff."

Riviera relished the opportunity to spend time in America. Through his travels with Dr. Feelgood and taking time out there, especially in Los Angeles, he was familiar with the underground scene and had made plenty of contacts. So, to return to his favourite haunts with his own punk group and chalk up another first for Stiff was a prospect he couldn't resist. On 8 April 1977 at CBGBs, The Damned became the first British punk band to play in the US.

Riviera and staff from the Stiff office flew to New York to see the band play the shows booked by Advancedale. They had cause to expect big things as they prepared to see The Damned play two sets on four consecutive nights at the legendary hole-in-the-wall in the city's East Village. *Damned Damned Damned* had entered the UK album chart on 12 March, beginning a ten-week run that would peak at No. 36. Dave Vanian had adorned the cover of *NME* on 19 March wiping his eye with a large piece of meat. "Old Wave Meats New Wave", ran the headline. Punk was rearing its ugly head in the mainstream and Stiff had one of its most outrageous bands in the chart. Not with a trashy, throwaway single, but an LP that sounded as startling as it looked.

If the band's eyes weren't out on stalks after taking their first ever flight, they were when they reached the dressing room. "When we got there," explains Scabies, "there were three large-breasted, scantily clad women in the dressing room and lots of flowers and cakes, and Jake said, 'This is from The Rolling Stones. Welcome to New York'. I've since found out that actually what it was about was Glen Colson was working for The Rolling Stones and thought it would be a good story for the Stones to be associated with, and so he did it. So, it wasn't really that Mick and Keith did this."

Ex-Charisma publicist Colson was working in America for Rolling Stones' manager Peter Rudge and encountered Riviera and Robinson when they met with Rudge, who wanted to manage Graham Parker. When the gigs at CBGBs were confirmed, they called Colson and asked him to get his pals from the New York media down to the club in The Bowery.

"I went down there and Jake introduced me to Rat Scabies," says Colson. "Jake said, 'This is Glen Colson, my pal' and Rat said, 'So fucking what?' I just thought, 'Bloody hell, that's nice, I've done all this work.' I got all the *New York Times* and the *Trouser Press* there because they were all pals of mine, and the *New York Times* called him Mr Scabies. All the girls in the office had bought cakes and they wanted to sleep with the band because they'd been reading about them in the *Melody Maker*. The *Melody Maker* was quite an underground, hip paper, and all the music people in New York read it. It was far hipper than anything you can ever imagine. It was like *Rolling Stone* was to England; it was revered there. And they'd all given cakes to the band hoping that they could sleep with them later on in the evening, and the band came out and threw them all over the press. It's quite a small gig, CBGBs, so it probably only held about 200 people. They were pretty good; they reminded me of The Who, because they were crazy and the power coming off the stage."

Support at CBGBs came from The Dead Boys, who hailed from Cleveland, Ohio. Notorious for their lewd, aggressive stage shows, they were fronted by Stiv Bators, who would later form Lords Of The New Church with Brian James. "We got this message before we left saying, 'The Dead Boys are gonna kick your ass when you come over,'" says James. "We were like, 'Who the fuck are these Dead Boys? Who are they?' It was like, 'They're real tough guys' and we're thinking, oh shit, here we go. Having just seen *Mean Streets*, I thought, all right, okay, so this is what rough New York is all about, is it? So, we get there and they're just like us. They played great rock 'n' roll and with them playing – because we would do two shows a night – steadily over the course of the three days both bands were playing better and better."

Stiff's original intention was for the band to only play in New York, says Scabies. But word had got out of their thundering performances at CBGBs and they were invited to play two shows on the next two nights at the Rathskeller in Boston, known as The Rat. In one of their Boston shows, the band reportedly brought out chairs and tables on to the stage and proceeded to eat pizza. This was possibly a sideswipe at CBGBs, where people were served hot food at tables while they were playing.

Riviera was also on great form, delivering another of his withering put-downs when the venue tried to short-change the group. "The guy tried to stiff us on the money because we were on a percentage of the door," says Scabies. "I just remember Jake going, 'I didn't notice anyone in there with only one leg.' 'What do you mean?' 'Well, you've paid me for twenty three and a half people!'"

The Damned then heard that if they were prepared to fly west, there was a dream show on the table: a slot supporting Television at the Whisky A Go Go. Money was tight, but Riviera did his sums and reckoned the prestigious date would just about cover their trip to LA. But the artfully edgy New York band refused to have them on their bill. The snub was a bitter blow.

Scabies says: "We went to see them and I remember Jake throwing a lot of abuse. 'Show us your tits!' I think that's what he shouted. The tragic thing about it actually was that we really liked Television and 'Little Johnny Jewel' was what everybody really talked about. That was the first punk single or one of them. They were something else and they gave punk an absolute musical credibility. But their attitude was so punk because it was completely out there, with 'Little Johnny Jewel' specifically.

"There is some good stuff on *Marquee Moon*, but the kind of griminess that Richard Hell put on it just wasn't there. It was like freeform jazz that made sense and it was kind of intellectual. And I was really pleased. 'Okay, I'm in a punk band and everyone's saying punk bands are three chords. But these guys are really accomplished and you could put them on any stage anywhere.' So, when they said, 'You can't do it', we were actually quite gutted. I know we got a bit spiteful about it. But that was one of the reasons we were a bit spiteful, because we thought they'd be on our side. I doubt they'd even heard us. I think it was more our reputation preceding us and Tom Verlaine saying, 'I'm not having a fucking freak show going on before me'."

Discovering they had been booted off the bill on their arrival in LA, The Damned had no money to stay in a hotel, leaving Riviera to thumb through his contact numbers and make some calls. As a result, Tomata du Plenty and Tommy Gear, the singer and keyboard player respectively from local punk band The Screamers – invited them to crash on the floor of their flat for the night. A bit more Jake-style hustling and the band had two nights at The Starwood and the offer of another place to stay.

Marina Muhlfriedel, alias Marina Del Rey, played keyboards with the mostly all-girl pop/punk group Backstage Pass, who had got to know Riviera when Dr. Feelgood had played LA. They were inspired by groups on the local underground scene like The Germs and The Screamers and came along after The Runaways and before The Go-Go's, who would eventually sign to Stiff. When the likes of The Ramones, Blondie, Television and The Damned were in town, they lived up to the group's name, turning up at after-parties and in musicians' hotel rooms.

"They were supposed to be making money when they got to California and they weren't really earning anything," says Del Rey. "So, there was a period when Jake moved in and he was trying to get Genny [Body of Backstage Pass] and I to answer the phone 'Stiff'. Jake and Brian moved in, and then Rat was with us, but then he moved in with Spock [Backstage Pass bass player] and they were together. He gave her the name Mistress Spock because she was a real sci-fi girl and that was when she went from being Joanna to Spock."

For an unplanned trip, The Damned made a lasting impression. At one of the hastily arranged shows at The Starwood, Sensible walked on stage stark naked and proceeded to play his bass, while Vanian emerged wearing a gas mask and waving road flares over the audience, singeing people's hair. For a finale, Scabies pulled out some lighter fuel and set light to the drum kit belonging to support band The Quick. Pictures of the infamous show were captured by local rock photographer Jenny Lens and her picture of a nude Sensible ended up being turned into a pin badge in the UK.

After their final US show at Mabuhay Gardens in San Francisco on 21 April 1977, The Damned returned to London, only to set off for gigs in Paris, Lyon, Brussels and Copenhagen. Riviera stayed behind for a month to soak up the Californian sun and hang out with Del Rey and other friends he had made in LA. Although she began seeing Riviera on and off at the time, she admits being taken aback at his argumentative demeanour.

"I met Jake for the second time at a party for The Pretty Things at Jayne Mansfield's house and left with him and had the biggest argument of my life with a stranger," she says. "He was laying into me about being a rich, spoilt girl from Beverly Hills. It was the craziest thing and I was so upset. I ran into Pete Thomas that night and Pete said, 'Don't worry because anyone Jake yells at is probably going to turn into his best friend'."

Backstage Pass had begun as "a bit of a joke" and it was only as a result of some cajoling on Riviera's part that they played their first public shows. "By the time we got really involved with Jake," says Del Ray "Jake said, 'If you don't go out and play, you're not a band'. You can get all the press everywhere in the world, but until you play, it's just bullshit, you know. Jake booked a showcase for us at the old Columbia lot and we had never played live before, we'd barely played at all. All of a sudden we're in this huge room, Fleetwood Mac were rehearsing in the next room, and there's all these people there and all this drink, and Jake sort of kicked our butts to go out and do it and we did it. And I think our first real gig was opening for Devo at Mabuhay in San Francisco and our second or third gig was opening for Elvis at the Whisky. My feeling is that he let us open because he just didn't want an opening band that was going to detract anything from Elvis."

Genevieve Schorr, alias Genny Body, shared the flat with Del Rey and says Riviera wasn't so interested in The Damned as securing an American record deal for his primary concern, Elvis Costello. "He was staying with us and he would get on the telephone to Island Records and start yelling at them," she says. "He was trying to get Elvis a record deal."

As the watering holes that had served up pub rock began to throb to an edgier, almost alien sound, musicians were drawn to the capital. While the complacent bosses of the more established record companies adopted an "I see no ships" approach to punk's advancing fleet, Riviera and Robinson's criteria stood firm: if something excited them, it deserved a chance. Music fans first and foremost, they made their own exciting discoveries first hand in the pubs and venues where they spent their evenings. And again they displayed an uncanny knack of unearthing musicians with a truly unique gift for song writing.

Tim Smith and girlfriend Gaye Black were there at the right time to take advantage of punk, but not the right place. The couple were at art college in Torquay, a far cry from the capital. Nevertheless, Smith formed Sleaze, the first group to roadtest his rough-hewn compositions. Eventually, his fellow band members ousted him because they wanted to do covers, but by then he'd met Black, who was interested in learning the bass. Smith saw edgier groups like the Feelgoods as the antidote to "fat blokes playing down the pub", and the two of them set off for London with big dreams and a handful of guitar chords.

Their ambition of forming their own band was fulfilled almost immediately after they met guitarist Howard Pickup and drummer Laurie Driver. Then, four days before Christmas 1976, The Adverts – and a plethora of other bands looking for a place to play – got a lucky break. An infamous gay club named Chaguarama's in Covent Garden had been given a lick of paint and a new name, The Roxy, by its new proprietor Andy Czezowski. The club in Neal Street became an instant gathering point for punks and provided the perfect platform for those who had learned four chords or less.

The Adverts made their first appearance there on 15 January 1977, supporting Generation X. However, it was the three successive Monday nights in February supporting The Damned that catapulted them into prominence and saw Gaye Advert being hailed as the "first woman of punk". "The Adverts were a great band," says Brian James. "Andy gave them a chance at The Roxy and the first gig they did was totally shambolic. But you could see that Tim had a talent, Gaye looked good, and you could see the other two guys had promise and they were very keen, and they were watching everything Tim was doing. It was a classic new band, with one guy who knew what he wanted. So, I recommended them and told Jake, 'Go down and check out this band The Adverts at The Roxy', and Jake came down and liked them – well liked the way Gaye looked anyway – and put out 'One Chord Wonders'."

"That was the amazing thing about a company like Stiff," enthuses Smith. "That when all the record labels were still sitting in their offices trying to figure out what was going to be the next big thing, Jake was down at The Roxy finding out what was going on and seeing what bands were playing live. That was a big difference between a dynamic record company like Stiff and the majors. The bigger labels didn't want to respond. They were dragged kicking and screaming into liking punk rock just because they saw there was no way to resist it anymore. Whereas Jake and Dave liked the idea of it. Obviously they had come from pub rock, which they liked. They liked the idea of musicians just playing, without all that commercial crap around it. They created their own commercial thing in their own sort of way. But the bands they were interested in were the ones that went out there and did it, the rest of the major labels were just interested in the money really."

The Adverts signed a one-single deal with Stiff and "One Chord Wonders" (BUY 13), released on 29 April 1977, exemplified Stiff's finest qualities. From the group's raucous delivery and Larry Wallis' no frills production at Pathway to Bubbles' arresting pop art sleeve, it was bang on the money. The record showed that Stiff had its finger on the pulse and knew just how to package its exhilarating records. Which is why, contrary to the band's wishes, Gaye Advert's face was chosen for the iconic front cover.

Smith recalls how the band were surprised, not to say hoodwinked, by this choice of image: "When we had been doing the recordings at Pathway, we got taken out to a building site across the road and did a photo session there, all hanging around in the dark amongst the rubble, and we believed that was going to be the cover. I think that ended up on the back of it. So, when we went down to see what they'd come up with for the cover, we were a bit surprised to see just a picture of Gaye on the front.

"As I've said many times, it's such an iconic picture, what can you say? It's a brilliant cover, so you can't turn it down. But it wasn't what we were expecting. We were expecting the band hanging around in the dark amongst the rubble looking like a gang, because we wanted to put across the image that we were a band. None of us, and particularly Gaye, liked the idea we were being promoted as just the beautiful iconic female figure on the front. Once you are stuck with that, you are stuck with it for good – as we were."

Bubbles' decision to use a cropped close-up of her face resulted in one of punk's most enduring sleeves. The monotone design harked back to Bubbles' 1970 album sleeve for heavy blues rock band Red Dirt on the Fontana label. That cover featuring the face of a native American was black and white, all except for red lines dripping from the forehead. It was a stroke of genius from Stiff's perspective, but pushing her to the forefront caused problems within a group.

"It was popular," says Advert, "but it wasn't really what we needed at the time, because I didn't want to be picked on for being female and other members of the band didn't want me getting all the attention. It didn't help anything really."

"It caused a bit of friction, the usual band competition: the drummer wasn't happy about that, particularly about Gaye being picked out from the rest," Smith admits. "Well, you know, none of us were happy; Gaye didn't want it. But there we were, saddled and, at the same time, blessed with a brilliant sleeve that laid out what, for loads of people, was the band."

If the sleeve was brilliantly conceived, so too was the poster for their subsequent nationwide tour. "The Damned Can Now Play Three Chords, The Adverts Can Play One. Hear All Four Of Them At ..." Stiff's stablemates lifted the roof at 30 venues. They travelled in the same minibus, with Riviera and Lowe sometimes tagging along, and covered the whole country. The timing was perfect. Punk had exploded and was dominating the front covers of the music press. The Damned had been gigging solidly for several months and their album was selling well. The Adverts meanwhile had recorded a session for John Peel on 25 April and had released a staggering debut single. On stage each night, the two groups vied to blow each other away.

The expedition, however, was not without controversy. As with the Anarchy Tour, panic among councils and other public authorities about punk gigs meant dates were canned. A show in Stafford was called off with four hours' notice after police refused to attend; another in Southampton went the same way when porters and bar staff downed tools in protest at the booking. Other gigs were called off amid similar unease and matters weren't made any easier when skinheads attacked Lincoln Drill Hall on 7 June, resulting in terrifying scenes.

"We ended up having to hide in the dressing room while skinheads tried to batter down the door," Smith remembers vividly. "We came out at the end afterwards to find the tyres of the van had been let down in the back alley behind the venue and there was a gang up at either end of the alleyway waiting to come and beat us up. So, it was a bit weird, two punk bands having to call the police to stop ourselves getting killed. But it was quite nasty because, at that particular gig, gangs of skinheads were waiting on the road between the station and the venue trying to pick off punk stragglers to beat them up, so it was not very nice really. I mean, you were fearing for your life."

Advert adds: "The kids had smashed all the windows in the minibus by the time we'd got back out to it. It was mad. When you were in the venue, you couldn't actually see anybody, you could just hear them trying to batter the door down. You didn't know if it was a whole army or a dozen or what. It was frightening."

The Adverts had left Stiff within a month of the tour's last date. Robinson had hoped the group would stick around and fought hard to keep hold of them, says Smith. But by this time The Adverts had their own manager, Michael Dempsey, and he felt they would be better served by a bigger label.

Smith says of their decision to quit Stiff: "I think the main reason was because we were always going to be second in the list to The Damned, who were obviously the punk band who had been with Stiff for a while and who Stiff would have put all their resources into. So, we were always going to be the support band to The Damned and the band that had less exposure than them. I think Michael's tactic to go to another label where we were the punk band and they would give us all their attention was absolutely correct. Anchor were a major label because they had funding from ABC, the American label, and they had an A&R team who were very keen on us and wanted to commit to the band."

The Adverts did what Stiff had failed to do in its first year in operation with their first release on Anchor Records. "Gary Gilmore's Eyes" entered the UK chart at No. 27, sandwiched between Hot Chocolate and The Dooleys, and a month later it reached its highest position of No. 18. When their debut album *Crossing The Red Sea With The Adverts* was released on Bright Records, it enjoyed one week in the UK chart at No. 38. Their departure from Stiff had been vindicated.

Advancedale artists promoted from the office at Alexander Street had also scored hits. Graham Parker's "Pink Parker" EP had got to No. 24 in March 1977. Meanwhile, Dave Edmunds – who had snubbed Stiff for Led Zeppelin's Swan Song label – achieved the same chart position with "I Knew The Bride".

Stiff's first year had seen it attract widespread press attention and release a battery of incredible records. But, for all that, it had not made even a fleeting impression on the UK chart and with its operational costs growing, commercial success was needed.

Happily, one of the very first artists to sign for Stiff was about to put that right.

4

Elvis Is King

Declan MacManus stood up from his seat nervously anticipating the doors of the rattling London Underground carriage opening at Royal Oak Station. It was a weekday afternoon and he had thrown another "sickie" from the Elizabeth Arden cosmetics company in West London, where he worked mostly by himself, an arrangement which quite suited the geeky looking computer operator. In his hand was a cassette tape of songs he'd recorded that he wanted to take to a label he'd read about in the paper. The label, of course, was Stiff.

"A charming girl opened the door and politely received my hand-written tape box and that was that. No big interview, no audition, no cigar-chomping mogul," recalled MacManus, now known to the world as Elvis Costello. [21]

At 22, MacManus had a wife and a two-year-old son waiting at home when he came off his shift at the decidedly unglamorous looking cosmetics factory in Wales Farm Road, North Acton. Settling down and taking on such commitments at such a young age was common in the Britain of the mid-seventies. However, such social conformity now seems rather anomalous with a pub rock performer who aspired to carve out a living from his notebooks of scribbled songs.

Music was in his blood. His father, Ronald Patrick Ross MacManus (known as Ross) taught himself to read music, sang, and picked up the trumpet, inspired by musicians he heard on his jazz and bebop records. He learned his chops in the swing bands which thrived during World War II, but it was his voice that landed him his big break. A talent spotter for the Joe Loss Orchestra pricked up his ears when he came across him performing one night and he was snapped up as one of three leading vocalists with the famous band leader.

So, when Declan Patrick was born on 25 August 1954 to Ross and Lillian, it was into a household steeped in music. When his dad went on summer seasons with the orchestra, a wide-eyed Declan would sometimes get to clamber aboard the tour bus and, more often, he would be taken on the short journey to watch him perform at the Hammersmith Palais. He recalled these precious young memories in a BBC documentary about the celebrated venue, screened shortly after its closure in 2007.

Ross enjoyed some success after going solo in 1968, chalking up a minor hit in Germany and backed by The Joe Loss Blue Beats. However, it was through a classic television advert that his voice was enshrined in the memories of anyone who lived through the 1970s. It was his breathy crooning about the "Secret Lemonade Drinker" who crept down to the fridge in his pyjamas in the memorable R. White's commercial. Listen carefully and you will hear his son providing backing vocals.

MacManus Jr had paid his dues by the time he set off for Stiff. He had dragged his guitar around bars and small clubs for several years and enjoyed some prominence on the London pub rock scene with his band Flip City. Ultimately though, it had led to nothing. Dave Robinson had raised Flip City's hopes by talking about releasing "Third Rate Romance", one of MacManus's compositions, as a one-off single – only to drop the idea. The group split up soon after. Undeterred, MacManus plugged on with only his amplified acoustic guitar for support. Live music fans who got their regular fix at small clubs or pubs away from the centre of the capital, such as The Half Moon in Putney or The Swan in Kingston, will have been fortunate enough to have seen one of these very early solo performances.

Among those MacManus badgered to plug his gigs and play his songs was Radio London DJ Charlie Gillett, who had kick-started the career of Graham Parker. He had also sent him a demo tape containing six original songs he had recorded in his bedroom using a four-track tape recorder. Most of them had been written late at night, so as not to disturb his wife and baby son, and also on the tube train on his way to work. The songs, which were among fifteen he recorded to convince record companies to sign him, were: "Cheap Reward"; "Jump Up"; "Mystery Dance"; "Wave A White Flag"; "Blame It On Cain", and "Poison Moon" (these songs would resurface as a bootleg single entitled The Honky Tonk demos, much sought after by fans).

On 15 August 1976, Gillett gave D.P. Costello, as MacManus was then known, his first airplay. Despite the basic nature of the recordings and the almost brutal rawness of the vocals, Costello clearly wasn't short of self-belief. Gillett later told his listeners the letter that had arrived with the tape "D.P." sent in said "something along the lines of, 'Here's a tape and I hope that one day I'll be famous enough so it will be worth auctioning the tape off on *Honky Tonk'*. Well I'm not going to do that; I'm going to keep it. And here's another song called 'Lip Service'".

But whereas such welcome airplay had instantly led to a major record deal for Graham Parker, Costello's radio debut brought no such rewards. And, as the cocky computer operator tramped from one record company to another, he was continually knocked back. They "tolerated" the unannounced auditions he sprang on them, but casually took calls from "their wives or bookies" [21] as his piercing voice and the strings of his acoustic guitar cut through their plush offices. Given the unavoidable comparisons between the two artists, Costello and Parker, from age and appearance down to their gritty vocal delivery, his rejection by every major label in town must have been hard to swallow. This was spelled out in "I'm Not Angry" in which he sings of the "vanity factory" (Elizabeth Arden) where he once worked.

The only consolation of his humdrum job, aside from the regular money, was that he could work on his songs and even pluck away at his guitar on quiet shifts. Costello recalls: "I used to work evenings when it was at the end of the month and the payroll stuff was due. I'd stay late, sometimes work 36 hours on coffee and write two or three songs and read the music press." [22]

The demo Costello hand delivered to Alexander Street was the first Stiff received when it opened for business. So, while Robinson would later casually toss the precious tapes of budding songwriters in the bin to cries of "Rubbish!" this one from an artist he had recorded at the Hope & Anchor was guaranteed an attentive audience. Commenting on the style of these early compositions, Costello confesses that he was uneasy with imitating some American singers and songwriters.

Conflicting accounts of initial reactions to his demo have been given over the years. In an interview with the *NME*'s Nick Kent published on 25 August 1977, Riviera said: "I immediately put it on and thought, 'God, this is fuckin' good' – but at the same time I was hesitating because after all it was the first tape and I wanted to get a better perspective."

Robinson meanwhile has said Riviera was dismissive of the tape when he heard it and he was the one who wanted to sign him. "Elvis Costello went to every single major in town before he came to us, but he was on my list anyway, so it didn't really matter in my book," he said. [5] But, as Robinson had recorded him a year or so earlier at the Hope & Anchor and had him on his "list", why then had it taken the singer visiting Alexander Street in person and handing his tape to whoever happened to be there?

"He [Robinson] was quite surprised when I turned out to be the same person," said Costello. [24] "When I submitted the tapes to Stiff, he didn't realise it was the same person who'd done the earlier tape ... It turned out he already had over an hour of me on tape and didn't know it."

Sean Tyla was a regular visitor to Stiff in those days and he remembers Robinson inviting him to give his feedback on the tape. Riviera had wanted to sign Costello from the off, but that day at Alexander Street, Robinson had "vilified" his demos, according to Tyla: "Robinson was not as enthusiastic as his partner and invited me up to the top floor listening room and asked for my opinion. I must admit I was surprised to be consulted." [16]

Interestingly, Nick Lowe too remembered Stiff seeing his potential, not as an artist, but as a songwriter in the first instance. Riviera had apparently picked up on "Mystery Dance" and could hear its thudding beat, instantly singable chorus and fifties-style rock 'n' roll guitar solo being performed by his friend and collaborator Dave Edmunds. He called Costello. Stiff was impressed with his tape, he said, but the singer would have to wait for a week while the label weighed up other demos that had been sent in. A week later Riviera called him in to see them.

Speaking less than a year later about his long-awaited deal, Costello said: "I didn't go in and say, 'Look, I've got these songs and, well, with a bit of patching up and a good producer, I might make a good record'. I went in and said, 'I've got some great fucking songs, record them and release them.' Stiff were the only ones that showed that kind of faith in me." [25]

But one obvious challenge faced Riviera and Robinson: how were they going to market him to the masses? With his horn-rimmed glasses and brushed back hair, he looked more like a nerdy college student than a pop star. As for his name, D.P. Costello hardly fitted with the exciting, cutting-edge operation they envisioned. Stiff wanted not only to ignite some careers, but detonate a device that would blow a bloody great hole in the music industry. How could Costello be primed to do just that?

Costello, like other artists, took to dropping in at the Stiff office. The endless banter and frantic bouncing of ideas within the office was the ideal environment to provide the answer. "Here, put these on", said Robinson thrusting into his hand a pair of thick-framed Buddy Holly glasses. Stories abound about where the christening of "Elvis" took place, but the name certainly came from the man who had already reinvented himself. Costello recalled: "'This'll be great', Jake just said, 'We're going to call you Elvis. Ha ha ha!'. And I thought it was just one of those mad things that would pass off and, of course, it didn't. Then it became a matter of honour as to whether we could carry it off." [26]

"Suzanne [Spiro] was the one that got him the glasses," says Attraction Bruce Thomas. "She was an advertising set stylist before she went to work at Stiff and she said, 'We'll get you some glasses' and did the Buddy Holly on acid thing. It was going to be Elvis Costello or Jerry Lee Abbott."

Ian Gomm, who first met Costello when he came to watch Brinsley Schwarz, called in at Alexander Street one day to find him being reinvented. "I gave him a lift to the Tube station, Declan, who had now been renamed Elvis. I remember him coming out of this office and looking really quite bemused with this pair of bloody glasses on," he says. "As I said, 'Do you want a lift to the station?' somebody shouted, 'And keep those fucking glasses on, Elvis!'"

Following its launch the previous summer, and subsequent run of singles, Stiff was keen to keep up the momentum with new acts – especially ones that might attract the interest of the press. Costello was pointed in the direction of Nick Lowe and Barry Farmer at Pathway and, as he didn't have a band, Stiff had a brainwave for these embryonic studio sessions.

Along with The Damned, Graham Parker and Dave Edmunds, Advancedale's management roster also boasted country rock band Clover, who hailed from the Bay Area of San Francisco. Some of them would later re-emerge as Huey Lewis & The News, one of the transatlantic success stories of the eighties. But in 1976 they were certainly not hip. If anything, they were a band out of time.

Riviera and Robinson had high hopes for them. But the longhaired troupe had failed to get a foothold in the UK and had found themselves kicking their heels at a country retreat. Headley Grange in east Hampshire had once been a poorhouse, but by the 1960s it was playing home to the rich and famous. Led Zeppelin recorded and composed there and it was where Robert Plant wrote most of the lyrics to "Stairway To Heaven". It was here, in the cold and damp of this tumbledown manor, that the Marin County cowboys and Costello were crashing as they prepared for their Stiff recording sessions

Costello needed no introduction to the music of his newly acquired backing band. Rummaging through the racks in a secondhand record shop in Wandsworth, he'd unearthed a vinyl copy of Clover's album *Fourty Niner* that was missing its sleeve and played it until he knew every note. Some of his own compositions had more than a slight country lilt to them, "Radio Sweetheart" and "Stranger In The House" to name but two, reflecting his admiration for the likes of Merle Haggard, George Jones and the Flying Burrito Brothers. So, when Costello unexpectedly found himself in the cramped confines of Pathway with musicians he admired, he felt a little apprehensive at the idea of directing them.

Costello said: "Given my almost complete lack of studio experience and the cult status of Clover, it was pretty intimidating to ask for changes in the arrangements, but it is not as if we had the resources to belabour anything in the recording process. *My Aim Is True* was recorded in six, four-hour sessions, yielding the original 12-track sequence and three completed out-takes. It transformed me from someone who recorded in his bedroom to a pop singer with an odd name, who had the chance to appear on television and radio, perform on club and theatre stages, and eventually make his way in the world. The recordings with Clover were the first thing most people heard with my new name attached and whatever naïveté I now detect in my own performances, their impact, and the debt I owe to the players, is undeniable." [27]

The results of these first sessions toward the end of 1976 would eventually find their way on to a bootleg LP called *Our Aim Is True*, so authentic looking with its black and white chequered sleeve that many thought it a Stiff marketing device. For fans, it still stands as a fascinating glimpse into the development of one of the most extraordinary artists of his generation. Teetering on the threshold of fame, the voice being accompanied by these American visitors gives little hint of the belligerent, finger jabbing figure who would soon be unleashed by the label. The songs are those of a singer/songwriter with an acoustic guitar, not the agitator with an electric one – more denim jacket than skinny tie.

But although he may have looked and sounded more pub rock mutineer than new wave warhead, Stiff had heard enough to know it wanted not just a single, but an album. Sessions continued with the west coast band, disguised as The Shamrocks due to contractual issues. Crammed into Pathway were: John McFee, lead and pedal steel guitar; Sean Hopper, keyboards; John Ciambiotti, bass guitar, and Mickey Shine, drums. Vocalist and harmonica player Huey Lewis was surplus to requirements, so went on holiday. The recording sessions took place over three days and were followed by three days of overdubbing and a further three days mixing. The twelve tracks were completed on 26 January 1977.

"He [Costello] was very mature. He'd had his background with his father's big bands and that sort of thing, so I think he knew how to carry himself with professional musicians," Barry Farmer remembers. "It was very much a professional gig with them. It was a lot of fun, but they came in and worked extremely hard. They did it very quickly and they did a great job of it. And certainly, in the circumstances, I think Elvis was getting pretty much what he hoped he would get. I really enjoyed it.

"They all sounded like real songs, not like some. There were quite a lot of songs or recordings made there which were kind of 'Oh yeah.' But these all sounded very well honed and the lyrics were so well structured. There were a couple of people that came along not so long after Costello, who obviously picked up ideas from him, but had missed the point. Costello very much had elements of an English Dylan, in that he was very clever at using short phrases to tell a big story. One line would have a great weight of image behind it and he was very clever at that. Whereas other people tried the same thing and just got clever and wordy, he'd get it right."

Although "Mystery Dance" had grabbed Riviera's attention when he first heard the tape, it was another less obvious one that was chosen as his debut single. "Less Than Zero" had been penned after Costello watched a television interview with an arrogant and unrepentant Oswald Mosley, leader of the British Union Of Fascists. The references to "Mr Oswald" caused some American listeners to misconstrue the lyrics, assuming them to be about Lee Harvey Oswald. Consequently, Costello wrote a "Dallas version" about President John F. Kennedy's assassin.

"Less Than Zero" was released on 18 March 1977 as Stiff BUY 11, with "Radio Sweetheart" on side two. Its monochrome sleeve was as sparse as the record's three chord intro. The name of Stiff's new prodigy was written in large block capitals, above a photo of a rake-thin bloke, with his hands self-consciously stuffed into the pockets of his corduroys and one foot pointing towards the other. Staring out awkwardly through his specs, Costello looked more like a supply teacher than a pop star in waiting. An image makeover was in order.

On the other side of the sleeve, the forceful marketing of the label was maintained, with Stiff's logo and full address featured, along with the slogan "Reversing Into Tomorrow". Riviera and Robinson's management company also got a mention, with those who bought the record being informed that Elvis Costello was "an Advancedale Artist". And the initiated, who knew to scour the run-off grooves carefully, found the words "Elvis Is King" etched by Porky Peckham. And on the reverse? "Elvis Is King On This Side Too." The cover may not have been wildly exciting, but it was 100% Stiff.

What the media would make of this oddity on a swaggering new label was anyone's guess. However, Stiff's cuttings books were building up nicely by now and "Less Than Zero" attracted some notices. Reactions were mixed, however. Appraising the single in *Melody Maker*, Caroline Coon drew comparisons with Jonathan Richman and the "Graham Parker/Bruce Springsteen school of modern rock". Despite it being promising with "ideas streaming from both sides", she concluded: "This is album material. Not for the chart." The teacups must have really started flying at Alexander Street when *Sounds* landed on the desk complete with Jonh [*sic*] Ingham's scathing review:

> It's spot the rip-off time as a cross between Graham Parker and Brinsley Schwarz (the group) takes a wander through the pop history books in search of suitable riffs. The B-side is a little more palatable, but why bother when there's still albums that do it far better.

Ouch!

Costello may have shared a management company with Graham Parker, but such comparisons must have rankled. After all, Advancedale's prized asset had enjoyed critical acclaim after his spin on *Honky Tonk*. And, as if Parker and his band weren't casting enough of a shadow over Costello's arrival, they celebrated a Top 30 hit with a cover of The Trammps' "Hold Back The Night" in the month "Less Than Zero" – which stiffed – was released.

For someone who would later become known for his refusal to do interviews, Costello had plenty to say as Stiff sprung him from the traps. Was he embittered? Damn right he was. But ready to play the music biz game? Over his dead body. In a spiky interview with Chas De Whalley from *Sounds*, his unapologetically aggressive stance was in keeping with that of his brash label. He refused to have his picture taken – "I want to keep my own face. I don't want anyone to know what I look like" – leaving the photographer with no option than to take paparazzi-style shots. He snapped him skulking outside the front door of 32 Alexander Street, ironically right next to a poster promoting Graham Parker's hit EP!

If some observers reckoned Stiff had picked the wrong song to launch its new artist, it couldn't have been faulted for its next choice. "Alison" was an achingly beautiful lament in which he yearned for an old friend who was married, but unhappy. Accepted more than three decades later as one of the finest songs in the Costello songbook, its plaintive chorus also provided him with the title of the album that was soon to follow.

Costello's own marriage was crumbling, but he was still wearing his ring as he crouched in a corner on the cover of the single. Again, Stiff had plumped for a black and white image with the title of the single and its flip-side "Welcome To The Working Week" in modest type along the top. A ripped up photograph of "Alison" featured on the back.

"Alison" was released in the same month as the Clash's "Remote Control" and the Sex Pistols' Silver Jubilee diatribe "God Save The Queen". Everything was moving at breakneck speed and singer songwriters with acoustic guitars were at risk of being drowned out. But Costello had no such fears. His songs were different; he was different. "I listen to all kinds of things and naturally some come out in my songs," he told Chas De Whalley. "But I've never rewritten anybody else's song and I'll argue the toss with anybody that I sound like me. My album *My Aim Is True* will prove it when it comes out next month."

Despite Costello's bravado, his debut album would not appear in the shops for another three months because of a bitter dispute between Stiff and its distributor, Island. Relations between the two labels had not so much cooled as completely frozen over. As millions celebrated the Queen's Silver Jubilee weekend on 4 and 5 June 1977, Island stopped all promotion and distribution on behalf of Stiff and there were rumours Stiff employees had been barred from Island's offices. So, as Stiff stood on the verge of releasing its most hotly anticipated record to date, it couldn't get its product into the shops.

Maybe he had spent too long in the sun during his month-long vacation in the US, but when Riviera bumped into a *Sounds* reporter in London's Nashville Rooms in West Kensington, he spent the evening airing the company's dirty washing. He had dumped Island Records, he told them. "'I tore up the contract and threw it down the bog', was the least colourful comment he made all night," said a subsequent report. "The others were not only unprintable but libellous too." [28]

Island was reported to have paid £17,000 for its stake in the rights of the Stiff catalogue and, when relations broke down, had demanded it back. It was also said to have ordered compensation be paid in lieu of the costs it had incurred in setting up the promotion and distribution arrangements for Stiff's product. Only *Damned Damned Damned* had made the chart by then, indicating Island had not yet recouped its outlay. According to the revealing *Sounds* article, awash with information from inside sources, "Island want their dues in hard cash and, unless Stiff are wealthier than their pokey little offices suggest, they just ain't got it," it reported. [28] So badly had the relationship deteriorated that Riviera was rumoured to be preparing to fly out to the Bahamas to negotiate with Chris Blackwell face-to-face. After all, Stiff faced being left out of pocket and stuck with boxes of records it had no way of paying for or getting into shops.

There was a flip side. Island's chart successes had been few and far between and the publicity around Bob Marley and Eddie & The Hot Rods had not reflected in sales. The label had also reduced the number of sales reps it had out on the road in order to make savings, suggesting furrowed brows on both sides. But if Riviera was worried, he didn't show it. Quite the reverse. He told *Sounds* that Stiff was preparing to go it alone again, and was involved in discussions with other independents about establishing a nationwide distribution system that would negate the need for the deal with Island.

"I could go straight back to work tomorrow, if I could get my records back," said Riviera. Stiff's co-owner added rather ominously: "We might even have to wind everything up completely until our contract runs out."[28] Island refused to comment while negotiations were taking place.

Tales of Riviera's verbal sparring matches with his counterparts at Island were the stuff of legend. Glen Colson, who Riviera brought in to help promote Costello, recounts an occasion when it wasn't just verbal: "One time we were in Dingwalls and there was a marketing guy that worked for Island called Knocker Knowles. There was also a guy called Matthew Kaufman who had a record label [Beserkley] and he was there as well and we were all chatting and Jake poured a glass of beer over this Knocker Knowles' head.

"This guy was like a fucking boxer and you'd never find someone like him in a record company any more. I used to get on okay with him, but Jake said, 'You haven't got The Damned in the Top 20 this week, so you're going to get some beer over your head'. And he punched Jake and knocked all his teeth out and Jake sued Dingwalls and they gave him some money to get some crowns. And then he blamed me for not jumping in and helping him. I said, 'I didn't pour fucking beer over this lunatic's head'. He only punched him a couple of times and then he went down like a sack of spuds. I just picked him up and that was it. He deserved it."

Things had started out so well when the deal had been signed back in February. To mark the new arrangement, one morning Costello played for Island staff in the label's studio in Basing Street. Tanked up on cans of extra strong lager, Riviera led a party from Alexander Street for the occasion, and Colson recalls him making a typically bullish, yet prophetic, speech: "'Forget all about your Steve Winwoods, and all your arty farty, this is the man that's gonna fucking do it'. Costello went into about five songs and everybody was just up against the wall because it was loud in this small room. It was exciting."

Once, Riviera turned up at a restaurant, marched up to the table and demanded that the person he was meeting name three songs from Elvis Costello's new record. When he couldn't, he walked out.

When the deal with Island was first agreed, Island press officer Rob Partridge suggested Island and Stiff employees get together over lunch to mark the partnership. But Riviera, who had a loathing of corporate-style events, refused to get involved. Colson recalls: "Jake called me up and said, 'You're having lunch with the Island lot today in this Italian restaurant down in Kensington, and you're taking all the roadies of all the bands. And you're gonna tell them they work in the company, they are the workers of Stiff.' So, I show up with about fifteen of these roadies, and they are about the worst fucking behaved bunch in the world. And there were about six or seven people from Island at the top and I could see them looking over at me and thinking, 'What's going on?' People were saying, 'Oh, I've never eaten avocado before' and they were eating the skin just to wind them up!

"Kosmo [Vinyl] was there and probably that Dez Brown guy, and lots of other roadies. We had a huge lunch and I'm sure they didn't want to pay for it. They were desperate for me to pay, but I just told them I had no money on me. But this lunch lasted for about three hours. It was like the last days of Rome; these roadies were just going fucking crazy. That's what he's like. He didn't want to have a get-together."

Not a single record was released by Stiff during June and July 1977 due to the stand-off with Island. The release of "Alison" at the tail-end of May began a period of inactivity which would not end until Costello's next single was issued on 5 August. The impasse meant the scheduled release of *My Aim Is True* was delayed. But Costello was incapable of sitting still and Stiff knew it couldn't afford to. The enforced delay was used to deal with another pressing issue.

Costello, unlike most Stiff acts, had yet to be seen performing by most of those seeking out his records and reading about him. He did return to his old pub rock haunt, The Nashville Rooms, to support The Rumour on Friday 27 and Saturday 28 May 1977. Two short, sharp sets were delivered not with an acoustic guitar, but a Fender electric plugged into a small amp. He clearly made a big impression on the *Melody Maker's* Allan Jones, as it prompted him to do a full-length interview. Costello may not have wanted anyone to see his face, but Stiff needed its mystery man to get himself out there if the album – whenever it was released – was to sell. For that, he would need his own group. And fast.

Costello told Jones in an office above Alexander Street: "The group I want will be a lot sparser than the album sound. I just want bass, drum, guitar – my guitar – and for keyboards we'll probably go for a Vox or Farfisa sound. I want to get away from the conventional group sound". Tellingly, he added: "There are going to be no fucking soloists in my band. The songs are the most important thing."

The drummer was the first vacancy to be filled, laying a rock solid foundation for Costello to build on. Pete Thomas had relocated to the US after the break-up of Chilli Willi & The Red Hot Peppers to team up with country songwriter and singer John Stewart, composer of The Monkees' No.1 hit "Daydream Believer". He was still just 22 and living in Topanga Canyon in the Santa Monica Mountains, near Los Angeles, along with his sister Philippa among others. But in the summer of 1977 Riviera turned up with a plan to bring him home.

"He showed up in America with The Damned," says Thomas, "and he came round to my house in LA and we went for a walk in the park and he played me Elvis' demos. He said, 'God, I've got this guy who I think is gonna be great', and I really liked it. Then he said, 'Well, if you happen to come back to England, you know, I might be able to wangle something.' And, one way or another, I managed to get back to England. I cut all my hair off, got a leather jacket and a skinny tie."

At the time, there had been the possibility of Thomas returning to England to team up with Dr. Feelgood. So did Jake, as has been claimed, get the Canvey band to pay for his flight, only to then steal him from under their noses? "It had very little to do with me," says Thomas coyly, "but somehow I was back in England doing some things and then there were other possibilities. It might be an example of Jake's entrepreneurial skills or something like that. It was a clever way of getting me back." Riviera must have had a grin the length of Sunset Strip.

Although not well acquainted, Thomas and Costello had met on the pub rock scene. "I think I saw Flip City at The Kensington and Elvis used to come and see Chilli Willi," says Thomas. "I think I met him once or something. He was just this bloke that used to come along. But I knew who he was and I think he quite liked Chilli Willi. That whole pub rock thing was based on those American bands. Some people liked the New Orleans more, some people – like Paul Carrack – liked the funkier stuff. But everyone was basically playing American-style stuff."

Stiff Records require organist/synthesiser player and bass player. Both able to sing, for rocking pop combo. Must be broad-minded. Young or old 01-229 7146 or 1147.

So read the tiny advert hidden away in the *Melody Maker* classifieds on 4 June 1977. Applicants were auditioned at a small rehearsal space in Putney, with The Rumour's rhythm section of Steve Goulding on drums and Andrew Bodnar on bass duties.

Bruce Thomas was a seasoned bass player who had done sessions with singer/songwriters, including Bridget St John, Richard Thompson, Iain Matthews and Andy Roberts. He had played on the original version of "Ray Of Light", later transformed into a trance-like, dance-floor hit by Madonna, and played with Sutherland Brothers And Quiver, an outfit much admired by Costello. But his long hair, flared trousers and personal music tastes were a long way from the band Costello and his ultra-hip label had in mind. When he dialled the number, it was the receptionist – and his future wife – who landed him an audition.

"When I rang up they said, 'Who are your favourite bands?' and I said, 'Steely Dan and Graham Parker'," he says. "And I heard Elvis's voice in the background saying, 'Get rid of him', and the woman who was on the phone said, 'I think you should give him a chance', which was ironic because I would end up marrying her."

Pete Thomas couldn't sit in on the auditions but, fortuitously for Bruce, he had already recommended him. "I got in with Elvis one day and someone said that Bruce Thomas had answered the ad," says the drummer. "I used to love Quiver, Bruce's previous band. I used to go and see them when I was 15 and I thought Bruce Thomas was the greatest bass player. So, when someone said 'Bruce Thomas has just called', I just went, 'Oh for fuck's sake, this guy is fucking brilliant'. I think Elvis spotted that I was enthusiastic, and it was like, 'All right, we'll get him in'. Obviously he was great, so that worked."

The hippie-looking bassist was aware of his namesake from Chilli Willi, but knew nothing of Flip City or Elvis Costello. So, he did his homework, buying the singles Stiff had already released and working out the bass parts. Bruce Thomas remembers: "I went and did the audition, and they were all there in their tight black jeans and I had flares and earth shoes on, looking like Dennis Waterman or somebody really uncool, with big lapels and that kind of thing. They were all like looking at me and I thought, I'd better go and get my hair cut and get these trouser legs taken in.

"Steve [Goulding] was playing the drums at the audition. I think they'd already decided on Steve Nieve, mainly because he went to the audition, thought he was joining an Elvis Presley tribute act, drank a bottle of sherry and fell asleep on the floor. So, he got the job. I knew

Pete, and thereby Jake, very slightly, because he was their roadie. I'd learned some of the songs and Jake had checked me out because I reputedly had a volatile nature, I can't imagine why!

"The song that did it for me actually, the song I thought, 'I want to play that on stage', was 'Mystery Dance' because I thought, I've worked out the moves. I was working on my feet. Playing it was a piece of cake. I was more bothered about the bloomin' shakes. So, I thought, this is okay. Then, of course, I had to learn songs John Ciambiotti had done the bass parts for. I used to like Clover. They were a bit of a cult band; they were one of the cooler of those American bands."

The keyboard player who ended up out for the count on the floor of Pathway had not acquired his stage name. That day, he was still Steve Nason. Just 19 and with no previous experience in bands, he was a prodigious talent. He had trained at London's Royal College of Music and at the Costello audition he did enough to simultaneously pass and pass out. So, with the classically trained pianist with a wild streak and a long-haired bassist schooled in folk and country rock, the "rocking pop combo" was complete. Costello quit his job at Elizabeth Arden on 5 July, praying his yet-to-be-released album would enable him to continue to provide for his wife and son. Stiff meanwhile was pinning its hopes on him providing the commercial success that had so far eluded it.

While Elvis Costello was signed to both Stiff and Advancedale, there was no disputing he was Riviera's man. Graham Parker remained Robinson's primary concern from a management perspective, but when the auditions finished in Putney, and Costello emerged with his answer to The Rumour, it was Riviera who was ready with a plan. The next single, "(The Angels Wanna Wear My) Red Shoes", and the long-awaited album were due for release and people needed to start being exposed to Stiff's great white hope sooner rather than later.

Costello and his group spent time getting to know each other, playing songs in London ahead of some warm-up shows. These were not to be in the capital – where the usual suspects from the music press might come along and slate them before they'd had time to gel – but in the West Country. Riviera again called Sue Barber, as he had done for Brinsley Schwarz, and the group were despatched to Camelford, Cornwall, for a week to rehearse. Rehearsals took place four miles up the road in Davidstow Village Hall, a former Nissen hut which was part of an RAF base during World War II.

If things were moving at a lightning pace, so was Costello. Not only did he run his new group through numbers from the album he had recorded with Clover, he also wanted to work up songs that would feature on his second album. The Cornish sessions, fuelled by adrenalin and potent local scrumpy, proved one thing beyond all doubt. Both Costello and Stiff had hit the jackpot.

"That was a furiously creative period and there were no restrictions," says Pete Thomas. "He'd play 'Lipstick Vogue' and I'm like, 'Well it could go like this'. And it was, 'Fine, okay, that's that one'. It wasn't like, 'I don't know, maybe we should calm it down'. So it was really exciting and we all seemed to enjoy it. We were all like 21 or 22, apart from Bruce, whose age we never did know. I guess someone had his passport, but you know, he mucked in. It was just really good fun."

The raw power of this new group was unleashed for the first time on Thursday 14 July at The Garden, "The South West's Top Rock Centre", in Penzance. For just £1, those who were there got to see the historic first public performance by Elvis Costello and his new band. Headlining was sometime cross-dressing American punk Wayne County (later Jayne County) and The Electric Chairs, who were just months away from releasing their fabulously trashy 45 "(If You Don't Want To Fuck Me Baby) Fuck Off'. Staff from Alexander Street had made the long trek to catch the showcase gig, crammed into a van and sitting on furniture they had brought from the office. Some of them had to restrain holidaymaker Captain Sensible from leaping on the stage mid-set to jam with Costello and crew. "The whole idea was 'destroy'," comments Pete Thomas. "It was all about going on stage and flattening people. Costello was Mr Angry. I don't think he was really. I think it was sort of expected. In retrospect, he is a really clever bloke and he'd dropped it. 'Right, we've got The Jam, we've got the Sex Pistols, we've got The Clash. We can fit into this.'"

Adds Bruce Thomas: "He [Wayne County] was going, 'Who are you guys?' and we said, 'This is our first gig', and he said, 'Fuck!'."

The following night they made an appearance at Woods Leisure Centre in Plymouth. It speaks volumes about the level of interest already generated around Costello that *Record Mirror*'s Chris Rushton made the journey to this West Country outpost on a Friday evening to review a try-out show. He described Elvis as: "Slightly stroppy creep

of a school prefect – the type that gets beaten up after school hours."
He went on to hail the band's "machine-like performance".

While in Cornwall, the band spent a day in a small studio and re-
recorded *My Aim Is True*. Stiff's plan was to release this version after
the initial pressing recorded with Clover had sold out, although this
was eventually abandoned. They also played a show at Davidstow
Village Hall where they had rehearsed. Their thundering new wave
felt more like a tsunami in the sleepy Cornish village. Riviera was
blown away. "That's fucking world class," he raved to Bruce Thomas.
"That's a world-class band". Thomas looked at him and replied:
"Yeah, I know."

Better drilled than an army platoon, and with Riviera as their
bellowing sergeant major, they were ready to embark on their first
national tour, starting at Rafters in Manchester on 21 July. Taking to
the stage after support from punk outfit The Lurkers, they packed
twenty songs into their first official concert. The set featured songs
from *My Aim Is True* (which would be released the following day),
and his second album. With punk raging and so many new artists
and groups for the media to salivate over, publicity was critical for
the singer who, several weeks before, had said he wanted to hide his
identity. So, before playing this opening show, Stiff had managed to
land Costello his first TV appearance on Granada's *What's On*, hosted
by Tony Wilson.

Riviera was now Costello's *de facto* manager and it was at this point
he had drafted in Glen Colson to help increase the singer's media
profile. Colson had never met Costello or seen him play when he was
told to accompany him to Manchester.

Colson remembers "I'd been working with Stiff for about a week or
two and Riviera said, 'I want you to take him and meet him at King's
Cross. I've told him what train to get – here's the tickets.' So, I was
waiting and he was late. The train was beginning to move and I could
see this funny chap with an amp and a guitar running up the platform.
I caught up with him and said, 'Elvis?' and he said, 'Yeah, Glen?' I
grabbed his guitar and he had the amp and we ran and got on this
train. We talked all the way, I mean full belt. I mean, he loves talking
and I love talking, so it was non-stop and by the time we got there
he'd lost his voice. We were doing this show and it was in Granada
Studios where *Coronation Street* was filmed and this magazine show
was very, very strange. It was Tony Wilson, Edna O'Brien – who is

very good looking, a siren type – and there was a snake charmer. When we went for make-up, Elvis said that he wanted me to get him a glass of honey with ginger and hot whisky. I nipped out and got him that and he drank it. He said his dad did it all the time because his dad was a singer. There was this snake charmer wandering around with these fucking great boa constrictors and everything. I said to him, 'How are you going to play?' and he said. 'Well I've got this amp'.

"So, I said, 'Well, okay'. Later on, I hung out with Billy Bragg and I realised that you can actually make quite a good noise with an electric guitar and singing. We got in the studio and a lot of people were laughing because he looked quite gawky in those days. They were all saying to me, 'What's he going to do?'. I said, 'He's going to sing'. So they said, 'Well put the amp over there', and I thought, 'I don't know what the fuck this is going to be like', and I was getting a bit embarrassed by then. I thought it was going to be dreadful, this fucking racket. I'd never ever seen anybody play with an amp – not by themselves like a folk singer. I think he sang '(The Angels Wanna Wear My) Red Shoes', and he was absolutely brilliant, because he had this fantastic voice and he could scream as well and really emote. It was powerful, it was really good, it was better than everybody. And everybody in the studio just stopped and turned round and listened to him."

Elvis Costello and his new group made their much-anticipated London debut at Dingwalls in Camden Lock on 26 July 1977. That morning at Alexander Street, a stunt was being planned – with *Melody Maker* journalist Allan Jones in attendance and taking notes. American label CBS was holding a convention at the Hilton Hotel in London's exclusive Park Lane. These important people would be taking a break for lunch, right? So, what better opportunity for the maverick label that wanted to stick two fingers up to the major labels to do just that – and in full public view?

Placards were made and a posse, made up of Stiff employees and Graham Parker roadies, set off for the Hilton. Costello, accompanied by Riviera and some of his band, rocked up outside. He put down a small, battery-powered practice amp, plugged in his Fender guitar, and launched into "Welcome To The Working Week". Bemused passers-by who stopped to listen included A&R man Gregg Geller, Columbia publicist Hope Antman, later to become his wife, and rock journalist Lisa Robinson. "Speaking only for myself I can say I was intrigued by what I saw and, especially, heard," says Geller of the legendary stunt. "Prior to this incident I hadn't been completely certain that there was, in fact, an actual person named Elvis Costello. There was a rumour that he was merely one of a number of recording guises of Nick Lowe."

All was going to plan until a police officer asked Costello to move on and when he tried to keep playing, he was arrested. This posed a potential problem as he was due to attend a soundcheck later that afternoon. Luckily, he was released in time to get to Camden Lock for what was billed in music press ads as "The very first London performance of Stiff recording star Elvis Costello". His run-in with the law meant he had to appear bleary-eyed before magistrates the following morning and was fined £5 for "selling records in the street". Financially embarrassed, he pleaded for time to pay, a request they granted. It was a small price to pay. Three months later CBS/Columbia signed Elvis Costello, granting *My Aim Is True* a release in America on a major label. The man who signed him confirms the Hilton Hotel episode was pivotal.

"It was certainly the start of the process," says Geller. "I always made it a point to return from London with a stack of the latest UK releases. Someone, and I'm pretty sure it was Dick Wingate, returned from the Stiff offices with a bunch of *My Aim Is True*, which had just been released, and gave me a copy. On returning home, with the memory of the London Hilton incident still fresh in my mind, it was the first thing I put on my turntable – and there it stayed. I fell in love with the album and soon decided I wanted to sign Elvis."

In his autobiography *Howling At The Moon*, the hard-living chief executive of CBS Walter Yetnikoff leaves no room for any doubt. He said he was running late to a meeting when Lisa Robinson implored him to stop and listen, and he disappeared back into the hotel. He was making a big mistake, she insisted, and the "gawky guy with glasses" he had glimpsed for a few seconds had hits in him. "Fine, I'll tell my A&R man to sign him," replied an exasperated Yetnikoff. "As a result of that reasoned adjudication, Elvis Costello came to Columbia Records," wrote Yetnikoff.

The stunt landed Costello on the front cover of *Melody Maker* the following week, just as Stiff must have hoped. A bobby in full uniform was captured in the foreground of the picture, about to make his headline-grabbing arrest. Someone carrying a sandwich board declaring "Welcome To London Home Of Stiff Records" was outside the hotel entrance. The news story on the front segued neatly into a full-length, fly-on-the-wall feature entitled "A Day In The Life Of A Bunch Of Stiffs", written by Allan Jones.

If one record perfectly encapsulated the ethos of Stiff Records, it was *My Aim Is True*. Combining Barney Bubbles' iconic designs, Riviera's ingenious marketing slogans, Stiff's irreverence and a unique artist, it did what the major labels had failed to do for years. It acknowledged that music fans deserved better and tapped into Britain's deep-rooted culture of buying and collecting records. The Stiff template had been created and the bar set high.

Although Chris Gabrin had produced the black and white shots that had adorned the sleeves of "Less Than Zero" and "Alison", it was Keith Morris who was invited to do the shoot for the album under Bubbles' direction. Bubbles reportedly threw Elvis Presley-like shapes around the room as the other Elvis struck a variety of poses against a pale backdrop. A picture of awkwardness in a jacket, open-neck shirt and tie, turned-up jeans, and National Health glasses, Costello was a geek years before it was chic. A vibrant yellow screen was placed over him for the initial run of 10,000, ensuring it would stand out in the racks and window displays of record shops.

Then, when the album began to catch fire, Stiff made a discovery that would result in a collector's dream. Riviera had gone with Bubbles to oversee the first run and found out that using different coloured inks wouldn't cost more. He then demanded that every run of 5,000 copies be printed in a different colour.

For Riviera, this was what the major labels, with their dull groups and even duller records, didn't get. As well as music fans, there were record fans. Some people would love Costello's album and having a copy on their turntable would suffice. But others would desire more than that – if it was made available – and if the blue sleeve had to be hunted down, all the better. Stiff knew this and with *My Aim Is True* it pulled off a trick it would reprise on later releases. As an additional incentive, the first 1,000 copies contained a poster urging the customer to "Help Us Hype Elvis". If the customer returned the enclosed sheet to Alexander Street, they could have a complimentary copy sent out to a friend. This was a ploy apparently used by eccentric American composer and singer Van Dyke Parks.

The marketing was predictably aggressive and must have cost an arm and a leg. Stiff booked out the centre pages of *Melody Maker*,

NME and *Sounds* for their editions on 23 July 1977 – the day after the album's release. Each paper carried a section of a black and white promo poster, so those who wanted it for their bedroom wall would have to buy all three papers. A one-page advert in the *NME* a fortnight later simply had a picture of the record with the words BUY IT in giant letters above. Other labels – and their artists – must have been aghast at this carpet-bombing of the music press. How can they afford it? They may have wondered. The answer was that they probably couldn't.

One of Stiff's strengths was its ability to think on its feet and just as everything was going to plan that was put to the test. Elvis Presley was found dead on the bathroom floor of his Graceland home on 16 August at the age of 42. Amid worldwide grief and wall-to-wall tributes and obituaries in the press, any mention of Stiff's phoney Elvis could have backfired. Some of the national dailies shelved features on Costello they had in the pipeline to avoid any backlash, but it was too late for Stiff to withdraw the album, so they made a virtue out of necessity. The sleeve carried the words "Elvis Is King" in block letters within the chequered border. Stiff reacted as only Stiff could. "The King Is Dead, Long Live The King" ran a new slogan, making a virtue of Presley's untimely death. The *NME* had considered running "Elvis & Elvis: Which One Is A Stiff Artist?" as a cover line, but thought better of it before going to press.

Any fears that Presley's demise might derail the other Elvis, just as he looked as if his pounding of the pub rock beat was about to be rewarded, proved unfounded. *My Aim Is True* delivered Stiff its first hit record. A reported 11,000 copies were sold in its first three days and it enjoyed a twelve-week run in the UK album chart, reaching No.14. Costello and Stiff were on the map. Scores were being settled.

The press couldn't get enough of Costello who, egged on by Riviera, was letting them do the chasing. *Sounds* filled its front page with his picture on 7 August. "At last a hero for all you weeds with glasses" ran the headline above an interview with Stiff's emerging star. The writer referred to Costello having spurned two thirds of the music press and the difficulties he'd encountered in getting to speak to him. Costello, like his hot-tempered handler, was characteristically hostile. "People don't take Stiff Records seriously," he complained. "If it's CBS or some other big company, it's a great sales campaign, with Stiff they call it gimmicks. People just treat you like a joke. People don't think I exist, they think I'm Nick Lowe."

With his face becoming more and more familiar and Costello none too keen to give much about his past away, some of his ex-work mates from the cosmetics firm were coming out of the woodwork, recalls Colson: "I never talked to him about it, and I never even told him that these girls were calling up from Elizabeth Arden. They were threatening to go to the press and tell the press who he was. Because I didn't tell anybody who he was. I didn't let on and nobody wanted people to know that he was a computer bloody guy at Elizabeth Arden. So, I had to send all these albums over to the factory to keep them quiet. It was all very secretive and even the fact that his father was this singer in Joe Loss and that he'd sung R. White's lemonade advert. All that was kept very secret."

The interest whipping around Costello and his group had become a tornado by the time the band appeared at The Nashville Rooms on 7 August. With *My Aim Is True* receiving rave reviews and only space for about 400 to cram into the venue, the queue to get in snaked right around the block.

Colson says: "What happened that night was very strange because Jake said to me, 'Get all the nationals down'. I knew about four or five of the guys who worked on the nationals and I got them down. I said to Jake, 'How am I going to get them in?' and he said, 'You can't, it's full up now'. I said, 'Can I come in?' and he said, 'No, it's full up'. So, even I couldn't fucking get in the gig! And these guys [journalists] actually got arrested for arguing … It couldn't have been better for Jake: 'Journalists Arrested At Elvis Gig'. No one could get in and there was huge excitement."

Dave Robinson took to the microphone to personally introduce the band and apologise for the ruckus outside the venue: "Good evening ladies and gentlemen. We're sorry for all the aggravation getting in here tonight, but there's so many policemen trying to get in, we had a lot of trouble getting everybody else in. Anyway, I'd like to introduce you to Elvis Costello and The Attractions."

Pop's anti-hero was the hottest ticket in town. And his record label was on fire.

5

Whole Wide World

Few with even a passing interest in British pop music could have failed to have heard of Stiff Records as it celebrated its first birthday in August 1977. The music papers had afforded the label and its acts widespread coverage, with The Damned and Elvis Costello making the front covers. John Peel, the barometer of cool at Broadcasting House, had been an enthusiastic supporter. As the music industry's youngest and most unruly child, Stiff had certainly been both seen and heard.

But despite all the attention and kudos, not one of its fifteen singles had troubled the UK Top 40. Singles like "So It Goes" and "Alison" now stand as classics and many mistakenly assume they were hits on their release. If Stiff was to be more than a source of bemusement and curiosity for the major labels, it was going to have to step up to the next level.

By the summer of 1977, Riviera and Robinson had been joined by another figure with plenty of experience and industry nous. Paul Conroy was added to the payroll earlier in the year, joining secretaries Cynthia Lole and Suzanne Spiro at its modest headquarters, as general manager. Conroy had begun his career with Terry King Associates, booking bands like Genesis, Lindisfarne and Caravan, and set up a booking agency at Charisma Records. A familiar face on the pub rock scene, he was friendly with Riviera, having been the agent for Chilli Willi & The Red Hot Peppers and helped pull together the Naughty Rhythms Tour. He also knew Robinson from his days at the Hope & Anchor and had once unexpectedly found himself sharing space with him at 32 Alexander Street.

"Peter Jenner and Andrew King and I took that front room when I was managing the Kursaals [Flyers]," explains Conroy. "I needed a place in central London because I was living in Kingston at the time and one day I got in there and found Dave and Rosemary shacked up in the back room. Peter Jenner said to me, 'Oh Dave wanted to ... you didn't need all the space, did you?' So, I opened up the door when I got in the office and there was Dave with a sleeping bag on the floor."

Still only in his twenties, Conroy had been plotting a path out of the music industry when Stiff's offer came. He would spend six years at the label and play a significant role in its expansion and success. He remembers how it came about: "The Kursaals played in The Roundhouse, and I've got the poster on my wall: Sunday Outing, with Kursaals top of the bill, Crazy Cavan & The Rhythm Rockers, and right down the bottom this band called The Clash. They came on stage and that's when I got out of managing the Kursaals. I was going back to college to be a mature student when Jake approached me originally. Then Jake and Dave took me down to the New Born café in Westbourne Park Road and offered me money beyond my wildest dreams. Well it wasn't actually, it was £40 a week! My family were disgusted. I was about 28 and they thought I should have taken the college route because I'd done teacher training and I was going to do American Studies at Exeter. It took a long while for them to realise there was a route for me in showbiz.

A few months after starting, Conroy was joined in the damp, windowless basement of the Bayswater terrace by musician turned label manager, Alan Cowderoy. In the sixties he had co-founded UK prog band Gracious, whose first album was released on Vertigo. Two years after the band split up, he joined Phonogram as manager of the Vertigo label established in 1969 as its conduit for adult oriented rock. But in September 1977, the one-time prog rocker threw his lot in with the new wave of Stiff.

"I knew Robbo through Clover when I was at Phonogram and running the Vertigo label, and then subsequently Graham Parker & The Rumour," recalls Cowderoy. "He would be pressing us to do what we wouldn't do normally and he understood the only way we were going to get a picture sleeve on a seven-inch release would be to call it an EP. So, we had to produce this thing called 'The Pink Parker', which was on pink vinyl, and the only place that would press the pink coloured vinyl in those days was in Holland. It was a monumental problem and Robbo would love coming up with those kind of challenges. We did the *Graham Parker Live at Marble Arch* album, so it was a kind of testing ground, and at the same time he was bringing in the first Stiff singles like 'So It Goes'. He said, 'Look at the packaging, this is what you should be doing' and eventually he just said, 'Come over to Stiff'.

"I had a company car, a pension plan and a good salary at Phonogram and I was offered half that and no car and no pension to go to Stiff. I was at that age of 26 or 27 and I just thought, 'This sounds exciting and if I don't do something now, I could be stuck here at Phonogram.'"

Working at 32 Alexander Street wasn't for the faint-hearted, as another of its new recruits quickly discovered. Philippa Thomas, sister of drummer Pete, joined Stiff after leaving the sunny canyons of Los Angeles for London. She had stayed on in LA for around six months after her brother had flown home to join The Attractions. While on America's west coast, she had immersed herself in the underground scene and for a while had lived in a shack behind the Whisky A Go Go. She'd become particularly close to Backstage Pass, and local clothes designer Toni Laumer, who would eventually marry Jake Riviera. She remembers Riviera raving about Stiff on his visits to the city and loving the records he brought with him from England.

"I remember Jake as exploding with enthusiasm for this new label, slagging off all hippies and bands like the Eagles," she says. "He gave me The Damned album, singles and *My Aim Is True*, which I played to death and proceeded to play at any party, slagging off what was on the turntable, throwing LPs out of the window and forcing American people to listen to the two Stiff Albums."

In September 1977, Thomas was offered a job at Stiff for £25 a week, cash-in-hand, doing everything from answering the phone and running to the nearby shop to creating window displays and selling merchandise at gigs. On her arrival, she was immediately struck by her shabby surroundings and the brash way the label did business.

"In the toilet/sink area were piles of Pink Floyd and Roy Harper posters," she remembers. "Next to them sat Barney Bubbles working on a shelf next to the sink. In the basement Paul Conroy and Alan Cowderoy worked in almost complete darkness. The front of the ground floor consisted of a reception/waiting area and backroom occupied by Jake and Dave. All the furniture was dilapidated and people waiting to go into the back room sat on old aircraft seats.

"I was encouraged to adopt a bolshie telephone manner when answering calls: for example, 'Who are you and what do you want?'

On my first day I managed to throw away a cheque for, I think, £3,000, an advance from Island. After much rampaging Dave tipped up the bin in the street and retrieved it – a good start! I think I got told off.

"I worked in front office with Cynthia Lole and Suzanne Spiro, both of whom left shortly afterwards; Cynthia to work with Jake and Suzanne to set up a shop. One day, Jake got really cross and smashed a hammer on the desk; it made a big hole, never to be repaired. My first job in the morning was to go down to Ron's, the corner shop, and get three bottles of cider and some 'dog' [sausage] rolls from the glass display cabinet ... After a gig and all night drive, stopping off at a Wimpy, The Damned turned up and took over my job on the front desk. Apart from Dave Vanian, the others were covered in tomato ketchup. The trepidation felt by those who were waiting to go into the back office for a meeting was intense. There was usually a lot of shouting from the back office and those coming out often seemed downcast and pissed off."

Bubbles didn't work out of the office all the time, but the unruly environment of Alexander Street proved too much even for him on one occasion, as Alan Cowderoy recalled:

"He worked in a little room underneath the loo and either Dave or Jake was in there one morning having a wee and they missed and it was all coming through the floorboards and going all across his artwork. Barney came out screaming at them to stop!" [6]

Chris Morton also testifies to the volatile atmosphere at Stiff and says that while Riviera and Robinson were different, they were both aggressive characters, their intimidating style rooted in past frustrations: "They both had an axe to grind, they both had a chip on their shoulders and they both had scars," he says. "It was the same for me. I've always been very anti-authoritarian and that's why I fitted in well. The 'fuck you' attitude was the best thing I had and the next best thing was my imagination. They both had a long-running hurt from how the system and the regular record companies had fucked them over or taken them for granted."

That summer, with the company celebrating its first anniversary, things finally began to take off for Stiff. On 6 August 1977, *My Aim Is True* entered the UK album chart and began its climb to its peak position of No. 14. Throughout that month, Elvis Costello and The Attractions left audiences reeling with electrifying live shows that confirmed them as one of the most dynamic acts around. The band's tour schedule included a "hometown" gig at Eric's in Liverpool with Nick Lowe and Dave Edmunds, and a two-day trip to Belgium to appear at the Bilzen Festival with The Clash and Stiff stable-mates The Damned. Such was the impact of the album, live shows and the nationwide publicity they were attracting, they were invited to do a live recording of "Red Shoes" for *Top Of The Pops* – almost two months after its release.

Costello was the first Stiff act to appear on *TOTP*. As the band were playing dates in Scotland, this meant flying to London, recording the song at the BBC's Shepherd's Bush studios, and then catching a flight to Edinburgh. But due to a commercial airline strike, they had to board a six-seat chartered plane for a flight that would stay with Costello for years to come. "I remember there was a fog and we were in this little crop-spraying Cessna," says Bruce Thomas. "It came down through the clouds and we were about 40 feet above this caravan site and it just pulled back on the joystick. And I think that's when Elvis got his fear of flying, because that was very hairy."

"Red Shoes" ended a drought of more than two months without a Stiff single being issued. However, with the Island distribution deal now in place and Stiff confident its records would reach the shops, it prepared to unveil one of the most idiosyncratic acts on its roster.

Wreckless Eric had been drinking when he stumbled into the Stiff office and apologetically handed over his home-made tape to a long-haired American bloke. The cassette he'd used to record his rough demo was destined for the Stiff dumper, he figured.

Recalling his first encounter with Stiff, he says: "I went on the Tube and I had to get to Royal Oak. God it was a complicated journey and I ended up going to a lot of pubs on the way. I had my last week's pay and a tax rebate, so I had to have a few drinks – it was Dutch courage at the time. I had the beginnings of a maturing drink problem, basically. I got there eventually and I was trying to find the street. In my mind it was going to be up three flights of grubby stairs that got narrower as you went up and eventually you go into some grubby office and there would be a couple of hippies in there or something. I don't know why I thought this. But when I went along Alexander Street there were all these big white houses on one side and shops on the other. I was looking for the number and I was halfway past it before I realised and I thought, 'Fuck, there's people in there and they're looking out'. So, I thought, 'Right, you can't fuck about here. You can't just sidle past because that's not going to look good.

"So, I thought, 'Okay', opened the door, kicked it open and there's all these people and I thought, "I'll just ignore them, face front". There's a huge, hippie kind of bloke, a mountain man with big gingery hair and a gingery beard and he turns out to be an American. He's going, 'Can I help you?' I said, 'I suppose I'm one of those cunts who brings tapes into record companies.' He said, 'Oh great, yeah.' And everyone's stopped talking. I'm thinking, 'Just face the front, face the front, don't look at anyone.' I said, 'Right, there it is', and he's going, 'Wait. Don't you want to give us your address and your number and everything because we might like it?' I said, 'Yeah, I suppose I could.' I mean, I was really cool. I said, 'Yeah, all right, I'll do that' and I wrote it all down and gave it to him. Then I just turned around and walked out. I walked back and was trying to find my way home and I was thinking, 'What the fuck have I done?'

"It was Huey Lewis that I'd handed it to, but I didn't know that at the time. Nick Lowe [who he also didn't recognise] was in there talking to The Damned and they all just looked at me like, 'Fuck me, he's weird'. He took it and went upstairs with it and had a listen and he came rushing down the stairs, 'Jake, Jake, you've got to hear this.' So, Jake goes up and they listened to it and they heard 'Whole Wide World'. And Jake just went, 'Where did he go? Well find him!' And I was long gone."

A little bloke with the look of a street urchin and a reedy voice, Wreckless Eric cut an odd figure, even at Alexander Street. He had a young face and could have passed as a nephew of Ian Dury. His clothes were more War On Want than the King's Road, and a plastic carrier bag and a can of strong lager were the former art student's only other accoutrements.

Eric Goulden was born in Newhaven, Sussex on 18 May 1954. On leaving school, he left home for art college in Bristol and it was there he began drinking heavily. When the foundation course came to an end and he had to do a diploma course, he plumped for Fine Art (painting and sculpture). He decided to head north and was offered a place at Hull College of Art. He didn't even know where Hull was and had to look it up on a map.

Together with other aspiring musicians he got to know around the college scene, Wreckless formed a shambolic ensemble called Addis & The Flip Tops, so named because they had begun by using an Addis Flip Top bin for a drum. They played a garden fête for a school for disturbed children, the college disco – anywhere that would put them on. They even had a go at writing their own songs.

In both his songwriting and his desire to perform, Wreckless had taken inspiration from seeing Kilburn & The High Roads at Hove Town Hall during the summer of 1974. And, as with most people who got to see Dury's bizarre troupe, the experience stayed with him. "In a way, they couldn't play that well," said Wreckless. "They could play nearly well enough to do what they were doing, but it worked. I thought they must have all met in a home or something. You looked at them and thought, 'They're not normal, these people'." [6]

By the time he graduated and relocated to London, Addis & The Flip Tops had been binned. Wreckless looked for work and somewhere to live and at night went to gigs at the 100 Club, Marquee, The Roundhouse and other happening venues. The closest he came to working in pop was when he got a job as quality control inspector at the Corona Lemonade factory near Wandsworth.

He put an advert in the window of his local news agent in a bid to join a band and answered an ad in *Melody Maker* for a rhythm guitarist with a group called Flying Tigers. None of this came to anything, but he explains how an article in another edition of the same music paper would change the course of his life:

"I was in this pub around the corner getting slaughtered at lunchtime and I read this thing about Stiff Records. I was fully aware of Brinsley Schwarz, Ducks Deluxe, Bees Make Honey, Kilburn & The High Roads and everyone else, and it was obvious there were new trends going on. You could tell; they were funny times. There was an article in the *Melody Maker* and it had a picture of the first Stiff record, which was "Heart Of The City". There was Jake talking about Stiff Records and Nick Lowe talking about his record. I was very interested because Link Wray had supposedly made records in a chicken coop, so this was a romantic idea. The idea of Decca Records or something did not really appeal to me. But when I read about them, I was just captivated. I couldn't stop thinking about it."

At the time Wreckless hand-delivered his cassette to Stiff, he was short on self-confidence. When Riviera heard the demo Wreckless had made on his girlfriend's brown and cream cassette recorder, containing every song he'd got, he had been knocked out and immediately wanted to put one of them out as a single. "I didn't know Jake Riviera at the time," Wreckless recalls, "but I thought the wrath of something equally monstrous would come down upon me. Anyway, the next day I was sitting in the flat and suddenly the phone rings and this voice says, 'Can I speak to Eric?' And I said, 'Oh, that's me, yes. What?' He said, 'This is Jake Riviera here calling from Stiff Records', and I said, 'Look, you don't have to send it [the tape] back. I mean, you can re-use it if you like; just stick some tape over the holes'. He said, 'No, we really like it and we would like you to come and see us, if that would be okay, and talk to us about making a record'. I'm freaking out and thinking, 'I must have banged my head'. He said, 'Could you come in and see us? What are you doing this afternoon? Can you come over?' I said, 'Oh, yeah okay. Where is it? Oh yeah, it's where I took the tape'."

In a dreamlike state, Wreckless arrived back at the offices where he was greeted by a tall guy in a suit. He said how much he liked the tape and that the song Stiff wanted to make into a record was "Whole Wide World". He would be producing the release. Wreckless had come up with the lyrics for the song while sitting on a street bench two summers before. A paen to his dream girl out there somewhere in the world, it was oddly poignant and, like those written by his mentor Ian Dury, had some unforgettable rhymes.

Musically, it couldn't have been simpler, the whole song played on a guitar, alternating between the E and A chords. Most record companies probably would have ejected the tape as soon as they heard his voice, if the tape had made it that far. But Stiff wasn't most companies and if anyone could spot a gifted songwriter, it was Riviera and Robinson.

Wreckless was confused, mistakenly thinking the young guy with the suit was the office boy. It was only when he took a record off a shelf and said, "That's my one, the first one we put out", that Wreckless realised this was Nick Lowe. As he stood in the cluttered office papered with posters promoting its artists, Riviera and Robinson tumbled in and apologised for being late. Robinson was carrying a golf club and swung it back as if to hit him on the head. Wreckless recalls: "I'm thinking, 'He's not really going to kill me because he's got this record company going and that would be pretty stupid to do something like that and I haven't done anything to piss him off yet. Then again, if he's going to knock my head off, there's not much I can do about it, so I might as well enjoy it!'"

Lowe then tapped up Wreckless for the change in his pocket, added it to what he had and then sent Suzanne Spiro out for a bottle of cider. A bemused Wreckless was then ushered to an upstairs room to do an audition on an acoustic guitar. He was then asked when he was free to go to Pathway Studios and do some recording. The man who'd just jacked in his job at the Corona factory was being added to the Stiff production line.

Says Wreckless: "On the day of recording, I got a taxi because I had to take my guitar and amplifier, which I then found out I hadn't needed to do, because the studio had one. I got there at the appointed time and I felt very nervous because I didn't know what a recording studio was like. I imagined it would be this enormous thing like a factory with a load of loud speakers at one end. But it was this pokey little place, really rank. Steve Goulding was there to play the drums and Nick said, 'Well, I've got this idea for it and I'd like to try it. If it doesn't work, we can do it the way you've been doing it.' I said, 'Yeah, all right.' He said, 'What I'll do is, I'll play the guitar on it, and if you want to put anything on it later, you can.'

"They got the backing track together and it was the guitar and the drums, and then the bass went on, which was really super. It was all done on the A string, so it was really dumb and he was playing it in a way that was dumb. And there were tambourines and hand-claps and stuff, and then we had to get a vocal on it. They gave me joints and drink and Nick decided we'd come back and do that. Then we went off to The Red Cow to see The Damned. We went in Baz's [Barry Farmer's] Morris van. I came back the next week to do the vocal."

Wreckless Eric was in and out of Pathway working on his own debut release – in between sojourns to the pub – and when he and Elvis Costello crossed paths, it threw up an idea which reveals something about how Stiff saw itself. Both Riviera and Robinson knew their rock 'n' roll history and had seen how the hit factories of the fifties and sixties packaged up their star acts. They were happy to steal, but only from the best, and it was thought to have been the Chess label from which they took the idea of a record with Costello on one side and Wreckless on the other. In 1964, Chess paired rock 'n' roll pioneers Bo Diddley and Chuck Berry on an album entitled *Two Great Guitars*. The record was released on the subsidiary label Checker, and was one of the first such "super sessions" to enter the market.

The plan to record the two men on one album was eventually dropped, although there is some disagreement as to why. Costello asserted it was because he recorded enough demos whilst Eric was in the pub to render the idea redundant.

Wreckless strongly refutes this version of events and sees Costello's remarks as belittling: "I used to not be into what he did and think he could be a bit much at times, but still have a respect for him. But when I read that, I lost all respect for him. In his situation, what he had written was to kind of make himself appear more. I mean it's inaccurate. There was a point where when I went back to do the vocal, he was finishing off 'Mystery Dance'. And they did that and then while Nick was fixing something in the control room, Elvis played something to me that was so 'I'm clever'. I just thought, 'Oh my God'.

"Anyway, the original plan was for me and him to make the album together and he was DP Costello and Jake had this idea that one side would be called 'Wreckless Meets DP' like 'Chuck Meets Bo'. I mean, I used to go in and I was never very pushy and I think that there were a lot of very pushy people suddenly around. Also, I was not from London. I was new to London and I didn't like London. It didn't really thrill me and I found it difficult to be somewhere so large and competitive in a way. I mean, there were all these kind of pub rock people, these big hairy men strutting about!"

Any idea they might cohabit the same piece of vinyl was certainly short-lived. Costello had huge ambitions and Riviera knew he could fulfil them.

Wreckless was exhilarated by the recording of "Whole Wide World" under Lowe's patient tutelage. However, the weeks that followed proved an anti-climax. There were no immediate plans to release the record, for which he hadn't yet recorded a B-side anyway. So, he was left kicking his heels while punk exploded and Stiff focused its attentions on The Damned. Needing ready cash while he awaited stardom, Wreckless signed up with Manpower Services, doing labouring jobs in a variety of storerooms and basements, and cleaning toilets at the Tarmac Roadstone depot in Greenwich. He also cleared tables in the cafeteria of Swan & Edgar's department store in Piccadilly Circus, later to become Tower Records, where his own releases would be sold. In between clearing away customers' coffee cups and saucers and wiping down surfaces with a cloth, he and his girlfriend huddled together around the convector heater in their freezing flat.

But while he shivered through winter and wondered when he'd finally get to record a B-side for his single, he made a new acquaintance who would give him the encouragement he so badly needed. Stiff organised a gig at Victoria Palace Theatre on 26 October 1976. Graham Parker & The Rumour were headlining, Tyla Gang and The Damned were playing support and the Stiff posse was out in force. Wreckless had to meet up with Riviera and Robinson beforehand in a nearby pub, so he wouldn't have to pay to get in and he took it all in with childlike wonder.

He was thrilled when Nick Lowe introduced him to Lee Brilleaux, one of his heroes, and bowled over when he told Wreckless how pleased he was to meet him at last. Lew Lewis, who'd just been thrown out of Eddie & The Hot Rods, and Dave Edmunds also shook the hand of Stiff's almost apologetic newcomer that night. Better still, there was an aftershow party in the artists' bar, something at which Wreckless had never before found himself. As the in-crowd toasted a great show and knocked back the drinks, Wreckless came face-to-face with Ian Dury.

Wreckless remembers: "I was talking to Nick Lowe and he said, 'There's someone you ought to meet over there', and it was Ian. Denise Roudette [Dury's girlfriend] was with him looking fantastic. It was astonishing – there he was. I had seen him from a distance, I had seen him on stage, and I had a copy of *Handsome*, which was autographed, and 'Crippled With Nerves'. I just said, 'You're fantastic, you're the best'. I think he thought I was taking the piss. His minder Fred Rowe was standing nearby and Ian started shouting 'Fred, Fred', and I thought he would have thrown me out. But Denise said to Ian, 'No, he means it'. So, we got talking about lyrics and then Ian told me to go round and see him in his gaff." [6]

Ian Dury had grown up in the Upminster area of Essex, at the eastern end of the London Underground's District Line. His father Bill was a bus driver and then a chauffeur, his mother Peggy a health visitor. However, their very different social backgrounds caused tension in the marriage and, after they separated, Dury had been raised by his mum and her two sisters.

At the age of just 7 he contracted polio after swimming with a friend in an open-air pool on Southend seafront. The disease very nearly took his life and paralysed his left side. He spent an incredible eighteen months in hospital before being sent to Chailey Heritage Craft School near Haywards Heath in East Sussex, a harsh institution which catered for children with a range of disabilities. "Men Made Here" boasted a sign above the door. Some, however, left scarred, and without question, it was Chailey that shaped the person Ian Dury became.

In his Kilburns days, Dury had lived with his wife Betty, a talented artist, and their children Jemima and Baxter in a rural village in Buckinghamshire. But by the time he was introduced to Wreckless he was no longer living with his family, and was sharing a flat with his teenage girlfriend Denise Roudette at Oval Mansions – or "Catshit Mansions" as he called it. He'd met Roudette when she'd come backstage after a Kilburns gig and after they began a relationship, she had roadied and provided backing vocals for the band.

The night Wreckless called to see the performer, who had so entranced him during his summer break from college, was a momentous one for another reason. Not wanting to arrive too early, Wreckless had nipped into a pub and watched Bill Grundy provoke the Sex Pistols into their infamous tirade of expletives, prompting viewers up and down the country to choke on their tea.

When he got to Oval Mansions, he found Dury and another guy called Chaz [future Blockhead, Chaz Jankel] putting the finishing touches to a song called "Sweet Gene Vincent". A cardboard cut-out of Dury's rock 'n' roll idol was propped up in his sitting room, and scattered about were giant sheets of scribbled lyrics, which Dury would eventually copy out on an old typewriter.

At 34, Dury was more of an uncle to Wreckless. They shared a love of art and had both studied Fine Art at college. But Dury had been a teacher, had a wife and two children, and was a comparatively old hand in the music business. He had done his time on the pub circuit and Kilburn & The High Roads had released their album on the Pye label.

Roudette was doing some rudimentary bass playing at the time and she started practising with Wreckless. Her relationship with Dury had always been pretty stormy and, from his nearby flat, Fred "Spider" Rowe, Dury's minder, would hear them going at it hammer and tongs. On one occasion, she confiscated his leg irons and hurled them off the balcony!

Rowe recalls: "She used to say to me, 'I like to get him on his good leg so I can give him a whack and I know he can't support himself on the other leg'. So, she'd give him a whack on the shin and because he couldn't put his arm out to save himself, he would go straight down and he loved it." [6]

During one brief separation, Roudette had camped out in Wreckless' sitting room. "Denise moved back in with Ian and then Ian wanted to come round and hear what we were doing," said Wreckless. "Perhaps he thought Denise and I were conducting some sort of torrid affair, I don't know. He sort of tagged along with us and said, 'I need to come round again with some drums'. Suddenly we got a fire-damaged Olympic drum kit, which had been removed from the back of a second-hand shop by Fred Rowe. I would be making some money by clipping hedges in the morning and they would come round in the afternoon and we would play. We were this little Bohemian combo and life was very charming." [6]

Months went by before a record with Wreckless' name on it was finally released on April Fools' Day 1977. "Whole Wide World" was included on a compilation entitled *A Bunch Of Stiffs* (SEEZ 2), an attempt to cash in on the arrival of new wave. As it hit shops a month or so before the dispute with Island, it helped sate the appetite for Stiff product in the meantime, although only four of the artists were actually signed to the label: Lowe, Costello, Tyla Gang and Wreckless. Costello's debut single "Less Than Zero" was also included, although the intro on this recording came from keyboard session player Stan Shaw, and not the singer's guitar.

"Undertakers To The Industry. If They're Dead We'll Sign 'Em" read the funereal inscription on the sleeve. A slavering creature, part-bat, part-werewolf rising up from a cemetery adorned the other side, the names of the artists dotted around its wings and claws. Riviera and Robinson had mooted the idea of a record featuring their friends from the pub rock circuit when they first launched Stiff, and this was effectively it. Graham Parker & The Rumour's "Back To Schooldays" was included, although it was omitted from the sleeve credits for legal reasons. The Takeaways were a Stiff supergroup starring Sean Tyla, Larry Wallis, Dave Edmunds, CP Lee and Nick Lowe, while Stone's Masonry featured Martin Stone and Paul "Bassman" Riley.

A Bunch Of Stiffs was also a way of showcasing Advancedale clients, with not only Costello, Parker and Lowe, but Dave Edmunds involved. His song "Jo Jo Gunne" was listed, but he was also disguised as Jill Read for his cover of The Chantels' "Maybe". The song was also released as a single in France and Holland, backed with "Wang Dang Doodle" by The Takeaways. "Jill, If You're Out There, Write To Us For Your Royalties" read a tongue-in-cheek message written across the sleeve.

Delighted at the news of the record, Wreckless popped into Alexander Street and asked for a copy. Mistaking him for a customer, the woman he spoke to said, "We've got it in, but it's not on sale yet". "Oh, see I'm on it," he replied. Recognising him, she gave him one of the newly-pressed copies and clutching it proudly, he headed off home.

On the day the compilation was released, Stiff cemented its reputation as a champion of the offbeat and eccentric by issuing a record by veteran comedian Max Wall, the first of a number of comic performers who would record for it. "England's Glory" had been written by Dury and pianist Rod Melvin when they were in the Kilburns and was a master class in lyrical rhyme, a precursor to "Reasons To Be Cheerful" that celebrated Dury's Britain. A wonderful pencil drawing of Wall by Humphrey Ocean provided the cover's artistic centrepiece, with Barney Bubbles' ink providing the finishing touches to the black and white cover (this was the only Stiff record on which Bubbles received a named credit). The lyrics, which were vintage Dury, were displayed on the back. "Max Wall Rocks", Porky Peckham inscribed into the run-out grooves on side A, and "Max Wall Rolls" on the flip.

Sales were almost non-existent and Stiff eventually gave away the piles of unsold copies with the *Hits Greatest Stiffs* compilation (FIST1). On signing with Island, the first ten Stiff singles had been instantly deleted, so this was a convenient way of breathing new life into these releases at a time when Island was increasing its audience reach. As "Less Than Zero" and "White Line Fever" had already been included on *A Bunch Of Stiffs*, their respective B-sides "Radio Sweetheart" and "Leavin' Here" got an unexpected run-out here.

The inner sleeve pictured a woman with a T-shirt bearing the slogan "If It Ain't Stiff", and clutching a few previous Stiff releases. "Clutter Your Home With Stiff Records" the owner of this collection was urged. But with typical Stiff perversity, the other side promoted "some fine records on other labels you might enjoy". Recommendations by those at Alexander Street included Abba, Elvis Presley, Lee Dorsey, MC5, Jonathan Richman & The Modern Lovers, and Nick Drake, as well as a compilation LP by fellow independent Chiswick. Other record companies must have been gobsmacked.

Thrillingly for Wreckless, it was "Whole Wide World" that made an immediate impact, as he discovered when he tuned in to John Peel on the day he had picked up his complimentary copy. Wreckless recalls: "I was listening to John Peel and he said, 'I've got this great compilation album that's just come out on Stiff Records, and this is without a doubt the greatest track, it's just fantastic' [mimics guitar intro to "Whole Wide World"]. It was me and it was on John Peel. I just didn't know what had happened, it was so shocking. It was kind of beyond pleasure or exciting or elating. It was just the world had done something weird at that moment. There it was on fucking radio on John Peel. I'd been listening to John Peel religiously since I was thirteen, so I was somewhat confused."

Stiff was keen to seize the moment and Wreckless and crew were despatched to the studio to record "Semaphore Signals" as a B-side. "Whole Wide World" became BUY 16 on 19 August 1977, having been held in the queue with *My Aim Is True* while the Island deal was hammered out. It remains one of Stiff's defining records.

It seemed ironic that Wreckless, who had been in such awe of Dury, had got his record out first. But a week later his friend and collaborator made his own stellar debut on Stiff. The underlying riff had been plundered from one of the jazz musicians Dury so admired, but "Sex & Drugs & Rock 'n' Roll" was one of the most extraordinary songs he would ever write. From his recognition of the hedonistic holy trinity and artful rhyming lyrics to its jazz/funk feel, it encapsulated Dury's extraordinary talents in little more than three minutes. The flip-side "Razzle In My Pocket" was quirkily charming and the perfect foil for the uproarious A-side. In his best wide-boy drawl, Dury recounted an afternoon "on the nick" at a local shopping arcade, in search of girly magazines.

The safety-pin earring he wore on the front cover might have been punk chic, but the dark eye make-up and his doleful expression recalled the silent film icon Harold Lloyd. Here was a true performer, already in his mid-thirties and with a family, who owed his influences not to American proto-punks, but to rock 'n' roll and jazz legends, and Music Hall stage acts like Max Miller. Although audiences would take up the song as an anthem celebrating such age-old pleasures, that wasn't Dury's intended message.

"With this song, I was trying to suggest there was more to life than either of those three: sex, drugs and rock 'n' roll, or pulling a lever in a factory," Dury explained years later. "Of course, when I go out and perform the song, everyone sings along and you can't stop 'em! People say to me, 'Now there's AIDS about, don't you think that song was awful?' and I explain that the song was always a question mark over those activities." [32]

It was an instant success. *NME* declared it Single Of The Week under the heading "Seminal Punk Makes A Score" and its chart supplied by Rough Trade Records showed it at No. 2 shortly after its release. Stiff sold around 19,000 copies, but then inexplicably deleted it. When the press and record buyers questioned the move, Stiff was defiant, insisting: "We're a record company – not a museum."

Alan Cowderoy explains: "The whole policy at Stiff was to put out a single and then delete the single, whether or not it was a success. It would only have a limited lifespan. On the one hand that's great because it got people buying early and perhaps gave the record an earlier chart position. People were concerned that the shops might run out of copies or that the picture sleeve might not be available after the first run. So, the shops themselves were much more animated and were keen to take the stock from us and the public were out there trying to buy it early on.

"But if we hadn't adopted that policy of deleting records and had 'Sex & Drugs & Rock 'n' Roll' on *New Boots And Panties!!*, it would have helped our cause a lot. I organised our releases in Europe and we pressed up 'Sex & Drugs & Rock 'n' Roll' as a twelve-inch. There were floods of imports coming into this country, where it was no longer available. Everybody wanted 'Sex & Drugs & Rock 'n' Roll', and I think we could have put it on the album at that time." [6]

Predictably, the record was banned by the BBC and made no impression on the UK chart. Dury and Wreckless were the proud owners of the label's two biggest non-hits. But Stiff ploughed on, putting to the test Dave Robinson's belief that if you "throw enough shit against the wall, some of it will stick". Both artists had albums in the pipeline and a plot was being hatched that would really give these industry underdogs the platform they deserved. Meanwhile, another newly-signed act was in the wings, and Stiff had a new label design ready to go.

The Yachts mostly hailed from Liverpool, although singer Henry Priestman was originally from Hull and had been studying at the art college at the same time as Wreckless. Previously known as

Albert Dock And The Cod Warriors, eventually shortened to plain old Albert Dock, the group became something much more focused after Henry and co-vocalist John Campbell saw Roogalator, The Stranglers and other bands in London. They slimmed down from an unwieldy ensemble to a sleeker five-piece outfit. Priestman also began writing his own songs on the suggestion of Clive Langer from Deaf School, a group made up of students and staff from Liverpool Art College.

It was when The Yachts supported Elvis Costello at Eric's in Liverpool that they were spotted by Paul Conroy and invited to do a couple of shows with Costello at The Nashville, where he had a four-week residency. "Thinking about it now, if Stiff hadn't been at that gig and Elvis hadn't played, our lives would have been very different," says Priestman. "At the first gig, I used Steve Nieve's keyboard and I didn't know they had a standby switch on their amps. So, we ran on and shouted 'Yachts', and it just shows how green we were. It was our first gig out of the city and it was like, 'What's going on here?' It was really helpful to have that approval of being on with Costello. Then, as soon as we came off after that second gig we did at The Nashville Rooms, Paul Conroy said, 'Right, we want you to go and do a single'."

"Suffice To Say" was recorded at Pathway, with former Kursaal Flyers drummer Will Birch making his production debut, and it was easy to see why Stiff had picked them up. In just three minutes and fifteen seconds, The Yachts and their young producer had captured the zeal and sense of purpose of the new wave. This was pop, but not as people knew it. The song had only been written a month before it was recorded and was one of about four of the group's own songs. It was released on 23 September 1977, bearing the new grey Stiff label that would appear on countless hit records. But it failed to chart.

"They got it in the States more than in Britain," says Priestman. "Some people loved Yachts and still do, and I still listen to it now going, 'Well, I wouldn't have bought it'. But I'm proud of it. It was tongue-in-cheek and new wave, but they really loved it in America. I was 21 or whatever and I remember thinking, 'Here we go!' We were third in the Most Added Song on the *Billboard* chart that week, after Bob Dylan's 'Saved' and something else. They really got it, in the way they got The Police, but they didn't get the more punky things".

Almost twenty singles had been released by Stiff in its first year of operation, none of which had charted, and aside from the odd TV appearance by Elvis Costello, it wasn't receiving the kind of coverage that was needed to convert its underground successes into mainstream hits. So, to propel Stiff forward, Robinson and Riviera decided to resurrect something from the past.

Ian Dury said: "First of all I heard them talking about doing another tour like the Naughty Rhythms and I just leant in between them and said, 'I'll have some of that lads', and they said, 'Okay'."[5] Stiff's Greatest Stiffs would be a nationwide jaunt in the style of the Naughty Rhythms Tour and the Motown and other package tours of the sixties. Riviera and Robinson knew their music history and were always willing to adopt concepts from previous eras, such as EPs. If concert packages had been good enough for the likes of Pink Floyd and Smokey Robinson & The Miracles, they were good enough for Stiff.

Dury had got himself on the bill after eavesdropping on Riviera and Robinson's conversation. His fellow travellers would be Elvis Costello, Nick Lowe, Larry Wallis and Wreckless Eric. The latter's backing group consisted of Dury on drums, Roudette on bass and Davey Payne on saxophone, but Stiff wanted to see this unusual combo perform before the bus set off. "They wanted to make sure I could cut it," says Wreckless.

The first warm-up gig was at Barbarella's in Birmingham and Dave Robinson was there in person to announce over the microphone the "surprise guest appearance by Stiff recording artist Wreckless Eric". The volley of spittle that greeted their set confirmed the audience's approval. The following night they were at Oxford Polytechnic supporting traditional rockers the George Hatcher Band, where the audience were unsurprisingly less receptive to this odd collective. Then it was back to Alexander Street for a pre-tour meeting for everyone involved. Wreckless was nervous.

"I think Jake might have made an appearance, but Dave did most of the talking," remembers Wreckless. "He said how it was going to be, how the billing was going to happen and how the sound checks were going to go. And he said, 'Eric, I want you to stop behind, I want to have a talk with you'. I thought, 'Fuck me, what's going to happen?' Because we didn't go down well with George Hatcher's audience. But he said, 'I think you're going to do pretty well on the Stiff tour and I'd like to manage you. It would be a good idea for you because we're already looking after the record'."

Ian Dury had some arrangements of his own to make before he hit the road. He had come to be heavily reliant on minder Fred Rowe, who helped him on and off stage and was on-hand to protect him when his behaviour got him into trouble. An ex-con and a menacing figure, he was a reassuring presence for Dury whose disability made him vulnerable. When the tour was confirmed, Dury took it for granted his chaperone would go too. But to his chagrin, Rowe said his work and family had to come first and that he couldn't go off on tour with him. In the end, it took Dave Robinson himself to persuade him.

Rowe remembers: "At that time, I was with a glazing firm. It was work and I had two kids to look after, so I needed the money. Ian said, 'We're going on the Stiff tour.' So, I said, 'I can't go on tour Ian, I've got Clare and Alfie to look after and I've got to make a buck to feed them an' that'. He said, 'Well I'm not going then.' I said, 'What do you mean, you're not going? You're putting a gun to me. Come on Ian, for fuck's sake.' At the time, I'd been with him for three or four months, and during the course of that time. I'd done any task that was required, and he sort of depended on me a bit too much. I said, 'Well, the thing is Ian, if you don't go on the tour, don't go on it, because I can't come.'

"So, Robbo came round and started working me over. He said, 'Come on now Frederick' and he went on and on. So, I saw my ex-wife and said, 'Will you take care of the kids? I've got to go ...' 'Oh, it's rock 'n' roll is it? You're going on tour and leaving me?' Robbo said, 'You've got to come Frederick, because if Ian don't come, blah, blah, blah.' Anyway, I said to him, 'I'll do it, I will go. But this is the last thing. Fuck it. I'm not doing no more.' He said, 'We'll pay you £50 a week.' I was doing the glazing for about £160 a week take home. 'Don't worry,' he said. 'We'll make sure Val has got money to feed the kids.'"

Not for the first time, as his band members would confirm, Ian Dury had got his way, and he was flanked by his bodyguard as he set out on Stiff's package tour of Britain. But before the bus even pulled away from Alexander Street on a cold October day, something happened that rocked Stiff to its foundations.

—

Stiff's Greatest Stiffs was just days away from its curtain raiser when Paul Conroy popped into the office one Saturday. As summer had turned into autumn, the future for Stiff couldn't have looked more hopeful. But on 24 September 1977, the bomb which had been ominously ticking away at Stiff finally exploded. The Riviera and Robinson Show was over. It was clear from the empty bottles Conroy found lying on the

An early poster showcasing Stiff's first releases.
It was typical of things to come. (*Stiff Records*)

Top left: Nick Lowe behind the camera. (*Courtesy of Dick Wingate*)

Top right: Graham Parker only cut one album for Stiff, but he was managed by Dave Robinson for a number of years. (*Pictorial Press Ltd/Alamy*)

Above: The famous "Double B Side". Tyla Gang's "Styrofoam". (*Courtesy of Urban*)

Top: The original bunch of Stiffs: Elvis Costello, Nick Lowe, Wreckless Eric, Larry Wallis and Ian Dury. (*Chris Gabrin/Redferns*)

Above: The traditional concert finale for the Stiff's Greatest Stiffs tour. Elvis looks unimpressed. (*PYMCA/Alamy*)

Top left: Jake Riviera at the Stiff office, July 1977.
Two months later he would be gone. (*Douglas Doig/Stringer*)

Top right: Barney Bubbles was a design genius. Without him, the Stiff story
would have been very different. (*Chalkie Davies/Getty Images*)

Above left: Dave Robinson seen here in his days as
Brinsley Schwarz's manager. (*Courtesy of Ian Gomm*)

Above right: Record plugger Sonnie Rae and press officer Andy Murray at
Stiff HQ. The pictures on the wall suggest it was taken in 1978. (*Unknown*)

Top: The Damned sign to Stiff. Riviera and Robinson join in the fun.
(*Estate of Keith Morris/Redferns/Getty Images*)

Above left: Rare Elvis Costello photo taken at end of US tour party (Ukranian
Ballroom, East Village, NYC, Dec 1977). Left to right: Eileen Schneider
(Columbia press); Gregg Geller (A&R, Columbia Records); Hope Antman
(Head of Columbia press); Dick Wingate (EC's Product/Marketing Manager
at Columbia). (*Courtesy of Dick Wingate*)

Above right: Dartboard to promote Elvis' first album produced
by CBS America. (*Courtesy of Dick Wingate*)

Above: Canvey Island legend
Lew Lewis. (*Photo by Nigel Dick*)

Top right: Rachel Sweet in the studio.
(*Photo by Nigel Dick*)

Right: American advert for
Ian Dury's first album and tour.
(*John Blaney's collection*)

Opposite: Poster advertising
the second Stiff package tour.
(*Stiff Records*)

BE STIFF TOUR '78

OCTOBER 10 TO NOVEMBER 19

MICKEY JUPP	LENE LOVICH	WRECKLESS ERIC	RACHEL SWEET	JONA LEWIE

TRAVEL BY TRAIN

Top: The Be Stiff Tour at The Bottom Line, NYC. L–R: Wreckless Eric, Rachel Sweet, Lene Lovich, Les Chappell. (*Bob Leafe/Frank White Photo Agency*)

Above: Memorabilia produced for the Be Stiff Tour. (*Unknown*)

Right: The old train used on the Be Stiff Tour (see page 165). (*Photo by Graham Smith*)

pavement outside the Stiff office that some drinking had been going on inside. Given Riviera's propensity for hurling bottles through windows, this was nothing out of the ordinary. But the events that had unfolded at its Bayswater offices that afternoon were seismic.

Conroy recalls: "I had gone to see QPR play because I used to see them play every other Saturday, for my sins. I think Alan [Cowderoy] was in the office and I came back to do some work; I don't know if we were going out that night. It was a Saturday afternoon when they decided that they weren't going to continue. They'd sat in the office. Alan was downstairs, so he didn't hear much of what was going on really. I came back to the office and saw Jake go off, and he said, 'You'll find out' or something like that. And Dave came out and it was like, 'Oh fuck'.

"Although I hadn't given up as much of a well-paid job or things like that, I felt a bit pissed off at the time because Jake had been the one who'd really persuaded me to come in because creatively he was such a powerhouse and had great visuals and things. And apart from the fact we knew the glaziers' bills would be less if Jake left – because cider bottles used to go through the window quite often at Alexander Street – it wasn't going to be so much fun. And it was like, 'How are we going to keep this company going?' Dave sat and talked to us at the time because we didn't know what the fuck was going to happen then and whether Dave would be able to continue, even with all our help."

From the outset, it had been a stormy relationship and those who worked at Stiff knew it was not built to last. The personalities of Riviera and Robinson were simply too big for the same organisation and just a year after they had launched Stiff together, they had agreed to split. Riviera was to join Radar, a label recently started by Andrew Lauder. Worse still, he was taking Elvis Costello and Nick Lowe with him. That left Robinson with Wreckless Eric, Ian Dury, Larry Wallis and The Damned.

Bad news travels fast and the music press were quickly on the story. "Stiff's Riviera In Mystery Split" revealed *Melody Maker*, while its rival ran the headline of "We Here At *NME* Are Worried About Stiff" above an article in Adrian Thrills' regular gossip column on 8 October. His article also reported that Riviera had dissolved their joint management company Advancedale. Riviera was uncharacteristically reticent, telling the journalist: "Under the terms of my parting with Stiff, I'm not allowed to say anything about the details of the split for two weeks." Robinson couldn't be reached for a comment.

Paul Conroy had been contacted by *NME*, but he clearly didn't have all the information, saying he thought it was likely Costello and Lowe would remain on Stiff. Riviera meanwhile hinted he was not only looking for deals in the US for his clients, but also in the UK. Far from opting to stay out of things, Island Records director Dave Domleo supplied a comment that offered cold comfort for Robinson. "Who Stiff have on their label is up to them," he said. "We don't have any authority over who they sign. Logically though, it would seem a better working situation if they retained the contracts of Lowe and Costello."

The press reports were the first some of the artists knew about the dramatic turn of events. Ian Dury, however, had sensed something was wrong and had advised Wreckless to speak to Riviera. Sitting outside the pub next to Stiff's offices one afternoon, he spotted Riviera and asked him what was going on.

"Jake was running down the street with some stuff," says Wreckless. "I remember him turning to us as he was carrying all these papers and throwing them into the back of his car, and saying, 'Now I'm getting fucking sued'. In the middle of it all, I said, 'Jake, could I have a talk with you?' And he said, 'Yes. I owe that to you. There's stuff going on'. He went from ranting and shouting at people, to just being really gentle. He just sat there and it was a bit like, 'Mummy and daddy haven't been getting on too well and we're getting a divorce'. He said, 'Things aren't going well and basically I'm leaving Stiff Records and setting up something else. I'll be setting up a record company, management and publishing, basically all the things that you need. I should offer you a pitch really.' I said 'Well, I'm not asking for one,' because I didn't think that was right. I think he would have taken me with him.

"Dave had The Damned, Ian Dury and me, and Jake had Nick Lowe, Elvis Costello and The Yachts. So, they got three acts apiece. No one knew what was going to happen with Ian. No one had any idea that he was going to get that huge. Their biggest act was The Damned, who were fabulous."

If there was surprise at the news at Alexander Street, it was not at the fact that it had happened, but the timing. The pair had been in advanced negotiations with CBS Records for a production-distribution deal that would have set the company up for five years. The US giant had its sights on Elvis Costello, and was also interested in Nick Lowe. So, what led to the break up as Stiff stood on the verge of a major deal?

Theories abound among those who were there at the time. One insider suspects Costello was unwittingly at the root of the trouble and that whatever agreement was being discussed with CBS, Riviera wasn't prepared to go 50-50 on his prize asset. Another reports a huge bust-up on a flight back to Britain about the future direction of the label and its finances.

Glen Colson, who was close to Riviera at the time, says: "Jake was going to give him [Robinson] Stiff, so he [Robinson] probably thought, 'In exchange, you're taking Nick because he's your best friend, you're taking Barney because he's your best friend as well, you're taking Glen who's your new best friend, you might as well take Elvis as well because you discovered him.' I don't think Dave Robinson had anything to do with Elvis whatsoever. I think it was all Jake's doing. The whole marketing of Elvis was Jake and Barney, so all I did was step in and stoke the fire up … CBS Columbia wanted to sign Elvis and they were talked into signing the whole label and then I think maybe Jake thought, 'I don't want all the other people. I'll just cut a deal'."

Speaking in the BBC Four documentary, Riviera said he and Robinson simply had different ambitions. "Dave wanted to play golf with Richard Branson and own racehorses and fly helicopters and stuff, and direct films," he said caustically. "All of which he got to do, you know. Whereas I just wanted to tear it up."

Whatever the reasons, Robinson was shell-shocked. Just when Stiff appeared to have acquired what it needed to really take the majors on, its entire future was in the balance. He didn't know how Island was going to react to the news that Elvis Costello would be leaving Stiff. The music press headlines were bound to create unease among creditors, and The Damned, Wreckless Eric and Ian Dury looked unlikely saviours. It was a bitter blow.

But according to Robinson, he had suggested that Riviera take Costello with him to Radar when they agreed to split. "Jake leaving Stiff had a huge effect and quite honestly, Elvis had signed to Stiff Records and I gave him Elvis because I thought he wouldn't be able to make a living," said Robinson. "I said 'You take Elvis'. Nick came with Jake because he was in the Brinsleys. I was very unhappy. It was the worst possible time and it was really stupid. I had worked hard and Jake had worked hard, but it was obvious to me there was some other agenda and I didn't know what it was. I didn't want to actually say, 'You stupid cunt'. I wanted to get a letter between us to solve this as quickly as possible. I had experience of partnerships breaking up in difficult areas. I said, 'You have Elvis'. I liked Elvis, I thought he was great, but I thought he needed something. He gave me a very sad story, whether it was right or wrong.

"It was a key time because we were on the cusp of making a very large deal in America, and when I say 'on the cusp', they had agreed our terms. It was a licence deal and the finance we had always yearned. We had always been hassling from one cheque to the next, just like any independent. I spent a few days around the office panicking and the accounting guy had disappeared around the same time. I found his drawers full of receipts and I couldn't make head nor tail of his accounts. So, they weren't up to date and he disappeared subsequently. I think he turned up and I shouted at him and he disappeared again. We found out anyway that we owed about £150,000. The Americans didn't want the deal for a while and eventually we convinced them that the label would survive in a cut-down version. So, instead of getting the large sum of money – I think they were going to pay us $350,000 – and because Elvis was leaving who was one of the things they liked, we got something less." [5]

The sudden schism made for an unsettling atmosphere at Alexander Street and a testing time for artists and staff alike. Philippa Thomas was faced with a particular dilemma. She had a strong friendship with Riviera and his girlfriend, and her brother Pete was a member of the departing Attractions. However, she also felt a loyalty towards Robinson and Stiff. "I felt a bit of a split allegiance, because my brother went with Jake," says Thomas. "I was very friendly with Jake, and I was a bit, 'Why can't I go?' But Dave really picked himself up and continued on his own, really. I think he had quite a lot of irons in the fire; the management of Graham Parker and quite a lot of things going on at the same time."

The news that Costello and Lowe were leaving to start anew at Radar caused unease among Stiff's remaining artists. It was clear Riviera had big plans for his two star names, leaving some of those on Stiff's books to contemplate whether the grass would be greener at the brand new label.

Little over a year after Stiff's formation, Riviera and Robinson had agreed to part company and Stiff was about to take five acts on the road, two of whom, Costello and Lowe, were off to another label. With Larry Wallis effectively along for the ride, Stiff needed Ian Dury and Wreckless Eric to come good.

6

Dumping Music On The People ... In Your Town!

Dreary autumn rain tipped down on an assortment of musicians as they scampered from the Stiff offices to Trevor Wiffen's waiting green Ford coach. Philippa Thomas was at the hub of the activity in the office, making phone calls and rushing to and fro with last minute messages for the departing crew. Dave Edmunds held his suitcase above his head to avoid a soaking and made a mad dash for the coach doors as it prepared to leave. Stiff's Greatest Stiffs were about to be unleashed on the British public and the sense of anticipation at Alexander Street was palpable.

Eighteen musicians boarded the bus at 4pm on Monday 3 October and two hours behind was a second coach stuffed with journalists who'd been corralled by Glen Colson. Their destination was the town hall in High Wycombe, the Buckinghamshire town where Ian Dury had attended, and loathed, the grammar school. The sell-out show would be the first of 25 up and down the country, concluding at Lancaster University on bonfire night. It would prove an explosive affair, both on and off stage.

Media coverage was critical if tickets were to sell. Many hours had been spent in the office on a co-ordinated marketing campaign to get the word out in the weeks and days before the tour kicked off. As ever, the music press had lapped it up. A photograph of the five artists hitting the road almost filled the cover of *Melody Maker* on the first day of the tour. Stiff's scruffy Herberts also found themselves leering out of the cover of *Time Out,* ahead of the show at London's Lyceum Ballroom.

Sounds donated some space on page six to the "bunch of live stiffs", reporting that it was Elvis Costello who would be leading the tour and joined by the other four acts. "Collect This Paper" urged the special edition cover, the corner of which was stamped with the classic Stiff ruse of a fake apology. "Suddenly everything's collectible. Records obviously – limited editions, 12-inchers, official bootlegs, promo singles, green, pink, white, purple vinyl – but scores of other things too," it read. "Beatles', Stones' books, posters, tickets, tee shirts – even copies of the *Radio Times*. Yes, and even *NME*. 1976 copies can fetch 20p; some from the sixties sell for £2. Can you afford to throw *anything* away? The record as artefact has become the standard ploy of the record business in 1977."

A giant poster with pictures of each of the five artists was produced with the tagline "Dumping Music On The People … In Your Town!" Events on and off stage would be filmed by Stiff with a view to it being released. The small print disclosed that all the acts would play sets of equal length, but the playing order would change nightly. In an egalitarian mood, Stiff had decided on a rotating bill that would see the five acts taking turns to top the shop. Revealingly, it was Costello who was handed the final slot at the rehearsals which took place at Manticore Studios in Fulham's North End Road on the afternoons of Saturday 1 and Sunday 2 October. A surviving schedule for the tour shows Wreckless going first and Dury and Lowe alternating at the weekend run-throughs

At High Wycombe, things got off to an inauspicious start when the press entourage were escorted to the front of the queue, only to be told by promoter Ron Watts they'd have to pay to get in. Riviera was furious and left Glen Colson to sort it out. Another first night shock for Colson was the discovery that, although he'd done the publicity for *New Boots And Panties!!* and had taken on Kosmo Vinyl to help champion Ian Dury, Pete Jenner and Andrew King had also added Irish promoter and publicist BP Fallon to "Team Ian". The stakes were high and the 35-year-old performer needed to seize the moment.

Wreckless opened the show with a 20-minute set, *Record Mirror*'s Tim Lott finding him "witty and intense" and "not just a warm-up". Then came Ian Dury and his band, which was followed in turn by Nick Lowe, who had clearly dressed for the occasion. He was resplendent in a green suit covered with question marks. He took to the stage carrying a twin-necked guitar accompanied by a rather incongruous looking band. He went straight for the jugular with "Shake And Pop" and followed it with the grinding "Music For Money" (both of which would appear on his debut album for Radar, *Jesus Of Cool*). During his slot, Larry Wallis took over the microphone to deliver a short set of his own.

Topping the bill was Costello, the artist the audience probably knew the most about following the waves made by *My Aim Is True*. But if the sneering figure with short-cropped hair and a black bomber jacket wasn't what they expected to see, his set definitely wasn't what they'd expected to hear. Although his debut album had only been released about two months earlier, the restless songwriter had already moved on. And when disappointed fans shouted out for the songs he'd recorded with Clover, he told them to "buy the fucking record", treating them instead to songs from an album that wouldn't even be released on Stiff. "Elvis deliberately cut his own throat by doing a set of songs nobody had ever heard before," recalled Colson. [6]

On the night, it was Dury and The Blockheads who turned reviewers' heads, serving notice that Costello wasn't the only act worthy of top billing. Those in attendance got to witness a landmark moment in the emergence of new wave and an occasion from which Dury would never look back.

In a bowler hat and overcoat, and with more stage props than Tommy Cooper, Dury was more Vaudeville than punk, more variety performer than pop singer. Elvis Costello may have looked more Pure Pop For Now People than a bloke in an old coat with a carrier bag, but no one on the Stiff's Greatest Stiffs bill was more serious about things than Ian Dury and he had the press eating out of his hand.

"Ian was just such a larger than life character," comments Jankel. "Journalists lapped it up, they'd never seen anything like it. In a way, he was like Charlie Chaplin, but he had something to talk about, he had an agenda, a real agenda, and no one had ever really ever heard lyrics like that. He walked into a room and everybody's eyes were on him, and I think this was so different to anybody else. Musicians could write great songs and so on, but they didn't have his presence."

For years, Dury had toiled with the Kilburns, honing his songs, attire and cockney geezer persona. With The Blockheads, he had a group that brought an urgency to the remarkable lyrics he wrote out on vast sheets of paper in his flat. He also had an album hailed as a triumph by the critics; a volcanic eruption of funk, punk and Music Hall.

New Boots And Panties!! (the only items of clothing Dury would buy as new) was unveiled by Stiff on 30 September 1977. Chris Gabrin's black and white photograph, on its now iconic cover, captured Dury with his young son Baxter standing outside a shop selling women's and men's clothes. A collage of pictures from his earlier days in the Kilburns adorned the inner sleeve and a shot of Dury and his friend Humphrey Ocean was used on one of a series of ingenious advertisements. These, along with the album artwork, were produced by Barney Bubbles. "This Man Is Ready For The Mincer" ran the message across the top of one." "Ian Dury. It's taken him five years in an abattoir, an asylum and a hospital to discover it takes longer to get up north the slow way. Genius is pain."

Dury and Jankel had gone into a small studio in Wimbledon called Alvic in the spring of 1977 to record demos of some songs they'd co-written. Jankel had played the bass, piano and guitar parts, while Dury sang and played drums. At the time, Dury had also been collaborating with American journalist and musician Steve Nugent, presenting him with sheets of scribbled lyrics. So, he also joined them at Alvic to help work on the fruits of their labours, including: "Billericay Dickie", "Plaistow Patricia", "My Old Man" and "Blackmail Man".

It was a chance remark during these embryonic sessions that connected Ian Dury with the rest of the musicians who would become The Blockheads. The studio engineer told him about a tight rhythm section which was using the studio and suggested he get in touch. Bassist Norman Watt-Roy and drummer Charley Charles were in Loving Awareness, a kind of hippie concept group. But it hadn't caught on and they were hiring themselves out as session musicians. The pair gelled immediately with Dury and Jankel and completed the demos within a matter of days.

The recording of the album began the following week at The Workhouse Studio in the Old Kent Road, 50% of which was owned by Blackhill and 50% by Manfred Mann. To really bring Dury's extraordinary songs to life on record, other ex-Kilburns Davey Payne and Ed Speight supplied sax and "ballad guitar". Jazz pianist Geoff Castle meanwhile came in to play Moog synthesiser on the opening track "Wake Up And Make Love With Me".

Blackhill was overjoyed by the outcome and peddled the 10-track record around the established record labels. But none of them was imaginative or brave enough to take it on and Dury's managers finally decided to take it downstairs to Stiff. Robinson had previously expressed an interest in Dury but been told by Jenner and King they would be taking him elsewhere. So, it was doubly satisfying when they came back to him with the album the major labels had rejected.

"Stiff was aimed at people whose arses were hanging out in the industry and couldn't get a look in," said Dury. "We were the unemployables really.

We didn't fit into any of their stupid categories, since the record industry is run by shoe salesmen and drug dealers. We took *New Boots* ... to every single label, but they were just fucking stupid – they still are."[5]

———

When it came to performing his songs on the Stiff's Greatest Stiffs tour, Dury's rhythm section suggested he try their bandmates from Loving Awareness, keyboard player Mickey Gallagher and guitarist Johnny Turnbull. They agreed and Dury boarded the coach with what amounted to a ready-made group. It was the moment of truth. After years of trudging around the pub circuit, he had no intention of living up to the name of his new label. Dury and his blistering new band blew the audience away.

Sounds writer Vivien Goldman admonished Costello for his "totally self-absorbed way of lecturing the audience like a parrot in NHS specs" and preferred Wreckless Eric. But she was in thrall to Dury, who despite losing his voice, "managed to grip the onlookers by the appropriate areas". "Even if people don't know Ian's songs," she enthused, "they can enjoy them 'cos they've got Music Hall/fairground/end-of-the-pier roots that elicit a Pavlovian instant fun response. See him if you can."

Colson said: "No one really knew how big Dury was going to be. The first night of the Stiffs tour, Ian blew everybody away and everybody knew from that night onwards he was going to be enormous. I had taken all the press down there to see Elvis Costello and give all the other guys a bit of press just to keep them happy. But it turned out that Ian totally stole the show and nobody I had taken down there was remotely interested in Elvis Costello because he had had his bit of fame and they all chased after Dury. Ian was put on the cover of *NME* and he shot from absolutely nowhere to being on the covers of papers overnight." [6]

Wreckless was too drunk to turn the tour to his advantage, and instead looked on in awe as Dury grabbed his chance. "Ian was going to be top dog at Stiff Records, definitely, and it was fucking obvious," says Eric. "At the first gig at High Wycombe Town Hall someone said, 'Your guitar solos are too long' and someone else said something, and Ian said, 'What's this, a fucking debate or a rock 'n' roll concert?' He had it down. There was a lot of sharpness. I lost my sharpness on that tour. I started off sharp, but lost it."

At Aberystwyth the following day, the bands arrived to find a mountain of filled rolls, sandwiches and bags of crisps laid out. Pete Thomas had an idea. One of the numbers in Lowe's set was "Let's Eat", and as he brought the show to a close with it, his tour-mates began lobbing the food into the crowd. "We all lined up behind the amplifiers," says Bruce Thomas, "and as soon as he went 'Let's Eat', it all went over in waves, like a World War II Salvo – or 'salvoloy!' Of course, within about ten seconds it all started coming back, not over the amps to us – but at the band. There was this glorious image of Nick Lowe with a bit of buttered bread stuck to the side of his face. That's probably where I got the idea for Ian Dury's fried egg. That's the thing I remember most about the Stiff tour, more than the music, a bit of the aggro stuff."

Those looking on from the beer-drenched floors of the colleges, civic halls and other venues along the way, could have been forgiven for seeing Stiff's touring troupe as one big happy family. Musicians who appeared in one band line-up popped up again in another. Wreckless Eric's New Rockets featured Ian Dury on drums, Denise Roudette on bass and Davey Payne on saxophone. Meanwhile, Larry Wallis's Psychedelic Rowdies and Nick Lowe's Last Chicken In The Shop shared the same six musicians: Wallis and Lowe, Penny Tobin on keyboards, Dave Edmunds on guitar, and Terry Williams and Pete Thomas on drums. Williams also played with Rockpile. Only The Blockheads and The Attractions appeared as standalone acts. In another apparent display of harmony, each night everyone piled back on stage at the end for a rousing finale of "Sex & Drugs & Rock 'n' Roll". The song title neatly encapsulated the tour's spirit of excess, but the public solidarity was deceptive.

The concept of a rotating bill was novel, but it almost instantly became the cause of resentment. At the centre of it was a power struggle between the artists with the biggest egos – Costello and Dury. Both saw themselves as the most important act on the bill and openly coveted the headline slot. Practical considerations also played a part in the nightly schedule being reviewed just a few dates into the expedition. Dury argued that he needed a rest between drumming for Wreckless and his own set. Likewise, Pete Thomas wanted a decent break between playing with Lowe and Costello.

Lowe was more interested in finishing his set and getting to the nearest pub than topping the bill, as was Edmunds. Wreckless was too drink-addled to be competitive. It also became clear early on that, of the five acts, Costello and Dury were best equipped to bring the shows to a climax and send the punters away buzzing. So, with the help of Dave Robinson, a compromise had to be hammered out involving two running orders. The first was Lowe/Wallis, Wreckless, Costello and Dury; the second Wreckless, Lowe/Wallis, Dury and Costello.

"That tour caused a lot of friction, because as soon as you put artists on stage, it's all very well with this 'You're on next', but it didn't work that way and you could see that Jake was floating more off to the Elvis side," explains Conroy. "Then, of course, you had Ian Dury with Peter Jenner and Andrew King coming in – and Kosmo – and it all started to fracture. And, of course, Eric didn't really have a manager as such. It goes on in the film and people have said, it became serious. It wasn't just, 'We're all having a laugh and we'll have a few beers with the late night, 24-Hour Club.' Elvis was certainly taking it very seriously and so was Ian. Those two were extremely competitive with each other and Nick was along for the ride ...

"You had Edmunds in there and you had Larry Wallis, who was happy to be away from ... well, he wasn't happy to be away from his snakes, was he? But your normal record or management company could not have put that together in many ways, it was such a weird amalgam. Larry had come from The Pink Fairies, Nick had come from the Brinsleys, Eric had come up from Brighton with a plastic bag, and Elvis had only just recently given up his job at the cosmetics factory. It was that chemistry. But as soon as they started getting out on the road, there was definitely a more competitive spirit from certain acts."

The changed arrangements did nothing to suppress the enmity that existed between Costello and Dury. If anything, it grew as the tour went on. They shared the same record label and, likely, a professional respect. But once they hit the road, it was all about who won. At High Wycombe, Ian and The Blockheads had drawn first blood. The pair kept their distance. Dury was busy bonding with his new band and Costello, although he partied along the way, would often crash out on his own, writing lyrics in the notebook he carried with him at all times. On stage, the rivalry drove each of them to deliver a performance more electrifying than the other's.

Mickey Gallagher says: "It was controversial and it was better to have controversy on that tour than it was to have a nice friendly bus full of punks travelling around the country. A bit of aggression, a bit of competition was always there. There is a great clip in the film of Ian coming off stage in Newcastle. Elvis and us used to rotate who was top of the bill and I think we were on first that day. Ian is coming off stage and Elvis walks towards the stage to go on, and as he walks past, Ian goes, 'It's yours tonight, Elvis', like he's graciously giving it to him. That was all part of the vibe of it."

Recalling the backstage animosity between them, Fred Rowe recalls: "Elvis started having little pops at Ian, and Ian is another wordsmith. So, Ian had a pop at Elvis, who said, 'You're only talking like that because you've got this trained gorilla by you'. That was me. I said, 'Hold on, I'm his friend, there's no need to get irate about it. We're just having a conversation.' Anyway, he swallowed that and Ian gave him a few jabs what he couldn't answer and he ran off."

Costello's feared handler, Riviera, made the odd appearance on the tour and left his unmistakable mark. As he prepared to take Costello away from Stiff to Radar, his loyalty towards him was now stronger than ever. He subjected BP Fallon to a humiliating dressing down in front of open-mouthed onlookers after he committed the crime of throwing Stiff badges into the crowd during Costello's set at High Wycombe, distracting the audience from watching the singer. The legendary red mist descended again during the dispute about the rotating bill, causing Riviera to lock horns with Robinson at Glasgow Apollo.

Rowe looked on open-mouthed: "As it went on – I think it was about the fourth gig – Ian was going on third and they dropped down one. Then further into the tour, two or three more gigs, Leicester or somewhere, Ian come second in the pecking order to Elvis. Then we got to Glasgow and Jake Riviera, who showed up a couple of times on the tour, was mouthing off to Robbo, and Robbo was really slaughtering him with verbals. The fans, according to Robbo, also liked Nick Lowe and to have Elvis after Ian was not a good idea because they was all wound up by Ian and his showmanship. Then they get Elvis on – a good singer, a good artist – but he wasn't like Ian. He [Dury] was a very entertaining bloke, he was telling people jokes and squirting water at them an' that and they loved it.

"Of course, Jake got the hump when Robbo said, 'Do you think it would be better to put Ian on last?'. Robbo never lost his temper like Jake did. Jake was fucking fuming and Robbo was just smiling and jabbing him with verbal right-handers an' that. I was absolutely enthralled by this. Fucking hell, there's two public schoolboys here.

I'm a crook and these were people I'd never experienced in my life before. All I used to talk to were crooks and here was two posh kids having a ruck in a way I'd never seen before in my life. The two blokes would come to blows and there'd be blood everywhere, but they were doing it verbally and I was so impressed. Jake went away with his head down, beaten, absolutely knocked out. Mike Tyson couldn't have done a better job!"

Costello's own camp was crackling with tension, largely due to the presence of the "Tour Nurse" Fay Hart, A.K.A. Farrah Fuck-it Minor. A well-known face on the alternative Los Angeles scene, she knew Riviera's friends in Backstage Pass. She was born in Macclesfield, Cheshire, but had grown up in the US and she was a close confident of Riviera's partner Toni Laumer (an out-and-out extrovert). Hart had caught Jake's attention on his trips to LA and had been invited to join the Stiff's Greatest Stiffs tour. "I remember she was a pioneer of the see-through mini-skirt and basically Jake spotted her as being clever and stylish and funny and an ideas person," remembers Pete Thomas. "I can't remember quite how she got to England, but then her and Steve hooked up."

Hart would later go on to marry Steve Nieve and have two children with him. During the course of the tour, however, she also became friendly with both Costello and Bruce Thomas, creating an uncomfortable situation. After the penultimate gig at Newcastle Polytechnic, an exhausted Costello sat on the fire escape of the Swallow Hotel and scribbled the lyrics to "Pump It Up", a reaction to the rampant excess being exhibited on the tour. Bruce Thomas claims the song is also about Hart.

In the film, which Stiff failed to get released, Hart is seen forcibly having her breasts exposed by two members of The Attractions. "Get your tits out before the film runs out," says a voice off-camera as Pete Thomas grapples with her and manages to pull up her top before the pair tumble to the floor laughing. In a separate scene, he performs the same trick with the help of Bruce Thomas.

Such antics were recorded in a newsletter handwritten and then photocopied and distributed by Hart. The second issue entitled What Did I Do Last Nite reported the following incidents:

* "Well wasn't Glasgow fun? There was a bit of aggravation in the dressing room which led Elvis to threaten a bouncer with the jagged

edge of an orange juice tin while Bruce was frantically jumping about gritting his teeth."

* "Congratulations Davey [Payne] for the brilliant way you got the message across that you don't like cold tea – communication is such an art" [He overturned an entire table, sending crockery and glass flying].

* "Pete Thomas has gotten quite serious about the art of dropping his trousers for everyone's enjoyment. It wasn't enough that he shocked 200 students while they were calmly watching TV – he was next seen with bare bum pressed against the coach window while driving down the M1!"

* "Jake Riviera was proudly and loudly protecting his interest in Norwich. I overheard him calmly screaming at a fat bearded student type about the lack of sandwiches ... 'just because you're the most boring, the fattest, the most beardest, the most hippyest etc ...' The next thing I saw him whizzing by with a box of sandwiches. Another demonstration in communication."

A "special bulletin" in the same diary announced "the 24-Hour Club is now defunct. I think it was the mini-bars in the hotel in Glasgow that did them in". News of its demise, however, was a little premature. This hard-core band of party animals had a loose membership and some fell by the wayside. But among its members in chief were Larry Wallis, Pete Thomas, Dave Edmunds, Nick Lowe, Terry Williams and Kosmo Vinyl.

"The deal was that at any time, day or night, if two or more members turned up at your room, seat on the bus, anywhere at all, it was firmly against club rules to refuse a drink and a party," says Larry. "Of course, we founders had a reputation to live up to, and so we were pretty messed-up practically all the time. But never gave in, not once. At times it was the best fun, and at others death would have been welcome. But whatcha gonna do?"

Bruce Thomas says of the behind-scenes mayhem: "You couldn't decline a drink if someone was still up and drinking. It morphed into The Attractions' white boot gang, where The Attractions all bought white cowboy boots one day. We went to some other hotel, got pissed, lost our clothes and walked back home down the motorway in white boots and towels wrapped round us, like centurions. People don't realise The Attractions were fairly hardcore for about three years."

Some kept away from the mayhem. The Blockheads were more interested in smoking joints and chilling out than running up and down hotel corridors and wrenching mini bars off walls. And anyway, Dury didn't like his group drinking before shows. The Attractions were well up for marathon boozing sessions, but Costello had little appetite for this clichéd rock 'n' roll behaviour. Wreckless recalls in his autobiography that while Larry Wallis was running around a hotel in Leeds wearing a policeman's helmet and everyone was roaring drunk, Elvis was "in Woolworths buying up rare copies of 'God Save The Queen' on the EMI label, which had somehow found their way into a bargain bin".

As for tour manager Dez Brown, he was teetotal and viewed as the tour killjoy. In a scene filmed on the bus, he incurs the wrath of some of the passengers for refusing to let them pull in at a pub. One mocks him as "the Ice Queen of tour management"; Kosmo pathetically claws at the window as the prospect of more alcohol is squashed.

Pete Thomas, recalling the former equipment handler for the Pink Fairies, says: "He never washed. Dez had a real hum going and he also had some extraordinary power over women. I mean, Dez was just non-stop, which is rather hard to put together with this smell. Jake had these rules just to annoy people. Like, no one was allowed on stage in shorts or with a beard or with a T-shirt with any other band's name on, and there were all these sort of things which created this great kind of edgy vibe. I think maybe Dez took it a bit far and took the humour out of it sometimes. But he was all right. He's up in San Francisco and he still comes to the shows."

Inevitably there were casualties along the way and a couple of the troupe were taken to hospital. Wreckless, who was almost permanently pissed, on and off-stage, was taken to a private doctor after performing at Brighton Top Rank. He was advised to rest up for a week and went to his parents' nearby home, ruling him out of the next few dates. Otherwise, the bus trundled on from venue to venue and the tour passed without a major incident ... until Manchester, that is.

Wallis recounts the drama that unfolded at the Post House Hotel after the show at Salford University: "Very late one night, Dave Edmunds and myself were haunting the hotel looking for action, and I got a real craving for milk and cookies. We decided that Dez's room was the place to be, so we banged on his door. He opened it and told us to go away, but we barged on in. I guess he must have had company, as he physically tried to manhandle us out, and as I was holding a pint mug of milk in one hand, and a plate of chocolate biscuits in the other, somehow the mug shattered and Dez cut his feet quite badly.

"I toddled off to bed, and when I woke up, Pete Thomas had already left our room, which was unusual, and then it all came back to me. Wow, I didn't know where to turn, but I had no choice but to face the music. When I went down to the bar for a liquid breakfast, you could cut the atmosphere with a knife; no-one would meet my gaze, I felt as sick as a dog. I went over to Dez, and apologised. He was really good about it. I went to the bar and stood next to Nick, who told me I was off the tour. 'I know', I said. It seemed only right. Nick said that if only I had apologised to Dez, and I told him I already had. This brought about a change in Basher's attitude, and he became very kind to me.

"Edmunds had already got a taxi to the station but, truth be told, I don't think he was very happy on that tour anyway, and he'd found a good reason to leave, i.e. I was getting the sack. We boarded the bus and headed for the station to try and head Dave off at the pass, and Nick sat next to me, to show his support for an idiot. We never caught Dave, but he re-joined us at the next gig. Dez and I remained good friends, thank God. What a palaver!"

Remarkably, Lowe had slept through the drama and had awoken to find blood and broken glass all over the floor – reportedly the inspiration for his 1978 hit single "I Love The Sound Of Breaking Glass". "Dez is carved up," he is caught saying in the film, "it looks like Sharon Tate up there, you know, blood all over the place. There's a note by [my] bed, 'Nick, you missed the sound of breaking glass, make sure you have your boots on when you get out of bed'".

On stage, Wallis's showstopper was "Police Car". Written while the frazzle-haired composer was high as a kite watching TV, it invoked seventies cop shows like The Sweeney. A mainstay of the tour, it was included on the *Hits Greatest Stiffs* album, recorded on the label's mobile studio. It also became Wallis's one and only record for Stiff when it was released as a single on 28 October 1977.

Staring out from the sleeve in his trademark shades, the ex-Pink Fairy had ensured his place in Stiff's Hall Of Fame with a song that seemed to capture the prevailing mood in 1977. The single's cruise through flashing lights and late-night liquor stores with shotguns under the seat was all over in less than three and a half minutes. Eddie & The Hot Rods provided the backing for the recording, which was done at Electric Landlady Studios A.K.A. Pathway.

Like so many of Stiff's classic early singles, it didn't lay a glove on the charts. But it was enthusiastically taken up by a bunch of bands, becoming an underground anthem of sorts.

Wallis casts his mind back to the hallucinogenic evening that inspired the song: "I was living in a church with a bunch of architects, but my girlfriend Rose and I lived in the church hall at the back of the place, like a couple of vampires. We lived on Jim Beam, amphetamine sulphate, hash and fish fingers. Someone had built a very high platform, where we basically lived. It had all we needed: a bed, a Sony Trinitron, two shot glasses, a mirror, blade, and drinking straws.

"One Friday evening, as usual, we were as stoned as two boogie owls, and watching Angie Dickinson in *Police Woman,* when suddenly there was a close-up of a police car roaring towards the camera. Its radiator grille, to my stoned eyes, was a big grin, and its siren was screaming, 'I'm a Police Car'. I immediately stopped watching the show, and fifteen minutes later, tops, 'I'm a Police Car' was completely written."

The transformation of this chemically-induced composition into another smoking Stiff release came when Dez Brown heard it while calling round one Sunday afternoon. "I played him the song and he knew how shy I was," says Wallis, "so he gave me half a Mandrax and suggested we go visit Nick and Jake at their pad in Queensgate Terrace. When we had been there for a while and had a few glasses of wine – Dez didn't drink, the cunning swine – Dez suddenly announced, 'Hey, Lazza's got a great new tune!'

"This was his plan all along, and against my protestations, a guitar was thrust into my hands. In front of Nick, Jake, Jake's girlfriend Toni, and possibly Chrissie Hynde, I had to squawk my way through the song. A couple of days later, I met up with the Rods guys in Pathway, we ran through the thing, maybe twice, and banged it down. The Rods really knew what they were doing and a jolly good time was had by all. Now it's gotten a life of its own, and I think the song has had a more successful career than I have!"

In early 1978, Wallis recorded a solo album for Stiff called *Leather Forever*. Playing on the record were Deke Leonard, a former member of the Welsh psychedelic rockers Man, Big George Webley, who played bass on the Tyla Gang album *Yachtless*, and Pete Thomas. However, delays and label politics meant it was never released.

The same fate was to befall Nick Lowe's proposed album *Aerials Over Orkney*. Instead, the last glimpse Stiff fans got of one of its founding members was his face printed on the label of the Goffin and King penned single "Halfway To Paradise" – the push-out centre punching a huge hole through one side of his nose. In an interview shortly after he left Stiff, Lowe disowned the record as "garbage" and said Riviera had wanted to put it out while he was touring with Rockpile to "keep the ball rolling".

"With the last single, I'd been getting a hard time from Stiff," said Lowe [unknown article]. "They thought the songs I'd been doing weren't commercial enough, the words were too off the wall. So, I said I would do someone else's song. I'd always liked 'Halfway To Paradise' and I had a real good arrangement, but I got hustled into doing it quickly. The version that came out wasn't finished, the vocals are terrible: it's not badly sung, it's just flat! They're not actually screwing me up or anything like that, that's not the reason why I left Stiff. I left because it's not fun anymore."

Lowe was in a bad place at the time and in no mood to be a Greatest Stiff. His relationship with Dave Edmunds had also started to fracture. To all intents and purposes, they were the best of mates. Edmunds had released Lowe's song "I Knew The Bride" as a single on Swan Song and it was ostensibly a Rockpile record. But behind the scenes all was not well. Rockpile had embarked on an American tour with Bad Company in May that year and ended up being thrown off and replaced with The Outlaws. When Bad Company's label owner Peter Grant became Edmunds' manager, he insisted there was no bad blood and offered Lowe a contract. But Grant didn't see eye-to-eye with Lowe's manager Riviera, and the fact Rockpile's two vocalists were serving different labels and managers inevitably caused friction. Lowe walked out on Rockpile and when he embarked on the Stiff tour there was no sign of Rockpile guitarist Billy Bremner in his Last Chicken In The Shop group. The incongruous sight of guitar maestro Dave Edmunds behind a drum kit and Attractions drummer Pete Thomas playing guitar indicated just how little attention Lowe was paying to the tour.

For all the space the music press devoted to the tour, it still hadn't spawned a hit single. People had raucously sung along to "Sex & Drugs & Rock 'n' Roll" – a phrase that has gone on to become universal shorthand for the excesses of the industry – and scurried around venue floors trying to pick up the series of badges that spelled out the song. But not enough folks had gone out and bought the single, which was left off *New Boots And Panties!!*. "Whole Wide World", another popular number with audiences, had had to make do with critical, rather than commercial, success.

Then, on Guy Fawkes' Day, the final day of the tour, Stiff blasted into the UK's mainstream pop consciousness for the first time. When the all-important Top 40 was announced, one of the highlights of the week for music fans in 1977, Elvis Costello's "Watching The Detectives" was at No. 33, an unexpectedly sinister filling in an easy listening sandwich of Boney M and The Commodores. A couple of *Top Of The Pops* appearances later and it rose to No.15, a parting gift to the label that had taken a punt on him when the major labels had rejected him out of hand. Had Dave Robinson committed hari-kari by suggesting that Riviera take Elvis with him? Time would tell.

The label's first non-stiff, which had been released on 14 October, came in at least three different sleeves. On the coloured picture sleeve designed by Barney Bubbles, Elvis stared intently down the lens. The back featured a picture of the whole band, even though only Steve Nieve had played on it, and an obviously worthless "Stiff Single Voucher". "I think you know what I mean" read Porky Peckham's mysterious inscription in the run-off grooves on the A-side. "Little Triggers But Big Tears" said the etching on the other, a reference to two of their unreleased songs

A plain Stiff sleeve was also released, but the most prized release for collectors was the one carrying the entries for the name Stiff from the London telephone directory, with the label's address and number circled. An added selling point was that the B-side featured two previously unreleased live versions of "Blame It On Cain", and "Mystery Dance", recorded at The Nashville Rooms on 7 August that same year.

Recorded under the watchful and admiring eye of Nick Lowe, "Watching The Detectives" was a disconcerting record, a nail-biting tale of domestic unease. The opening few seconds are unusually sparse for a single that was released as punk was raging. Steve Goulding's tumbling drums guarantee the listener's attention and Andrew Bodnar's bass plucks out an almost hypnotic introduction before a rhythm guitar provides a reggae beat. Costello's twanging guitar then interjects with the jagged-edged riff for which it would be best remembered.

As well as being a landmark for Stiff, "Watching The Detectives" was a watershed for the experimenting songwriter. "'Detectives' was very important because it was the first song that proved to me that I could write in a whole new style," said Elvis. [30]

The show at The Lyceum Ballroom in London's Strand on 28 October was sold out and saw the London-based music press posse out in force. And when Ian Dury beckoned people on from the wings to join him for "Sex & Drugs ...", the cameras were rolling to capture the perfect finale for Dave Robinson's much-vaunted movie. "Humphrey Ocean, where are you? Come and dance with us," growls the singer as he lurches forward and grabs the microphone. Urging the audience to show its appreciation for all the artists, as the credits roll on the screen, he calls out for Costello and Lowe when they don't appear. As balloons are batted around the auditorium, they reluctantly emerge for the show's grand finale, Costello's body language speaking volumes. Sharing a microphone with Dury, he stands with his arms folded in his checked jacket, reluctantly wording the chorus.

Dury had won the hearts of the media and while Costello undeniably had a red-hot band, the Blockheads were the surprise package, the dark horse from the Stiff stable. "Ian may have come out on top a little bit," says Pete Thomas. "I mean, The Blockheads were really great. We were good, but we were all out of our brains."

Like Lowe, Costello was now joined at the hip with Riviera, and it was he who would shape his career not just for the days ahead, but for almost the next twenty years.

With Dave Robinson left holding the Stiff baby and its two most promising acts about to leave, there was to be a final blow before one of the most eventful years in pop history was out. If some were worried that the label wouldn't survive their departure, events unfolding within another of its acts only vindicated their fears.

Tensions were running high in The Damned. The group had been touring non-stop since the first album and they were exhausted. There had been little time to spend coming up with material for the follow-up, which Stiff was bugging them for. There was also irritation at the increased involvement of Brian James' photographer girlfriend Erica Echenberg in the group and strong opposition to his insistence on bringing in a second guitarist. He figured a second player would lift the burden of playing the lead riffs and solos and allow the band to throw off the 1-2-3-4 straight-jacket of punk and be more experimental.

An ad had been placed and Captain and Rat took the calls in the Stiff offices. "We'd say, 'Are you the greatest in the world?'" said Sensible. "If they said 'No', we put the phone down on them. If they said 'Yes' then there were five or six more questions they had to answer in the right way or else the phone would go down." [31]

Those who talked their way through to the auditions were left in no doubt as to what they would be letting themselves in for. "Some of the people who came for the actual auditions were really dreadful," said Sensible. "After two or three, we thought, 'We'll have to liven this up a bit. They'd put the guitar on, plug in and we'd all pull our trousers down. If they didn't mind that, then we'd start gobbing at them while they were playing. This one guy was really grooving on it. He was shrieking with laughter while he was playing, doing this tricky routine while we were naked and gobbing at him. We said, 'That was marvellous. We'll definitely put you on the shortlist'. By the next evening, we said, 'We gotta get that lunatic back'". [31]

That lunatic was Lu Edmunds and he made his debut with The Damned at the second Mont De Marsan festival. During the same month, the band began work on their second album for Stiff, *Music For Pleasure*, but it was to be a far from enjoyable process. Firstly, Pink Floyd's former singer Syd Barrett spurned the group's invitation to produce the record. With the ethereal Barrett having eluded them, they settled on the arguably odder choice of Floyd drummer Nick Mason. Pink Floyd owned Britannia Row Studios in Islington, where the album was recorded, and they and The Damned shared the same publisher.

James explains how this unlikely marriage arose: "I'm an old Syd Barrett fan, as is Captain, and I think it was more a joke. 'Hey, it would be great to have Syd Barrett do it, wouldn't it?' and Peter [Barnes, Floyd's music publisher] was like, 'Yeah, if you can get two words out of him. His brother looks after him and he wouldn't be capable of doing it'. Then, in true Stiff fashion, it was like, 'Ah, but talking of the Floyd, I wonder if any of the others would fancy doing it, and they've got a studio haven't they and it would be cheap'. Jake says, 'When can we do it?' and it was like, 'Huh, I ain't got no songs. Ever since I met you Jake, we've been doing nothing but gig, so I ain't got nothing'. Jake mumbles and then goes, '[Dave] Edmunds, come in here. You still got that acoustic guitar? Sell it to BJ here because he's got to go off and write some songs for a new album'. I said, 'You know, I can't write songs like that, they've got to come out'.

"I don't know why he [Nick Mason] agreed to do it to be honest. Obviously he didn't need the money, he's in bloody Pink Floyd. I don't get it. Maybe he just did it as a favour to Peter Barnes or something. But he obviously didn't know what the fuck to do. He didn't know how to mic things up, so the noise that you hear in the studio sounded like what you'd hear in the control room. The thing is, you walk into the gentleman's toilets at Britannia Row and you can fit the whole of Pathway in there. It was just this lush, plush, vast place. It was like being in the bloody Intercontinental Hotel."

For the group, the surprise highlight of the recording sessions was the involvement of saxophone player Lol Coxhill, who had previously played with Nick Mason. "He used to turn up with these knitted toys on a pair of roller skates that he'd walk along and treat them as if they were real children," says Rat. "He'd go and buy them ice-creams and things like that. And what a phenomenal player. That track he was on ['You Know'] is outstanding and his timing was much more in tune with what Brian was wanting to do in a lot of ways: that hypnotic riff that's got this underground atmosphere running through that you'd only hear in a drug den full of hookers in Detroit, that kind of sleaze."

Recording sessions were put on hold on September 7 for the wedding of Dave and Laurie Vanian. Elvis Costello and Nick Lowe were among the guests. The honeymoon began in Sussex and continued as The Damned began a European tour. "Problem Child", written by James and Scabies, was the first single from the new album, issued on 30 September. But the tale of delinquency followed in the footsteps of its two predecessors, failing to enter the UK chart, making its rowdy presence felt only on the *NME* one. Given the success of their debut, this was a backward step.

If Stiff was now seen by some as a sinking ship, news of a Rat leaping from it only cemented that impression. The shock exit of The Damned's hell-raising drummer was reported in the same issue of *NME* as the upheaval within the label. Scabies, the paper said, had been unhappy in the band for some time, and was rumoured to be joining The Heartbreakers following the departure of Jerry Nolan. Now Stiff's sole punk representatives on earth, The Damned were on tour in Europe and the walkout had come days after violence involving neo-fascists broke out ten minutes into their first gig at a hall near Nancy in France. British punk bands were a target for such groups in Europe, prompting Paul Conroy to tell *NME*: "It's getting so political at continental gigs now, it makes you wonder if it's worth touring there."

Before going on stage for the second gig of the tour at Colmar, Scabies had ransacked the mini-bar and shovelled down a load of speed. Once back at the hotel, he started wrecking the lobby and climbed on to a window ledge, leading to press speculation that he had tried to kill himself. It was all too much and Scabies headed back to England, crashing at the flat of Johnny Moped's drummer Dave Berk. Berk meanwhile headed the other way to take over his seat for the remainder of the tour. *Music For Pleasure* had become anything but.

"I tried to quit before the album and Jake said that I should not let the band and the record company and everybody else down and I should do the record," says Scabies. "And if I still felt like leaving, that's what I should do, which is what happened. Jake had left, Robbo was in charge, we still hadn't been paid anything or even seen a piece of paper with a number on it. And we were getting more and more frustrated with that. I was getting very frustrated with the fact that we were touring all the time and life didn't get any better. It was still sitting in a van and sharing rooms and bad food. I thought, 'If this is success, there's not much to it, is there?' We were on £30 a week or something, but it wasn't an X-Factor deal. It was, 'Here's £30 a week and that's your lot, mate'. Even then, that wasn't much more than you'd get on the dole. You have this Tinsel Town image when you're a kid of what it's going to be like to be a musician, and actually you end up being pretty bored most of the time, the food's never that great, you never really got quite enough money to buy any weed or anything. And I'm sure that's a deliberate thing, because as soon as musicians get money they usually blow it. I just knew with the album that we'd made and with the changes at Stiff Records, it wasn't for me."

Barney Bubbles' cover art was sadly the most memorable feature of *Music For Pleasure*, the band's own dissatisfaction with it mirrored by the critics when it was released in November. Scabies had left, but the gigs continued. When the album hit the shops, The Damned were on tour with The Dead Boys, and Jon Moss, who would go on to join Culture Club, was behind The Damned's kit. A second single, "Don't Cry Wolf" was pressed up on pink vinyl, with the old black and white Stiff label, and in the now familiar phone directory bag. But The Damned would no longer be needing Stiff's number.

Just as relations between band members had deteriorated, there was little love lost between the group and Stiff. They'd always had a great rapport with Riviera and the bombshell that he was leaving and they were being handed over to Robinson had been a blow. Their dwindling record sales, coupled with the fact they were frequently a nightmare to deal with, hardly gave Robinson cause for celebration either.

By the end of 1977, The Damned were seen as punk's also-rans. The Clash's debut album had reached No. 12 and they'd scored a No. 28 hit with "Complete Control". The Stranglers had enjoyed Top 10 smashes with "Peaches" and "Something Better Change", while *The Stranglers IV: Rattus Norvegicus* had got to No.4 in the album chart. As for the Sex Pistols, their debut album *Never Mind The Bollocks* had entered the chart at No. 1 and singles "God Save The Queen", "Pretty Vacant" and "Holidays In The Sun" had made the Top Ten. In terms of commercial success, Riviera had been given a pasting by his nemesis Malcolm McLaren.

There was also the little matter of money. The Damned's initial records had sold well, but they insisted they'd barely seen a penny. Robinson countered that the money from the 45,000 copies of their debut album had simply been used to pay the bills for the trail of destruction the group had left at hotels and venues. With sales of *Music For Pleasure* drying up at about 20,000 copies and neither of the singles charting, the bottom line didn't make happy reading. Five days before Christmas, The Damned left Stiff.

"It was mutually agreed," says James. "We put out *Music For Pleasure* and we had no real manager then because Jake was our manager, not Dave Robinson. It was like, 'It's run its course now'. I don't even know if we sat down with Robbo and said, 'Look, let's leave it now'. That was the end of that year – that was it. So, I got in touch with a friend of mine, a guy called Alan Edwards, who was a press guy in them days, and asked him if he wanted to manage The Damned, and he said he'd give it a shot. I just got more disillusioned. Rat had left, we'd started up The Damned together, so I split the band up, and then those guys got back together at a later date."

He adds: "I think they [Stiff] used us. We gave the label profile and brought some money into the label, and at the final reckoning they figured 'Next. Out'. Basically, that was it, pretty much. I know that to this day that Captain – I don't know if he could even look Robinson in the eye – finds it hard to talk to Jake."

Scabies observes: "By this time Paul Conroy had come into the frame as well and he was starting to build Stiff with people around him that had other talents. And I think they just knew the album wasn't going to appeal to them, fans particularly, and it wasn't going to break through into the mainstream. And why spend all their time and resources doing that when actually they were then, at that point, being inundated with young hopefuls and demo tapes? So I can understand it on a business level."

The Damned would resurface to enjoy mainstream success, but the question was, could Stiff do the same?

Financially, Stiff was under pressure at the beginning of 1978. It had expanded its premises, having added 28 Alexander Street to its existing base camp. Both the art department and the press office had moved into the newly rented space, while Robinson, Conroy and Cowderoy continued to operate from No. 32.

Stiffs Greatest Stiffs was reputed to have lost £11,000, recouped only by sales of *My Aim Is True* and *New Boots And Panties!!*, and the only singles chart entry it had to show for its extravagant outing was from an artist who had just left. Added to that, some creditors, spooked by Riviera's shock departure with Costello and Lowe, were banging on the door and demanding their money. "Stiff: Where There's Life Before Death" joked one of its plethora of slogans. Such dark humour was beginning to sound like a prophecy.

Dave Robinson, commenting later on the aftermath from Riviera's exit, said: "People who could have been unpleasant, like Chris Blackwell of Island, gave us a hand and ran with us, and while an awful lot of creditors wanted their money immediately – we managed to talk them out of it – a lot of others waited, and that's what kept us going." [38]

Stiff had proved a curiosity rather than any real threat to the major labels. But record companies being what they were, their deepest fear was that their competitors would get in on a new phenomenon first, and the rise of new wave had got the shrewder operators reaching for their surfboards. Radar was effectively set up as the new wave arm of Warner and the fact it enjoyed such major clout in the UK was one of the main attractions for Riviera. From Radar's perspective, Riviera had a lot going for him too. When Andrew Lauder took him out for a Greek lunch and let him in on his new label, Radar had no artists. So when Riviera asked if he was interested in signing Elvis Costello and Nick Lowe, it was a "no brainer".

By his own admission, Nick Lowe's debut album for his new record company was a collection of bits and pieces he had lying around, as opposed to any planned project. But Radar ADA1, his first single from it and the label's maiden release hit the jackpot. "I Love The Sound Of Breaking Glass" smashed its way into the charts on 11 March 1978 and reached No. 7. More gallingly still for those watching from Alexander Street, one week later Elvis Costello arrived in the singles chart with his first Radar release "(I Don't Want To Go To) Chelsea". It got to No.16.

With The Damned no longer around and the label's coffers practically empty, Stiff prepared to launch Operation Dury – starting in the US. *My Aim Is True* had been released and distributed in America by CBS and a similar licensing arrangement was going to be needed for *New Boots And Panties!!*. So, when Ian Dury & The Blockheads were invited on a coast-to-coast tour of the States supporting former Velvet Underground star Lou Reed in the spring of 1978, it presented the ideal opportunity to nail a deal. And they got one, from Arista.

"In America, big deals come out of the barrel of a smoking gun," said Andrew King. "It is no good having records, you have to have great records and a gun. Deals get done out of fear. People like Arista don't do deals because they think your stuff is wonderful; they do deals because they are frightened that someone else is going to do the deal. It is all done through terror." [6]

Clive Davis, then president of Arista, clearly didn't like Ian Dury & The Blockheads. But that was no matter. They were sizzling hot in Britain, where *New Boots And Panties!!* was selling by the truck load, and Arista agreed to give it an American release. When the Lou Reed tour pulled into New York to play The Bottom Line, Kosmo Vinyl pulled out all the stops to try and get Davis to come along. He was even more reluctant than he might have been, as he had already planned to go to the Lincoln Center to see the Metropolitan Opera or some other high-brow show. Begrudgingly, however, he agreed to see Arista's new acquisition perform, with catastrophic consequences.

Chaz Jankel, who had only joined the band for this date, relates what happened: "Clive Davis was told not to come back stage until at least ten or fifteen minutes after the band had come off stage because after gigs they needed time to change and they were all a bit wound up. But he didn't take that into consideration, he just bowled back into the dressing room where we were just taking our shirts off.

Kosmo quite impetuously grabbed the back of Clive Davis's shirt and started yanking it to one side and Davis goes, 'Ere, lad I told you, it's a Brooks Brothers'.

"And this was the worst thing that could happen to Clive Davis because he hated anybody manhandling him. He stormed out of the room and he was really angry and the net result was the next day he called Dave Robinson and said, 'All business deals are off between you and me. I was insulted and manhandled last night and I can't believe what's just happened. You'll never work in this country again'. And that was it."

Relations between Lou Reed and Ian Dury's camps were precarious over the six weeks of the tour, which took place in March and April 1978. Surly and aloof, Reed never came to the sound checks and "spent the whole time in his hotel room watching old videos of himself", according to Andrew King. He was also resentful of the publicity this jumped-up British pub rocker was attracting on what was his tour.

The feeling was mutual though. "Arista thought we'd get an open-minded audience supporting this famous American lounge lizard Lou Reed," commented Dury. "But he had a pot belly and trainers and was about as subversive as a packet of crisps." [32]

The tour included a week of shows at a club in San Francisco and among the celebrities who came along were Rod Stewart and Ronnie Wood. Backstage, they got chatting to the Blockheads and their crew and, unimpressed with the way the band were getting treated by Reed, sprang a surprise on their preening rock star host.

Fred Rowe recalls: "He [Rod Stewart] came in and I said, 'They're a bunch of cunts, they think they're the bollocks and because we get a good reception, the band's getting the hump'. He said, 'We'll sort them out then. Come in here Fred and watch the door'. He twisted all the knobs they tuned the guitars with and that was great because when they went on, it was an awful fucking sound. He [Lou] said, 'Just a minute. The room is too hot' or 'the room is too cold' – all this bollocsing about. But Rod had done it and he [Reed] was fucking livid."

One of those who got the chance to meet Dury on his first American trip was Liam Sternberg. A musician and songwriter from Ohio, who would later write his name into Stiff history, he encountered him when the tour rolled into Cleveland – an occasion he would never forget. "It was my chance to meet someone from Stiff, so I thought,

'Great'," remembers Sternberg. "So I met Ian Dury and Kosmo Vinyl. I didn't meet the band; I met them later. Ian [Horne] the sound man was trying to chat up two girls from Akron and he was plying them with drink, only they went off to the ladies room and never came back and he was stuck with the bill. And the bar bill was $100. The waitress presented him with this bar bill and he said, 'Wait, now I'm not paying that. These girls were drinking it all. They owe the money.' She was almost crying and she said, 'Look, if you don't pay the bill, I'm going to get stuck with it.'

"Kosmo said, 'What's the trouble here? I'll pay the bill. I've got tons of money. I'm a rich rock star'. And Ian [Dury] goes, 'Money doesn't mean anything to me. I'll pay the bill'. Kosmo says, 'No, I'm paying the bill' and brings out a $100 bill. Ian says, 'No, I'm paying the bill mate,' and he brings out a $100 bill. Kosmo says, 'This money means nothing, I'm paying it', and he took a lighter and he burned this $100. The waitress's eyes are getting as big as saucers, and Ian went, 'Money means nothing to me' and takes the money and eats it. He ate a $100 bill! So eventually they paid the waitress and everything was cool."

Audience reactions in America varied greatly. Some were blown away by Dury and The Blockheads, finding them more entertaining than the headlining act. Others, in more conservative parts, found his swearing, bawdy tales of dubious characters and apparent endorsement of "Sex & Drugs & Rock 'n' Roll" hard to stomach. US Irish Republicans meanwhile found the Union Jack he'd had embossed on his front teeth before he left, plain offensive. *New Boots And Panties!!* failed to make the impression it did in Britain and Arista was quick to drop him.

Back home, however, things were about to take off for Dury and for Stiff. "What A Waste", a song that had not featured on the album, had been released as a single and entered the chart on 6 May 1978 at No. 37. In a double-whammy for Dave Robinson, Graham Parker was also among the new entries with "Hey Lord, Don't Ask Me Questions".

An unshaven Ian Dury, with his hair cropped closer than ever and wearing eye-shadow, made his first appearance on *Top Of The Pops* the following week with his record at No. 35. "It's going to go a lot, lot higher, I can promise," presenter Dave Lee Travis forecast. He was right. Three weeks later, Stiff BUY 27 was No. 9. The importance of Ian Dury's success with *New Boots And Panties!!* and "What A Waste" cannot be emphasised enough. Had he faded into obscurity, Stiff could have gone the same way, and few would have backed Wreckless Eric to be its saviour.

Nigel Dick, a press officer at Stiff at the time, says: "I arrived pretty much the week that Elvis and Nick formally announced that they were leaving the company, which was quite a bombshell for everybody. It was like, 'How are we going to survive? It's all going to come to nothing.' Then luckily *New Boots And Panties!!* took off, and that basically provided the money on which the company survived for the next 18 months."

7

Be Stiff

In late January 1978, Stiff literally flew into a blizzard; the Great Blizzard, as it's vividly remembered in Ohio. Heavy snow and near-hurricane strength winds combined to wreak havoc on transport, schools and businesses, bringing them to a standstill for days on end. Akron, OH, is the capital of America's tyre industry, but there was no need for tyres that week. The roads were empty, silent. Giant snowdrifts buried cars, and even houses, in the historic snowstorm.

Any record company, English or otherwise, venturing into North East Ohio in such treacherous conditions would need one heck of a reason for doing so. And Stiff did – Devo. The oddball's oddball group, they had a nervy, spasming sound which dispensed with traditional rhythms and chord progressions. The result was an almost alien kind of music that sounded as if it had emerged from a laboratory rather than a studio.

Devo took their intriguing name from "de-evolution", a tongue-in-cheek theory that, despite technological and other advances, man was regressing and displaying a herd mentality. The breeding ground for this was the campus at Kent State University in Ohio, particularly its Commuter's Cafeteria, and the basements of nearby Akron. Gerald Casale and Bob Lewis were among the intellectual students who embraced it. They read strange literature on the subject; a 1948 Wonder Woman comic book featuring a De-evolution machine and a little known religious tract called *Jocko-Homo Heavenbound*. But reading about it and discussing it wasn't enough for these reverse Charles Darwins.

Lewis says: "Once we came up with the joking theory of de-evolution – it was a joke at the time, subsequent events have proved it was not such a joke after all – we applied it to various arts; not just music, but poetry and literature. I did some Devo journalism that was trying to have the same playful, mocking spirit and to try, in a kind of reverse psychology, to elevate the human and warn people about the perils of technology. Without being Luddites, you can still be aware of the danger. Once we had that, applying that to music was not that difficult, especially because at the time we were doing it – and this was closer to the early seventies – there were bands like Yes and Emerson, Lake and Palmer, where every song had to have a fifteen minute jam and it was kind of dinosaur rock. So, we said, 'Well let's try to make things almost childishly simple in how we arrange the music and how we craft the song.'"

A humorous idea may have given Devo its name, but it was something entirely serious that gave birth to the band. An event that not only changed the lives of these young men in Ohio, but also shook the world. On 4 May 1970, a group of students were holding a protest about the Vietnam War on the campus hillside at Kent State University when the Ohio National Guard opened fire. Amid the mayhem four students were killed. Two of them were friends of Jerry Casale and he watched them die and it changed his life. "I was a white hippie boy and when I saw exit wounds from M1 rifles out of the backs of two people I knew," he said. "That day was Devo. It might have been the most Devo day in my life." [36]

Lewis observes: "If it hadn't been for the shootings, I don't know if the band would ever have happened. Jerry was on his way to a masters in fine arts and I think he would most likely have gone into graphic arts, and I was going to go be an anthropologist and dig up stuff."

Jerry Casale and Lewis were in the initial band that formed in 1973, along with Mark Mothersbaugh, Jerry's brother Bob – by then a radiologist – and some other friends. The membership fluctuated until eventually settling on what would become the classic line-up of Bob and Jerry Casale, Mark and Bob Mothersbaugh, and Alan Myers. Devo first came to prominence through a short promotional film called "In The Beginning Was The End: The Truth About De-evolution". Made in May 1976, it was directed by music video pioneer Chuck Statler, who had met Mark and Jerry Casale at Kent State, and won a prize at the Ann Arbor Film Festival the following year. It was subsequently screened to audiences routinely before Devo shows.

The film also introduced the fictional figure Booji Boy (pronounced Boogie Boy) who would take centre stage in Devo's visuals throughout their career. Speaking with a childlike high-pitched voice and wearing an orange nuclear protection suit and a baby mask, he is seen running up a fire escape and delivering secret papers to a man with military stripes at the beginning of the track "Jocko Homo". "In the past, this information has been suppressed," says the military leader, sitting at the end of a long table. "But now it can be told, every man, woman and mutant on this planet shall know the truth about De-evolution," he says. "Oh Dad, we're all Devo," squeaks Booji Boy. Watch this film now and it stands as a reminder that the conceptual Ohio group were years ahead of their time: such story-telling visuals didn't become the norm in the industry until the dawn of the eighties.

Devo released "Mongoloid"/"Jocko Homo" as a single on their Booji Boy label in 1977. "Are we not men?" came the question. "We are Devo" came the automaton-like reply. When it was picked up by Los Angeles independent Bomp Records, word of this quirky quintet got out. The race to sign them was on.

Devo knew little of Stiff, but it knew of them. The record was being sold through independent shops in France, the Netherlands, Germany, Denmark, London and elsewhere. Bob Lewis had been hitting the phones to record companies in an attempt to get the group a deal. The long-distance call to Ohio from Stiff came from Paul Conroy.

"I think they'd heard the single," says Lewis. "This was before we had recorded in Europe, and I think they were interested in trying to get an act in New York. We only played CBGBs once, but we went back and played Max's Kansas City two or three times, so it's possible somebody saw us there."

Stiff wasn't the only label that wanted to sign them. Island and Warner Bros. were on the case and had made serious offers, reportedly running into six figures. But the deadpan Midwesterners weren't phased by the attention. They waited patiently, weighed things up and read books like Clive Davis' *Inside The Record Business* to avoid being screwed over.

The group played three nights at Max's Kansas City in December 1977, sharing the bill with Suicide and fellow Ohio-ites, The Cramps. As they packed up their van ahead of the drive to New York, they packed up 5,000 copies of "Jocko Homo" which they had arranged to deliver to Stiff's office. Devo had now outgrown its Booji Boy label and Stiff had agreed to take on distribution of the record in the UK.

Lewis recalls how: "Mark [Mothersbaugh] and I went to a little office they had in New York City and we met with Dave Robinson, dropped the records off, and spent the afternoon talking to him. I don't know if we sketched out exactly what the parameters of our relationship were going to be, but we knew that we didn't want to sign with them exclusively, because we had bigger fish on the line. But we didn't know how long that process would be, so I think we sold them 5,000 copies of 'Jocko Homo' and then we also made the deal for 'Be Stiff' and 'Satisfaction'. We've got cashflow out of it now and the warning shot to whomever was interested was that if you're interested, you'd better speak up because we're not going to just sit by the phone waiting for the call for the date. We're out to do other things too".

Dave Robinson flew out to snowbound Ohio to hold meetings with Devo a month later. So too did Island's suave supremo Chris Blackwell, although he was ill-prepared for the sub-zero conditions. He'd flown in from the Bahamas wearing beach clothes and sat shivering in the back seat of the car as he was driven away from the airport. Once in Akron, he was accompanied to a department store to kit him out in some winter clothes. Then it was on to the apartment rented by Bob Mothersbaugh and his girlfriend Susan for the serious discussions around a deal.

Jerry Casale and Mothersbaugh liked Blackwell and the Island deal was a generous one. But it was a British-based company which meant reduced foreign royalty rates on sales in America – the place they were likely to sell the vast majority of their records. The band were playing with a strong hand. Brian Eno and David Bowie had both championed them and, as they had no way of financing an album, Eno had offered to step in and make the record with them in Germany. Better still, Bowie would produce it. Aware of the intense competition and eager to impress, Chris Blackwell spent time with Devo and hung out with other acts from Akron's flourishing underground scene. He then returned to the Caribbean, leaving the band to mull things over.

Warner's deal looked even better on paper. But there was a *caveat*. Bowie's own company, which he had named The Bewlay Brothers, after a track from *Hunky Dory*, would receive some of the money via a production deal. And if Devo agreed to Warner's terms, Bowie's lawyer Stan Diamond would represent them free of charge. In the event, Bowie didn't produce the album, but this apparent conflict of interest was just one of their reservations about the deal. Devo were determined not to repeat the mistake made by groups down the years and get tied up in a deal they would later regret.

Another label then entered the fray. Richard Branson, president of Virgin, was in Jamaica and wanted to fly them out there to talk over a deal. Mark Mothersbaugh and Bob Casale packed their summer clothes and headed to the Caribbean ... and a different world. Ushered into a large hotel room, they were greeted by the multi-millionaire, his aides, and a huge pile of marijuana on a table. A joint was passed around and Casale and Mothersbaugh took their turns. As they chatted to their hosts and the effects of the high grade hash started to kick in, Richard Branson dropped a bombshell. Johnny Rotten wanted to join Devo and he was in the next room. If Devo were up for it, they could go straight out on the beach and announce it to the British music press, who were there waiting. Stunned and stoned, they politely declined and returned to their hotel room convinced they had burned any bridges with Virgin.

Stiff meanwhile got on with the business of distributing the group's single. "Jocko Homo"/"Mongoloid" was released on 28 February 1978 on Booji Boy, with the label stating it was "Shipped by Stiff Records". Shrink-wrapped, it came in an imaginative gatefold sleeve with the lyrics printed inside. The 5,000 imported from the US were distributed and then further pressings were done in the UK.

Devo didn't trouble the Top 40 with their first sortie into the British market, but "Jocko Homo" did get to No. 62. One of the most distinctive records ever released by Stiff, indeed by any label, it sold around 18,000 copies in all, including Europe and Japan, a handsome return given its modest production back in Ohio. Lewis used the phone at his parents' home to arrange distribution with foreign independent record companies at all times of the day and night.

Stiff was keen for Devo to support the record by doing some shows in the UK and, with temporary visas arranged and an album recorded, they landed in London on 6 March. Johnny Rotten may not have been out front to face the volley of spittle and violent scenes as Richard Branson had wanted, but they blew the place away. They did the same over the next few shows and, by the time they got back to Akron, the Virgin boss wanted them more badly than ever. Upping his offer, he dangled the extra carrot of a film production package as part of the deal. Branson also agreed to split the world's territories into two separate contracts – just as Devo had demanded. They'd done their research and wanted to spread their risk. They signed with Virgin.

Warner declared war. After all, hadn't the album been made with the whole idea that it would be released on Warner? Hadn't they given the band spending money in Germany? The two companies slugged it out in court and ended up in a huddle outside. A compromise was reached. Richard Branson agreed to tear up his contract and sign the group for Europe, allowing Warner to sign them for the US and the rest of the world's territories. Devo had ended up being represented by two record labels with massive clout.

But Bob Lewis says the relationship with Warner was never the same: "When we went to Germany, we went under the auspices of Bowie's production company," he says. "Bowie had a deal with Warner, so the idea was we would be on Warner, through Bewlay Brothers, when that album came out. Plus, he had also said he would produce it. When it came time to produce it he was busy with his jet-set life and so poor old Brian Eno was sacrificed to the gods of the studio. He had to go spend eight weeks with the boys in some godforsaken part of Germany. In his book, I guess he talks about some of the frustrations he had. He was trying to bring some of his more new wave or enlightened methods of randomness into the process. But no, no, the boys were not having any of that because at that point, it was all about control, control, control.

"So Branson hypnotises them and then they do that and Warner Brothers says, 'No this is not going to happen'. From that point on when they went out to California, Warner had big acts like the freakin' Eagles and those were the people who were going to get the attention and the money and we were like a sideline for them. And once you've already cheated on your boyfriend, before you're even going steady, they were pissed, and I think it harmed things long term. Let's face it, the big record companies were not very artist friendly for the most, and that's why you needed to have a champion in the organisation to help take care of you."

Sadly, Stiff couldn't compete with such corporate might and *Are We Not Men? We Are Devo* was released on Virgin in the UK. But its distribution deal for the UK still stood and, for their second offering, Devo bowled another curved ball. They had taken The Rolling Stones "(I Can't Get No) Satisfaction" and, in an act many would see as sacrilege, deconstructed it to the point of it being almost unrecognisable. The legendary riff, one of the most famous in rock history, had been surgically removed and replaced by a discordant twanging; the Stones' steady rock beat transplanted for a disjointed, spluttering one. "That was really one of those serendipities where Mark Mothersbaugh had been in some cover bands that played a lot of Rolling Stones songs and he really liked Keith Richards' rhythm guitar playing," says Lewis. "So, he just started playing the riff and the one thing he could do was to take normal music and mutate it. So, we made it robotic rather than sensual, if that makes sense. I do agree that it's a cover that's up there."

The Stiff publicity machine went into overdrive. "Buy Now Before Deletion" advised a poster for BOY 1, which went on sale in a picture bag and in both 7 and 12-inch formats. Philippa Thomas and Terry Razor took to the streets of London in white boiler suits and sunglasses and mimicked the hand and arm signals the band were making in the photograph that had appeared on the front of *Melody Maker* on 25 February. One photograph from the Stiff stunt shows them posing outside Virgin Records & Tapes in Oxford Street, while another captured them swinging from a lamp post. Full-page ads were taken out in the music press.

The third single released as part of the Stiff deal appeared to have been penned specially for Devo's English pals. But "Be Stiff" was written by Jerry Casale and Bob Lewis in 1974. "It was a satire of fear-driven, uptight people in America ... nothing ever changes," said Jerry Casale.[37] Nevertheless, the song produced during the sessions in Germany with Brian Eno couldn't have been a more fitting anthem. The single, which spent just one week at No.71, was followed two months later by the "B Stiff" EP, which brought together all the tracks from the releases issued via Stiff: "Jocko Homo", "Mongoloid", "Satisfaction (I Can't Get Me No)", "Sloppy (I Saw My Baby Getting)", "Be Stiff" and "Social Fools". Devo's brief association with the label was at an end and it would play out the rest of its career on the majors. But their legacy to Stiff extended beyond three memorable 45s.

When Dave Robinson flew into that Ohio whiteout, it wasn't just to woo Devo. Stiff had discovered, through its initial dialogue with the group, that beneath Akron's rubber-coated surface was a diverse underground scene. Bob Lewis had told Paul Conroy about other musicians they knew like Chris Butler, who had lived down the hall from himself and Jerry Casale in an apartment building when they were first starting Devo. Liam Sternberg, a songwriter and key figure on the local scene, was another name that was dropped. Stiff arrived in town hoping to find a mini-Motown buried beneath the snow.

"Because we had pretty much decided that while we wanted to have a limited relationship with Stiff," says Lewis, "they weren't where we were ultimately going to be and for that reason we felt we could share the wealth a little bit with the other local bands."

As a musician, songwriter and talent scout, Sternberg was plugged right into the Akron scene. Under the exotic stage name of Pietro Nardini, he played guitar for local group, Jane Aire & The Belvederes. It was Sternberg who was credited with discovering singer Jane Ashley, who had been performing with disco groups and wanted a separate identity for her new wave activities.

Ashley says: "I was really good friends with Liam Sternberg, first off, and I was also really good friends with some people from Devo and Tin Huey and various other groups that didn't break out on the European market, but did Stateside, like Chris Butler from The Waitresses. So, people were really just doing their thing and I was just learning my craft, and I was on the road with a nine piece disco band, touring all over the States. Then Liam would meet me on the road or back in Akron to do various recordings, the early recordings for Stiff. And because that was a disco thing, that's why I changed my name from Jane Ashley to Jane Aire, so there'd be two separate entities. Liam thought of the name of The Belvederes to go with that."

Punk had been taken up in Akron, but the British new wave ethic had struck a deeper chord, says Sternberg: "What had a big influence was Blondie in a way because that came out independently in a sense, and then a lot of other stuff coming out of New York and out of CBGBs. Everybody was realising they could make their own records because the record industry was stuck tight with huge deals and huge stars, where you could put your cocaine bill on a studio tab. It was crazy and you couldn't get into it. People just wanted to make records. It's really fun to make records, even if you can press 1,000 of them at least you've got 'em. If you can't sell them then maybe you can give them to your friends, it's something to do. That was the spirit of Akron: make underground records, press them yourself. And Stiff was definitely that kind of label."

Groups like The Waitresses, Tin Huey, The Bizarros and Chi Pig had given Akron a reputation for having a fertile underground scene. Yet, in contrast with The Ramones or Television, news of the intriguing sounds emanating from basements, garages and bars from this Midwest city's clutch of acts hadn't reached Europe. Stiff – with Sternberg's encouragement – was going to change all that.

"Paul [Conroy] had a great idea to market Akron and do an Akron compilation. So, they called me again and Dave said, 'Well look, we're going to come in. Can you arrange for us to meet Devo?' I said, 'Yes, that's no problem'. So, I picked them up. There was a raging snow storm and I almost killed them both in the car. They got here and I set up a meeting with Devo and then they had several meetings with Devo, and Dave said to me in the hotel, 'Look here's (I don't remember exactly what he gave me) $800. Make an Akron album. Get all these groups together. Find them and make an album.'

"So, I had to learn about publishing contracts, record contracts, the crash course in the music business, and we got that together. It was wonderful. Even now I can't imagine it, I suppose some things still work on cash, but it was really cash and 'do it on your honour'. 'Maybe this guy's going to run off with the cash'. We don't care."

The Akron Compilation, the record that resulted from this casual hotel cash handover, was bizarre even by Stiff standards. It was also one of the most imaginative and fun records conceived by the label. Chris Morton played up its reputation as the rubber city and made a virtue out of the fact it was a weird, humdrum place. A bleak, snow covered parking lot, the same one seen at the start of Devo's "Jocko Homo" video, was chosen for the mock Akron postcard on the sleeve. Covering the wall behind the vehicles was a giant mural bearing the slogan "Shine On America" and Lady Liberty shining a great light. The painting covered the entire brick side of the Great Falls Employment Agency, owned by Mark Mothersbaugh's father. Students at the local high school had been responsible for the project as part of the US bicentenary in 1976. But by the time the photograph appeared on the sleeve of a record supposedly showcasing the best of Akron, some of its lower sections were missing, exposing the grimy wall beneath.

"The place is basically strange," says Sternberg. "It's so boring and they [Stiff] never made it out to be anything other than a boring lousy place. This was the key to a lot of their marketing at the time, their way of presenting things. It was very anti what the late hippie movement was doing. The very end of the hippie movement coincided with the beginnings of punk."

Above the photo, Morton added a rubber tyre with Akron spelled out in its tread. Better still, it gave off a smell of burning rubber if you scratched it. On the back cover, the names of the ten featured acts were worked into a diagram showing the steps in the manufacturing process for rubber. A barrage balloon on the front of the sleeve read Stiff Records Presents and the rear displayed the album's prefix GET 3. For the inner sleeve, there was an aerial shot of Akron on one side and one of a guy hard at work at one of its famous tyre plants, with inset pictures of the acts on the other. Side A was entitled "Tireside" with images of the city in the centre label. Side B was "Plateside" and consisted of sketches of places and events associated with Akron: Goodyear Air Dock; Soap Box Derby; The American Golf Classic.

Morton's design was so inventive, *NME* gave it a "highly recommended" award that year and he still remembers the project with fondness. "I've got a couple of copies and they still smell a bit – it's brilliant," says Morton. "We had a lot of bother getting it done as well; there were about four or five attempts to get a smell and the first smells were just disgusting and not at all like rubber, so it was quite fun. But I'm very proud of that cover. The whole thing was a fake. It was like a sub-plot version of Phil Spector. It was Liam Sternberg – he had a hand in everything. There were real people, there, but he was the mastermind behind it all." Many real acts from Akron did feature, of course.

While there may have been much excitement at Stiff when *The Akron Compilation* rolled out at the end of June 1978, it ground to a halt commercially. Some saw it as a victory of design over content; some simply didn't know what to make of it. Dave Robinson was disappointed at its poor sales and called a meeting in the office. He demanded to know why it wasn't selling better and, after an awkward silence, Nigel Dick put up his hand. "Right, why isn't it selling?" demanded Dave. Looking nervously around, Nigel replied, "Because it's crap". "That's irrelevant!" Robinson fired back.

Jane Aire & The Belvederes had been the first of the up-and-coming acts from the Akron compilation to be picked out by Stiff for an individual release. "Yankee Wheels", written and produced by Liam Sternberg, was issued on 14 April. "Aire Today Gone Tomorrow," Porky Peckham scratched into the run-out grooves of the B-side, a prophecy that was fulfilled when the single flopped and she signed to Virgin. The vocalist would return to Stiff, but in the meantime, the label would focus its attention on other new artists it had welcomed on board.

Rachel Sweet had just turned 16, went to Firestone Senior High School in Akron and, in her sneakers and blue denims, looked for all the world like an all-American teenager. Except she wasn't. Not by a long chalk. Sweet seemed an incongruous addition to a small independent label in England synonymous with gnarled old pub rockers and end-of-the-pier humour. But then only Stiff would sign an unknown kid from Ohio with a penchant for country and a distaste of punk in 1978.

Sweet had been a precocious child. She had performed in public for the first time at the age of 5 after her journalist grandfather persuaded her to enter the talent contest at the *Akron Beacon Journal's* annual picnic. Winning gave her a taste for performance and soon the Sweet's youngest daughter began doing amateur TV talent shows and summer theatre productions. Her parents took her to New York, signed her with a child manager and four agents and she successfully auditioned for TV commercials.

On a family vacation to Florida she walked into a club and insisted she be given an audition. Impressed, she was allowed to sing that night alongside the rather more experienced Frankie Valli and was even paid. Her powerful young voice came to the attention of another celebrity – actor Mickey Rooney – after her father passed some of her recordings to a studio. He enthusiastically invited her to join him on a ten week tour of supper clubs, travelling across America by bus. Although he wasn't quite so bowled over by his 10-year-old warm-up act when he took to the stage to find the audience chanting her name. "Can't. She's in bed," said the Hollywood star. Sweet, in fact, was standing in the wings watching.

Bill Cosby was the next superstar to endorse her prodigious talents: they performed two shows a night every night for three weeks in the Reno/Tahoe area, accompanied by a full orchestra. The girl from the home of Firestone Tyres could certainly withstand the rigours of the road.

At 11, she took a detour into country music and recorded "Faded Rose" for Premiere Records. "I got interested in a field that would accept me," she said. "Tanya Tucker was doing it. I didn't see any rock 'n' roll acts that were 12 or 13." [33] In Nashville, she did some demos and got on Derrick Records, a label based in Texas. And she looked like she was on her way when her first single; a cover of Fred Rose's "We Live In Two Different Worlds", reached No. 94 on the US Country

Charts. The next ones didn't and major labels told her to try them again when she was 18.

Back in Akron, she refocused her attentions on her studies, setting her sights on becoming a lawyer. She also began spending time in Liam Sternberg's basement. Writing songs which he wanted to send over to Stiff in England, he asked her to provide vocals for the demos. She thought little more about it until "Tourist Boys" and "Truckstop Queen", two of the tracks on his basement tape, wound up on *The Akron Compilation*. "The next thing I knew, I was getting reviews for an album I didn't even know I was on," she said. [33]

Sensing a star in the making, Dave Robinson flew over to see her at a country event and signed her to a two-year contract. Then tragedy struck. Her mother Judy, who had encouraged her to take up the piano as a child and played her all her Elvis Presley records, died of cancer. The recording of the album had to be delayed while the family mourned her. Sweet was still not 16. In the meantime, experienced players from the Stiff scene began working on rhythm tracks ahead of her arrival in London. Sweet and her older sister Lia boarded a flight for London four weeks later. In spite of what she'd been through and arriving in a country she didn't know, she belted out the songs like a seasoned pro.

Liam Sternberg praises Sweet: "She was a really courageous girl because her mum had died and she came about four weeks afterwards to record and came with her sister. We stuck her in a studio with The Blockheads. That was great because those guys can really play. Charley Charles and Norman Watt-Roy. Man, what a pumping bass! And Davey Payne on sax, I mean, forget about it. Then the Graham Parker horn section were on some of the tracks. I didn't realise how good it was. I don't know what I was thinking. I knew it was musically good, but I didn't really know how good it was. Try to find that now – you can't. She sang four lead vocals in about an hour. She started at about three in the morning because the band took a long time to set up and everything and had to do the tracks. It was really late in the studio, but she knocked them off really good."

Sternberg's songbook was to provide the material for the record and, despite being twice her age, his lyrics tapped into the teen chatter you'd expect from a girl still at high school. But although she did justice to his compositions, Stiff didn't hear a hit. The problem was that four weeks of studio time had already been spent. "This was the Wednesday and we had to have the test pressings the following Monday," said a spokesperson. "We booked the Island studios for Thursday afternoon and spent Wednesday looking for songs. Thursday morning we told Liam and Rachel they were in the studio that evening." [34]

With time ticking away, other faces from the Stiff scene came in to accompany her on these last-minute tracks: Andrew Bodnar, Brinsley Schwarz, The Rumour's horn section, and a session drummer.

As Stiff would do so many times, it reached into the past to find future hits. A reconnaissance mission around secondhand record shops in London threw up two tried-and-tested 45s: Dusty Springfield's "Stay A While" (the follow-up to "I Only Want To Be With You") and Carla Thomas's 1966 reading of Isaac Hayes' Stax track "B-A-B-Y". The latter was also chosen as the first single to be taken from her debut album *Fool Around.* "Stranger In The House" had been written by Elvis Costello and recorded by George Jones, and proved a perfect choice for a singer right at home with country. "Pin A Medal On Mary" meanwhile was penned by Will Birch and John Wicks from The Records.

"They routined the songs, went in, recorded them, had them mixed and finished in about five hours," said a Stiff spokesperson. "They're the standout tracks on the album. It's the old story ...". [34]

A piercing shriek was let out to eerie effect in "Cuckoo Clock", the closest thing to new wave found within the grooves of *Fool Around.* The voice, the kind that makes you fear for your windows, belonged to a singer from the Alexander Street scene brought in for just that one number. But she was no bit-part player at Stiff. In fact, she'd had her own debut released before Sweet's plane had landed.

Lene Lovich had also been born in the US, although that was where the similarities with Rachel Sweet ended. From her upbringing and family life to her style of singing and stage persona, they couldn't have been more different. She was born Lili-Marlene Premilovich on 30 March 1949, and grew up with her brother and two sisters in a poor, black neighbourhood in downtown Detroit, Michigan, amid violence and unrest. At home, her Serbian father's mental health problems made for a tense atmosphere and the children came to bond even more closely with their English mother (her maiden name was Norfolk, by coincidence the English county in which Lene has lived for many years).

Lovich says of her childhood: "I don't really like to say this because it sounds a little sad, but I was always the odd one out as one of very few white kids in a black neighbourhood, which for a start was a bit weird. Now that's not a racist thing, not at all. In fact, I thought I was black until I was about 8 and I always knew there was something different about me."

But as neighbours rowed furiously with each other and anger simmered in this post-war tinderbox, another sound could be heard. Music. The shy, self-conscious youngster had found something she could immerse herself in and another survival tool. Listening to Stevie Wonder on the radio and trying to mimic the dance steps of The Temptations and The Drifters out in the streets, this was a world she could disappear into. She also began making up her own comic songs to entertain or annoy her brother and sisters. "I didn't have any idea that I would ever be involved in music but I was always very close to it," says Lovich. "I did used to make up songs as a child. I had to live very much in my imagination. I was never the popular one at school at all. It wasn't until I saw *The Addams Family* and I thought, 'Wednesday – that's me!' I just didn't fit in and it might sound a little sad, but you learn to keep your thoughts within you."

With her father's mental health making life hell for the family, her mother moved back to England with the children. They settled in her native Hull, a peaceful idyll compared to the riot-torn neighbourhoods of Detroit. Lene, like many other teenagers of her generation, felt the pull of art college. She made friends with people involved in fringe theatre and one of them taught her how to play saxophone. More significantly, she met guitarist and songwriter Les Chappell, who would become both her romantic and creative partner.

After art college, Lovich got a gig with a hotel band playing in Europe, and she and Chappell then threw in their lot with The Diversions. They scored a novelty hit with "Fattie Bum Bum" in September 1975, which was written by Carl Malcolm. He had a bigger hit with it the same year as he got to No.8 in the charts, with The Diversions only making it to No. 34. An album was also recorded for Polydor, but never released. For the same label, and under her own name, she also released a three-track single in 1976, "I Saw Mommy Kissing

Santa Claus"/ "The Christmas Song (Merry Christmas To You)"/ "Happy Christmas".

Lovich was convinced there was a band out there for her and wrote to Charlie Gillett. As part of his radio show, the disc jockey and author read out messages from musicians looking for groups or bands in search of new recruits. Gillett dutifully gave her a mention and nothing happened. But timing is everything and hers couldn't have been better.

Gillett and Gordon Nelki were setting up Oval Records. They knew various songwriters and musicians who were doing their own things, so they decided to pool their talents in one big collective. Lovich and Chappell got wind of this and offered their services and those of drummer Bobby Irwin from London band The Sinceros. "Can you sing?" the greenhorn label owners wanted to know. "Everybody hates my voice" she told them. They eventually talked her round and began trying to find songs her unusual voice would suit. One of them was "I Think We're Alone Now", written by Ritchie Cordell, and a major hit on the US Billboard for Tommy James & The Shondells in 1967. Lovich had never heard the record so couldn't be influenced by the original. The group rehearsed it, played it live and then recorded a demo and it was added to a tape of original songs by Bobby Henry.

Gillett recalled: "The whole idea was to form this collective called the Oval Exiles and to take them round to three or four record companies. Dave Robinson listened politely to all the stuff on the tape, but only when he heard that song did he light up and said, 'We want to put it out next month'. We said we didn't even have a B-side. He told us to get it done and we had to call Lene up and she wrote 'Lucky Number' overnight as the B-side." [5]

Not only did Stiff need to replenish its stock of artists following the departure of Riviera with Costello and Lowe, it had still to release a single record by a woman as 1978 arrived. Lovich's wasn't the first; that honour went to Jane Aire's "Yankee Wheels". But that summer "I Think We're Alone Now" was released. Stiff is believed to have pressed up around 5,000 copies of the single, which wasn't formally issued, but sold via mail order. From the record itself, with its 1960s production, to the monotone cover that emerged from the art department, it was clear she was a unique artist. Dressed in a French resistance-style coat and dark glasses, her arms were level with her shoulders, her hands holding out her long plaits. Over the large puddle in front of which she was standing, her name was spelled out on a line of barbed wire.

Robinson demanded an album and Lovich and Chappell were joined in the studio by Irwin and his Sinceros colleague Ron Francois on bass. Keyboards were supplied by Nick Plytas, who had been in Roogalator and the Tom Robinson Band, and Jeff Smith from The Diversions. At Charlie Gillett's suggestion, the record was entitled *Stateless*, after he heard her talking about her passport. This embellishment of her back story would only make her more mysterious and of interest to the music press. Stiff played it for all it was worth.

> *"For security reasons, Lene Lovich (not her real name), must remain in the shadows," read a brochure produced by Stiff for record dealers. "She is stateless, and her presence in this country is only possible through elaborate subterfuge courtesy of the Stiff Secret Service. Her new album may resolve some of the issues hanging over the head of this enigmatic figure. It is believed that the current interest in Lene from both the Latvian and Lithuanian Governments is not unconnected with some incredible tapes reclining in the Stiff vaults – the result of a clandestine trip behind the Iron Curtain. Lene sings and plays saxophone."*

Lovich throws light on this story: "Well it was partly true, because I didn't have a passport at the time and being from mixed parentage I wasn't sure what was going to happen to me, where I was going to live. They [Stiff] stretched the truth as they did very well and made a lot of it. But it was just a fun idea. It was actually Charlie Gillett's idea to call it *Stateless*. There were two album covers. There was one which looked like me running down an alleyway, almost looking like Edvard Munch's *Scream*. Then there was another one that was taken by Brian Griffin, which was a very posed portrait. I was totally pleased. I spent a lot of time talking to Chris Morton, although not giving him any ideas whatever, he had all the ideas to hand. I was just in awe of the whole art department and what they were doing and I really related to that, being from an art background."

It was in the summer of 1978, while Lovich was recording *Stateless*, that *Top Of The Pops* viewers got their first look at Siouxsie & The Banshees when they entered the chart with "Hong Kong Garden". Their debut single for Polydor got to No. 7. Never before had a female singer with such a formidable presence and outlandish look graced the show. Only Patti Smith and Debbie Harry had come close. New wave bands were increasingly infiltrating the UK singles chart: The Jam on Polydor; X-Ray Spex on EMI International; Buzzcocks on United Artists, Undertones on Sire; Boomtown Rats on Ensign. But by mid-1978, there was not one such outfit on Stiff who were more than ever, banking on highly individual and intriguing solo artists.

———

Jona Lewie had been around the block. He'd been a professional musician since 1970 and even had a hit record, making him the only artist to arrive at Stiff at this point having already appeared on *Top Of The Pops*. A pianist with a penchant for boogie and blues, he had a highly distinctive, laid-back vocal style and a line in smart suits. As eccentric as the day was long, he was made for Stiff.

Born John Lewis on 14 March 1947 in Southampton, he had grown up in South London listening to jazz and blues records and learned to play his grandmother's piano. By his late teens he was so accomplished he was invited to play as a session musician with big American touring acts like Arthur "Big Boy" Crudup and Juke Boy Bonner. When he travelled to the States as part of a placement for his sociology degree, he rang up Nick Perls at Yazoo Records and ended up on the album he was recording.

His first band proper was Brett Marvin & The Thunderbolts and although they didn't enjoy mainstream success, one of his songs "Sea Side Shuffle" was released under the name Terry Dactyl & The Dinosaurs, and scored a surprise hit. The accordion-led, jug band romp got to No. 2 in summer 1972. Two singles and an album followed before these dinosaurs became extinct. Continuing to record on his own for Sonnet Records under the name Jona Lewie, he then reappeared in The Jive Bombers who asked him to front the group, using his own songs.

Through his former college friend Thunder Thompson, Lewie met Martin Stone, which is how he ended up one day at Jake Riviera's Kensington flat. And it was when The Jive Bombers found themselves on the same bill as Graham Parker & The Rumour that he met Parker's avuncular manager. Recalling their first meeting, Lewie says: "He knew my name, I don't know how, and he said, 'Hey Jona, that song you did at the end – that's a hit!' The song in question was 'Hallelujah Europa'."

This introduction happened in 1976, but it was two years later that Lewie was invited into the Stiff fold. Just as with Costello and Lovich,

Charlie Gillett was the conduit. Lewie had released several singles on Sonnet Records, including "The Swan" and "Piggy Back Sue", and Gillett gave them an airing on his *Honky Tonk* show. Gillett also sat on the panel for *Time Out* magazine's alternative Top 10 and, as a result, they made the list.

Stiff wasn't so impressed. "I had already been to see them and handed in a demo," says Lewie, "which was politely rejected by Paul Conroy: 'Sorry, we are not interested in your music at this time. Please consider us again'". A typical standard rejection and he'll never live it down. "After Nick [Lowe] had to leave – it was too much for him – I got to know Jake quite well. I got to know later that in a parting shot to Dave, Jake had apparently said, 'Sign Jona'. So, they both knew about me and he was offering Dave, as a gesture, something that might be helpful in replenishing the loss created by the removal of two acts."

With recommendations from Gillett and a departing Riviera, and perhaps casting his mind back to "Hallelujah Europa", Robinson decided to see if Lewie could deliver another "Sea Side Shuffle" for Stiff. When Jona picked up the call from Alexander Street he was told it was very urgent and that Stiff needed him to come over as soon as he could. The label that had turned him down was now in hot pursuit, as Lewie explains: "So I went up and saw him and he was a bit pissed. These were heady times, Jake had just gone and taken two key acts. I was always beavering away and, as it happens, I had many quarter inch tapes with piano/vocal demos, millions of them – well 50! Anyway, a couple of months later, we went through all those and discussed which ones he wanted me to do as an album.

"I don't think we'd even signed anything yet. I didn't even sign a contract until I was half way through the first album: that's how 'Wild West' it was. I had a couple of massive rows with Dave before I signed anything. It was never easy. And even once I was signed, you were made to feel you were on unstable ground, that there was no future, no security. There were times when it looked like maybe they'd throw me out. People think success is easy, but it's so hard. I signed before the album was released, otherwise he [Dave] would never have released it."

Dave Robinson, recalling his visits to Alexander Street, said: "Jona Lewie used to have meetings with me and I couldn't get him out of the office. Lights would be out, people had gone home, I would put on my fucking pyjamas." [5]

A single came first and it was as quirky as expected. "The Baby She's On The Street" hit the street at the end of June 1978, the first in a long run of singles Lewie would record for the label. Backed by the marvellously titled "Denny Laine's Valet", it was produced by Lewie himself. Opening with a foot-stomping, boogie-woogie piano, the lyrics were almost impossible to hear because of his intentionally opaque delivery, and only the presence of a keyboard gave it a hint of modernity. But it was as catchy as hell and Robinson sensed a hit.

"Dave Robinson picked up on the indecipherability of the lyric and he liked the number because being a record company man, he was always looking for things that would hopefully be as successful as possible," says Lewie. "At the time, 'Wuthering Heights' by Kate Bush had come out, which also had a kind of indecipherability and he cited that track when he wanted to release 'The Baby She's On The Street' as a single. Where that comes from is me being completely influenced by country blues artists in America."

But Jona Lewie was to be denied a hit with his first record, making it three misses in a row for Stiff following the triumph of "What A Waste". The Box Tops' "Cry Like A Baby" had made no impact in the UK, although it fared much better in Europe. A throwaway single by Humphrey Ocean & The Hardy Annuals entitled "Whoops-A-Daisy" was, like Max Wall's, destined to gather dust in the Stiff stockroom. 500 copies of each were pressed up in red, blue, green, white and clear vinyl, making it one for Stiff's most avid collectors.

Robinson had filled the vacuum left by Costello and Lowe the previous year and with some pretty arresting artists at that. News of Stiff's death had been greatly exaggerated. It was time, Stiff figured, to push on with another major offensive; one that provided the opportunity to unveil another of its recent arrivals.

Mickey Jupp hailed from the Southend scene which had spawned Dr. Feelgood and the Kursaal Flyers and had been playing and singing in bands since finishing art college. Born in Worthing, Sussex, he fronted R&B group The Orioles in the mid-sixties. But he was best known for his band Legend, which recorded an album for Bell Records and then another two for Vertigo before splitting up.

Relocating to Southend-on-Sea, he found himself involved in the pub scene that was exploding in the Essex town, and his name had been one of those on Dave Robinson's mind when Stiff was launched. After all, Robinson greatly prized songwriters and Jupp had been responsible for several Dr. Feelgood songs, including "Cheque Book" from *Down By The Jetty*, and "Down At The Doctors", which skirted the singles chart in the autumn of 1978. For whatever reason, the veteran performer ended up behind Sean Tyla and Canvey Islander Lew Lewis and others from the pub rock scene, and didn't come aboard until two years later.

His debut album *Juppanese* was recorded at Pebble Beach Studios in Worthing. Procol Harum's Gary Brooker came in to produce and play and a tonne more experience was added with Chris Spedding on guitar, Bruce Lynch on bass, and Dave Mattacks on drums. But Stiff didn't much care for the first four tracks that emerged from the sessions: Nick Lowe would produce and Rockpile would back Jupp on the rest of the record.

Jupp says of the altercation: "I was happy with the way it was going with Gary. Stiff weren't. I should have put one or both of my feet down, but I didn't and so I had to tell Gary – who I considered to be a good friend – that he was off the case. Of course, shortly afterwards, we had to go back to him – cap in hand – and ask him to finish the tracks that he'd started."

What Jupp didn't know when he signed was that he was about to become involved in Stiff's biggest throw of the dice yet – the Be Stiff Route 78 tour. Just like the Greatest Stiffs expedition, five acts would be thrown together and cover the length and breadth of the land. Lovich, Lewie, Sweet and Jupp were all chosen for the line-up, with Wreckless Eric the only participant from the previous tour. This time, rather than travelling by bus, they would go by train!

Even by Stiff's standards, this was a audacious mission. The estimated cost of this extravagant outing was £100,000. A British Rail InterCity train was emblazoned with Be Stiff Tour 78 in giant lettering along its carriages, and venues and hotels were booked along the route. Pulling in at Bristol for the opening show at the university on 10 October, the Stiff train then stopped off at 33 venues from Wick Assembly Hall and Strathpeffer Spa Pavilion in Scotland to Sophia Gardens in Cardiff and the Bournemouth Village Bowl, taking in Dublin and Belfast *en route*. It would close at the Lyceum Ballroom in London. Then it was off to New York for four shows at The Bottom Line.

Paul Conroy says: "That tour happened because it was all part and parcel of Jake leaving and we'd got a little bit further down the line. I'd said to Dave about doing a train tour because I'd seen The Grateful Dead had toured America on a train and that seemed a cool thing to do."

Sponsorship money had been prised out of PolyGram, the Bron Agency, Ensign Records and the *NME* by Stiff to try and minimise costs. *Sounds* meanwhile invested £35,000 on a ten-week promotional campaign that included national press advertising, commercial radio spots, specialist press ads, flyposting and promotion at festivals and college campuses. In collaboration with Stiff, *Sounds* also produced a compilation called *Can't Start Dancing*, featuring tracks from all the acts from the tour, as well as Ian Dury and The Rumour, who were then signed to the label in their own right. Robinson had also vetoed a brand spanking new train offered by British Rail in favour of a rickety set of old carriages. Financially Robinson was effectively betting Stiff's entire future on five oddities who wouldn't have got past the reception desk at any other label.

"By this time next year we could be writing a Stiff obituary," he joked in an interview with the *Radio Times* ahead of an *Omnibus* TV programme dealing with the packaging, promotion and selling of records. But he was as phlegmatic as ever about his latest venture. "The record business is a big gamble all the time," he said. "I don't know how many mistakes a major company can afford to make, but we can afford very few."

For an office team already worked off their feet, the Be Stiff tour would stretch things to the limit. Not just financially, but practically. There was the huge logistical operation of getting a large crew of people on and off trains, and to and from venues and hotels, to a tight schedule. The personnel list on the official itinerary counted 23 artists and band members. The seventeen non-performers included tour manager John "Kellogs" Kalinowski, Kosmo Vinyl, who helped with music press and acted as MC, and Philippa Thomas and Terry Razor on the merchandise stall. Sweet was accompanied by her sister Lia and, to ensure she didn't fall behind in her academic studies back home, her tutor Cath Cinnamon.

Experienced session players played on *Fool Around*, but on the road Dave Robinson wanted a band behind the teenager which would look the part. The Records not only backed Sweet on stage, but also did their own set at the shows, giving the audience even more value for money. Reviewing one show, *NME* lauded their opening slot as "the finest of the evening".

"Funnily enough there wasn't the whole thing then of young people making session music as there is now," says Andy Murray, who had only joined Stiff in July 1978 after Paul Conroy called him. "Liam [Sternberg] had assembled a band of more or less those kind of guys who were very good musicians but were not young, and Dave rightly said, 'Look, let's not do that. The Records are not happening, they are not in the charts at the moment, they are available – let's just have them'. And it worked very well. There was Hugh Gower on lead guitar, Will Birch on drums, Phil Brown on bass, and John Wicks on rhythm guitar and lead vocals."

Andy Murray was tasked with coordinating the tour. Together with Conroy, he drew up a marketing plan that was more ambitious than anything Stiff had previously attempted. Stiff would release each of the albums recorded by the five acts on exactly the same day – 13 October. Not only that, but in a canny move guaranteed to get collectors of the label salivating, each would have a different colour vinyl, as well as the standard black. *The Wonderful World Of Wreckless Eric* came in green, *Fool Around* in white, *Stateless* in red, *Juppanese* in blue, in yellow Jona Lewie's offering was *On The Other Hand There's A Fist*. Finally, the albums were available in picture disc – a relatively new practice – for only £4.99. Such an ambitious undertaking would have presented a production challenge to any record company.

Stiff also pressed up 1,000 dealer albums with two songs by each artist. "You're extremely lucky to get this – you probably don't deserve it", read each side of the label. Record stores could take their pick from an array of window dressing: posters, mobiles, cut-outs, train sets, badges and bumper stickers. Browser cards were also made up so the respective records could be filed under Stiff and the records marked "File under Stiff" just to avoid any confusion. Dealers were also sent concert tickets. Full-page adverts appeared in *Sounds*, *Melody Maker*, *NME*, *Music Week*, *Record Business* and *Radio and Record News* and other specialist press.

A special Stiff Albums Sales Brochure was produced for dealers, including a potted history of each artist and a list of selling points. Anyone buying any of the new release albums would be able to buy another at a reduced rate and each album would feature on the inner sleeve of the other. A single would be trailered two weeks before the release of the album, advised the brochure, although this wasn't the case for Lovich or Lewie. The planned releases of Lovich's "Home"/ "Writing On The Wall" (BUY 35) and Lewie's "Hallelujah Europa (Part 1)" / "Hallelujah Europa (Part 2)" (BUY 37) never happened.

This imaginative and brilliantly coordinated promotional campaign won Stiff an honour at the *Music Week* Awards held the following year. Andy Murray had put the Be Stiff tour forward for Marketing Campaign of the Year and the judges were suitably impressed with the intricate planning that had gone into it, the branding, different formats, coloured vinyl, picture discs and other elements. But because the album sales hadn't been anywhere as impressive, they created a new category – Top Promotion of the Year.

In keeping with Stiff's self-deprecatory style, Conroy, Cowderoy and Murray dressed up as undertakers, with top hats and all. Their joint acceptance speech made the industry bigwigs sit up even more, as Murray recalls: "Of course, Paul can't work to a script, so he gets the award and goes, 'Well, we won this because we're the best fucking record company and we've the best fucking records!' It was a real HM Bateman moment because a black tie lunch was what it was in those days, so that was very Stiff. It was a real industry awards with everyone in bow ties and us dressed like undertakers and it actually got a bit of a shock laugh."

Working out of a basement room with just a telephone, a desk and a filing cabinet, Murray had to hit the ground running and had little time to acclimatise to Stiff's hand-to-mouth operation. As well as helping to promote Sweet as one of the Be Stiff performers, he had also agreed to put her and her sister Lia up in the flat he rented with his mate Paul, who worked for the promoter Harvey Goldsmith.

As Murray recalls: "Dave was saying, 'We've got to get somewhere for Rachel. Where's Rachel going to stay?'. I said, 'I've got a spare room'. 'Well I wanna see it.' So he came round to have a look, interviewed Paul to see if he was a reasonable, mature, balanced human being, which he wasn't at the time. He was out seeing rock bands every night and doing various things. They [Rachel and Lia] were very nice, although they did scratch my Meatloaf album. I'd bought it on import because I was a big Todd Rundgren fan [Rundgren produced Meatloaf's *Bat Out Of Hell*], and it wasn't big for another year later.

And they loved it and all they would do was play it. ('Andy. It's only a record.') So, from that point of view, they were terrible. I recall that Dick [Rachel's father] was around enough of the time to realise they were being looked after. So, funnily enough, given this is the seventies and obviously a hugely sexist time, I don't recall anyone ever trying to chat up the pair of them."

At the official photoshoot for the tour, the travelling band of musicians posed in front of the train, bearing its proud Stiff livery, as it prepared to leave from Olympia Station. Murray wasn't there. He was on a train heading to Bristol where a personal appearance by the five artists had been arranged at a local record shop. The shop was empty, but there was still plenty of time before he had to meet them at the train station and go with them on a bus to the store. On arrival, Dave Robinson had the foresight to run up the stairs of the shop and realising it's a wash-out, returned to announce, "No they're not ready for us. Let's just go to the gig". A PR own goal on the very first day was thus averted.

Music press headlines indicated some scepticism about the tour and made it clear that journalists would be monitoring its impact closely. "Can The Train Take The Strain?" [A play on the British Rail slogan at the time, "Let The Train Take The Strain"] *Sounds* asked on its front page, which carried a full picture of the un-famous five. "Last Train To Credibility City" read a headline a few weeks later. The importance of this high-risk venture delivering for the label bankrolling it was further underlined in the *NME*. "Be a killer or a real Stiff ... Why is Dave Robinson surveying a train load of amiable artists and praying for violence (In a manner of speaking)?" it wrote. *Melody Maker* put things in even starker terms. "When this is all over they've all got to go back to Stiff, and if they blow it, there'll be no Stiff to go back to" said the heading over a long feature and a picture of Lovich and Sweet playing cards in one of the carriages. Punning on Bob Dylan's legendary Rolling Thunder Revue, some wags dubbed it the "Rolling Chunder Revue".

Even by Stiff standards, this was a motley collection, and while it was all smiles at the station, not everyone was happy to be on board. Eric was a case in point. A year had passed since the Greatest Stiffs tour. Elvis, Nick and Ian had all enjoyed the sweet taste of chart success, casting an embittered Eric in the role of "also-ran". "Whole Wide World" and its follow-up "Reconnez Cherie" should both have been hits, but weren't. By Wreckless' own admission, his heavy drinking meant he hadn't taken full advantage of the first tour: he couldn't afford to make the same mistake on this outing.

Mickey Jupp had a reputation for being recalcitrant and was also a reluctant passenger. If he was an odd choice for this package tour, then "Old Rock 'n' Roller" as a single seemed even odder. "I didn't feel comfortable on that tour, but I never did when there's a lot a people around," he says. "I'm the same – if not worse – now. I guess my nervous system has been a huge drawback over the years."

Andy Murray comments: "'Old Rock 'n' Roller' was a bit of a funny choice. We liked Mickey Jupp because he was a retro rocker and he was great and the band were great. But it wasn't what was happening at the time on radio; it was neither punk nor flimsy pop. It was a bit old fashioned."

On the first tour, the battle between Costello and Dury to come out on top intensified their performances and the media lapped it up. Here, Stiff actively encouraged a sense of competition, not only releasing each of the artist's albums on the same day, but posting chart positions on the walls of the dressing rooms.

Speaking to *NME*, Robinson was unapologetic. "By the time we get to Belfast the knives will be out," he said. "The bottom line is we're a record company. We must sell records. If an act isn't ambitious, they're off the label. Last year Elvis started off doing 'Neat Neat Neat' and obscure country numbers. Dury was out to kill, to be top dog. When Elvis smelled the competition he went to his album. People must be ready to kill onstage. Lene is very ambitious." [35]

The only person who had a hit with a record released to coincide with the tour was Rachel Sweet. "B-A-B-Y" began getting played by radio stations while the train was still rattling along. For the 16-year-old singer performing in Britain for the first time, this was exciting news. But not everyone was pleased. "Rachel's single went on the Capital [Radio] play list and Eric's didn't and I mistakenly thought we were all in it together and there was a group ethos," says Murray. "There may well have been with the others, but there wasn't with Eric. He was very competitive, it turns out. All I said was, 'Rachel's single has gone on the Capital play list, isn't that good? Good for all of us.' Well this was the wrong thing to say and Eric was abusive and ripped my shirt."

Wreckless Eric's tour single, "Crying, Waiting, Hoping" was one of the last songs Buddy Holly recorded before his death in 1959.

It was coupled with a demo version of "I Wish It Would Rain", the finished recording of which was on the album. *The Wonderful World Of Wreckless Eric* had a truly retro feel thanks to its cover, which replicated *Jack Good's 'Oh Boy!'*, an album of songs from the teenage all-music show Good hosted on ITV in the fifties. Assorted Blockheads and other Stiff people can be recognised in the posed photograph, including then *NME* writer Danny Baker on the drum kit.

Wreckless, who was by now going out with Philippa Thomas, began the Be Stiff tour in a stronger position than he did the first. The album had some excellent songs and this time he had people turning up to see *him*. But while Sweet's polishing up of an old song came off, Wreckless was again denied a hit. Sales of the album were also disappointing and he was left bemoaning Stiff's tactics. "What caring label puts five albums out by five artists in the same day?" he questioned.[12]

If there was one overall winner from the Be Stiff shows in the UK, it was probably Lovich. On stage, she was kooky and beguiling, her band solid. In *Stateless,* she had an extraordinary record, a *smörgåsbord* of styles from the invigorating pop of "Say When", and "Lucky Number", to the achingly beautiful "Too Tender (To Touch)" and otherworldly "Sleeping Beauty". The critics were mostly impressed and so was label-mate Lewie: "Lene tended to be the most successful of the acts live and they were good live, there was no question about it. In a way, they were more prepared than all the others because she had presence with her performance, her dress, going back to Bowie, and was colourful and well meaning."

Lovich found the whole experience a learning curve: "It was a wonderful education because we didn't have to play for very long, just do maybe half an hour or twenty minutes, and you just learned from all the other people. To start with, I think Dave said it was only Eric and Mickey Jupp go on last. It was not a complete rotation to start with because we had to prove that we were capable. I don't think even Stiff knew what the hell we were going to do. So, it wasn't until they saw us on stage that they decided we could have a rotation. Actually, you soon found out there was no extra fun being the last person on stage because half the audience had left to get the last bus and the other half were completely drunk, so somewhere in the middle was about the right place to be."

A red locomotive train with yellow aeroplane wings made for an eye-catching poster for the shows at New York's Bottom Line club between 17 and 20 December. The names of the five acts ran along the bottom, although Mickey Jupp's name had been crossed out – reportedly because he was afraid of flying. But on his non-involvement in the American leg, he says: "No way was I going to get dragged off to NY just before Christmas, thank you very much!" In the event, his band went without him and played anyway.

Lovich, for whom the British dates had mostly proved a launch pad, felt the "odd one out" in New York and that the others were better received. Lewie had been emboldened by the shows back in the UK and arrived at The Bottom Line determined the make an impression.

She remembers: "You had tables and chairs at The Bottom Line where people sat down to drink and have a little bit of food perhaps, that went right to the stage and right out to the little venue and I just ran out and ran along the tables where all their coffees and drinks and food was, jumped down on to the floor, went around and back on the stage again and carried on singing. And on one of the nights, I just threw myself into the audience. I've seen that happen with other people since, so I was quite brazen by then; I'd developed my act. It wasn't even an act, it was just impulse and desperation to try and make it and try and crack the States. In the sixties, the culture was, 'If you can make it in the States …' And indeed, my album was getting airplay all over America, apparently. But Stiff didn't manage to get a label deal with Arista and, frankly, they blew it."

Two days after the New York run, "B-A-B-Y" entered the UK chart, securing Stiff its third Top 40 hit. When the striking teen performer appeared on *Top Of The Pops* in jeans and a black shirt, with a formal white tie hanging loose, young male viewers jaws must have dropped. And with a soaring voice that belied her age and such an infectious pop song, her label must have been seeing her name up in lights. It was not to be. "B-A-B-Y" stalled at No. 35, a disappointing showing for the only hit record to result from the Be Stiff tour and the mammoth marketing campaign that went with it.

In the same chart, however, was another Stiff record. One that would deliver a smash hit and change the course of the label forever.

8

Hit Me!

Noel Edmunds was presenting *Top Of The Pops*. Boney M were dressed in fluffy, snowy white coats and singing "Mary's Boy Child – Oh My Lord", their No.1 Christmas record. Waiting at No.2 to topple these singing pom-poms were Village People, whose life-affirming disco anthem was the musical incarnation of New York's hedonistic Studio 54. But there was another unlikely contender for British pop music's coveted top spot.

On 23 December 1978, a sagging carpet was the only thing preventing a gobbing, pogo-ing mob from falling into the basement of the Ilford Odeon in East London. The subject of their delirium had just embarked on his sell-out Hankie Pantie Christmas Tour and a remarkable ascent of the Top 40 that would result in one of the most memorable chart-topping records of all time. Ian Dury was about to enter the big time. Stiff's saviour had finally arrived.

Speaking of "Hit Me With Your Rhythm Stick", Charlie Gillett called it one of Stiff's greatest achievements: "… to get that difficult, but brilliant, artist Ian Dury put into a context where you could do anything at all with him, and then to get that great record to be No 1." [12]

"Hit Me …" raised the bar for all future releases on Stiff, as well as delivering its first No.1. It was now major league. "The thing about having a No. 1 though, is that the criteria changes. Thereafter, you're looking up at that spot quite a lot," said Robinson. [12]

"Hit Me With Your Rhythm Stick" was released as BUY 38 in early December 1978. Everything about it was memorable, from Dury's rhyming patter to Norman Watt-Roy's nagging funk bass line and Davey Payne's rasping solo played through two saxophones. Radio stations loved it as did the public. Dury's masterpiece of alternative pop entered the UK chart at No. 30 on 16 December. The following week, it climbed to 13 and its upward momentum continued in January, taking it to No. 2, just one place behind "YMCA".

On 27 January 1979, Stiff and Ian Dury achieved what had seemed impossible. "Right now, it's No. 1 time," announced Dave Lee Travis on *Top Of The Pops*, "and yes, he's made it. Ian Dury & The Blockheads". The camera zoomed in on the band in tuxedos, frilled white shirts and black bow ties, their singer-cum-ringmaster wearing a white scarf, silver gloves and holding a walking cane on this most special of occasions.

Dury had been in southern France when the news came through that he was No.1. "We were on the beach in Cannes when 'Hit Me ...' went to number one," remembered Fred Rowe. "The hotel staff brought us a bottle of champagne on a tray and said to Ian, 'Your record "Hit Me ..." has gone to number one'. I remember when we first kicked off with Kilburn And The High Roads, Ian said, 'I can't sing' and I said, 'Yeah, but great lyrics Ian, I could listen to them all day'. He said, 'It might be a number one', and I said, 'I tell you what Ian. If you ever get a number one with this sort of work, I'll eat a piece of shit'. So, that day on the beach, Ian said to me, 'Ere, I'm going to find you a bit of shit around here to eat!'" [6]

"Hit Me ..." reportedly sold a million copies before disappearing from the UK chart after fifteen weeks. Stiff then deleted and re-issued it, shifting another 100,000 copies. The sleeve was as unusual as the record inside and vintage Barney Bubbles. On the back, the shapes combined to make a toy dog against the green square and a pink dog beneath made from cut out shapes. For the fold-out Hankie Pantie tour programme, Bubbles presented Dury's silhouette in matchsticks arranged on a red hankie. Never missing a trick, Stiff produced red handkerchiefs carrying his clever design and sold them at shows.

A naturally introverted and modest figure, Bubbles had followed Riviera to Radar and worked out of its offices overlooking Covent Garden, creating stunning artwork for Elvis Costello and Nick Lowe that would be revered for decades to come. He also remained a great admirer of Ian Dury and continued to produce unique record sleeves and promotional material for him in a freelance capacity. He was asked to contribute to a redesign of *NME* and had come up with the masthead, which is still in use today. Dury's songs, Stiff's marketing and Bubbles' designs were as potent a trinity as sex, drugs and rock 'n' roll itself.

"The whole artistic vibe of the place was from this mad designer in the basement," said Robinson. "I phoned him up once and said, 'I want a Blockheads logo and it's got to be black and white and square' and somebody in his office went, 'Wow!' and he'd said, 'I've done it'.

He did it while I was talking to him. He just made this little face with Blockheads and we still use that. We had these watches and when it was three o'clock it said Blockhead. It was all part and parcel of this incredible off-the-wall fun." [5]

Chris Morton, whom Robinson had appointed as Stiff's permanent art director shortly after Riviera's departure, was a great admirer of Bubbles' work. He remembers him as a captivating, but unpredictable and vulnerable figure who was already wrestling with some of the personal issues that would cause him to take his own life in 1983.

"He is probably the nearest thing I will ever know or understand to be a genius," says Morton. "It is a word that is horribly overused, but he really was unbelievably enigmatic. But he had these terrible mood swings, which did for him in the end. There were times when he would have the most amazing ideas and you'd be thinking, 'Fucking hell, look at this' and he'd be going, 'No, it's no good, nobody's going to like it'. At other times, he'd be unbelievably chirpy and bright, but there were big swings. The girlfriend he had for quite a long time has never got over him dying. 'Caramel Crunch' – that was her nickname.

"They were sleeping under the work bench and I can't remember who it was, whether it was Jake or somebody, but somebody went in one morning and caught them at it! I mean, Barney really was absolutely extraordinary."

Ian Dury & The Blockheads made a number of appearances on *Top Of The Pops* to perform their surprise hit, opting for a different look each time. For one, Dury and the drummer sported matching donkey jackets. Except it wasn't Charley Charles behind the kit – he'd gone missing. "I don't know where he was to this day – he just went missing," says plugger Sonnie Rae. "Robin Nash, affectionately known as Knob Rash, was running *Top Of The Pops* in those days, and he was calling and calling and I got summonsed and asked, 'Where is he?' and I said, 'Oh, just coming'. We dragged Spider [Rowe] into make-up, blacked him up, stuck a wig on him and stuck him on the drum kit. But they forgot to do his hands, which was really funny!"

To capitalise on Dury's success, Stiff would launch a full scale PR offensive that, despite their mutual distrust, would necessitate the collaboration of Stiff and Blackhill. Dury was the goose that had laid the golden egg and no promotional campaign would be too elaborate when it came to its number one act. But before that, the now flying label received an belated but hugely welcome boon from the Be Stiff tour.

Lene Lovich had been the surprise package of the station-to-station trip. An intriguing sight, her dark hair in plaits and her head adorned with an array of scarves and ribbons, she gave off an aura of mystique. Her music had a dark, Germanic feel that nodded more towards Bertolt Brecht than the Motown groups of her childhood; "Writing On The Wall" being a case in point.

What also made her music so removed from the norm was the way she used her voice, from short punctuated yells to Hammer House Of Horror screams. It was this unorthodox vocal style that would shoot her to stardom.

Stiff hadn't released a single by Lovich at the time of the Be Stiff tour, although *Stateless* had been one of the five albums issued on the same day. Lovich's rise to stardom was rapid, as she explains: "Stiff was small and able to react very quickly and make decisions quickly. I think that's why, once the tour had got started and our album was out there, the next single for me was 'Lucky Number'. I think that was because it went down well on stage. They didn't really know it was going to be a hit record and Dave Robinson told me several times it wasn't a proper song because there was no chorus. I have spoken to him since and he denies it and tries to make it appear he was the mastermind behind it all, but no. It had its own chorus, 'Ah Oh! Ah Oh!'. It's a new kind of chorus, but there it is.

"I think Dave Robinson had the front to put things out and have a go with things and I think you have to give him some credit for making it possible. It happened very quickly. We were out on tour after the Be Stiff tour and suddenly we heard. 'Oi, your record's doing quite good. You're going to have to do *Top Of The Pops*. We're going to have to fly you into London!' It was lovely – overnight. I knew it was the one thing that would impress my mum. It just happened so quick, you didn't have time to reason why and everything snowballed from that and suddenly you're in demand and we just didn't stop."

Lovich was one of its most colourful performers, but Stiff used black and white images of her to striking effect on records and promotional material. A picture shoot by Brian Griffin had produced the monochrome images chosen for *Stateless* and another of these was used on the cover of "Lucky Number". Released on 2 February 1979, long after the train tour had reached its final destination, it showed Lene with her pigtails holding an illuminated globe. The back cover had a white box which was supposed to reveal a number if subjected to radiated heat and anyone who found such a "lucky number" could claim a prize. "Home", another strong track from the album, supplied the B-side.

The video was classic Stiff. Employees were roped in to take part and the Island Records offices were used for filming. Says Nigel Dick: "There's a shot at the end of the 'Lucky Number' video where there's a bunch of people walking at you towards the subway that goes under Hyde Park and I think it's me, Conroy, Cowderoy, Andy Murray, Les and somebody else. Basically, we were a family."

The Be Stiff tour had alerted the media to the label's alluring new act and had led to a John Peel session on Radio 1. When "Lucky Number" was finally released, media requests poured in. A *Top Of The Pops* recording was followed by a session for Nicky Horne's show on London's Capital Radio and another on Granada TV's *What's On*. *NME*, meanwhile, ran a competition. Two more appearances on *Top Of The Pops* helped catapult Lovich to No.3. "Lucky Number" sold a reported 400,000 copies and spent eleven weeks in the UK chart.

Stateless had also charted and – keen to profit from the success of "Lucky Number" – Stiff released the high-tempo "Say When" as a single on 4 May. Lovich performed it with rapid arm movements which were mimicked by an ecstatic audience in the accompanying video made by Stiff Visions. Lovich and Stiff were clearly on a roll. *Sounds* named it Single of the Week and it entered the chart on 19 May. Five weeks later it had made No.19, ensuring two consecutive Top 20 hits for the new lady of Stiff.

Not only had Lovich found success at Stiff, but a place where she fitted in. "I loved it, I totally loved it because I felt, at last, there is a home for me and there are people who take me for what I am," she says. "It was wonderful. It really was like being in a family. It was just a fun atmosphere; no one really seemed to know what they were doing, which kind of took the pressure off. I'm sure they thought they knew what they were doing, but I don't know. There was probably no other record company in the world where you could just walk in and speak to the boss. Like, no problem, he was just another guy in the room. We used to hang out there and there were various people working in the Stiff shop. Everybody was friendly, nobody was up themselves and nobody thought they were better than anybody else, even if they had been there longer."

Stiff was eager to sign female acts after a first two years dominated by the boys. Liam Sternberg, having introduced Stiff to Rachel Sweet and Jane Aire, was also instrumental in the discovery of another. However, the 19-year-old vocalist with dark eye make-up and the most single of minds hadn't come to light in Akron, but South London.

Kirsty MacColl had music in her blood. Her father was folk legend Ewan MacColl, but he had been a distant figure during her childhood and split from her mother Jean Newlove when Kirsty was a toddler. He went on to marry Peggy Seeger, the half-sister of protest singer Pete, and performed and recorded with her. However, it was not the traditional strains of folk that stirred his young daughter, but the melodious pop of The Beach Boys and the story-telling songs of The Kinks. And her own career in the pop world which he so disdained would reflect her very different musical tastes.

Kirsty enrolled at Croydon College of Art in a bid to placate her parents, who both wanted her to go to university. But after six months she dropped out, hanging out in snooker halls and drifting in and out of temporary jobs. The closest she came to music was working in the mail order department of Bonaparte Records. But via her brother Hamish, she became close to a group called the Tooting Frooties and when they reinvented themselves as Drug Addix, MacColl joined, assuming the moniker of Mandy Doubt. An EP was released on Chiswick as part of a set called *Suburban Rock* (Billy Bragg's band Riff-Raff were one of the other releases). The record succeeded in getting Stiff's attention, but it wasn't the band it was interested in.

"Paul [Conroy] was the big enthusiast for her," remembers Sternberg. "Paul came up to me one day and said, 'I've found this singer, Kirsty MacColl. Have a listen because I think this is really great'. I didn't see it at first, but then I met her down in a pub in Chelsea and I really liked her."

MacColl said: "After I left [the band], Stiff Records called and said, 'We'd like you to come and play us anything you've got'. I said, 'I thought you didn't like the demos,' and they said, 'We hate the band, but we quite like you!' When they asked if I had any songs, I said, 'Oh yeah, loads!', even though I hadn't at all. Then I thought, 'Oh God, I'd better write something before I go to see them.'" [41]

One of the songs the teenager had quickly pulled together was "They Don't Know" and it was at Stiff's mobile studio – The China Shop – that she arrived to record it. Sternberg was there to produce and Lu Edmunds from The Damned was drafted in. His spontaneous solo was kept on the finished record, which became her debut release on 1 June 1979. A sublime pop song, it was simple but moving, and her searing cry of "Babeee" that cut in Spector-esque before the final verse served notice that Stiff had unearthed another raw talent. "Turn My Motor On", the B-side, was another of her songs that had been a feature of Drug Addix sets, and had reportedly been mooted as the single by Stiff before being switched.

BUY 47, as well as being the first record in MacColl's solo career, had the honour of being Stiff's first picture disc. In a pink jacket and a matching ribbon tied in her flame-coloured hair, Kirsty MacColl looked every bit the pop star. Rosemary Robinson was among those seen following MacColl down a flight of stairs on the black and white picture sleeve version. She recalls how: "She fitted perfectly. We didn't have any girls who wrote and had her kind of attitude, which was fairly in-your-face. She wasn't sweet. She wanted to interview the record company. She'd obviously come with an attitude." [41]

In the event, that "attitude" proved too much for Robinson and the two didn't hit it off. "They loved her, but Kirsty and Dave didn't get along," Sternberg says. "Kirsty and Dave was just not possible. She didn't want to sign a longer deal, so Dave didn't promote the record. It was like in the top three in airplay, but they didn't press any more. It got air-played to death and there were no records being sold because there were no records out there".

To be fair to Stiff, another factor had played a part. A strike by independent distributors coincided with its release, preventing copies that had been pressed up reaching the shops. MacColl, like other Stiff acts before and after her, was left to ponder her ill-fortune.

A second single had been scheduled for release in October 1979 and supplied with a BUY prefix. "You Caught Me Out" was co-written by MacColl and Boomtown Rats Pete Briquette and Simon Crowe, and members of the Irish band backed her on the record. But it was hampered by delays and numerous takes in the studio and ended up being shelved. It was a blow for MacColl, who was reeling from her break-up with boyfriend Rick Smith from Drug Addix. Despite being close to people at Stiff, including Robinson's personal assistant Annie Pitts, who paid for her to go to Spain on holiday, MacColl left.

"We didn't come to blows at all," said MacColl. "Most of my friends work at Stiff, but I wanted too much control really, or more control than I was getting. There were any number of things, but I think it was really because they didn't have my publishing." [41]

MacColl and Rachel Sweet both contributed backing vocals to Jane Aire's album *Jane Aire & The Belvederes*, which was released on Virgin. When Aire toured the UK with Lene Lovich to promote it, she asked MacColl to join her on stage doing backing vocals to help her overcome her debilitating stage-fright. "She was very nervous, she would throw up and found it very uncomfortable. At that time in her life, Kirsty was pretty angst-riddled. I loved her, but that was part of her nature," reflects Aire.

"Three years ago, I don't think marketing men were catered for before Stiff started," said Robinson. "Jake and I had a lot to do with the updating of the art departments and marketing managers at record companies. We also did well for the papers because we stimulated a lot of ads and now I find the papers haven't changed enough. They need some new blood, style and bite." [38]

A depression engulfed the record industry as the 1970s ended. Record label sales peaked in around 1978 and by 1979 they fell by a quarter. The cost of vinyl was pushed up as a consequence of the global oil crisis a few years earlier, prompting labels to start cutting back on their activities.

In August 1979, *Music Week* reported that around 600 jobs had fallen casualty to US record company mergers or cutbacks so far that year. But asked by the trade magazine *Record Business* if the so-called industry depression was affecting Stiff, Robinson was typically ebullient. "We are selling just as many records as before," he said. "Maybe your acts are too old, which is really what a lot of it is about to be honest. Three years ago, we had a big punk uplift and the A&R men were saying 'punk – I don't like it, it's noise, it's not musical' and your A&R men disappeared overnight, which is how it should be." [38]

So, whilst few of the established record companies were looking to expand, Stiff was broadening its horizons, and with hits being delivered by Ian Dury and Lene Lovich, there was little reason to question its optimism. By the summer, having conquered the British charts, Stiff set out to do the same on the other side of the Atlantic.

In June 1979, *Rolling Stone* announced Stiff was on the verge of production-distribution deals in the US via CBS. Ian Dury, Lene Lovich and Ian Gomm would all be released Stateside through Stiff/Epic, while Rachel Sweet would appear on Stiff/Columbia. Meanwhile, other artists like Wreckless Eric and Jona Lewie would appear on an independent label bearing only the Stiff logo.

Ian Dury's second album, *Do It Yourself*, accompanied ironically by a free copy of "Hit Me With Your Rhythm Stick", and a remixed version of *Stateless*, would be among the first fruits of the Stiff/Epic deal. So, too would be Ian Gomm's excellently titled *Gomm With The Wind*, a remixed and re-sequenced version of his British album *Summer Holiday*. Sweet's album *Fool Around* would be remixed and issued with two additional songs, "A Sad Song" and "I Go To Pieces". To celebrate the Transatlantic union, Dave Robinson and senior Epic figures chomped on hot dogs from a cart outside the CBS offices in New York.

Dick Wingate had worked at CBS and when he moved across to Epic, he managed to convince it that at least some of Stiff's artists should be released through the label. "Columbia really only wanted Rachel Sweet anyway," he says. "I wanted Ian Dury, Lene Lovich, and, to a lesser extent, Wreckless Eric and Ian Gomm. So, Rachel was signed directly to Columbia and we formed Stiff/Epic for the others."

Summer Holiday was released in the UK on Albion Records, the label set up by former Brinsleys manager Dai Davies. Gomm kept in touch with the Brinsleys' other long-term manager Dave Robinson and out of the blue he had received a call from the Stiff boss. "I've just done a six-album deal with Epic Records in America," Robinson told him. "I'm one album short. How about I put your one on it?" Gomm was taken aback, but happy for his record to have a US release.

"I said, 'Well yes, why not?'," recalls Gomm. "But in typical Dave Robinson style, he didn't quite get that. So, he drove all the way from London for about three and a half hours, because the motorways hadn't been built so much then [Gomm lives in Wales]. We were having our house-warming in the front room, and someone's at the door and it's bloody Dave Robinson. He came in and said, 'Have you thought about the deal yet?' and I said, 'Well, I said I'd do it. It's fine'. 'Oh great. Got any wine?' He drank a bottle of red wine straight down, sat in a chair and fell asleep. So all through the party, our friends were coming to me and going, 'Who's that guy in the corner?' 'Oh, he's in the record business you know'. Then I think about one o'clock in the morning everyone had gone and he woke up and said, 'Have I missed it?'"

One of Stiff's many marketing ploys at the time was to produce promo discs containing tracks and a question-and-answer session with an artist that radio stations could then present as an interview. So, before going out on a US tour, Gomm found himself sitting down for a cheesy chat with press officer Andy Murray in The China Shop, who relates how: "They had a little mobile recording caravan outside the office and I had to go down there and it was called 'Ian Gomm Talks'. Basically, they did it for a few other artists and they had a list of questions and I had to answer. 'Is this your first trip to America, Ian?' 'Yes, it is, and I'm really enjoying it.' [Gomm had joined Brinsley Schwarz after the Fillmore East gig] By the time I got to America, it was a five-week tour, I was on stage and every day was driving and then just promo. I just never stopped.

"I was talking to one of these DJs and I said, 'Ah, you've got "Ian Gomm Talks". Did you ever use it?' He said, 'Use it? We put it on at night, but we don't ask the questions it says on the back of the sleeve. Two nights ago I had it on. "Say, I got Ian Gomm in the studio. Tell me Ian, how long have you been homosexual and are you enjoying it?" and I'm going, 'Well, it's about five weeks now and I'm really enjoying it'. Typical Stiff isn't it?!'"

"Hold On" was released as a single and after being picked up by college radio stations, it became the first Stiff/Epic hit, reaching eighteen in the Billboard Hot 100. "My record was silky smooth, very Stiff really," says Gomm. "It was quite funny really because in America they loved it. In Holland and Sweden it did all right, but it couldn't get bloody arrested over here. But that's been the story of my life really."

Gomm toured the record extensively in the US in 1979, initially with Dire Straits on their Sultans Of Swing tour. He then enjoyed his own sell-out tour, supported by The Beat (the American not the English band). "Dave Robinson had done a deal with this company in New York called ARSE Management," says Gomm. "So we turn up and Epic have put tour money in and they had promptly handed it to ARSE Management and the guy just ran off with the money!"

As Robinson delved into his pub rock past in search of potential acts, some of Gomm's bandmates from Brinsley Schwarz had also arrived at Stiff. The Rumour released their own album *Max* for Phonogram and Stiff had picked up Graham Parker's accomplished band hoping they would have some success in their own right.

Their first single, "Frozen Years", was a compelling slice of electronic pop which reflected a shift away from guitar-based songs, as well as the plummeting temperatures during Britain's "winter of discontent".

Bob Andrews sang on the record which was a notable departure from those they had made with Parker. The record was a hit in Holland and the group appeared on the weekly Dutch TV show *TopPop*. In the UK, it simply melted away.

Says Andrews: "We had a lot of fun making that record and we thought at the time we were doing a lot of stuff that people were just getting into – all that electronic thing. I think some of the things we were trying to do were pretty 'out there' for the time. A lot of the punk stuff was just guitars. I guess the image was wrong, whatever we were. The Rumour was always that little bit older than everybody else, although not by much. We were 28 instead of being 22, and I think that was a big difference then. If you were over 25, you were considered an old man."

Its successor was "Emotional Traffic" (written by Andrews and his then wife Pat Mayberry). Stiff pressed up the record in the traffic light colours of red, orange and green, and five weeks later switched the A and B-sides. Both singles were taken from the album *Frogs, Sprouts, Clogs And Krauts,* the songwriting credits on which were shared around the band. However, great songs and marketing weren't enough and both singles and album failed to chart.

Weirdly, The Rumour briefly changed their name to The Duplicates and recorded another single for Stiff, "I Want To Make You Very Happy". Shortly afterwards, Andrews was dumped by the group and almost immediately recruited by Robinson as a producer. "I'd already started doing some production for Stiff with Jona Lewie, so it was a natural thing for me to carry on doing that," says Andrews. "I went to see Dave [Robinson] the day I got the sack from the Rumour and Dave said, "Don't worry about it, come on,' and off we went."

In 1980, The Rumour made one last attempt to achieve success away from Parker. *Purity Of Essence* was a mishmash of covers such as Randy Newman's "Have You Seen My Baby" and Love's "My Little Red Book", originals by Schwarz and other band members, and an unreleased Parker track. A cover of Nick Lowe's "I Don't Want The Night To End" was also released as a single. But even the usually winning touch of producer Alan Winstanley couldn't prevent The Rumour for being best remembered as Parker's backing band. Within a year, Robinson's pals from the Hope & Anchor had called it a day.

Ian Dury was Stiff Records' cash cow. The label had been on the ropes after the departure of Riviera, Costello and Lowe, and Dury's chart successes effectively ensured its survival. The one million plus sales of "Hit Me ..." catapulted Dury to fame and gave Stiff a platform from which it could give the major labels a real run for their money – fulfilling the original vision. So, as his follow-up to the platinum-selling *New Boots And Panties!!* neared completion, Stiff began plotting one of its most sophisticated ever marketing campaigns.

Musically, *Do It Yourself* was a different proposition to its predecessor. While *New Boots And Panties!!* had fused funk rhythms with punk energy and Music Hall, its follow-up was smoother and owed more to Dury's love of artists like John Coltrane, Charlie Mingus and Ornette Coleman and albums like Steely Dan's 1977 offering, *Aja*. Expectations at Alexander Street must have been high with the delivery of such a radio-friendly set on the back of a No. 1 hit.

However, in a perverse move, "Hit Me..." wasn't included and nor were any of the ten tracks picked out for release as a single. Blackhill's Andrew King said Dury always strongly resisted having singles on his albums. But he laid the blame for the decision not to issue the catchy opening track "Inbetweenies" as a single at Kosmo Vinyl's door.

"It wasn't quite as essential in marketing terms then as it is now to have a single on an album, because there was a much more genuine singles market then," King said. "There was also a sort of religious reason why it didn't become a single, for which I have always blamed Kosmo Vinyl. The Small Faces never had their singles on the album, and therefore we shouldn't either. I always felt that 'Inbetweenies' should have been a single and that would have turned *Do It Yourself* into a real hit. But it was on the album and therefore it couldn't be a single. Once Ian had said it, it was a point of pride and I have nothing against pride. But it was being proud of being completely bonkers as far as I was concerned." [6]

Dave Robinson sent a copy of the finished record to its producer Laurie Lewis and asked him to pick out a single. He told Robinson he couldn't hear one. "I loved some of the tracks very much and the track I particularly loved on it was 'Inbetweenies'," he said. "If I'd had to choose a song to be a single, that would have been it. At the time, Pink Floyd and Led Zeppelin didn't even do singles and from a marketing point of view it was suicide, but they were so big they could transcend all that." [6]

Single or no, Stiff pulled no punches in marketing the record – the thrust of which owed itself to Barney Bubbles' ingenious artwork. Even by his own painfully high standards, his design for the cover of *Do It Yourself* was a stroke of genius.

By 1979, millions of homes were papered with garish, patterned wallpaper and the album title prompted Bubbles to look through Crown's sample books for ideas. Initially, he suggested Stiff release the record in a handful of different wallpaper colours and styles. Thrilled at what was such a wonderfully Stiff concept, Robinson said they should use the whole book so that its licensees could have the option of their own unique sleeve. Robinson reportedly came to a deal with Crown that Stiff could reproduce the patterns providing the order number appeared on the sleeve. In the end, 28 different sleeves were produced, ten in the UK. Bubbles ran amok with the DIY theme. Drill holes were added to each letter of the title which ran across the top of the sleeve and he created Tommy, a talking toolbox with fold-out compartments making up its face. The inspired graphic was prominently displayed beneath the band's name and the album's tracks, and was also used on stickers and other promotional material. "It's for all the family to enjoy" read the tagline.

A grid of black and white, booth-style shots on the inner sleeve featured not only Dury and The Blockheads, but others including Andrew King, Peter Jenner, Kosmo Vinyl and Fred Rowe. Chris Gabrin returned to shoot the back cover image. As with *New Boots And Panties!!*, he was drawn to a shop-front. This time he had found a wig shop to line the group up outside in sailor's hats, side-on to the camera. A grinning and immaculately dressed Rowe stood facing out, his bald pate completing the intended joke. Apparently the shop's owner didn't see the funny side and sued for £15,000.

Stiff went into overdrive to market the record and its biggest artist. Paint pots with the Blockheads logo splurged across them, badges, wallpaper and wallpaper ties were produced and sent to record shops and the media. Posters were displayed along escalators at 150 London Underground stations and thousands of other sites across the country. In a special tie-in with *Do It Yourself* magazine, a Stiff representative was despatched to DIY shops to organise window displays. Full-page ads were not just taken out in the rock press, as was standard for Stiff, but also with *Music Week*, *Time Out*, *The Observer* colour supplement and *The Guardian*. A spokesperson added: "In true Stiff tradition, there will be a certain amount of pirate activity surrounding the album release."

It would be these stunts, carried out guerrilla-style, for which Stiff's most audacious campaign to date would be remembered, with Nigel Dick as fall guy: "I was involved in the Ian Dury wallpaper stunts. At six o'clock in the morning, I found myself down at the South Bank climbing over a chicken wire fence to break into *Melody Maker* offices. I was appalled and I was thinking, 'If I get caught, my mother is going to fucking kill me!' But there was the fear of, 'If I don't do it Robbo's going to fucking kill me,' so you went along with it because you were part of the team. I papered two strips and I think somebody actually let me in. I do remember this fear and I remember they were in some old Nissen huts on the South Bank somewhere. It was before they were made to go and work out of the IPC offices in that huge building, and I seem to remember sticking two pieces of extremely ugly wallpaper up on the wall. Of course, it didn't last beyond 9.30 in the morning."

Had *New Boots And Panties!!* not enjoyed such phenomenal success, the sales of its successor would have been seen in a similar light. Advance orders saw it storm into the UK album chart and it climbed to No.2. In all, it sold 200,000 copies and gave Dury his second platinum album. However, its twenty-week stay was a comparatively brief one and equated to just one fifth of the time *New Boots ...* occupied the listings.

The record did help raise Stiff's profile elsewhere in Europe. In Germany, where Stiff had a licensing deal with Teldec, it built on the impact of "Hit Me..." reaching a respectable No. 23, and the band embarked on a European tour that summer. Those who took part do not remember it fondly. Dury had not responded well to being famous and was on a massive power trip. So tyrannical was he in the studio during the recording of the album, that Jankel had phoned him and told him to stay away from the sessions. Blackhill also found its client increasingly infuriating, but the success he had enjoyed made his unreasonable demands difficult to refuse.

Andrew King commented: "If we had released 'Inbetweenies' as a single and it had all gone on, it would have been all right because we could have used this month's income to pay it off. That was the beginning of the end. It was a huge tour and they did wonderful gigs, but in retrospect, we were hard at work constructing our own coffin." [6]

Commenting on Dury's state of mind during this period, Chaz Jankel says: "Ian always wanted to determine the pace of it all. He wasn't working for his management, they were working for him. Also, because he was disabled, it was draining and he was carrying a lot of all this. He wanted to be top dog, but a lot of responsibility came with that. He had a full band, he had kids he wasn't living with, he had a girlfriend, he had drink to deal with, and he had an addiction to sleeping pills, which actually really fucked him up. That was the heavyweight shit that really messed him up. It was a very hectic life and part of him liked to live on the edge all the time, the beatnik, very arty way of life. But it takes its toll and as time went by, post-Stiff days, you'd see him sitting at his desk just contemplating life. He didn't want to rush any more.

"Maybe he also felt he'd better get on with it because he was 34 when we made *New Boots And Panties!!*, he was no spring chicken, and he probably thought, 'I'll give it a go'. For a while it was very intense and then it evaporated. From my own point of view, I couldn't be around him all the time because it was just too intense, so I said, 'That's it' and I actually moved continents! I went to live in LA. He respected me more ultimately for it because I wouldn't sit in his pocket. The terrible thing was that if he did that to people, then I think ultimately he took advantage of them and that friendship. Although when people talk about that, one always has to take into account that he could be a wonderful friend as well."

It was as the Blockheads toured Europe with their overbearing front man that they recorded a song that would become another non-album hit and that contained some of his most memorable lyrics ever. "Reasons To Be Cheerful (Part 3)" was written in a Rome hotel and cut at the RCA studios there after an incident caused the Italian shows to be cancelled. Electricity had shot up a lighting roadie's arm after he leaned over a mixing desk and touched a microphone stand. Another roadie had leapt across the stage and kicked him off the equipment, effectively saving his life. Then, as the band were unloading gear outside a venue, they were confronted by a gang of youths and a major fight was only just averted. "Reasons To be Cheerful" came to Dury as he contemplated the episode. "The phrase came because Charlie was still alive – that was the reason for being cheerful," said Ian. "It's a bit like saying, 'Count your blessings'." [32]

Stiff had excelled itself with the promotional campaign for *Do It Yourself* and "Reasons To Be Cheerful" prompted another stunt.

This time, Andy Murray and Kosmo Vinyl's sister Carol dressed up as a clown and a fairy and went out and about to spread the word. Released on 27 July, with "Common As Muck" on the B-side, it got plenty of airplay and entered the chart.

In 1979, *Top Of The Pops* recorded its highest audience of 19 million viewers as the light entertainment luvvies that had set the conservative tone of the show were swamped by the incoming new wave. The Skids spat at the Nolan Sisters backstage and Generation X urinated off the roof at The Dooleys. Where albums had once reigned supreme, single sales hit a record high of 79 million that year.

A more fertile environment could not have been imagined by Stiff, although the industrial unrest spreading across Britain at the time threatened to sabotage its chances. "Reasons To Be Cheerful" reached No. 6 on 11 August only for the next edition of *Top Of The Pops* to be cancelled by a technicians' strike. The following week – the video sent down to the BBC having not been played after all – it reached No.3 and the Boomtown Rats "I Don't Like Mondays" was replaced at No.1 by Cliff Richard's "We Don't Talk Any More".

"Dave Robinson went bananas and blamed me, but it was nothing to do with me," said Laurie Lewis. "But if it had gone on the telly that week it would have gone to No.1, no question." [6]

9

Nutty Boys

Arguably the most momentous event in Stiff's history happened in the summer of 1979. Friday 17 August, to be exact. But it wasn't the recording of a future chart hit or a boardroom business deal that changed its course forever ... it was Dave Robinson's wedding.

Predictably, the Irishman's nuptials were a right old knees-up. The now-demolished Clarendon Ballroom, in Hammersmith Broadway, was packed with famous faces celebrating the marriage of Robinson to Rosemary O'Connor. They'd been together for several years and had a baby son, Max. Rosemary was a familiar face to Stiff employees and artists alike, having travelled on the Greatest Stiffs tour and featuring in the resulting road movie. "I sat next to Rosemary Robinson quite a lot and she was a right old gossip," remembers Bruce Thomas. "She wanted to know everything that was going on, so I used to feed her all sorts of shit."

The newly-weds had enjoyed a brief honeymoon in Nassau, courtesy of Island boss Chris Blackwell, before returning to London to tie the knot. Unbeknown to Robinson, staff at Alexander Street had been putting together a rather special wedding gift. Jock Scot ("poet and tragedian") armed with a tape recorder, had approached as many people as he could, from musicians to employees and music industry acquaintances, and got them to contribute short messages. These were then spliced together for a seven-inch record pressed up specially for the occasion, named "Kongratulationz".

The cartoon-style sleeve featured the couple, their baby son and the dog, with Robinson himself depicted as a pig. "In this event, I see no problems" read the speech bubble beside Robbo's head, presumably one of his oft-used phrases. A message on the other side of the commemorative sleeve read: "Apologies to all friends not included on this recording. We tried to get through but you obviously haven't paid your phone bills." The commemorative disc was given a prefix of Max 1 and was credited on the label to The Dulcet Tones of Jock Scot. It remains one of the rarest Stiff records in existence.

It wasn't one of Stiff's in-house designers who provided the satirical sleeve, but Edwin Pouncey, a freelance artist working as Savage Pencil. "I seem to remember that someone at Stiff rang me up out of the blue and asked me to do the cover as a surprise for Dave and Rosemary Robinson," says Pouncey, who still has his copy. "At the time, I was drawing a strip for *Sounds* called Rock 'N' Roll Zoo that commented on the punk scene and music industry. The characters were usually depicted as cartoon animals. I was asked to include their baby and dog as part of the design. I never got a response from the Robinsons; why would I? But I heard later from a Stiff source that Dave was not amused. Whether they actually liked it or not, however, I never really knew."

"Not amused"? Word has it that Robinson was fuming and desperately tried to retrieve the records, which were given out to wedding guests. Listen to some of the contributions from those put on the spot by Scot and it's not difficult to see why. Those still working at Stiff clearly didn't want to upset the boss and were suitably tactful when the microphone was suddenly thrust at them. But not everyone was so polite. Here's one of the tamer ones.

Jock: *"Knocker Knowles, the well-known stud from Island Records, between shafting nubiles, has managed to catch his breath for a moment. This is the man who knocked out Jake Riviera, I'm sure he's got something worthwhile to say."*

Knocker: *"Can't stand the geezer. Err, yes, he deserves to be married. Love and cuddles, Knocker."*

The reception at The Clarendon had the feel of an industry bash. Phil Lynott, Graham Parker & The Rumour, Elvis Costello, Ian Dury, Nick Lowe and Rachel Sweet all turned out, along with Stiff employees and faces from the London music scene. In true Stiff style, it made it into the diary columns of the music press. There was plenty to write about.

In the lead-up to the evening's festivities and with imaginations in the office well and truly fired, ex-prog rocker Alan Cowderoy came up with the idea of putting together a house-band especially for the occasion. Andy Murray agreed to play guitar and Nigel Dick the bass in Stiff's own wedding band. Dick had unexpectedly shown off his guitar skills at the Be Stiff end of tour party, jumping up on stage to jam with Wreckless Eric and his band. And he and Murray had both ended up playing guitar in front of 3,000 drunken Aussies, when The Sports had played at Alexandra Palace on ANZAC Day and invited them up on stage.

Rob Keyloch from the Stiff mobile studio (The China Shop) was commandeered to play drums and Liam Sternberg as an additional guitarist. Nick Garnett, then general manager of Virgin Music Publishing and a mate of Murray's, was enlisted as second drummer. None of them fancied singing, so Mary Bird, the girlfriend of Lene Lovich's future drummer Justin Hildreth, and Jock Scot, completed the line-up. A couple of rehearsals took place before The Stiff All-Stars nervously climbed on to the stage at the somewhat shabby venue to play their set of rock 'n' roll covers.

Some of their colleagues might have sniggered into their drinks at the sight of this hastily assembled group. But as they walked off the tiny stage, Ted Carroll from Chiswick collared Nigel Dick and asked if they wanted to record a single. Dick, suspecting it was the drink talking, checked with him a few days later and the label boss confirmed he was serious. The Stiff All-Stars had a record deal, although not with the label from which they had taken their name.

Says Dick: "Like at many record labels, there was a bunch of us who were musicians and who wanted to be rock stars, and for whatever reason we didn't have the luck, the chops, the looks or the ability, but we wanted to play. So, that's what we did. A lot of people used to laugh at us and giggle at us behind our backs, but I think on some level some of them secretly admired us. We did TV shows, we actually did quite a lot of places around London, like The Marquee in Wardour Street. We got to live the rock 'n' roll dream between seven and nine o'clock of an evening, and then had to rush back to the office to work in the morning. We put out four singles in the heyday of singles. It was an amazing experience."

Headlining at Robinson's wedding were The Inmates, a garage band whose debut single, a cover of The Standells' "Dirty Water", had just been released. Signed to Radar, they found themselves jockeying for position with the likes of Yachts and Bram Tchaikovsky as Elvis

Costello, and the label to which he defected, basked in the glow of his No. 2 hit "Oliver's Army". Several months later, they would make it into the Top 40 themselves with a cover of Jimmy McCracklin's "The Walk".

But one other act entertained the guests that night, a group Robinson had an ulterior motive in adding to the bill. A bunch of mates from around North London, Madness had only played their first gig a few months earlier, and were one of a number of groups who were beginning to revive ska. Armed with some melodic songs and boundless energy, they had appeared on Alan Cowderoy and Paul Conroy's radars. But as Robinson had been in Los Angeles overseeing the career of Rachel Sweet and then on tour in Australia with Graham Parker & The Rumour, he'd not had a chance to see this exciting new prospect for himself. His wedding reception presented the perfect opportunity.

Mark Bedford, the group's bassist, remembers: "It was all a bit frantic and Stiff had started having a bit of success. He was getting married, so he was all caught up in that and in his gruff old way he said, 'I haven't got time. I can't get down to see you play, but I want to see you because I don't want to send someone down there … come and play at my wedding'. And he did the great thing, which of course tempts all bands at that early stage, he got out some cash and said, 'I'll give you some money to play at the wedding'. So, that's what we did. It was at the old Clarendon in Hammersmith, and I now realise it had everyone there. Elvis Costello, Jake Riviera and all the people we then came to know who worked at Stiff were there.

"I think we played for about half an hour and we played pretty much the set we would have done at The Hope & Anchor or The Nashville. So it included not only 'The Prince' and 'Madness', but 'My Girl' and most of that first album. In those days, the songs were so short, so it would all be over in half an hour. Cathal [Chas Smash] was still working in Ashford at the time and he came up for the gig and he danced and did his thing. And I remember he cut his hand on something and he was dancing and we were looking down and starting seeing these drops of blood on us and thinking, 'Jesus, what's happening'. It was quite a weird experience really. I think the qualifier for Dave Robinson was that Elvis Costello started dancing, and Dave said, 'I couldn't believe it. If Elvis Costello is dancing then you must be doing something right.' So that's what started it and I think people from Stiff did come and see us at gigs afterwards for a little bit."

Guitarist Chris Foreman adds: "I think some of the Stiff people had seen us and they didn't like us because we weren't 'musos'. But he [Robinson] saw something in us and we did his wedding and it was a good laugh. Elvis Costello was there and I think we dragged him on stage with us. He was a hero of ours, of course, but we weren't too intimidated by him. I do remember we had this brilliant dressing room that had a two-tone carpet, you know, black and white squares, and I said, 'We should do a video in here' and we did 'Bed And Breakfast Man' in there."

Melody Maker reported on the wedding itself, with the headline, "Nick Lowe and Dave Robinson wed – official", cleverly reflecting the fact that love was obviously in the air and Basher had also just tied the knot with Carlene Carter. The singer was the daughter of country music legends Carl Smith and June Carter, and her mother had later married Johnny Cash. Lowe and his long-term girlfriend had taken their marriage vows in Los Angeles while Rockpile were on the west coast leg of a US tour playing support to Blondie. Lowe's hit single "Cruel To Be Kind" was released shortly afterwards and the official video featured actual footage from the wedding.

Madness took their name from a song by Cecil Bustamente Campbell, A.K.A. Prince Buster, and their music was heavily influenced by the foot-stomping music that originated in Jamaica in the fifties. White kids growing up on bleak estates in North London, they had got their passion for music after discovering the records of Roland Alphonso, The Skatalites and The Maytals. Their own twist on ska, however, had also been informed by the urgency of punk and the theatrics of a performer who was as English as jellied eels: Ian Dury.

One night, Foreman and his mate Lee Thompson had wandered into The Tally Ho to find Kilburn & The High Roads playing. The group and its rather sinister-looking singer left an indelible impression on the two lads and they turned up at another gig, bringing another mate, Mike Barson, with them. The three of them began hanging out together and largely inspired by Dury's strange collective, they formed a sax, organ and guitar trio. They experimented with this line-up for a while, before recruiting drummer John Hasler, vocalist Dikron, and Cathal Smyth, "Chas Smash", on bass guitar. And when a friend held a birthday party at his house on 30 June 1977, they played their first ever show. They called themselves The Invaders. Although not a member at that stage, Suggs was at the party and was to take over vocal duties from Dikron before being sacked from the band, although he was re-instated in 1978.

If some of their songs had a fairground feel, then the line-up certainly proved a merry-go-round. By the time they played for the second time, only half of them were still around and the musical chairs went on for a year and a half before the group finally settled on the line-up pop fans around the world would come to know and love. The Invaders played their final gig at the London Filmmakers Co-op in Gloucester Avenue on 1 January 1979, with only a handful of people in attendance. Three months later the band arrived at the Music Machine to support Sore Throat, and discovered Thompson had advertised them as Morris & The Minors, a reference to the vans they rattled around in. No one liked it and it was decided to change it there and then. After bouncing about a few ideas, Foreman suggested Madness.

Then a six-piece outfit, they began gigging more regularly at the Dublin Castle, Hope & Anchor and The Nashville, and it wasn't long before word of this exciting group playing speeded-up ska reached the music press. Ska was being given a second lease of life and the epicentre of activity was Coventry, the multi-cultural city to which many immigrants had gravitated in the fifties and sixties. Musicians there, black and white, were fusing its infectious rhythms with the attitude of punk and new wave to create a vibrant sound that made it fresh and relevant to the disillusioned youth of Britain. The fact most school kids had never even heard of ska made it even more alluring and, for added appeal, these bands had something to say.

One group epitomised ska's new-found voice and political purpose: The Specials. Their set mixed souped-up covers of songs like "The Guns Of Navarone" by The Skatalites and "Longshot Kick The Bucket" by The Pioneers, with gritty original songs about life in broken Britain. Keyboard player Jerry Dammers was not only alive to the potential of the group, but the whole ska scene. Stiff and Rough Trade had shown what could be achieved by small indie labels and, with the same DIY ethos, he formed 2 Tone Records. Chrysalis Records had wanted to sign The Specials, but instead the entrepreneurial musician negotiated a deal for the label. Chrysalis would finance fifteen singles a year and issue at least ten.

Madness was oblivious to the existence of another band playing exactly the same kind of music as them until they ended up on the same bill at the Rock Against Racism gig at Dave Robinson's old haunt of the Hope & Anchor. The Specials invited them to support them at their next London gig at The Nashville and names and addresses were exchanged. Dammers had discovered the perfect addition for his embryonic label.

2 Tone's inaugural single coupled "Gangsters" by The Special AKA vs "The Selecter". It went straight into the chart and, as word of the cool new label with the black and white man began to spread among British kids, Madness got their turn. "The Prince" – released on 2 Tone Records in August 1979, the month after "Gangsters" – was Lee Thompson's tribute to Prince Buster, while the B-side was their cover of "Madness". Both tracks were recorded at the old Stiff favourite of Pathway. On 5 September 1979, Madness made their first appearance on *Top Of The Pops*, and ten days later "The Prince" entered the chart at No. 37. Less than a year after playing their first gig together, Madness were a hit group and record labels, including Warner, Chrysalis and Elton John's Rocket, were banging at their door.

Young and inexperienced they may have been, but Madness had a manager they trusted in one-time member John Hasler and weren't remotely phased by the attention from well-known labels. The fact they already had a hit record also strengthened their bargaining position. Mike Barson's diary confirms they met with Robinson four days after playing at his wedding. He had struck the pianist as "a man of mucho action and no red tape" and had "talked a lot of sense as to what we should do". But Robinson faced tough competition for their signatures and the band held talks with other labels in the weeks that followed.

"We were on 2 Tone, we had a single in the Top 20, so everybody wanted us – everybody," Chris Foreman enthuses. "I was 23 and the youngest band member was probably 17 or 18, but we went to record companies and they said, 'We'll give you two hundred and fifty grand' and we weren't interested. We liked Stiff and we met him [Robinson] in a pub, instead of an office. Stiff were in Alexander Street, which was like someone's house, it was just brilliant. It was the antithesis of other record companies.

"We went to Chrysalis and the guy said to his secretary, 'Have we got a copy of the Madness single?'. He hadn't even heard it and he was going to give us two hundred grand, and we knew even then: 'We're going to have to pay that two hundred grand back'. We weren't impressed. Generally, me and Mike, or Suggs, would go and meet someone; it wouldn't be all six of us. Some people, like Lee, weren't interested at all. But we met Robbo and we liked him, he was down to earth, and he's the top guy. It's not like you're meeting some A&R man. He said, 'Okay, I'll give you ten grand, just so you can all give your jobs up', and he gave us ten grand. I was working at the Post Office and I went sick or something indefinitely, and some time later they wrote me a letter saying I owed them money. So, that was the way it was in that little building."

Bedford too was particularly struck by the fact that in contrast to other labels, their discussions with Stiff involved meeting the guy who ran the label: "From our understanding at the time, you didn't get to see the hierarchy of a record label, but with Stiff there was none of that. Dave was the head of the label and he would show up with the guy in the post room. There was that very democratic thing with Stiff. As we had a lawyer, there was a bit of playing off a couple of companies against each other and I think Dave always says that we 'did' him. At the very last minute, the lawyer threw in the classic lawyer tactic of saying, 'Right Dave, I think they want to sign, but just come in with ...'. I can't actually remember the formal details of the deal, but one thing I do remember which appealed to us, was that Dave had a plan of when to put the record out and he practically gave us a date, straight away."

On 1 October 1979, for an advance of £10,000, Madness signed to Stiff Records in the UK and Sire in the US. The cheque was sufficient for them to pack in their day jobs and set up a bank account at William & Glynn's bank in Camden (they were turned away by other banks for being too scruffy!). The Irishman's charm and anti-corporate style had proved more alluring than the big money offers of Chrysalis and other established companies. Stiff's bold marketing and its association with Elvis Costello and Ian Dury (both of whom were idols for the band) suggested it would be a good fit for an act with a strong visual identity. From Stiff's vantage point, it had a group that had already proved its chart potential and that could provide a route into the extremely lucrative youth market.

Madness were moving on from 2 Tone after just one record. But the band knew from the songs they were producing that it wasn't its natural home. "We had already written that first album," says Bedford. "It was all there, all of us had contributed to that. It was an assembly of all our influences, which weren't all 2 Tone or early ska and reggae. We knew from what we'd written that there would be pop songs on it."

The two tracks on their 2 Tone single and another called "My Girl" had emerged from a recording session overseen by the producer and songwriter Clive Langer. He had played in the art rock outfit Deaf School with Mike Barson's brother Ben and was pursuing a solo career with his own outfit Clive Langer & The Boxes, who were signed to Radar. Deaf School had turned up in the audience at the Hope & Anchor once. For his studio sessions with Madness, Langer had teamed up with Alan Winstanley, who had done some production and engineering for Radar. The resulting album was so successful that the duo would produce almost all their subsequent records and their partnership would span decades.

When a nationwide 2 Tone tour set off in October, Madness were on board. Robinson, seeing a bunch of lads who needed a firm hand, wasted no time in putting his stamp on things. Hasler was still managing the band with help from The Specials' handler Rick Rodgers at Trigger Management. His office was based above a shoe shop on the Kentish Town Road and was a regular hang-out for the band. But Robinson had decided they needed someone more "professional" helping out. So, when rehearsals began for some warm-up gigs ahead of the 2 Tone tour, they discovered he had brought in John "Kellogs" Kalinowski as tour manager.

Some of the dates on the tour were marred by outbreaks of violence. Despite the multi-racial composition of The Specials and The Selecter, ska attracted skinheads and at some venues the bands ran the gauntlet of Nazi chants. Robinson had fired Kellogs after arrests were made and young fans taken to hospital during a show at Hatfield Polytechnic when he wasn't around. But he was reinstated after Madness rallied to his defence and Thompson reportedly got him to apologise on behalf of the whole band. "We went off on the 2 Tone tour with Kellogs tour managing and we got to quite like him because he knew stuff," says Foreman. "He seemed quite aggressive, but he was a hippie really."

Before the tour, it had been agreed Madness would leave early to go on a US tour and, after 29 dates, Dexys Midnight Runners took their place. As The Specials played "Blank Expression" at Ayr Pavilion, the Nutty Boys walked across the stage carrying suitcases and waving goodbye to the audience.

Foreman recalls: "We badly wanted to go to America. Robbo didn't care because Stiff didn't have a presence in America. They had a label and, in retrospect, we should have stayed with Stiff in America. But we just thought, 'Well they're not doing anything', and Seymour Stein at Sire Records was after us, and we just loved him. He was great; a real character. He used to take us out for meals, but he knew music and he was a lovely guy. So, we signed with Sire and we went to America".

From the monotone photo of the band doing their "nutty train" on the cover to its seamless blend of ska and pop, *One Step Beyond* was a triumph. Madness would make better albums, but they would never make a more important one. Released on 26 October 1979, less than a month after they'd signed, it had a bumper fourteen tracks and the sticker on the front told fans to "Pay no more than £3.99" for the privilege. Dave Robinson had his sights firmly set on those long-overlooked pocket money purchases.

In a classic piece of Stiff design, nearly as inventive as 2 Tone's Walt Jabsco, a pork pie hat was placed above a giant letter M, creating a Madness man. The logo, with the name Madness written along its edge, appeared on the back cover, along with various pictures of unofficial band member Chas Smash dancing, and would be reproduced on button badges, T-shirts, patches and posters. The inner sleeve featured photo-booth pictures of fans who'd been asked by one of the music papers to send them in.

In late 1979, however, it was singles in colourful bags and bearing photographs of the bands they'd seen on *Top Of The Pops* that were most eagerly awaited by young record buyers. So, it was critical the right song was plucked from the album and released as a 45, especially as they would be released on the same day. Dave Robinson's money was on the title track.

"One Step Beyond" was an instant smash. The Nutty Boys stomped their way into the chart at No.22 in November 1979 and reached No. 7 during an incredible fourteen-week run. The Selecter and The Specials were also flying high, with "On My Radio" and "A Message To You (Rudy)" respectively making the Top 10. Kids who hadn't even heard of ska until the release of these records were suddenly in thrall to this raw, rather strange music from a faraway land. And Stiff had bagged one of the most exciting acts behind this unexpected revival.

The insistent spoken intro to the Prince Buster cover had been borrowed from another entitled "The Scorcher" and lent the song perfectly to an accompanying video. MTV was still almost two years away and the video had not yet assumed the seminal role it would later play in the commercial success of singles. But Stiff was ahead of the game. Robinson had always seen the pop music and short films as being complementary. For "New Rose", three years earlier, The Damned had been filmed playing live, with the camera veering wildly from one band member to another. Artists on the Stiff package tours had been filmed both on and off stage for promotional road movies that Robinson was personally very excited about, although in the event they were never released. A very visual label, Stiff had sought out visual acts, and in Madness it had a band that was pure television gold.

With 2 Tone blowing the dust off records by some of Kingston's finest, Stiff saw a window of opportunity. While the first artist to have a reggae hit in the UK was Madness's hero Prince Buster, the second had been Desmond Dekker. His guttural, gospel-influenced voice cut through the airwaves in the summer of 1967 when "007" scored a Top 20 hit for Dekker and his band The Aces. But it was "Israelites", released almost two years later and Britain's first No. 1 reggae record, that turned him into Jamaica's first worldwide star.

Within months of his chart-topper, "It Mek" made No. 7 and his searing rendition of reggae legend Jimmy Cliff's "You Can Get It If You Really Want It" got to No. 2 in the summer of 1970. When *The Harder They Come* hit cinema screens starring Cliff and featuring his soundtrack, reggae's popularity soared. But Dekker's didn't, despite "007" being included on it. He did return to the chart in 1975 with a re-release of "Israelites" and then "Sing A Little Song". His career faded though and there was little record company interest in him until the ska revival of 1979 got Stiff thinking. If he topped the charts once, he could do it again, figured Robinson. Stiff's press officer, Nigel Dick, was instrumental in helping get the re-recorded "Israelites" (BUY 70) some chart action. Not an easy task when all the press wanted was to interview Madness.

"I knew as much about him as everybody else did: he was the bloke who did 'Israelites'," Dick rightly recalls. "I rang round the papers and I couldn't get anybody who was interested in interviewing him. I thought, 'Fuck, I've got to get a story out on him somehow', and he was a lovely bloke. So, I said, 'Well Desmond, could you do me a favour and come by the office on Tuesday afternoon and I'll interview you'. So, I did this interview with him and I found out all this stuff, like he basically discovered Bob Marley. They used to work together in a tin factory...

"There was all this fantastic stuff about his first tour with the Israelites, and all the rest of it. So, I wrote the article myself, as if it was an interview with Desmond, and all these people said, 'Yeah, I mean, Desmond, what the fuck, not interested'. And then I started seeing this article published in all these magazines, written by these other people. It was like, 'I wrote that you bastard!' But after the initial fit of pique, and when I actually had a perspective on it, I thought, actually I've just done my job. It doesn't matter who wrote the story."

Dekker's back-story might have been entertaining, but BUY 70 proved one step beyond for "Israelites". Stiff had to settle for a No. 12 hit in Belgium and hope that Madness could take full advantage of the ska renaissance.

Madness had signed on the dotted line with Stiff just eight days before pen was put to paper on another important contract, namely a new distribution deal with CBS Records. Stiff had originally signed a two-year deal with Island, which was distributed by EMI, in early 1977, but this was renegotiated and a new three-year one signed, in July 1977. *My Aim Is True* being its first beneficiary. But when financial problems at EMI led to it being taken over by Thorn, this handed Stiff the opportunity to switch its distribution to CBS before the contract was up.

Fatefully for Lene Lovich, her single "Bird Song" was scheduled for release, three days after the deal was signed. It ended up being distributed by both EMI and CBS, and the momentum she had built with "Lucky Number" and "Say When" was lost. A haunting song and a video to match, filmed at the historic St Pancras Church on Euston Road, it received some airplay and she performed it on *Top Of The Pops*. But after entering the chart at 39, it came to an abrupt halt.

A significant development happened before the year was out. Stiff moved house. Alexander Street had served it well and held many memories for staff and artists alike. Commercial success meant it had outgrown its original home, however, and if it was to continue expanding, larger quarters were required. Stiff didn't go far, relocating to 9-11 Woodfield Road in Westbourne Park on 3 December 1979. The premises had previously housed Front Line, the reggae subsidiary of Virgin Records established in 1978. Shortly before Stiff's arrival, it had been used to store thousands of cardboard cut-outs of the train robber Ronnie Biggs. The glamorised criminal had featured on "No One Is Innocent", a single recorded by the remnants of the Sex Pistols and released on Virgin. To help spread the word about its big move, Stiff designed and produced a cardboard give-away that included a map, its new address, and the photographs and job titles of everyone in the office.

Stiff was certainly thinking big as the removal vans arrived. Plans were being drawn up to charter a 747 and take Ian Dury, Lene Lovich, Madness, Rachel Sweet and Wreckless Eric on a world tour, reported *Melody Maker*. The label had confirmed preparations were underway, but wouldn't release details as "many things are a bit shaky at the moment".

Without doubt, 1979 had been Stiff's most successful year. The big hits that had eluded it in its first two years had finally arrived and the Elcotgrange accounts reflected its dramatic change in fortunes. Its turnover had rocketed from £715,871 in 1978 to £2,509,088 in 1979, and the money generated by its operations had risen from £34,218 to £93,935. Bigger hits meanwhile meant big royalties, and in one year the amount due to artists had increased from £61,351 to £207,449.

Though Stiff's strike rate had improved, for every "Hit Me …" or "One Step Beyond" there were many more singles that had added to the label's costs and failed dismally. Of the 52 singles released up to and including "One Step Beyond", only eight had made the Top 40. A case in point was "Peppermint Lump", a single by 11-year-old Angela Porter, performing as Angie. She was at stage school and had popped up on TV shows like *Rod Hull And Emu* and *Nationwide* when she made her singing debut courtesy of Stiff. The two songs on the record had been written by James Asher, then a staff writer for Pete Townshend's production and publishing company, Eel Pie. The legendary guitarist had been impressed by the songs when he heard them and ended up singing and playing on the record, as well as arranging and producing it. The front cover of the single showed Angie, in school uniform complete with straw boater, and Townshend, nonchalantly leaning against a tree. Released immediately after Ian Dury's "Reasons To Be Cheerful", its sales gave Stiff no reasons to continue with the youngster.

Stiff's penchant for the comedic that had begun with Max Wall had continued with acts like Binky Baker & The Pit Orchestra. Baker, DJ Anne Nightingale's husband, released his single "Toe Knee Black Burn" towards the end of 1978, a send-up of Radio 1's cheesy disc jockey. BUY 41 unsurprisingly sank without trace (it's only lyrics are the title itself repeated throughout the song, stressing different syllables of the DJ's name), but not before *Sounds* slated it and questioned why Stiff was wasting its time on such releases. The record was "an unfortunate example of the current directionless of Stiff", commented the magazine. "Really, when they've got geniuses like Wreckless Eric and Rachel Sweet, why do they bother with jokes where you stop smiling after the first bar and a half?" questioned the reviewer.

Despite two Stiff tours, five singles, two albums, costly adverts in the music press and no shortage of media attention, Wreckless still hadn't troubled the charts. "Hit And Miss Judy" had been a radio-friendly slice of pop, released on orange vinyl and on 7-inch and 12-inch to increase its appeal. But miss it did, further deepening Wreckless's sense of frustration.

Rachel Sweet, like Wreckless, had attracted her fair share of publicity. A photograph of the 16-year-old doing her homework in a train compartment had filled the cover of *Sounds* in April 1979, months after the Be Stiff Tour. The interview with her covered three pages. Asked if she knew what her next record would be, Sweet replied: "Probably. It won't be another oldie. I don't want to be stereotyped. You get a girl comes out with two records that are oldies and right away everybody thinks that's all you do." But perhaps believing it had hit on a winning formula with her brassy cover of "B-A-B-Y", Stiff had followed it up with two more: Del Shannon's "I Go To Pieces", and Elvis Presley's "Baby Let's Play House".

The headline above the *Sounds* feature had been telling, listing the things that Rachel Sweet was not. "Stiff's alternative to Little Jimmy Osmond", "Five foot nothing of red-hot jail bait", and "A child with the body of a woman, the passions of a tigress", were just some of the epithets the music paper came up with. A makeover was required and when her second album *Protect The Innocent* appeared in February 1980, Stiff had clearly decided she was something entirely different. The bouncy, fresh-faced teen image some had accused her label of cynically exploiting had been replaced by that of a sultry young woman. Dressed in shiny black leather, in the dark photograph by Brian Griffin, she held a girl in a chair, her black gloves covering her mouth. The transformation was marked and the intentions behind it utterly transparent.

In the studio, there was a complete change of personnel. Liam Sternberg had been dumped in favour of post-punk producer Martin Rushent and Alan Winstanley, soon to be Clive Langer's production associate for Madness. Backing on this occasion was rumoured to have been provided by Fingerprintz, the band that had played with her for the Be Stiff shows in New York. Sweet's desire to have more original material on the album was achieved with two of her own songs and two co-compositions among the twelve tracks. Where sixties soul, country and pop influenced *Fool Around*, here the songs were darker and leaned more towards new wave. Covers traversed an array of styles, from The Velvet Underground's "New Age" and The Damned's "New Rose", to Graham Parker's "Fool's Gold" and Robert Palmer's "Jealous".

Two singles were taken from *Protect The Innocent* as Stiff showed its determination to break Sweet. Sadly, while the B-side "I've Got A Reason" was used in a BASF TV commercial, the A-side "Fool's Gold" was ignored. "Spellbound" by Fingerprintz' Jimmie O'Neill was then given the disco treatment, but what he succeeded in delivering for Lovich with "Say When", he couldn't repeat for the girl she had played cards with on the train. It signalled the end of her time at Stiff and she picked up her career with CBS. Her duet with Rex Smith on "Everlasting Love" reached No. 35 in the UK, equalling the performance of "B-A-B-Y".

Liam Sternberg cites poor management and unsuitable material for Sweet's lack of success in the UK. "Stiff immediately wanted to straighten her out, which they did and it was horrible," he says. "It never happened for her because she was given crap repertoire by terrible A&R people and that's it. And she never had good management. That's very important, because an artist can be quite fragile and easily swayed, however strong their art is. They can be bent out of whack and they need a manager to protect them and their field of creative action. People will say anything about music: everybody's an expert in music."

Second albums are generally said to be difficult and those on Stiff's roster were doing nothing to challenge the theory. Dury, Wreckless and Sweet's follow-ups had failed to live up to the promise of their debuts and consequently much was riding on *Flex*, Lene Lovich's successor to *Stateless*. Lovich's band had been touring almost solidly for a year and Ron Francoise, Bobby Irwin and Don Snow had left to play full-time with The Sinceros. Lovich and Chappell had now been joined by Justin Hildreth on drums and Mark Chaplin on bass. One-time Roogalator member Nick Plytas and American musician Dean Klevatt had meanwhile arrived to share keyboard duties. The *Stateless* production team of Lovich, Chappell and Roger Bechirian oversaw the sessions, although Alan Winstanley came in to finish things off when they ran out of time.

Lovich was one of Stiff's most photogenic artists and the sleeve for *Flex* captured her mysterious aura. Wearing a wedding dress, with her make-up and dark plaits providing the only contrast, she brought to mind Dickens' Miss Havisham, transported forwards in time. Photographer Brian Griffin's idea of doing the shoot inside a fermentation tank at the Guinness factory in Park Royal had further contributed to its oddly unsettling allure.

"We were inside the tank and it was massive," says Lovich. "It was really funny because you couldn't speak to each other because as soon as you uttered a word, the voice just went into a weird echo thing. So, you had to get right up next to each other and whisper in your ear. Actually, Brian and I never spoke much. It was just the most amazing photographic experience. I didn't feel any pressure. A lot of photographers wind me up, so that I end up looking like a monster. But Brian was just intuitive and somehow we just connected. We just did stuff; we didn't talk about it at all."

Commenting on the wedding dress and veil, Lovich says: "It wasn't a costume – it was just a load of old rags. I was very into curtains at the time because you always have a lot of volume, so I used to be buying lots of curtains. I probably went through a couple of years when I didn't have any normal clothes, just a suitcase full of bits."

Flex contained an enthralling set of songs. Lovich's shrill warbling and the baritone undercurrent of "Bird Song" made for a chilling opening. Her interpretation of The Four Seasons' "The Night" was as memorable as it was unexpected (this was released as a single in the US), and it was impossible not to get snagged on the pop hooks of "Wonderful One" and "Joan". Overall, however, it seemed less satisfying than *Stateless,* lacking a song with the poise of "Too Tender To Touch" or the pure pop class of "Lucky Number", and the critics didn't find it to their taste. It reached No.19 and spent just five weeks in the album chart. *Stateless,* by comparison, had stuck it out for three months.

"Angels" was deemed to have the best chance as a single and a video was filmed in the freezing cold one night in an alleyway beside Stiff's offices. Another shot from the Guinness factory, this time featuring Lovich and Chappell, made for an eye-catching cover. But it wasn't a hit. In a final attempt to salvage a hit from *Flex,* "What Will I Do Without You" (written by Chris Judge Smith) was issued as a single and with a bonus live four-track EP. But like "Angels", it peaked at 58.

A raft of one-off singles by unknown acts such as Michael O'Brien, Pointed Sticks, The GTs and The Feelies were all afforded BUY status, only to die a death. Another, the The 45s was said to have been Stiff's poorest selling single ever, failing to even register in the chart's lowest reaches. "The big labels survive by putting out a lot of product and hoping some of it sticks," Robinson had told one journalist. [40] Stiff, it appeared, was doing just the same.

Nigel Dick outlines the Catch-22 Stiff faced: "It probably realised it had to sell more records. Initially Stiff's records were distributed by Island, which in turn was distributed by EMI. What happens is that when something starts twitching, and maybe it could turn into a hit, then you ring up the people at Island and say, 'This new Kirsty MacColl track is being played a lot on the radio this week, and if we can get the records into all the Woolworths over the weekend, there is a chance we can get into the charts next week.' Then Island has to go to EMI and say, 'Can we have extra production capacity to press up these Kirsty MacColl records?' And then EMI has to go back to Island and say, 'Well, do you want us to press up Kirsty MacColl or do you want us to press up that new Tom Petty album?' Or, 'I thought you guys wanted to have another 50,000 U2 albums out this week?'

"So, eventually what happens is you do a deal directly with EMI. So you do a new deal with EMI – and eventually I think we had our deal with CBS – and you say to them, 'We have to have the ability for you to press up 100,000 records for us – per week if necessary. So, if CBS isn't doing very much business, then they'll ring you up and say, 'We've got space in our production capacity for 100,000 records, and you've only asked for 5,000 and unless you start using it, we're going to give it to somebody else'".

In a sea of misses, Madness sailed in with a hit. The band was ending the year on a high. November had seen them on their first American tour, playing clubs in New York, Boston and Philadelphia before flying west to perform in Los Angeles and finally San Francisco, where support came from hardcore punks The Dead Kennedys. Back on home soil in December, they had recorded a session for the BBC's *Old Grey Whistle Test*, presented by DJ Anne Nightingale. They appeared on the show with Jane Aire & The Belvederes and The Specials among others, and performed new songs, "Night Boat To Cairo" and "Embarrassment".

Four days before Christmas, Stiff released their second single, "My Girl". Founded on a steady ska beat, it was a sublime piece of pop by Mike Barson that vindicated both their decision to shake off the musical shackles of 2 Tone and Robinson's determination to sign them. The following day, Madness had a dream opportunity to promote the record to their younger fans with an appearance on BBC1's Saturday morning children's show *Multi-Coloured Swap Shop*.

A momentum was building and, as a sign of thing to come, the band which had been invited to play at Robinson's wedding just months before, were given the honour of playing *Top Of The Pops* into the eighties. Performing in front of a giant 1980 sign and dressed in white dinner jackets, black trousers and black bow ties, they were a confident band for a confident new decade. "My Girl" made No.1 in the UK and France.

Stiff's ship had come in.

10

America Gets Stiff

A map of the United States with an erection and the words "America Gets Stiff", was how the label announced its deal with Arista in *Billboard* magazine in February 1978. Stiff didn't pull its punches whatever its audience. But while it may have conquered the British charts and enjoyed No. 1 records in other parts of Europe, it had still to make an indent in America. Stiff vowed to take the US – and with some of its native acts.

Stiff's American headquarters were at 157 West 57th Street in Manhattan. Overseeing operations and then co-president of Stiff with Robinson was Allen Frey. A canny booking agent, he established a relationship with Pink Floyd in 1970 while living in England. When he moved back to the US the band went with him to the Ashley Famous Agency and he continued to book them right through the seventies. Frey also oversaw the careers of Rockpile, Costello and Parker in the US through A.R.S.E Management, and had set up the Stiff office there.

The distribution agreement Stiff had forged with CBS in the States and Island in the UK had been born out of necessity, not desire. So, it was no surprise when it announced the arrival of Stiff America.

"Stiff Label To Solo On Limited Basis" read the headline on the story in *Billboard* on 10 November 1979. Outside its arrangements with Columbia and Epic, both owned by CBS, it was going out on its own with a label that would be "independently pressed, distributed and marketed". All releases on this self-sufficient new label would be pressed and shipped in limited quantities and sold on a "cash on delivery" basis, with no provision to return unsold product. Each record wholesaled at $3.99. *Billboard* described the move as being similar to the approach taken by Virgin and Island when some of their releases were not deemed sufficiently commercial for Atlantic or Warners. These had instead been released through New Jersey-based distributor JEM, the parent company of Passport Records. Wreckless Eric got the honour of the launch album, and single with *The Whole Wide World* and "Take The Cash (K.A.S.H)".

By January 1980, Frey had a team of five people working with him, according to a Stiff family tree painstakingly traced by Nigel Dick and published in *Music Week*. General Manager was Barry Taylor, director of Stiff marketing Marion Harris, director of promotion Lynn Gilbert, and "office undertakers" Steve Bonano and Nancy Lizza. "Neatly situated across the street from the Russian Tea Room and Carnegie Hall, Stiff Records in NYC spends its day bravely converting the American music business and listening public to the 'Woodfield Rd' way of thinking," wrote Dick. "As yet it's early days, but the landslide is imminent." Such bravado was a characteristic of Stiff on both sides of the Atlantic and by this point Madness had played Stateside for the first time. What few could have predicted was that as the eighties dawned, it was New York City that would spawn the British label's most outrageous act.

Sleazy, deafeningly loud and shocking, The Plasmatics were every parent's worst nightmare. Spearheaded by Wendy O. Williams, an ex-porn star with peroxide blonde hair, suspenders and black gaffer tape on her nipples, they blew up Cadillacs, took sledgehammers to TVs and laid waste to guitars with chainsaws. Their terrifying stage shows, that included the mock hanging of rhythm guitarist Wes Beech, were a salacious cocktail of Alice Cooper mock-horror and car crash rock 'n' roll. Wherever and whenever they played, controversy was on the bill. Better still, from a Stiff perspective, publicity was guaranteed. One-time bass player Jean Beauvoir commented that:

Being in The Plasmatics as a rule was a danger and something we all took on. Wendy O Williams, our lead singer from Plasmatics, was a flamboyant, quite extravagant woman: foam on her breasts, a sledgehammer, black tights, I mean just outrageous. She'd do whatever she felt like doing. She'd help really bring the band to a different level by being just totally outrageous. [42]

Wendy Orlean Williams (christened to spell WOW) was born in New York, dropped out of high school and formed The Plasmatics after meeting Yale University art school graduate Rod Swenson. A face in New York's alternative scene in the late seventies, he put on live sex shows in two theatres in Times Square under the name Captain Kink. When the city's mayor launched a vice crackdown, he went back to his real name and used his fine arts degree background to make videos for Patti Smith, The Dead Boys and The Ramones, as well as other underground acts.

Swenson became involved with Williams after she replied to a casting call ad for his show "Captain Kink's Sex Fantasy Theater", and in early 1978 he started forming a band around her. Chins hit the floor when the group made their debut at CBGBs and within weeks word had spread like wildfire among New York's underground fraternity. The Plasmatics were born.

EPs were released on their own Vice Squad Records and fans queued around the block to see them at various New York venues. So notorious were the group's shows that, despite no commercial success, they headlined the 3,000-seater Palladium in New York in November 1979. Cavorting with her breasts out and in cut-off shorts and bright red boots, Williams and her band – Ritchie Stotts, lead guitar, Stu Deutsch drums, Wes Beech, rhythm guitar and Chosei Funahara, bass – made a devastating impact.

"Wendy gleefully picked up the sledge hammer and began smashing in the windows of the Cadillac," wrote Stanley Mieses, reviewing the show for *The New Yorker*. "Then what appeared to be sticks of explosive were shoved into the Caddy's interior and, boom, the doors and dashboard blew off."

The Plasmatics broke every taboo all in the one show and must have frightened the hell out of record companies in the US. But Stiff weren't so queasy. After flying out to New York to see the band for themselves and confirming the rumours were true, Stiff signed them. "Butcher Baby" was released as a single. The band filmed the video in a meat locker.

Salivating at the prospect of unleashing their shocking acquisition on the UK, Stiff organised a headline show at Hammersmith Odeon; the only British gig by the group. It was scheduled for 8 August 1980, with support from heavy metal group Vardis. The Plasmatics' debut album *New Hope For The Wretched* would be released at the same time. "Exploit The Plasmatics Before They Exploit You" urged *Sounds* above a caption competition. The stakes were high. First prize was a pair of tickets to the show, two T-shirts, and a piece of the car Williams would trash on stage. The runner-up would get tickets plus half the guitars she would sever with a chainsaw. There was also a booby prize for the five worst entries, "a genuine used (giggle) pair of gaffer tape strips as used by Wendy at a recent gig". All winners would receive a 12-inch copy of their single "Butcher Baby".

A frantic media scrum awaited the band when they touched down in London. Williams had changed into a nurse's uniform on board and emerged promising to "give a cultural enema to the British people". Before she could perform the procedure though, the Greater London Council had to carry out health and safety checks due to the group's fondness for pyrotechnics. Its officers were adamant: the exploding car sequence had to be cut from the show or it couldn't go ahead. Rod Swenson was furious and flatly refused to make any such concession or any other changes to the show. So, the gig was cancelled, leaving Stiff with costs running into thousands of pounds.

"The next day I put together a press conference and writers from every single major UK paper showed up with photographers – huge coverage," said Dick. "The band climbs on the plane, flies back to New York without playing a single note in the UK. And that was the release of *New Hope For The Wretched*." [42]

Fans in England couldn't see the band, but at least they could enjoy the record sleeve. A white Cadillac had come to a halt in a swimming pool. Williams sat on the roof, her breasts covered only with electrical tape. On the bonnet was Stotts in a giant life-belt, clutching his V-shaped guitar. He was dressed in a tutu, shiny blue tights and matching Mohican. Impressively, given The Plasmatics had never performed in the UK, the album reached No. 55. "Butcher Baby" – pressed on marbled and also blood-splattered vinyl – had achieved the exact same position that summer.

By the time another single, "Monkey Suit", was issued in the same vinyl, much of the initial hype had burned out and it proved to be the band's last UK release. A second album, *Beyond The Valley Of 1984* was released on Stiff America in 1981, and Williams continued to court controversy. She was arrested in Milwaukee for simulating masturbation with a sledgehammer and then charged with battery of a police officer as a result of the ensuing *mêlée*. She was later cleared. In Cleveland, she was held on obscenity charges and again acquitted. The Plasmatics landed a worldwide deal with Capitol Records and released a third studio album before being dropped. They disbanded the following year.

Pursuing a solo career, Williams was nominated for a Grammy for Best Female Rock Vocal Performance in 1985, and her influence would endure for longer than her equipment. However, her eventful life ended in tragedy. In 1998, her long-time partner Swenson returned to the home they shared in Connecticut to discover she had gone into nearby woods and shot herself. She was 48.

Commenting on the group's legacy, Beauvoir said: "I think what the band left behind in the music industry was very important in terms of theatrics and making artists feel they could go the extra mile and I kind of wish there was more of that these days." [42]

Around a year after The Plasmatics had made their CBGBs debut, Dave Robinson had been in the dive in New York's Bowery district to see a very different local band taking its tentative steps. Dirty Looks were a trio with short hair, skinny ties and the kind of new wave/power pop sound that was doing swift business in the UK. Hailing from Staten Island, vocalist and guitarist Patrick Barnes, bassist Marco Sin, and drummer Peter Parker had only played about ten gigs when they were spotted and snapped up by Stiff from under the noses of local A&R men.

Dirty Looks were whisked over to London to record an album produced by Tim Friese-Greene, who would emerge as the force behind Talk Talk. The eponymously titled album, which included the singles "Lie To Me" and "Let Go", was released in the UK that summer. To launch it in the US, the band and a film crew climbed aboard a flatbed truck and played outside the CBS/Epic offices in New York, entertaining office workers on their lunch break and attracting the attention of the NYPD. Incredibly, it sold 100,000 copies, making it Stiff's biggest-selling album ever in the US.

By contrast, *Dirty Looks* was a damp squib in Britain, and Stiff's loud trumpeting of the record drew fire from the *NME's* Paul Morley. His savage review provoked some lively correspondence with Nigel Dick, who had written the press release and loved the group. Dick remembers the spat: "I thought they were great and really had what it took, and he absolutely butchered their album in his review and made a big deal out of trivialising my press release. His conclusion was basically, 'This is a band pushed by a label which has come up with a load of comedians and during punk that was fine. But now we've all grown past that and realised what real value is.' I was trying to fight that. My response was, 'We are real music fans, we really care about music.' And his response to that was, 'I'm Paul Morley, what the fuck do you know about music?'"

In the glare of the Californian sun, another act with potentially huge appeal had appeared. The Go-Go's had honed their pop songs in the same scruffy Los Angeles venues Backstage Pass had passed through a couple of years earlier. The all-girl line-up had cut a five-song demo at the city's Gold Star Studios and appeared to tick every box. They sounded amazing, looked great, and wrote all their own material, an attribute highly prized by Robinson. Stiff were understandably quick to act.

When Madness played the Whisky A Go Go on Sunset Strip on 2 December 1979, the queens of the LA scene with a reputation for wild partying appeared on the $4 bill. The line-up was Belinda Carlisle, vocals, Jane Wiedlin, guitar, Kathy Valentine, bass, Charlotte Caffey, guitar and keyboards, and Gina Shock, drums. Musically – and for at least two of the respective band members, personally – there was an immediate chemistry.

"At sound check, I clicked with the group's lead singer, Graham McPherson, who went by the name Suggs," recalled Carlisle. "By show-time, we were flirting and having a good time watching each other on stage." [44] Nothing was to become of any potential romance, and anyway Suggs had a girlfriend back home in the shape of Bette Bright. However the mutual friendship that developed between the two bands caused Madness to ask the Go-Go's to be their support act on their UK tour, an offer which the girls readily accepted.

"We Got The Beat" was released in July 1980 – one of the most glorious two and a half minutes in Stiff's history. Announcing itself with Shock's tub-thumping drums, it was a textbook piece of power pop, the driving new wave rhythm cut through with Carlisle's sun-drenched Californian vocal. Inexplicably, despite the band's obvious appeal, high-profile support slots in the UK and a front cover of *Record Mirror*, the single didn't chart. But when copies reached the US they became hot property and IRS signed them up and released an album, *Beauty And The Beat*. It soared to No 1 in the US, spending more than a year in the *Billboard* chart, and "We Got The Beat" climbed to No. 2. Only Joan Jett & The Blackhearts' anthemic "I Love Rock 'n' Roll" denied it the top spot. Not for the first time, Stiff had to be content with the kudos and not the financial rewards.

One artist for whom America had proved a somewhat bruising experience was Graham Parker, represented Stateside by Mercury Records. For anyone who had followed his career and listened to his records, Graham Parker & The Rumour seemed a natural fit with Stiff. But despite playing a key role in his transformation from petrol pump attendant to an acclaimed artist playing large theatres, Robinson had not had the chance to sign him. Until 1979, that is.

Robinson had been delighted when Phonogram had given the precocious singer-songwriter a deal less than 24 hours after Charlie Gillett had played his demo. Phonogram was a big player and his debut album *Howlin' Wind* had been lavished with praise following its release on its Vertigo label in the summer of 1976. The record made the UK Top 20, as indeed did the subsequent *Heat Treatment* and *Stick To Me*. *Rolling Stone* named him artist of the year in 1977. Massive things had been expected of the British Bruce Springsteen and his red-hot group who seemed able to blend completely diverse genres into a cohesive and heady sound and had come to save rock 'n' roll. But while Elvis Costello rose triumphantly on the shoulders of punk, Parker had been elbowed to one side in the stampede. If ever there was a "Man Out Of Time" as Britain gobbed on its new heroes, it was he.

Parker says: "When I started I was with Mercury, who didn't give a shit, but I don't blame them as much as Dave did. The reason was there was no new wave, there was no punk, there was nowhere to put us. Even though *Rolling Stone* and a lot of hip critics liked us, those people were also hearing those obscure punk records, and hearing things from Akron that the public couldn't.

"So, they grabbed Graham Parker & The Rumour and they thought we were it. But there was no market. Then the Sex Pistols broke the wall, and suddenly Costello is that quirky, weird English guy, and I was kind of left in limbo. There was no marketing. It wasn't Mercury's fault *per se*. They were making money from their back catalogue, whoever was big on those labels. It would have been radio-friendly, AOR, what became called 'corporate rock', all to do with Journey and Boston and all this stuff. And that's what the radio played, and we didn't fit in."

He adds: "As late as '79, the record company was saying to Dave, 'We gotta break him in the Midwest. Let's put him on a tour opening for Journey'. We opened for Journey – after punk! We're still out there playing to 10,000 kids who were saying, 'Fuck off English faggots' because they don't know guys with short hair who aren't wearing satin bell-bottoms. They didn't get it – that was it. There were niches of up to a million in sales for people like The Clash and Elvis Costello. But we didn't fit that either."

Contrary to what some may have assumed, Parker's career wasn't snuffed out by punk. He continued to command large audiences, toured the world and when Bob Dylan played to an estimated 200,000 people at Blackbushe Aerodrome in Surrey in 1978, Parker was an invited guest. Arista paid him an advance of around £500,000 when Clive Davis signed him for the US in 1979, and his fifth album *Squeezing Out Sparks* gave him his highest *Billboard* chart placing of 40. In the UK it reached 18, Parker's then second-highest position. Many artists would have given their right arm for such sales figures, especially during a music industry slump.

Parker says: "I was still on Arista, but I was free in the UK because Phonogram still had my records: they had *Squeezing Out Sparks* in England still. It was a four-album deal; the live record didn't count. Everyone says I did the *Parkerilla* to break the deal, but I did it because everyone does a live album after they've done three studio albums. We still had to do four studio albums. But Mercury had let us go before *Squeezing Out Sparks*; that's what happened, thankfully. Phonogram wouldn't let us go. *Squeezing Out Sparks* came out on Phonogram in the UK and Arista in the States, then we were free, so he [Dave] said to me, 'How about coming out on Stiff?' And I thought, 'Well, you're a fucking successful label now, I'm not laughing at you anymore, it's not crackpot.'"

To mark his long-awaited freedom from Mercury Records in the US, Robinson came up with an idea. "Dave said, 'Write a whole album of hate songs about Mercury', and I wrote one, 'Mercury Poisoning'," says Parker. "So, they put that out on grey vinyl, another Dave idea, of course." The grudge record was released as a 12-inch promo in the US towards the end of 1979. The Stiff office anonymously posted 200 copies to the British media, in an attempt to stir up controversy back home. Disappointingly, no one took the bait.

If Parker was to bring to Stiff some of the commercial success he'd already had, Robinson knew he needed a sound to fit the times. *Squeezing Out Sparks* had been his most stripped-down album and the closest he'd come to new wave, calling to mind records like

Joe Jackson's debut *Look Sharp*. For an even more modern follow-up, Robinson teamed Parker with hot shot American producer Jimmy Iovine. He had come straight from working on Tom Petty's breakthrough album *Damn The Torpedoes,* which had yielded two singles that made the Top 15 of the *Billboard* Hot 100. He'd also produced the Patti Smith Group's album *Easter*, which included her hit "Because The Night".

"He'd been after me since '76," says Parker. "I met him at Stiff Records' first offices on Alexander Street. Dave introduced himself and said, 'You've got to meet Jimmy Iovine'. He'd talked about him before because Dave was obsessed with drum sounds and he said, 'This guy got the drum sound on "Because The Night", Patti Smith record, huge drum sound'. So, he introduced him to me and I was like, 'Hi'. Years later Jimmy said, 'I met Graham before we did the record, *The Up Escalator*, and he didn't say anything to me. I thought, "I guess this is punk"'. "I communicated in grunts," Parker explains. "I was like, 'Fuck everyone. I'm better than all of these people'. So, I really didn't respond to him. But when 1980 came along and he'd had a big hit with Tom Petty, *Damn The Torpedoes*, and Dave was still very actively involved in trying to get me to sound like something."

The Up Escalator, released on Stiff, became Parker's best performing album in the UK, reaching No. 11 and spending ten weeks on the chart. Bruce Springsteen was a guest vocalist and Danny Federici from his E Street Band played keyboards, along with Nicky Hopkins, following the departure of Bob Andrews. In what would prove to be his last record with The Rumour, they weren't credited on the cover. "They were credited on the back," says Parker. "But Dave said, 'We should just have you on the cover', and I said, 'That's okay with me', and The Rumour didn't seem to mind. They knew they'd been sort of hired to be my backing band."

What it didn't do was produce any hit singles. "Stupefaction" and the subsequent "Love Without Greed", backed with a live version of "Mercury Poisoning", did nothing commercially. "This record speaks for itself" read the matrix and so did the sales. The album would be his first and last for Stiff, although the label would issue one more thing before he moved on – a novel.

Years earlier, in his tripped-out, hippie phase, he'd written a sci-fi book entitled *The Great Trouser Mystery*. His attempt at fiction remained stored away in a drawer until, in 1980, Parker met an illustrator called

Willy Smax who had offered to work with him on it. Ever up for a new venture, Robinson excitedly offered to publish it through Stiff, and it was even reviewed on *The Old Grey Whistle Test*. However, the book marked the final chapter in Parker's long association with his manager. Robinson was sacked. Parker comments: "It was one of those things that I knew he was on the Stiff thing and I knew I'd have to fire him, as it were, and in 1980 that happened."

Three years after *My Aim Is True* moved 300,000 copies in the US, Stiff's American ambitions were very much alive. But by the autumn of 1980, there were matters of concern. *Billboard* reported in November the label had "reorganized its faltering American operation with a dual distribution deal". Stiff releases passed up by CBS would be handled in future through traditional independent distributors. Bruce Kirkland, a New Zealander who had been working for Stiff in London for 18 months, was sent to New York to oversee things. John Gillespie, formerly of Sire, would meanwhile supervise production.

Stiff, Kirkland told *Billboard*, had tried without success to sell records that CBS had not been interested in directly to dealers. Instead, it would now have formal deals with five distributors. Breaking Ian Gomm, Ian Dury and Lene Lovich on Stiff/Epic remained a priority. But that didn't mean it couldn't sell 20,000 or 40,000 units outside that agreement. Stiff's aim was to build a market through "college radio, dance rock clubs, and through shops specialising in this product", said Kirkland. "We are laying the groundwork for the future. Radio formats are going to change. AOR and Top 40 radio are all going through a change, and something will come out of it, and we will be ready for it."

Albums by The Plasmatics, Desmond Dekker, Jona Lewie and Any Trouble were being released in the US by Stiff the following week. In *Billboard*, Kirkland conceded that "everybody" was saying the timing was wrong. Radio formats were tied up and retailers were too committed to selling the major artists to experiment. "But we don't want our product to back up," said Kirkland. "And this is a new orientation for us. We have a new presser, a new jacket manufacturer as well, and this is our opportunity to feel our way in".

To create a fresh buzz around its new "product", Stiff was to resurrect a tried and tested formula. Son Of Stiff would be the third and final package tour. This time audiences would be treated to Dirty Looks, The Equators, Joe "King" Carrasco & The Crowns, Any Trouble and Tenpole Tudor, and their travels would take in the UK, Europe and the US. Interestingly, this was not the line-up *Melody Maker* had previously reported and nor was the tour on the same scale. Ian Dury, Madness, Lene Lovich, Rachel Sweet and Wreckless Eric were to have been sent on a "world tour in a chartered 747" calling in on the US, Europe, Asia and India. "Stiff hope to break bands on a worldwide basis in the same way that British tours established their acts here", said the article published in December 1979.

But when the time came to put the tour together, Stiff's priorities had clearly changed. Lovich hadn't capitalised on her initial chart successes, her relationship with Robinson had cooled, and she had no record to plug. Sweet's sensational start with "B-A-B-Y" had also proved to be her zenith and she was now Stiff's forgotten woman. Wreckless Eric's involvement in the previous two tours had not produced even a minor hit and a third throw of the dice would have made the bill look tired.

Stiff needed to break new acts if it were to service its rapidly increasing costs. Wreckless bitterly contested the label hadn't done enough to promote and support him. Stiff countered that it had gone above and beyond to get him the recognition and sales he deserved but, for whatever reason, commercial success hadn't happened. Ian Dury hated playing in the US, where there had proved to be a limited appetite for him, and Madness were riding the crest of a wave in Britain and had no need for such a platform.

The formula was the same: five acts, a rotating bill, press hitching a ride and a film-crew making a movie. But Son Of Stiff was different in one key respect – the acts were total unknowns. Paul Du Noyer in *NME* observed that "Stiff ain't what they used to be. This year's models seem to suffer when they're compared – as compared they inevitably are – to their predecessors of previous years."

Before the coach tour kicked off for real, each act played a show at The Marquee in London's Wardour Street, and punters could pay £1.50 to see one show or just £4 for all five. The UK tour began at Leeds University on 1 October 1980 and closed with four shows at venues in London. The Bandwagon then continued on to Europe, and after that, America. If journalists saw the tour as the least interesting, it was easily the most costly. Stiff was investing $200,000 in the ambitious expedition, according to *Billboard*.

Son Of Stiff did have one hugely charismatic figure, who, because of his impeccable punk credentials, was known to audiences. Edward Tudor Pole had a cameo role in *The Great Rock 'n' Roll Swindle*, Julien Temple's semi-fictional movie about The Sex Pistols. Trained at RADA, the well-spoken actor played a lunatic cinema attendant while performing "Who Killed Bambi?"

The leering singer then took to the microphone to lead the Pistols in the title song. In an extended diatribe he derided Elvis Presley, Mick Jagger, Bob Dylan and other leading rock figures, before starting on the Pistols themselves. In the film and on the accompanying soundtrack, the self-styled Tudor Pole also did vocals on a cover of Bill Haley's "Rock Around The Clock".

For a short spell in 1978, Tudor Pole had been considered as a possible replacement for John Lydon in the Sex Pistols. He survived four or five rehearsals in the room in Denmark Street where the group hung out and practised. "That was a blag – getting into the Sex Pistols for five or six weeks," says Tudor Pole. "A lot of adrenaline there, especially as I don't culturally come from the same place as any of them came from. That made it even more edgy. But Steve Jones; he was so nice to me. I thought, 'He's not going to like me because I'm not working class from Shepherd's Bush'. But he was a sweetheart."

However, the death of Sid Vicious on 2 February 1979 prompted an abrupt change of plan for him at Denmark Street. Says Tudor Pole: "When Sid Vicious died, I was no longer going to be the new singer of the Sex Pistols, because that all went down the pan. I said to Malcolm, 'I'm going to form my own group and I'll call it Tenpole Tudor', because he gave me that name, in a way. He said, 'Tenpole, we've done rock 'n' roll. I want you to come to Paris. I've got a friend there and I want you to make love to underage girls and sing at the same time'.

"I said, 'Oh come on, look. No I can't do that, Malcolm, I'd never get the horn!' He said, 'We'll see to that. Don't worry about that'. I said, 'How young?' He said, 'Only 15 or 14 – no younger'. I said, 'I don't fancy it, and anyway, when you're having a shag, you're not really in the mood for singing. It's a different ball game – no pun intended'. So anyway, he went off and God knows what he did … he needed a salve and a balm to his heartache because he was suddenly ousted from the controls. And he was a total artist himself, so it was like taking away Van Gogh's paints."

Tenpole Tudor had no difficulty getting gigs. On cramped stages, the lanky singer cut a colourful and theatrical figure, hurling himself around manically, throwing shapes that were as random as his clothes. Around him, guitarist Bob Kingston, bassist Dick Crippen and drummer Gary Long, created a suitably wild sound that fused rock 'n' roll, rockabilly and punk. They frequently played to rooms with about 50 people in them and often to the same faces. That changed overnight when *The Great Rock 'n' Roll Swindle* hit British cinemas, bestowing instant punk cachet on Tudor Pole and his group.

"We were playing at The Nashville and suddenly it was packed," says Tudor Pole. "Even Chrissie Hynde was in the audience at the front and she threw me her handkerchief. I thought, 'Makes a change'. It was really exciting. So, suddenly there was a bit of a buzz around the name and my dad had been on the bus and he's overheard a kid saying, 'Tenpole Tudor and Adam & The Ants – them two are the two great bands'. And I was pleased to hear that."

The noise around Tenpole Tudor was cranked up another notch when *Sounds'* Gary Bushell went to see and interview them, resulting in a double page spread in August 1980. "Pole-Axed" read the headline beneath a picture of the singer in a paint-splattered jacket, two-tone chequered trousers and Dr Martens in mid-kick.

Not long after the article appeared, Dave Robinson came to one of their shows, where he would make a characteristically canny move, as Tudor Pole says: "We were playing Dingwalls and we were quite hot at the time and lots of record company people were there that night, we'd heard. And we loved rockabilly, all rock 'n' roll, but there was a rockabilly in the audience who misunderstood what I was saying and thought I was taking the piss out of rockabilly. This was near the end of the gig. He hurled a glass at me and it hit my head, cut my forehead and blood was coming down and I remember thinking, 'Oh, this is so great, so punk'.

"We did 'My Girl' as an encore, a pretty straight version and we played it as best we could. There was a tiny little dressing room at Dingwalls and Dave Robinson was the only one who came backstage to see if I was all right and tend to my wound. It looked much worse than it felt; with all the adrenaline you don't feel it in the battle. Gigs were just like battle in a way. You're so pumped up, you're not going to feel anything. He came back and bathed it a bit, and I appreciated that. No other record company boss did, so that was one point in his favour."

Robinson went to see the band again and a meeting was arranged. The band's initial impression had been that he was a "nice guy", but in the Stiff office, Tudor Pole found the Irishman "really brutal and unsmiling, frightening – a little bit scary". As with Madness, Robinson wasn't offering more money than other labels. But he made it clear he meant business and that if they signed with Stiff, things would happen.

"He said; 'Well, how much do you need then, as an advance? Work out what you need.' 'Well, we need a van and then we need money for rehearsal rooms'. He said, 'Put it all down on a bit of paper and then hand it to me.' We were just kids, man. Our list was so feeble. It came to £15,000, and that included a van. So, we signed to Stiff Records for £1,000. We were in a pub not far from the Holloway Road, and he said, 'I want you to sign with Stiff, you've got a couple of weeks to do an album and then I want you to go on the Son Of Stiff tour. It's a three-month world tour, all round the northern hemisphere. All of Europe, America'. What greater temptation is there?"

The Son Of Stiff tour package was eclectic and rather disparate. A fortnight after shaking hands with Dave Robinson and recording an album, Tenpole Tudor found themselves on a bus with an odd assortment of acts. The Equators were a six-piece outfit from Handsworth in Birmingham, the vision of brothers Brian, Donald and Selvyn Bailey, and completed by Alphonso Renford, Cleveland Clarke and Dennis Fletcher. Formed in 1977 and influenced by groups like The Equals, they were well ahead of the game, playing a jumpy brand of ska two years before the arrival of 2 Tone, and watched by another local band still finding their sound, The Beat, as vocalist Dave Wakeling said: "... just when we thought we'd discovered something new, we discovered The Equators right in our home town of Birmingham, who had already come up with a similar formation ..." [45]

While 2 Tone may have seemed the most natural label for The Equators, they opted instead for Stiff and, unlike Tenpole Tudor, never regretted it. "We thought, 'Hey, we were playing this music before the 2 Tone thing came out. Why give it up to 2 Tone?'" said Donald Bailey." [45]

Also on the bus was Tex/Mex performer Joe "King" Carrasco, who was picked up by Stiff after his album released on the Hannibal label came to the attention of its A&R department. He had already released an album on Chiswick and had been well received by the press in the US. Stiff hoped his party style songs and full-on stage shows would have the same impact in the UK. To whet the public's appetite ahead of the tour, "Buena" was released as a single. "It's an exuberant call to accordion arms, aimed right at the feet, as in 'I theeenk he wants us to dance senor ...'" commented the *NME*.

Without question, the group with the greatest commercial potential wasn't from the US, but Manchester. Any Trouble had formed in around 1975 when singer and songwriter Clive Gregson went to teacher training college in Crewe. Initially a more traditional rock band with folk leanings, the arrival of new wave bands like Squeeze had heavily influenced their sound. In early 1979, they had gone into Pennine Sound, an eight-track studio in Oldham where Gregson had worked as an assistant engineer, and done a session paid for by bass player Phil Barnes' dad. From the five or six songs they cut that evening, pretty much live, "Yesterday's Love" and "Nice Girls" were picked out for a single. The record "sat around for a while", says Gregson, before being pressed up on the group's own label and sent out into the world.

When the band went along to a John Peel Roadshow at Manchester University, they handed him a copy. He played it a lot and when Andy Peebles also picked up on the record and played it every day for a week on his day-time Radio 1 show, things went crazy. Major record companies started calling Gregson at the dole office where he worked, offering the group a deal. A long queue quickly formed with Warner, EMI, RAK, Chrysalis and Stiff all in.

Initially, Paul Conroy and Nigel Dick travelled to The Commercial in Gregson's home town of Stalybridge to see them. The pub wasn't anything to write home about, but it was clear why Any Trouble were. Their reconnaissance mission complete, they drove back to London to give Robinson the thumbs up.

Gregson remembers: "Robbo just showed up like a whirlwind breath of something else really and we liked him. He was very charming, very funny, very Irish. Stiff was a really interesting group of people. Dave Whitehead now manages David Bowie, among other things, but at that point he was little more than a glorified motorcycle messenger at Stiff. Dave had driven Robbo up to Stalybridge or Stoke, whichever one it was, to see us. Robbo would just commandeer Dave and say: 'You're coming with me tonight, Whitehead. It doesn't matter what your plans are. We're going to Stoke and we're going to go see this band'. And he'd forced him to drive in the outside lane at 130 miles an hour to get there before Chrysalis. It made you feel special really, but I'm sure that was just the way he lived his life – it was crazy."

Any Trouble signed to Stiff in February 1980 and Robinson, still determined to break the label in the US, must have been delighted to have bagged a writer brimming over with radio-friendly songs. In the greater scheme of things, Stiff had barely made a pinprick on the American market. But Gregson's songs and pop sensibilities made him the kind of artist that could potentially get some commercial success there. Ian Gomm had scored the only *Billboard* hit for Stiff/Epic with the laid-back, melodic pop of "Hold On", and in Any Trouble, Robinson saw real possibilities.

Commenting more than 30 years later on the group's compatibility with Stiff, Gregson says: "I suppose if I look back on it dispassionately, which is almost impossible to do, it was a colossal mistake, because we were never a typical Stiff band in any way, shape or form. I also think if we had known more about the business, we would have probably realised that Stiff had absolutely no presence in the US at all, and if we stood a chance anywhere of selling some records, it was the US. So, with the best will in the world, we went with Stiff because we liked them as people, we liked what they were about, the whole deal. I think Robbo felt that maybe we were an act that could open some doors for them in America, and that may or may not be true. It didn't really happen because the whole way they went about it was complete bonkers really in typical Stiff fashion.

"Your typical Stiff act – if there was such a thing – was very musical but tended towards very strong visual images and identities, and we absolutely did not. We looked like four Herberts from Manchester who'd won *Jim'll Fix It* to be in a pop band! So, it wasn't really about the music."

Whatever their visual appeal, Any Trouble's single "Girls Are Always Right" was the only record released at the time of the tour to receive any radio play. The song was taken from the album *Where Are All The Nice Girls?* released the previous spring. Robinson had brought in John Wood to produce, hoping he could replicate the success he'd had with Squeeze. However, just like their debut "Yesterday's Love" and the Wood-produced follow-up "Second Choice", it was a miss.

The Equators had injected fresh zest into "Baby Come Back", which had served up a No.1 hit for The Equals in 1968. To produce the single, Stiff hired former Equals member Eddy Grant. He had already written and produced a Stiff single for his brother Rudolph, who performed as The Mexicano, and was signed after he topped the reggae charts for ten weeks with "Move Up Starsky". For Tenpole Tudor, "Three Bells In A Row" resulted in anything but a jackpot, while Dirty Looks saw "Tailin' You" become their third straight single to evade success. All in all, a very poor return on a tour that cost an arm and a leg.

Gregson says candidly: "I look back now and think, 'Bloody hell, what were we thinking? We must have been mad.' It made no creative or business sense at all. At that point we had a record – admittedly it was a cool record in the UK – but we had started to build an audience and we could pretty much tour on our own. It was a completely backward step for us because just at the point where we were starting to make some headway and become an established live act, flogging a well-respected record, we disappeared for three months and did this thing where you played with four other bands, doing 25 minutes a night. So, essentially, if you had really rabid fans, they might come. But they'd be disappointed because you weren't playing very much and they'd have to sit through four other acts – and the bill rotated every night. So it made no sense for us at all and at a point when we could have consolidated something, we dropped completely out of sight really."

Stiff plugger Sonnie Rae did her utmost to get the band heard and had a good rapport with them. But with video assuming a greater role in the progress of singles, they didn't look the part. "Any Trouble we had difficulty with, because they just looked so ordinary and people were really kicking back on the ordinariness of them," she says. "But I think Clive Gregson was a really good songwriter."

The debut album released in the spring had received a mixed reception in the UK and hadn't charted. Robinson, however, felt sure the radio-friendly style of *Where Are All the Nice Girls?* meant it could deliver the success in the US that Stiff, and plenty before them, had found so elusive. Reaction from radio stations there suggested he was right and when the group arrived in America, it was being widely played.

But, says Gregson, Stiff's decision to release it on its own recently-launched label was a fatal mistake: "It was the hottest airplay record in America in November 1980 – a record that nobody could buy, beyond the fact that we were playing the fucking life out of it right the way across the States! We were on this stupid tour which nobody knew we were on. It wasn't, 'Coming to your town – Any Trouble'; it was, 'Coming to your town – the Son Of Stiff tour'. So, they dropped the ball massively in that we had a record that actually stood a chance, which was killed because it didn't add up.

"Once it was all over the radio, they probably could have gone with a licence then, if Robbo had woken up. But Robbo was so bogged down with the Son Of Stiff tour at this point that I don't suppose anybody ever thought, 'Hang on a minute. Let's go and knock on EMI's door and say, "Take this up and make it a hit"'. There was never enough money in the world to break Stiff as a label in America. It was not going to happen. Many had died at the coalface trying it before, and subsequently Rough Trade America didn't last a whole long time."

Whilst not disturbing the charts, Son Of Stiff enjoyed plenty of activity on the road. The no-expense-spared movie Robinson had insisted on had the usual live footage and hi-jinx: a backstage food fight started by Ed Tudor Pole, drunken band members stumbling into a hotel, a crowned Joe "King" Carrasco giving an interview while in the bath.

"There was a lot of carnal lust in Hamburg," recalls Tudor Pole. "Dick [Crippen] said, 'She was dodgy that girl'. Anyway, Dick was right and I got mild VD off her. I discovered that a couple of weeks later, just after I'd been in bed with a girl from Marseilles. So I thought, 'Oh no, I would have given it to her'. So, I went along to a doctor in Lyon and he referred me to this place, like a garage. There was this bloke with green overalls and a syringe and that was it. Instantly cured. Anyway, cut to the Stiff Little Fingers tour last month at a gig in Leeds. This guy came up and said, 'It's me, Jack from Hamburg.' We'd met in Hamburg in 1981 on the Son Of Stiff tour, and I couldn't remember him. But anyway, I told him the story I've just told you and he said, 'Yes, I know, she did it deliberately!' I said, 'Why?' He said, 'Because she thought you were getting a little bit big for your boots.'"

In America, Tudor Pole almost sparked an international incident. The group hadn't gone down well in Detroit and they were determined to rectify things at the next show in Chicago on 8 December. They went down a storm and arrived back in their dressing room, drenched with sweat and blissfully unaware of events that had unfolded more than 700 miles away in New York City. Unfortunately, a press crew was waiting outside and, ignoring advice from other band members to give Tudor Pole time to wind down, they burst straight into the dressing room.

"This guy said, 'John Lennon has just been assassinated. I wonder if you'd like to make a remark?'" recalls Tudor Pole. "I said, 'He can fuck himself, the fucking old cunt!', obviously not thinking at all, but sort of being in character. I mean, I loved The Beatles and certainly John Lennon. Anyway, we got to Boston and someone said, 'Tudor Pole, we've got a message here from the John Lennon Preservation Society'. I was pretty frazzled by then after playing two and a half hours every night. And I was so scared in Boston, I ran around to make it difficult in case anyone was aiming at me."

Dick Crippen also remembers the episode vividly and the tight security that followed: "None of us knew what was going on. He was telling all these journalists to fuck off and they were all shouting, 'John Lennon's dead, what do you think about John Lennon' and he just made this remark, 'I don't care about John Lennon, he's just a bloody old hippie, now get out of my face', not really understanding what had happened.

"The next day it was plastered all over the *New York Times* and other newspapers. Obviously you're going to get the fanatics in America, so the next thing we know, we're getting people phoning up the venues, the record company and hotels we were staying in, saying if they see him they're going to kill him and he's on their list for assassination. Then we've got the FBI on to us saying they are going to supply an armed guard and Eddie is not to go out of his hotel room and he is to be escorted to the gigs. Eddie was basically confined to an hotel room and the dressing room and couldn't go out on his own anywhere. For him, the rest of that American tour must have been a complete nightmare."

A compilation 12-inch EP was released to coincide with the tour, featuring one track by each artist. But in America, it wasn't this, but another record that was getting people talking – and buying. According to the label, *The Wit And Wisdom Of Ronald Reagan* was issued on Magic Records in December 1980. But only one label could possibly have been behind a record that was 40 minutes of complete silence! "Warning: You may or may not hear something interesting on this record," read a *caveat* at the bottom of the back of the sleeve. An hilarious Stiff publicity stunt to beat them all, and one of its most fondly remembered, it hit record stores just weeks after Reagan's election on 4 November 1980. A perfect example of Stiff's marketing genius combined with superb design, it proved popular with both Stiff collectors and Americans who appreciated the dig at their president. Back at home, Robinson used it to taunt an already downcast Wreckless Eric, telling him, "I can a sell a record of total silence, but I can't sell a record of you".

Stiff Records fan and TV and radio host Jonathan Ross admired the imagination behind the stunt, but ultimately wanted the label to "make music". "If a record came out on Stiff, I would buy it because I kind of felt like I trusted the judgment of the people running that label to serve up something which at the very least would be interesting," he said. "They brought out an album, *The Wit And Wisdom Of Ronald Reagan* – you can imagine how difficult that is for me to pronounce, 'The Wit And Wisdom Of Ronald Reagan' – and it was a blank album, which is not a particularly good joke, but it sold an awful lot." [12]

In a telling comment, Robinson said: "It [Stiff Inc.] became a financial burden on the British company, though we did very well with *The Wit And Wisdom of Ronald Reagan*. I got the idea from the writer Richard Williams, who reviewed the wrong side of a vinyl test pressing. I thought it would be a great joke to do a record with nothing on it. We sold 40,000." [47]

The sun wouldn't set on Stiff America for another three years, but despite a gimmick record that would go down in legend, it was already proving a costly mistake.

11

Stop The Cavalry

Jona Lewie was the oddities' oddity. A deadpan, almost hangdog expression, a job interview jacket and tie and an accordion. If anyone seemed ill-equipped for the bright new, MTV obsessed world of the eighties, it was the man formerly known as Terry Dactyl. And when the Be Stiff train tour had come and gone without the even briefest flirtation with any commercial success, he looked nailed-on to live up to the Stiff press office's description of him as a "poverty stricken genius". All of which made it all the more surprising when he became the label's only act – aside from Madness and Ian Dury – to deliver a hit single in 1980.

As a plugger, it was Sonnie Rae's job to get Stiff's records played on radio and TV shows. This meant schmoozing with producers, presenters and the like and giving releases the big sell. Working on a shoestring budget that would have paled against those enjoyed by her counterparts on the major labels, the bubbly blonde chose carefully when booking restaurants for lunch appointments. "I built up a very good rapport with the radio and TV people," says Sonnie. "I didn't lie and, if I pushed the point, they trusted me enough to give me the benefit of the doubt and give things a second or third hearing. I also bought great lunches!"

Robinson had headhunted her from Sonnet in 1978 shortly before the Be Stiff tour hit the rails, and she worked closely with the press office to promote Lene Lovich, Wreckless, Kirsty MacColl, Jona Lewie and other artists. John Peel and his long-term producer John Walters had always been supportive of Stiff, along with Mike Hawkes, who produced the early evening Kid Jensen show. However, once "Hit Me ..." went to No.1, more mainstream disc jockeys and producers became amenable to playing releases that arrived in the post from Rae, often with beguiling messages. "Playlist now or I'll shoot the dog", warned the note she sent with the Any Trouble single "Second Choice". "I would write letters to go out with every single and the art department would make up a letterhead thing for me," she says. "I would choose something maybe from The Farside or a Gary Larson or something like that underneath it, often fairly tongue-in-cheek, which didn't go down very well with all the bands if they took themselves too seriously. So a fairly facetious letter would go out with every single."

By the middle of 1980, Jona Lewie had seen two singles bomb and the train tour hadn't been the breakthrough for him that it had been for Lovich and Sweet. If his next record flopped, then Stiff, and in turn Sonnie, would find it hard to justify investing time and money in promoting him. "You'll Always Find Me In The Kitchen At Parties" was, like its singer, a curiosity. Lewie had come up with this rambling chronicle of a bachelor in search of a girlfriend after Keith Trussell from the Brett Marvin band popped round to see him and left his lyric book behind. Spotting what he thought was a great idea for a song, he called him and asked if he could use it. He got the go-ahead and from that one thread, produced his third single for Stiff. With its prodding synthesisers, it was warmer and more contemporary than the bar-room piano of "The Baby She's On The Street", and the chorus sung by two female backing singers was hard to dislodge from the brain. Radio 1 loved it.

Lewie recalls the breakthrough moment: "It was a question of Sonnie going in there every week for about ten or eleven weeks to try and get on the playlist and she couldn't get arrested. So, here was Sonnie on the twelfth week, playing it to yet another record producer, and saying, 'Oh look, I've got this new artist on Stiff Records and we want to get it in the playlist'. And she was playing it and the door of the room was open, and who should walk down the corridor, going past, but a guy who played records on Radio 1 and who stopped and said, 'Christ, what's that? I like that'. He put his head round the corner and listened to the whole thing and when it stopped, he said, 'I'm going to make that my Record of the Week next week.' Boom! That's how ridiculous it is. You've just got to persevere. I think that was to be her last week; the last time she would be allowed to try and push that track. I think Stiff said, 'Right, look give it one more week. We've been twelve weeks now on this.' Who knows at the time? It's just one more track."

The "guy" in question was none other than Dave Lee Travis, better known to the nation as The Hairy Cornflake and presenter of Radio 1's breakfast show. True to his word, "Kitchen At Parties" was named his Record Of The Week, and Lewie finally returned to the UK Top 40, eight years after "Seaside Shuffle". It spent eleven weeks in the chart, climbing to No. 16, and was also a hit in Australia, New Zealand, Israel, Holland, Germany, Sweden and several other countries.

Top Of The Pops viewers seeing him for the first time were greeted by a bloke who looked like he was dressed for a wedding, and two attractive girls, one in a bright yellow dress, the other in an orange one. Few would have recognised the girl wearing yellow as KirstyMacColl, the stage-shy vocalist who had come and gone from Stiff, and who hadn't sung on the single itself. The record had been produced by Bob Andrews at the Old Kent Road Studios, the scene of *New Boots And Panties!!*, and it was his wife Pat Mayberry and Dave Robinson's other half Rosemary who had supplied the backing vocals.

"Kitchen At Parties", which years later would later be borrowed for an IKEA television commercial featuring Lewie himself, had all the hallmarks of a novelty song. But Lewie was to be no one-hit-wonder. By the end of the year, he had delivered an even bigger record, and one that would financially set him up for life. Robinson had a keen ear for a hit and he had immediately earmarked "Kitchen At Parties" as a single when he'd listened to the rough demos Lewie had brought in after being signed. However, he'd dismissed "Stop The Cavalry" as "just an anti-war song". On the cassette recording Robinson heard, Lewie had accompanied himself on the piano, giving the song a rather sparse feel. Convinced it had promise, Lewie went away and tried again using an eight-track recorder he had at home. This time Robinson heard a single.

The original draft actually had "gallantry" not "cavalry". The former sociology student's inspired decision to ditch the original piano accompaniment in favour of a Salvation Army-style brass band and sleigh bells gave the song a festive feel and his lyrics an unmistakably English setting.

"Looking back, I can't remember if 'Can you end the gallantry?' was just a way of fitting in the notes," says Lewie. "I thought, 'That fits' and then perhaps it mushroomed from there. Maybe it was that which turned it into a song that was referencing various war scenarios, and from there it went into how it would feel for a soldier as a person being in the situation. An horrific situation where you are daydreaming in your trench, waiting for the next period before you have to go out and fight again for another ten yards. It happens to be in December and you're cold and hungry and fed up, and your girlfriend is back home. The family are going to be having Christmas dinner soon and you think, 'I'm pissed off with all this. If I survive, when I get home I'm going to become the Prime Minister, not just of Britain, but the whole world. And if I win the election, I'm going to stop the cavalry, because none of the others seem to be able to do it.' That's sort of what he's saying to himself in his daydream."

Bob Andrews co-produced the song with Lewie and an initial mix was completed by October. But Robinson wasn't satisfied and with the lucrative Christmas market looming large, he demanded they go into a different studio to get it right. He hailed the reworked version a triumph, as did Clive Calder, whose company Zomba published the song. Although never intended as a Christmas song, its release towards the end of November and the lyrics made it one. A poignant video interspersed real photographs of war with shots of Lewie in the trenches and, in a dream, back at home in the arms of his girl.

On 6 December, to the delight of Lewie and everyone at Stiff, it went straight into the UK chart at No. 15. The next week it jumped to No. 3, one place behind St Winifred's School Choir's "There's No One Quite Like Grandma", with Abba's "Super Trouper" at No.1. However, with Britain still in mourning for John Lennon following his murder on 8 December, it was "(Just Like) Starting Over" that topped the charts on Christmas Day. "Stop The Cavalry" did, however, top the charts in France, Belgium and Austria and made him a star in other countries around the world.

Lewie recalls: "I was on my way back from Spain and at the station, on the way to the airport, I rang Stiff Records, because I was wondering about whether I should really go back or perhaps stay another week. I said, 'Oh Sonnie, hi. Should I come back, because I want to stay another week, I think'. 'Oh no, you must come. It's gone in at 69 and it's just gone up to 15.' 'What has?' 'Stop The Cavalry. It's going to be huge. Come back immediately'."

Ironically, the one-off record Stiff had issued to cash in on Christmas sank without trace. Elmo And Patsy's "Grandma Got Run Over By A Reindeer" was a cringe-inducing affair that had been released the previous year by a small independent on the west coast of America, where it had sold 20,000 copies. Anyone who had been following the label's fortunes since 1976 would have been forgiven for asking what on earth Robinson was doing. Earlier curiosities by the likes of Max Wall and Humphrey Ocean had been fun and in keeping with Stiff's own eccentric disposition. But this just looked crass and smacked of utter desperation. Aside from the Madness hit machine and Lewie's surprise smash, Stiff's strike rate was cause for genuine concern. "Grandma …" was the fourteenth single since "Baggy Trousers" and, of these, only one had made any impact on the chart. And in four-and-a-half years, Stiff had mustered just fourteen Top 40 hits. Quality and not quantity would be needed if the company was to prosper.

Pop had become a visual feast and a great video could make the difference. Robinson had always appreciated the importance of strong visuals in pop music and, as video threatened to kill the radio star, Stiff had a band that cried out to be on camera. Madness' videos would become as eagerly anticipated as the records themselves and were one of the reasons they appealed to such a young audience. But on their return from their second US tour, there had been little appetite in the group to film a video for "Night Boat To Cairo", as they were dead against another single being lifted from *One Step Beyond*. Robinson, who had a penchant for frontloading albums with singles, was understandably keen to try and squeeze yet another Top 10 hit from the album. In the end, a compromise had been reached and, reluctantly, the lads agreed to do a video.

Foreman says: "We thought there were too many songs off the album and we had an argument with Dave. He said, 'Well, we'll make it an EP', so we did three new songs. We always tried to make sure the B-sides were extra songs: most of my songs ended up as B-sides. So, we did this video for 'Night Boat To Cairo' at the last minute, in this studio with this blue screen. I always think it's a crap video, but everybody loves it. We'd just got gold discs, so we were horrendously drunk doing the video, and it got worse and worse. Dave knew that when you put the camera on, you've got to get it quick. You can't say, 'Can you do that again?'"

Thompson appeared in silhouette against a clichéd Egyptian backdrop, the booming of his saxophone heralding the Night Boat's departure. As the song burst into life, the lads, minus their singer, began marching around in pith helmets and safari shirts and shorts. Then, in the nick of time, Suggs leapt into view to deliver the unmistakable opening line.

The video was vintage Stiff and the response to the record vindicated Robinson's insistence on pilfering one more song from the album. "Night Boat To Cairo", a joint effort by Barson and Suggs, hit No. 6 and spent two months in the chart. Due to the concession the group negotiated out of Robinson, fans got three brand new songs into the bargain: "Deceives The Eye", "The Young And The Old", and "Don't Quote Me On That". The sleeve of BUY 71 featured the lads one above the other in a human tower. Madness fever was sweeping Britain.

Their latest filming obligations having been fulfilled, Madness took part in what amounted to a Stiff jamboree in France. At an indoor festival at Pavillon Baltard, near Paris, they shared the bill with Lene Lovich, Wreckless Eric and Lew Lewis, who had recently released his second single. The following month they set off on a tour of Britain, with Clive Langer & The Boxes and The Go-Go's in tow. Exhausted but exhilarated, they then took a break. New song titles were scrawled on a blackboard and they disappeared into a dark, windowless studio near Earls Court to begin rehearsals ahead of the recording of their second album. It would be called *Absolutely*.

The record had some strong material and there was no shortage of single material. Several of the songs, including "Embarrassment", "On The Beat Pete" and "In The Rain" had been road-tested in their live sets to good response. *Absolutely* also contained the song that would provide them with their visual *tour de force* – "Baggy Trousers".

Robinson, while running the label and all that entailed, nevertheless took a keen interest in the band's videos. So much so, he was behind the camera for the one that set every school playground rocking to the Madness sound. Most of the filming was done at Islip Street School in Kentish Town, the group performing in the school hall and on the playing field. Local kids were also filmed cycling and kicking a football next to the flats where Lee Thompson had grown up. But the video would be best remembered for the sight of the sax player in a pair of inflated trousers, taking to the air and flying about over the heads of his band members, playing as he went. The morning after it was first shown on *Top Of The Pops*, the video was the talk of school yards the country over.

"The one that really cemented us was 'Baggy Trousers'," says Foreman. "Dave did that and we just went down there and Lee wanted to fly through the air. He wanted to have these dummies that were us and he would kick our heads off. We thought that was a bit strong and so the dummies ended up in the pub. That video was like, 'This is it'. When we got the film back and Dave and us all sat down and looked at it, you couldn't see the wires, and that made us video legends."

"Baggy Trousers" sold more than 600,000 copies, making it the 12th bestselling single in the UK that year. The massive popularity of the song, and the unforgettable video that went with it, sent it to No.3 and kept it resident in the UK chart for four months.

Madness may have looked like lots of fun, but dealing with them was no picnic. *Top Of The Pops* dreaded the Nutty Boys coming in and had stern words with Stiff about their behaviour. In the month "Baggy Trousers" was released, they were banned from ITV kids' show *Tiswas* after Suggs and Smyth sprayed presenter Sally James with silly string and some of it got stuck to her false eyelashes. They had then tried to help her remove it and pulled an eyelash off.

Sonnie Rae found them so difficult, she begged Stiff to get someone else to take them on: "I worked with Madness in the beginning for three or four records, and I said to Robbo, 'I don't want to do this. Can we give them away please?' He said, 'They're our biggest act,' and I said, 'I don't care. I don't want to work with them, they are so unprofessional'. And they were; they were a nightmare. It's really difficult when you do live TV or something and I just couldn't get through to them. People were threatening never to have them on *Top Of The Pops* again and I felt it started reflecting on me lacking control, which of course I did. So, it was very hard, and when I said I didn't want to work with them again, that was that. They were very sweet. They apologised and bought me a pair of diamond earrings, but I said, 'I don't think I'm right for you'. In the end they went to Neil Ferris."

Foreman's view is: "We used to have a lot of run-ins with *Top Of The Pops* because we'd be late or whatever. I really think a lot of those shows – that show particularly – treated us like idiots. They'd make us get there really early, they'd keep us hanging around, and they used to go to the bass guitar on the guitar solo, they always did that. We were always getting in trouble and Sonnie Rae would be in tears.

The BBC said to Stiff, 'If Madness fuck up again, we're not going to have any Stiff acts on', and we thought that was really crap. They could have just said, 'We're not going to have Madness on'.

"They were biting the hand that feeds because, okay, 17 million people watched it, but they didn't tune in to see Tony Blackburn. We were the talent, we were what was selling it. These days people get treated really well. I'm not saying we needed champagne, but they used to stick us in this bloody horrible room in the BBC all day. But what happened was that our videos were so popular, there became this unwritten agreement with the BBC that when we put singles out, they would show the video."

Absolutely was released on 26 September 1980 and brought the kind of commercial success of which Stiff had always dreamed. It went straight in at No. 2 and stayed put on the chart for 43 weeks. The album also charted in other countries, although not America. As Robinson was quick to point out, this was the only territory where Madness were not represented by Stiff.

The album was a fourteen-track set that barely came up for breath. While it contained exactly the same number of songs as *One Step Beyond* and the same sense of urgency, this was a more mature collection by far, with social themes explored. Thompson had penned the words to "Embarrassment" following the reaction in his family to the news that his 17-year-old sister Tracy was carrying the child of a black man. *Absolutely* proved that musically and lyrically, Madness were growing up. To this day, many regard it as their most complete album.

"Embarrassment" was released on 14 November and went to No. 4, delivering Madness their fourth consecutive Top 10 hit of 1980. In the video, a solemn-looking Suggs delivered the lyrics in the dimly lit bar of the Embassy Club in London's Mayfair. Barson sat bolt upright at the piano, his hands and face pointedly blacked up. So successful was the song that it was still making its way out of the chart when Stiff released "The Return Of The Los Palmas 7" in January.

An instrumental that lasted less than two minutes seemed an incongruous choice for a pop single and the video had a decidedly homespun feel. The lads were filmed eating a fried breakfast at the Venus Café, a greasy spoon on the Golborne Road in West London. They then donned dinner suits and cowboy gear for a separate shoot at Kenwood Park in Hampstead. The clips were spliced together with random news footage for what was a typical Stiff production, but their fans clearly loved it. The cowboys swaggered their way to No. 7, ensuring the perfect start to 1981 and proving once again that together, Stiff and Madness had the Midas touch.

———

To say that Stiff was heavily reliant on Madness would have been a huge understatement. In the period between "My Girl" and "Work, Rest And Play" eight singles had been released, none of which had charted. Sandwiched between the monster hits of "Night Boat To Cairo" and "Baggy Trousers", Stiff had issued a dozen 45s, of which "Kitchen At Parties" was the only hit. And while *Absolutely* was one of the top 25 best-selling albums of 1980, other Stiff LPs of that year made almost no impact at all, with the notable exception of Graham Parker's *The Up Escalator*.

Stiff's accounts for the year to 31 March 1981 show a turnover of £3,396.250, compared with £2,509,088 the previous year. However, the funds generated from its operations came in at £26,990 against £93,935 in 1979, and after tax it had made a net loss of £6,172. In short, lavish ventures like Son Of Stiff, the rapidly expanding operation at Woodfield Road and the relentless promotion of acts that couldn't buy a hit were being bankrolled by Madness. A year of consolidation was fine, but Stiff needed more than one consistently successful act.

By 1981, Stiff's relationship with some of its best-known artists had begun to cool as they struggled to repeat their earlier successes. Lene Lovich was a case in point. "New Toy", released as a single in March 1981, was an über-modern piece of power pop written by Thomas Dolby, and he joined Lovich and her band to perform it on *Top Of The Pops*. However, what sounded like the certain hit single that was needed to re-ignite her career ended up stalling at No. 53. The fact that it was the first Stiff single released on cassette didn't help.

Lovich says: "It got a lot of attention on the radio. But you know, the whole chart situation at the time was weird. I don't know what happens now, but in those days they had chart shops. So, if somebody bought your record from a chart shop, it counted towards you going up the chart. And they could go to the other end of the street and buy it from another shop, and it wouldn't count. There was maybe a bit of manipulation, but the public didn't know, so they might be buying your records from the wrong shop.

"I know for a fact that when we had 'Say When' out, we actually sold more records and went down the charts, and obviously people who sold fewer records went up the chart. Then the radio stations lose confidence, 'Oh, the record's going down the chart', so you don't have the support any more. Clearly that's what happened. It could have been a much more popular record if that hadn't happened."

The outlook for her friend Wreckless Eric was more ominous still – he had become the label's forgotten man. His ability to pen unique songs that were both offbeat and yet radio-friendly hadn't diminished. In fact, "A Popsong" was exactly that. When that didn't translate into a hit song, Stiff took one last throw of the dice with "Broken Doll", a great single, co-written with guitarist Walter Hacon. Cliff Richard liked it so much he included it on his hit album *Wired For Sound* and EMI had planned to put it out as a single until Wreckless beat him to it. Sadly, it suffered the same fate as "Whole Wide World", "Reconnez Cherie", "Hit And Miss Judy" and other memorable songs from Stiff's ultimate square peg.

The photograph of the disillusioned singer staring out of the sleeve with a cigarette hanging out of his mouth seemed to say it all. Wreckless had long been aggrieved at what he saw as a lack of support and any real strategy from his label. He had once walked into the Stiff office having been touring in Australia and promoting *Big Smash!*, only for someone to ask, "Where have you been?". Before recording the album, Robinson had tried to team Wreckless up with songwriters Martin Page and Brian Fairweather who turned up to one meeting with very un-Stiff matching baseball jackets bearing the name "Fairweather Page". Later they would provide songs for the likes of Kim Carnes and Barbara Streisand and Page co-wrote Starship's 1985 hit "We Built This City". Their pairing with Wreckless, however, proved a mismatch and came to nothing.

Stiff was clearly at a loss to know what to do with him and while it pondered the issue, Wreckless began recording the songs for a new album. He had a hard-hitting band behind him this time: Pete Gosling on lead guitar, Walter Hacon on rhythm guitar, Dave Otway on drums, John Brown on bass and Malcolm Morley on keyboards and acoustic guitar. When they arrived for the sessions at Parkgate Studio, near Battle in East Sussex, a new residential section was under construction and they had to contend with banging and drilling as they worked.

After completing the songs somewhere quieter, they then set off on an American tour.

On their return to Britain, Robinson informed the flabbergasted singer that for the album's release, it would be coupled with a US compilation entitled *The Whole Wide World* as a double album. "As usual, Robinson took control of everything, including the remixing, the artwork (a striking Roy Lichtenstein Pop Art pastiche) and the title, *Big Smash!*" according to the sleeve notes for the *Hits, Misses, Rags And Tatters* compilation CD. As Eric has since commented: "I was given a choice of either *Upstairs Drinking Downstairs Dancing* or *Big Smash!* To be fair he did ask me if I had any ideas, but I didn't because I knew they'd never be as good as anything he'd come up with."

Robinson's handling of *Big Smash!* served only to deepen the artist's sense of frustration and injustice as Wreckless explains: "It was like, 'We're going to put it out as a double with this compilation that we had out in America', so I was very offended by that. It made me feel my new album wasn't good enough, which I don't think it was actually. But at the time it wasn't a good way to feel about it. But that other half of *Big Smash!*, the other stuff with the pathetic remix of 'Whole Wide World'… now why would you spend money remixing that? If you had a vision and an ear, you would know that's the mix and there's nothing you can do that's going to make it a better record. That's why Stiff America was set up with Allen Frey and then Dave put us with Epic Records. He had made this mistake with me, I suppose. Epic Records got on to it and we sold a fraction of the records. We'd get along to every other gig and the opening act had posters up and they had people from the record company and the radio coming in to interview them, and they were going off to do this, and so on."

Big Smash! was Wreckless Eric's last album for Stiff. It did achieve a position of No. 30 in the chart – his only ever Top 40 placing. However, this was partly because initial pressings in the UK came with *The Whole Wide World* greatest hits album, which had been released separately in the US. Just one month after entering the chart, it slipped out again. Three albums and seven singles later, Wreckless Eric and Stiff parted company.

Stiff employees totally reject his claims that the label didn't back him. Wreckless was the only artist on its roster who took part in two of the package tours, they point out. Full-page adverts for his records were taken out in the music press, just as they were for others.

Stiff had also kept faith with him for four years, even as his records failed to deliver a return – a loyalty he would not have enjoyed at other labels. "Eric stayed on the label and was certainly supported for another couple of years [post-Be Stiff], but didn't have hits," says Andy Murray. "But it wasn't for the lack of trying."

———

Another Stiff artist who seemed to have reached an impasse and was falling out of love with the label was Wreckless' friend and long-time supporter Ian Dury. By the end of 1981, he too would be gone. If those following the fortunes of Stiff had sensed an era coming to an end, it was with good reason. And if there was ever an inaptly named album, it was without question *Laughter.*

Fame had severely disagreed with Dury and those close to him found him more difficult than ever before. Chaz Jankel had left the band to pursue a solo career in the US and he had been replaced by the mad-eyed guitarist Wilko Johnson. Ian's often stormy relationship with Denise Roudette had been another casualty of what Andrew King had described as Ian's "number-one-itis". Adopting the kind of ostentatious rock star lifestyle more readily associated with Keith Moon, he rented a palatial property, complete with swimming pool, in the rural setting of Rolvendon in Kent. Here, with his burly minder Pete Rush, A.K.A. The Sulphate Strangler, and others on hand to do his bidding, he held court and partied into the small hours. Wrestling with an addiction to sleeping pills and still drinking heavily, Dury made for unpredictable company, being anything from hugely entertaining to downright unpleasant. Things were no different, possibly even worse, in the recording studio, and it is not with any fondness that The Blockheads look back on the recording sessions for his third and final Stiff album.

Mickey Gallagher recalls: "If he had a drink in the studio, it was fatal. He was probably at his horriblest during *Laughter,* really horrible. I remember sitting in the studio with the sound engineer Ian Horne and hearing the front door opening and hearing Ian's voice, and both of us froze and thought, 'Oh fuck, he's here'. Then he came in and we said, 'Oh, you all right Ian?' and he says, 'What's happening?' He sacked my keyboard roadie at the time for doing something naughty with drugs in the studio. He was a bit of a dictator. We used to call him 'The Raspberry' [raspberry ripple = cripple in Cockney rhyming slang] and after gigs everyone used to wait until he had gone." [6]

Davey Payne says of the sessions for *Laughter*: "When we first went in there, we were in there for a long time, and it was quite a good vibe because Ian didn't come in. The Blockheads were doing their thing, quite a lot of funky stuff, and it was quite good. And Ian came down thinking he was the genius and he could interfere … I would sometimes be doing some great solos and Johnny would be going, 'Yeah, Davey', and he would be kind of taking over and directing it a bit. He's a good musician, Johnny Turnbull; he really is. Ian would go, 'No, no', and it was for the sake of doing it more than anything. He almost got a sort of sadistic pleasure from being the boss. My lips would be swollen because I'd been playing so much and he'd say, 'No Davey, start again because I need it to come in here' and all your best things had gone. He did that a lot with everybody."

The first chance for Dury's fans to hear how the new Blockheads sounded came with "I Want To be Straight", a single that – in keeping with Dury album etiquette – wasn't on *Laughter*. Over a funky bass line, the band members introduced themselves in an unusual spoken introduction. Ian went last and then bellowed "And guess what?" before launching into the opening verse. Belying the mood in the studio, Ian appeared in the video with a clown's face and his old friend Humphrey Ocean, a highly-respected artist, sat sketching him as the band played.

Dury's tongue-in-cheek anthem to conformity had all the ingredients of his chart smashes: a solid funk rhythm, unusual lyrics and a soaring saxophone solo from Davey Payne. That "I Want To Be Straight" charted must have been a relief for all concerned at Stiff. However, its highest placing of 22 was a far cry from the performances of "Hit Me …" and "Reasons To Be Cheerful". Was the artist who had the entire industry in thrall just a year earlier beginning to lose his shine?

Stiff didn't need to wait long for its answer. *Laughter* was released in November 1980 and afforded all the usual promotional trimmings. One full-page press advert showed an abattoir worker with a bloodied apron holding up a turkey. Commercially, it turned out to be just that. The album didn't even make the UK Top 40, stalling at a dismal 48 and spending just a month in the chart. It did even worse in America, limping to 159 in the *Billboard* Top 200. "Sueperman's Big Sister", which had the honour of being BUY 100, completed a depressing *denouement* for Dury's period at Stiff. A patchy affair that lacked the urgent funk that enlivened so much of his music, it spent just three weeks in the chart and got no higher than 51.

Out on the road, Dury and his red-hot band continued to play to sell-out crowds, and in March 1981 they flew to Midem, a music industry bash in Cannes, to receive an award from the French pop station Europe Numero Un. In France, they were licensed to Barclay Records and during their visit they were invited to a reception at the Paris flat of label owner Eddie Barclay. Band members must have winced when they realised the irascible Dury was the guest of honour seated between Barclay and his beautiful, much younger film star girlfriend. They could only look on helplessly as Dury sabotaged his career in France.

"Ian and this girl were getting on really well," recalled Andrew King, "in fact so well that after a bit Ian said, 'This is fucking boring, shall we go somewhere else?', and she said, 'Yes, let's'. So, they got up to leave and Eddie said, 'Where are you going?' and Ian said, 'Well, I'm fucking off with your bird'. So Eddie said, 'You stupid ignorant man, sit down at once. Who do you think you are?' and Ian said, 'Eddie Barclay *tu es merde* [you are shit]', and Eddie Barclay said, 'Ian Dury, you will never sell another record in France', and that was pretty much the case. I don't know if he sold any, but he certainly never accounted for any sales there. I should have enjoyed it, but I didn't. I was crawling with embarrassment." [6]

Laughter had fulfilled Dury's obligations to Stiff and he was free to leave. The halcyon days of the Greatest Stiffs tour and the phenomenal success of *New Boots And Panties!!* and "Hit Me ..." suddenly seemed a distant memory. On a personal level, Dury seemed almost scarred by the recognition he had slogged away for years to achieve. Meanwhile, relations between Stiff and the now ailing Blackhill had turned decidedly chilly, and Dury was angling for a new deal with whichever label was offering the fattest pay check. Not put off by the very public slump in his career, Polydor stepped into the breach and signed Ian Dury. The Blockheads were coldly cast adrift.

Davey Payne, who was still in the group at the time, believes Dury's long-serving accountant encouraged him to ditch his band and hire cheaper session musicians. "The real reason was his accountant, Ronnie Harris, and he did the same thing with Dire Straits," he says. "We knew Terry Williams [ex-Man and Rockpile skins man who was in Straits from 1982–1988], who played drums, and he had the same story. You need the right band, as was proved with Ian. But once they start thinking they want some royalties, you drop them because you can get session musicians that will play for £100, it doesn't work. It doesn't with Mick Jagger and it didn't with Ian. He was almost like a manager to Ian and he used to run Andrew King down, saying, 'He couldn't manage a brown paper bag', all sort of things. Ronnie's okay, but I think he got it wrong. It went to Ian's head and he thought he was more important than he was."

Stiff without Dury and Dury without Stiff seemed unthinkable. The singer had been an integral part of the label from its early days and his association with Dave Robinson stretched back almost ten years. With Costello, Wreckless, Wallis and Lowe all gone, Dury was the only surviving member of the old gang at the label. But things had changed. Stiff was a very different operation from the one that had signed him back at Alexander Street, and changes were also afoot at Blackhill Enterprises. At the beginning of 1982, Andrew King joined Charisma, leaving Dury to be managed by Peter Jenner and Jenny Cotton under a new company, Cotton & Carruthers. Blackhill's demise resulted in a bonanza for Dury because while his publishing catalogue was separately held by Blackhill Music and would later be sold to Warner, it enabled him to buy his master recordings.

From a business perspective, however, Dury's departure was no bad thing for Stiff. Although the company's turnover had sky rocketed from £715,000 to almost £3.5 million in two years, and Madness were selling records for fun, paying out huge advances remained difficult to justify and made balancing the books all the more challenging. Stiff needed hit records and, as Polydor was to discover to its cost, Ian Dury had none left. Hefty advances against future royalties put pressure on the record company, not the artist.

Andy Murray, who was still at Stiff when Dury left, says: "Your manager has a lot in it to ask for a big advance because he gets 20% of the advance and in those days you would also get 20% of the recording budget, which stopped some years later when the artists sued and said, 'This is unfair', which it kind of is. So, there is a lot in it for the manager to get an advance and very little in it for the manager to say, 'Let's stick, for no money, with our pals of the last three or four albums because I'm sure that your genius is going to sell 10 million records more around the world and it'll all be great'.

"Sadly, there is a separate tendency, once you've taken the big cheque, that the creative pressure is somewhat off. So, it can be quite useful when you are up against it and the Dave Robinsons of this world say, 'There is no single on this album and it's not coming out until you write one'. Now, if you're Polydor and you've given Ian Dury £300,000, or whatever he got, you're not in a position then to tell the artist what to put on his record, because he goes, 'I've had your money. It's not my problem if you don't want to put it out'. So, it does actually change the creative dynamic."

Ian Dury would never again grace the UK Top 40 and his public profile would wane. Stiff meanwhile was about to net its biggest haul of hits yet.

12

Wunderbar

Make-up, coiffed hair and frilly shirts were de rigueur in 1981 – and that was just the men! Music and fashion had always gone hand-in-hand, but those tuning in to *Top of The Pops* as the eighties got under way could have been forgiven for wondering which had the upper hand. The Last Rites had long been read on punk and, in an unexpected twist, some of those who had been at its epicentre were re-emerging in these carefully manicured new groups. This was the year of the New Romantics, so the question was, how would a label with just one hit act keep sustaining itself in this new high-budget era of airbrushed pop?

Stiff had long recognised that British teenagers represented an overlooked and highly lucrative market. Sign the right act with the right look, as well as good pop songs, and pocket money was out there waiting to be spent. Not just on singles and albums either, but on other band merchandise. The 1980s would be the era of consumer spending and conspicuous consumption, for those that could afford it. Record companies needed to speculate to accumulate and Stiff couldn't afford the advances and royalty rates being paid out by some of its competitors. Even where it could, it didn't have the long term funding required to really break acts. No, Stiff needed to do what it had always done. Be alert for exciting new artists or bands, sign them up on short-term deals and let its graphic artists, pluggers and press team do the rest.

"I remember taking Paul Conroy to the airport one day," recalls Nigel Dick, "and he said, 'I'm going to see a band in Ireland'. He came back and I said, 'What were they like?' 'Oh, they were fucking brilliant, they're amazing, they're going to be so big.' I said, 'So we're signing them, right?' 'No, we can't afford to sign them.' And the band was U2. For a long time I thought he was daft, and then subsequently

I realised he was absolutely right. This was a band that needed a huge investment and we didn't have the money. It took Island three albums to break them, so on that level Stiff was very sensible."

The office at Woodfield Road was more like a factory shop floor than a record company. For the staff, it was a sweatshop. "Robbo really worked everybody hard," says musician Dave Stewart. "They had to be there at nine o'clock. He wouldn't let them take lunch breaks. He said, 'Bring in a sandwich'." A photograph of the office that accompanied a feature in *The Face* magazine in November 1980 suggested the all-hands-on-deck culture that defined Alexander Street had not been lost in the move to its new home, described in the headline as "A Garage Somewhere In London".

Disguising it as an anonymous business and keeping its location a closely-held secret meant staff no longer ran the gauntlet of fans seeking Stiff souvenirs and autographs. A large chalkboard on the wall was covered with scribbled information, ranging from gig dates to TV and radio appointments. "Dave Robinson, like any self-respecting managing director, pads around asking questions and losing things, pursued from time to time by his dog," wrote David Hepworth in his behind-the-scenes article.

Commenting on the difference between the major record companies and Stiff, Robinson made it clear that Stiff's principles had not changed one jot. "I've said this before, I know, but if they were really good, we wouldn't be here," he said. "It's not their lives. The groups that come in here, the music is their lives. The people who work here, the music is their lives. They don't go home until the job is finished. We fight against the English attitude, which is that a good excuse is as good as doing something." [46]

Quite how the Dubliner would have reacted had someone made such a remark about the Irish is open to debate. Certainly it was true that Stiff attracted employees who were passionate about music and who got a buzz out of working for a label that was flying by the seat of its pants. Part of the glamour of Stiff was the total absence of it, and the constant sense that the whole operation was teetering on the edge of a cliff. "We pay out a quarter of a million in royalties at the end of September and that will deplete us greatly," admitted Robinson. [46] "We don't have those kind of monies on hand. But Stiff was made in a certain kind of timber – and it wasn't to make me a wealthy man."

Top: Lene Lovich in classic pose. (*Photo by Nigel Dick*)

Above: A moody shot of Wreckless Eric. (*Photo by Nigel Dick*)

Top: Gold discs from Australia for *New Boots And Panties!!* and "Hit Me With Your Rhythm Stick". Nearly out of shot is Andy Murray. The others are L–R Alan Cowderoy, Peter Jenner (Dury's co-manager), Dave Robinson and Peter Hebbes of Festival Records, Australia. (*Photo by Nigel Dick*)

Above: Stiff marked its distribution deal with CBS/Epic at a hot dog stand in New York City. Dick Wingate is second left and Dave Robinson second right (See page 181). (*Courtesy of Dick Wingate*)

Top: Ian Dury & The Blockheads making friends in America.
(*Laurens Van Houten/Frank White Photo Agency*)

Above: A record produced for Dave Robinson's wedding with greetings
from "well wishers" in August 1979. Apparently, Robinson was not amused.
(*Photo by Tony Judge*)

WE AT STIFF HAVE RACHEL PREJUDICE

HERE TODAY, GOMM TOMORROW

Opposite top: The Son Of Stiff Tour, 1980. Joe "King" Carrasco wears the crown. Clive Gregson of Any Trouble is wearing the pink jacket. Eddie Tudor Pole is behind him. (*Courtesy of Joe "King" Carrasco*)

Opposite far left: Ian Gomm at The Whisky A Go Go. Ian has always been more appreciated in America than at home. (*Courtesy of Ian Gomm*)

Opposite left: Rachel Sweet in 1981 at the Fastlane, Asbury Park, NJ. It is now, sadly, demolished. (*Bob Leafe/Frank White Photo Agency*)

Top: Jona Lewie was on Stiff for five years. He scooped up an Ivor Novello Award for 1980's "Stop The Cavalry". (*Photo by Nigel Dick*)

Above: The Plasmatics liked to blow up the odd car on stage in America, but health and safety officials prevented their gig at Hammersmith Odeon from going ahead (see page 209). (*Bob Leafe/Frank White Photo Agency*)

Top left: Watch out Mike Barson! This falling piano nearly landed on someone's foot during the making of the "Shut Up" video (see page 277). (*Photo by Nigel Dick*)

Top right: Lee Thompson (mum) and Chas Smash (dad) on the set of the "Our House" video. (*Photo by Nigel Dick*)

Above: Suggs and Mark "Bedders" Bedford on stage in America. (*Superstock/Alamy*)

Top left: Shot of Tracey Ullman from 1983.
Her hits were a godsend to Stiff. (*AF archive/Alamy*)

Top right: The late Kirsty MacColl with Stiff press officer Nigel Dick.
(*Courtesy of Nigel Dick*)

Above: The Belle Stars were an important hit-making addition
to the Stiff stable in the 1980s. (*Photo by Nigel Dick*)

Top left: Did the late great Lee Brilleaux of Dr.Feelgood help fund Stiff initially (see page 33)? Either way, the Feelgoods' releases on Stiff ... stiffed. (*Chris George/Alamy*)

Top right: The Pogues circa 1985. Cait O'Riordan appears to be biting Shane MacGowan's shoulder. (*Superstock/Alamy*)

Above: Bringing things right up to date, author Richard Balls interviews Shane MacGowan for the book. No alcohol was consumed, obviously! (*Photo by Paul Ronan*)

Robinson inspired unswerving loyalty from many of those who worked for him, his highly regarded personal assistant Annie Pitts being a case in point. Stiff's managing director certainly put in the hours and expected nothing less from those who practically lived out of Woodfield Road. He also thought nothing of sacking people.

Nigel Dick remembers: "If you were a nine-to-five person, you just wouldn't last at Stiff really. I quite literally had Robbo ring me up at three o'clock in the morning and say, 'I want you to come down to my house, you've got to help me out.' So, you would get in the car and drive down to Brixton or wherever it was that he lived and you did what you had to do. Then you'd come into the office bleary-eyed in the morning and he says, 'You're late'. 'I was up at three o'clock in the morning. You had me driving all over London because you were drunk last night.'

"The other thing that links us all together is that, virtually without exception, we were all fired by Robbo. He would shout. I literally, without exaggeration, would lose sleep at nights worrying. I was worried I was going to be fired for four-and-a-half of my five years. It would be like, 'You have to get Graham Parker on the front page of the *NME* next week'. 'Well perhaps it's already booked, perhaps they've already done an exclusive with Chrissie Hynde'. 'I don't give a fuck. It's easy for an Englishman to say no.' Graham Parker still sends shivers down my spine because we released a Graham Parker album because he'd had five years at Phonogram, and Robbo said, 'Right, I'm going to pull him into the label because we can do all the stuff that they can't'. So, of course, then we had to prove it. And he says to me, 'I want a story on Graham Parker in every one of the Sunday magazines', you know, *The Observer* magazine, *The Sunday Times* magazine, and he tells me this three weeks before the album is coming out. In those days, all those magazines were printed in Hong Kong or somewhere six weeks before release, which meant you had to file the story eight weeks before release. So it was like, 'That issue has already gone to bed, that's just not going to happen'. But you couldn't tell him that. We used to call him *The Führer* and, having now read a lot about the end of the war in Germany, it was very much like, 'We have to attack, we have to attack.' And it was like, 'But we're in full retreat!'"

Chris Morton also frequently worked under frantic conditions, desperately trying to get artwork for advertisements completed for the music press' weekly deadlines. He also remembers Robinson as a hard taskmaster. "Dave was a fantastic bloke, but he used to say, 'Eat on the run, More-tone, you don't need to be stopping for lunch'. Then he got an ulcer and had to calm down a bit. But he would famously sit in the same T-shirt for 36 hours, with people bringing him in sandwiches, trying to get stuff done. He was an absolute workaholic and he expected everybody else to be ...

"It was chaotic, stopping and starting, everything changing extremely quickly. One minute you would be making a plan to do a poster for someone and the next minute somebody else would turn up and it would be a fantastic new tape they were playing, so you were thinking of an idea for a cover. The next minute you were working all night because you had to get the ads done for the *NME*. The hardest thing was getting the ads done on time. Dave was famously late for okaying ideas for ads and also they might get booked late ...

"The big hassle was getting the artwork done on time. It's one thing getting the artwork ready for a record cover because if you're a bit late, well the printer has to wait and you do it as fast as you can. But we used to end up making a rod for our own backs because we used to do different ads for *NME* and *Record Mirror* and *Sounds*. Then at the same time you'd have all the *Music Week* ads, the trade ads, which were more of a skewer in the back to record companies, whereas the *NME* ones were just taking the piss 'full on' because you were talking to the punters."

—▃▃

Tenpole Tudor – in chain mail and full battle cry – stormed into the UK chart with "Swords Of A Thousand Men". The Son Of Stiff tour had, albeit belatedly, delivered a hit. The rousing anthem began with a heraldic trumpet call played over a galloping bass and burst into life. Written towards the end of the tour and recorded hastily on their return to the UK, the group had no hand in the mixing of the record. But it made no odds. "Swords Of A Thousand Men" charged to No. 6, matching the performance of their debut single "Who Killed Bambi?" which was released by Virgin to cash in on the *Great Rock 'n' Roll Swindle* film. Stiff, as expected, went to town on the video. The band were filmed on location in full medieval regalia and brandishing swords and flags, and a picture taken from the shoot made for a great sleeve.

"Someone said Charles Fox, the theatrical costumiers, was having a sale of all their old stuff, because I knew about the theatre," says Ed Tudor Pole. "So, when I went along and saw all this medieval gear and tabards ... 'Oh man, I must buy them up.' Not thinking, 'Where the hell am I ever going to wear it?!' So, we got a herald's tabard with the big coat of arms, and that is how it all came together with punk knights and punk heraldry. So, it's a patriotic thing as well, in a good way."

Although Malcolm McLaren did not directly influence Tenpole Tudor's chosen image, Tudor Pole admits he was inspired by him. "I'd always loved knights as a kid," he says. "I wasn't seeing Malcolm by then, but I'd been his student long enough. There was a period I was going out with him often, and to go out with Malcolm was just to listen to him talking; he was so entertaining and funny. So, he was like a tutor."

Bob Andrews and Alan Winstanley co-produced the accompanying album *Eddie, Old Bob, Dick and Gary,* the tracks for which were recorded not long before the Son Of Stiff bus pulled away. When the finished tracks were presented to the band during the tour, they hated it. So vehement were Tudor Pole's protests, it was agreed he could re-record his vocals when they finally came off the road. They did and the album was released in April 1981. What the band didn't know, says Tudor Pole, is that Robinson had shipped the 2,000 copies Stiff had already pressed up to Europe. "That's why we've never got anywhere in Europe because really it does sound awful," he says. In the UK, the record reached a paltry No. 44, continuing the trend of poor performances by Stiff albums.

Despite the runaway success of "Swords Of A Thousand Men", Andrews was sacked by the band and never worked with them again. "I got into conflict with a lot of these people," says Andrews. "Jona was difficult to work with and I also tended to look at records and say, 'The band is not the be all and end all of these things'. So, when we did Tenpole Tudor and 'Swords Of A Thousand Men' we were at Basing Street Studios, and I said, 'Look, we've got to get a guitar solo on this thing', and they couldn't get one sorted out. So I played it, which completely put their noses out. It was a big hit, but they didn't want me back any more and I've had that all my production life."

Fortuitously for Stiff, what had all the hallmarks of a great British one-hit wonder wasn't. The equally uproarious "Wunderbar" yielded even more opportunities for Tudor Pole to wheel dementedly around the *Top Of The Pops* studio, arms flailing. More 1980s football terrace than medieval battlefield, it achieved a chart position of 16, a more than respectable return for both group and label.

Tudor Pole was elated to find himself back on *Top Of The Pops*. But he felt that by choosing "Wunderbar" as the next single, Stiff was deliberately marketing Tenpole Tudor as a novelty band. "The thing about 'Wunderbar' was we'd had a massive hit with 'Swords', which every 12-year-old in the land bought, but nobody much older," he says. "So we were being hired to play gigs for big money because we were in the Top Ten and no one was turning up. The promoters couldn't understand it. They'd say, 'You're the best band I've ever seen. I'll pay you. You're incredible. Why isn't anybody here?' It was only years later, I worked out it's a children's song. Well, I'd sing as if I had the mental age of a child anyway …

"We didn't want 'Wunderbar' to be the follow-up, we wanted 'Go Wilder'. He [Robinson] said, 'You don't want to be a one-hit wonder. "Wunderbar", that's a definite hit'. In a way, it sounds like a hit song. For any band, it's a novelty song. The trouble was, it was originally called 'Fall About', which was a far better lyric, and we changed it on a whim. We'd been playing 'Fall About' for years and it was one of our favourite live songs, everyone fell about. But on the way to the studio to make the single, on a whim we said, 'Let's call it "Wunderbar"'. 'Yeah, okay'. And that was it – committed. What a moment of folly. And then, of course, that's got all those connotations which are so uncool, and it's such a great song and we lost half our following – 'Fuck, they're just some fucking novelty comedy band' – partly aided and abetted by Robinson. But Robinson was right in the fact it was a hit single, but I think a pretty different bunch of people bought it to those who bought 'Swords'."

"Wunderbar", whoever bought it, had kept up the momentum following the band's flag-waving entrance earlier in the year. It had provided some welcome reassurance for Stiff that Madness wasn't its only commercially viable act. *Eddie, Old Bob, Dick and Gary*, aside from producing two hit singles, was the only non-Madness album to chart for the label that year. But when the Top 40 was announced on 26 September 1981, a week after "Wunderbar" slipped quietly out, Stiff had three records in it. Two weeks later they were occupying Nos 6, 7 and 8.

One of them was "Pretend" by Alvin Stardust. Born Bernard Jewry, he performed as Shane Fenton in the 1960s and had a string of hits such as "My Coo Ca Choo" and "Jealous Mind" as Alvin Stardust in the 1970s. He seemed an incongruous presence on a label that many associated with punk and new wave. But, given its financial concerns, this was no time for snobbery. Stiff needed hits, wherever they came from. The second was Madness with "Shut Up", the first single to be taken from their album 7. A nine-week run and No. 7 hit demonstrated the group's partnership with Langer and Winstanley remained as lucrative as ever. In the video, Suggs was a petty thief protesting his innocence with his band-mates dressed as uniformed police officers in hot pursuit, Keystone Cops-style. Highlights included a piano crashing to the ground and the group walking across a ceiling.

However, it was the third Stiff record in the Top 10 that unexpectedly supplied it with a No. 1 hit a week later. "The Tweets are in the runner-up No.2 position this week with 'The Birdie Song'," announced Kid Jensen in the chart countdown on *Top Of The Pops*. "And right now, congratulations to keyboardist Dave Stewart and vocalist Barbara Gaskin, who are at No. 1 with 'It's My Party'." Cue the sounding of a gong and an odd collage of sound that was as modern as it was intriguing.

Stewart stood in a T-shirt with cut-off sleeves and holding a giant keytar [a lightweight piano synthesiser that has a strap supporting it, giving the portability of a guitar]. Beside him was Gaskin, with massive red hoop earrings and hairstyle and outfit that recalled Scottish singer Aneka, whose "Japanese Boy" had been No. 1 just weeks before. Out of nowhere and, ironically, after so many of its artists struggled to chart, a duo not even signed to Stiff had come up with its second No. 1 record. "It was bizarre," says Gaskin. "We didn't expect it at all, we just did it for a laugh."

The song, written by John Gluck, Wally Gold and Herb Weiner and first recorded by Helen Shapiro, gave producer Quincy Jones one of his first hits. "I definitely knew the song, I think people of my age all did," says Gaskin. "Then Dave asked me to sing it and I thought it was slightly embarrassing, actually. We recorded it in an overnight session somewhere and I took my friend, who I went to school with, and we were just sneering about the idea really. But I really liked working with Dave and I knew that anything he did, I would like. So, I remember learning it and looking at the words and thinking, well this is a bit stupid, isn't it?"

Gaskin grew up in Hatfield, Hertfordshire. Moving to Canterbury to attend Kent University, she became the vocalist with folk rock group Spirogyra. She met guitarist Steve Hillage and he introduced her to

Dave Stewart. The two of them had been in the progressive band Uriel, which later became the organ-led trio, Egg. He had also added Hatfield & The North and National Health to his prog-littered CV, before hooking up with Bill Bruford, at which point he discovered synthesisers. After twelve years of playing in bands, he felt he needed a new challenge and he began arranging and producing songs.

One of the songs he was drawn to was the Jimmy Ruffin hit "What Becomes Of The Broken Hearted", composed by the songwriting team of James Dean, Paul Riser and William Weatherspoon. He told Barbara about it and she suggested that he get in contact with Colin Blunstone, who had been at school with her sister. He did so, and the former Zombies vocalist agreed to come on board, with any proceeds from the record to be split between them. They punted their reworked version of the Motown classic around, only to be turned away by EMI, Polydor and other major labels. Geoff Travis liked it and agreed to release it on Rough Trade. But when he played it to colleagues they hated it, preferring another cover of the same song that was also doing the rounds. The artwork having been produced and Stewart and Blunstone having agreed in good faith to go with Rough Trade, Travis offered to release it on their own label. In a nod to the song, Broken Records was formed.

Stewart's decidedly eighties interpretation of the song struck a chord with the public and another Travis, Radio 1's Dave Lee, began playing it. Such was the demand that record shops quickly began to run out and Rough Trade's fleet of vans simply couldn't keep pace. Stewart also detected that some of the staff weren't too interested in such a commercial record and didn't see a need for their sales teams to be proactively contacting shops.

Travis, admitting Rough Trade wasn't doing the record justice, graciously offered to tear up the agreement, sell off any existing stock and hand the record back to Stewart, who says: "At that point, Robbo came on the scene. I think he, or someone from Stiff, must have heard the track on the radio and got in touch with John Marshall, my business guy, and said, 'Is there any chance?' So we went for a meeting up there and met Dave Robinson, Paul Conroy, who I knew already, and Alan Cowderoy, who was an extremely nice guy. I thought, 'I like these people, I like Robbo'".

Travis's loss was Robinson's gain. "What Becomes Of The Broken Hearted", catalogue number Broken 1, was released by Stiff in

February 1981 and spent ten weeks in the chart. It was the most unexpected of windfalls and Robinson – who had a fondness for cover versions – must have been especially pleased. Lene Lovich and other artists became infuriated with his insistence that they record other people's songs (he had a particular fondness for Motown numbers), something that occasionally strained their relationships with him. Robinson had always been extremely disparaging of musicians, whom he saw as ten-a-penny.

Stewart, however, he saw in a different light: "He [Robinson] said, 'To be honest David, musicians are like pebbles on the beach. What I'm interested in is producers.' He saw me as a producer because I put together this whole track. He had quite strong musical ideas, which he was very happy to put forward at the earliest opportunity. I really liked him. I liked his enthusiasm, he had this really positive outlook – 'Right, we're going to make this happen'. He was encouraging, he didn't talk down to you, he spoke to you as an equal. He was an intelligent bloke and when he was talking to you, he didn't make the mistake of thinking, 'Oh he's just another fucking musician, I'm going to patronise him'."

Robinson almost immediately introduced him to the team that would be selling his record. A smart move, as Stewart explains: "We went into a back room and there were four or five girls in there, all on the phone and saying, 'How are you? Have you got this record by Jona Lewie in the shop, you really need to get it? Why don't we send you some over?' I met them all and they were a nice bunch, and Dave said, 'You should hang out with them. Why don't you go to the pub?' So I said, 'Okay,' so we went to the pub and had a few pints and played darts and they were a really nice bunch and I got to know them a bit. It was a smart move by Robbo to introduce me to the sales team because then, because as we knew each other, when they rang up and they were saying about Dave Stewart's record, they actually knew me and had a little bit more reason to do it".

When Stewart gave the electronic treatment to "It's My Party" on the suggestion of a girlfriend, he didn't take it straight to Robinson; it didn't seem like an obvious fit with Stiff. However, history repeated itself, the major record companies didn't like it and Stiff did. As for a vocalist, Stewart had only ever envisaged one person singing it – Barbara Gaskin.

By August 1981, strangely-attired female singers were less of a phenomenon. Where Siouxsie Sioux and Lene Lovich had led, Hazel O'Connor and Toyah Wilcox had followed. Reflecting the more extrovert way in which women presented themselves in pop, Gaskin cut an enigmatic figure on the sleeve of the record. Sitting cross-legged, her heavily made-up eyes stared fixedly at the camera, and the long golden nails on the ends of her fingers completing the mysterious look. Amid the dry ice, Stewart wore a red boxing mask and gloves and held a fencing sword, props he had picked up at a martial arts shop in Soho.

A fencing duel featured in the video with Thomas Dolby, then practically unknown, playing the party wrecker who stole Judy. Mannequins made up the guest numbers. Stiff didn't try and direct the duo in relation to the record cover, although it did pay for a photographer and make-up adviser, says Gaskin. But the filming was a very different matter. "The video just took its theme from the equipment Dave had bought and it was all done in a day," she says. "Dave and I had worked out a storyboard, which Robbo completely ignored and just did what he wanted to do, which was fine. That happened quite a lot actually. It was a question of, 'Who's in charge here?' We thought we were and he thought he was. It caused a little bit of tension from time to time."

So phenomenal was the response to the record, the demand outstripped Stiff's supply and Robinson had to intervene. Recalling the single's meteoric ascension, Stewart says: "We used to get a phone call every Tuesday morning from Paul Conroy. He would call at about 10 o'clock when I was still in bed and say, 'Dave, it's No. 33.' Next Tuesday, 'Dave, it's No. 17', and then one week, 'It's No. 8.' It was like, 'Jesus Christ, we're in the Top 10.'

"But in that week a problem developed. The demand for it was so high they couldn't keep up with the pressings. We sold 40,000 in one day. They used to get a lot of sales to jukeboxes in those days: companies used to stock thousands of jukeboxes up and down the country – pubs and restaurants or whatever – and they'd come in and order 5,000. So, we ran out of pressings and I was really afraid it was going to be like Rough Trade, and it would just taper off. But Robbo had found a firm in Europe, maybe Holland or France, who could get some more pressings over to the UK. When the new pressings came in, there had been about a two-day hiatus where no sales had happened. All those back orders got sold on that one day. It was really good timing and it pushed it to No.1, because it was out-selling everything that week. I got the phone call the next Tuesday – 'Dave, it's No. 1.' 'Shit!'"

An exhausted Stewart had flown out to California to stay with a friend and catch his breath. No sooner had he arrived than his manager called to say he was wanted for the Christmas edition of *Top Of The Pops*. He was reluctant, but the opportunity to see Gaskin, with whom he had recently begun a relationship, swung it. Nigel Dick was waiting at Heathrow Airport to whisk him to the BBC studios, where another Stiff act was performing – although their identity was being kept secret. Frosty, Blob, Lump and Norman, A.K.A. The Snowmen, had dusted down party favourite "The Hokey Cokey" in an effort to make it a second happy Christmas in a row. Four giant Snowmen shook it all about on *Top Of The Pops* and the record went to No.18.

The gruff vocals and the fact one of the Snowmen was called Norman gave rise to the rumour that it was Ian Dury & The Blockheads. Sonnie says: "I just played that and people went, 'That's Ian Dury, isn't it?' and I would go, 'Ooh, I couldn't possibly say because it's a big secret. I don't know who it is'. I think they all thought it was Ian Dury, so I think that's why it got all the airplay it did." Sonnie says she believes the singer was a session player called Martin, while Nigel Dick admits to being one of the snowmen who led the *Top Of The Pops* audience in the "Hokey Cokey". "I believe I was Norman," he says. "It is possible that I also came up with the names, but it's a long time ago now. If memory serves me well, there were two guys who made the record, although I've forgotten their names. The fourth snowman was a friend of theirs."

Surprisingly, given the 750,000 copies Stiff had sold of "It's My Party", Robinson passed on the album subsequently recorded by Gaskin and Stewart. It wasn't an LP Robinson wanted – unless it was by Madness – but another single. The record never saw the light of day and the couple never performed a gig during their time with Stiff.

Stewart says: "Robbo kept saying to us, 'Look, we could release the album now and sell about 50,000 (and I thought, "Well that would suit me") or we can wait for you to have another hit and we could sell half a million.' So he was obsessed with more hits, more hits, and I hadn't gone into this game to produce hit records. I had gone into it to do songs I liked, so we did have a difference of philosophy. He did sit me down at one point and said, 'Right, look, if you really want to make this work, you've got to be thinking of these sort of product cycles.' He got a calendar out and said, 'I need your next single by then, we'll need to start promoting it then, and then we'll need a third single.' And so it went on and I thought, 'You know what, this is not really what I want to start getting into. I'm not a "product cycle" kind of bloke'."

"Perhaps we should have done what Robbo said," says Gaskin. "You have to have a trajectory and we were very slow getting a follow-up. He wanted them rattled out and, in commercial terms, that was probably the correct thing to do. But in terms of our musical life, it was the wrong thing to do. What we did instead was go into a studio and work on an album, and it took us ages and ages to do it, but we came out with a musical identity that persists to this day, I'm happy to say."

—

Robinson had seen the re-ignition of interest around ska and reggae sparked by 2 Tone as his chance to build a reggae platform within his enterprise. Although his initial attempts to gain a foothold in this lucrative market had been unsuccessful, he was determined to follow in Blackwell's footsteps through the Caribbean sand. And his ace in the hole was Desmond Dekker. Much had been expected of his 1980 Stiff release *Black And Dekker,* which included "Israelites" and "Many Rivers To Cross". Blessed with a title that later political correctness made seem unthinkable, the album failed to resurrect the career of the man who had played such a key role in popularising Jamaican ska and reggae in an otherwise pop and rock-centric Britain. In 1981 Stiff tried again, this time with the more suitably named *Compass Point.*

Keen to harness a more authentic sound, Stiff had flown Dekker out to Nassau in The Bahamas to work with a new producer. Robinson had taken Dekker to The Dominion Theatre in London to see Island artist Robert Palmer and to consider if he could work with him. He agreed and Stiff flew him out to Palmer's home in Nassau to start work on what would be a costly project. Recording sessions then took place at Compass Point Studios where Dekker was backed by a red-hot crew of musicians. The finished tracks were then mixed at Sterling Sound in New York City, adding yet more expense. None of the album's tracks were selected for single release. Instead, Will Birch was brought in to produce a cover of The Heptones' "Book Of Rules", and "Allamanna", which had featured on the Palmer-produced album, was used as the B-side. But there was no chart action for album or single. As the sun set on the ska renaissance that had been led by The Specials, The Selecter, Madness and others, it seemed like Dekker had missed the boat.

An insipid electro affair "Hot City" was released as a single in August 1983, in a last-ditch effort to wring a hit out of him. But Stiff's all-too-transparent attempt to serve up reggae for the masses failed miserably. Dekker continued to play live with The Rumour, with whom Stiff had originally teamed him up. But in 1984 he was declared bankrupt. He released a live album in the 1980s and teamed up with The Specials in 1993 for *King Of Kings,* a tribute to his musical heroes. Dekker was at his home in Croydon, when he died of a heart attack on 25 May 2006 aged 64.

Compass Point had come on the heels of The Equators' *Hot.* The group had gone down well with audiences on the Son Of Stiff Tour and Bob Andrews was brought in to produce their first album for Stiff. All eleven tracks were originals, the cover of "Baby Come Back" being omitted, and the usual Stiff press and marketing was applied. But this melting pot of a record received a lukewarm reception, consigning the band to a footnote in the Stiff story.

A second throw of the dice was also taken on their Son Of Stiff companions Dirty Looks. *Turn It Up* was, like the American group's debut, written entirely by Patrick Barnes and produced by Nick Garvey of The Motors. Their urgent brand of pop seemed in keeping with the times, with Elvis Costello, XTC and Squeeze all enjoying mainstream success. However, while the textbook pop of songs like "Daddy's Gone", "Do We Need It" and "Hit List" boded well for the American trio, they couldn't get on first base. "Dirty Looks' mistake was to use London only as a base for recording," wrote Bert Muirhead. "They should have settled there temporarily and built up some reputation in Britain." [34] They didn't and, when *Turn It Up* fell on deaf ears, Stiff and Epic dropped them.

Any Trouble were also in Stiff's Last Chance Saloon by 1981. *Wheels In Motion*, their second album, had plenty of pop appeal; "Trouble With Love" and "Open Fire" both sounded like hit material. But in the MTV era when a band's visual appeal was more important than ever, Any Trouble somehow didn't cut it. Squeeze's tousle-haired vocalist Glenn Tilbrook got away with wearing a pink, lounge-bar jacket to perform "Labelled With Love" on *Top Of The Pops.* Gregson sported an almost identical look on the Son of Stiff Tour and in the cheesy video for "Girls Are Always Right" and somehow didn't.

Producer John Wood's success with Squeeze hadn't rubbed off on Any Trouble when he had overseen things in the studio for their first

Stiff album. So, for the second album, it was decided to bring in ex-Gong bassist Mike Howlett, who had produced hits for Martha and the Muffins, Teardrop Explodes and Orchestral Manoeuvres in the Dark. "Yesterday's Love" was released as a single to trail the record. *Wheels In Motion* however ground to a halt.

Clive Gregson says candidly: "Squeeze made it. They came along earlier than us and I suppose you could argue they were much better than us, which was probably true. I've realised after 30-odd years in the music business, scuffing around doing what I do, that essentially it's not a meritocracy. People aren't successful because they're any good: people are successful because the public like them and if they don't like it, that's it – game over. So, I think the public were exposed to it, and I've never had any complaints at all about the effort that Stiff put in. The records were clearly visible and they were on the radio. We made videos that got shown on MTV or whatever the equivalents were back then. We did a fair bit of TV, we did all the stuff bands do, but it never caught on with the public."

Gregson recalls how Any Trouble's time at Stiff ended in brutal fashion: "We were on tour in the second half of '81 touring on *Wheels In Motion*, our second official Stiff record. My girlfriend at the time, Jane Kelly, worked for Stiff in the accounts department, and she phoned me up and said, 'They've dropped you!'. I didn't hear it from Robbo, of course. So, I said, 'Oh, all right'. It wasn't really surprising or a terrible shock. But it did give us an immediate problem in so far as we had no money and there was no tour support left and we were stuck in New York. I remember our manager coming in and saying to us, 'Well, we could just stay on the road. We've been offered some dates with Molly Hatchet', I think it was. We just thought, 'I don't think so. I think we'll just go back to England and give up'".

There was clearly a need for fresh blood at Stiff. Too often the records it had spent money producing were getting nowhere, and, in some cases, not being issued at all. A song by Lonesome Tone called "Mum, Dad, Love, Hate And Elvis" had been leased from Silent Records, and promo and radio copies had been pressed up as BUY 111. But it had never seen the light of day due to lack of airplay. Bubba Lou And The Highballs' "Love All Over The Place" had meanwhile been lined up as BUY 114 and promotional copies distributed, only for it to be scrapped. The next single that had made it off the Stiff production line (although perhaps it shouldn't have), was "The Turning Point" by John Otway. Stiff looked after his management in Britain and the US, and had already seen his rendition of Tom Jones' "Green Green Grass Of Home" sink like a stone. This suffered the same fate, further highlighting that there was too much BUYing and not enough buying.

Post-punk groups like Public Image Limited, Echo & The Bunnymen and Teardrop Explodes had begun making a real impact at other record labels. Stiff had no such bands and were keen to get a foothold in this flourishing market. When Department S arrived at Stiff, they put forward their biggest crowd-pleaser as the follow-up to their debut hit. They had scored a surprise hit with "Is Vic There?", reaching No. 22. The song had been recorded in Nick Lowe's sitting room in Shepherd's Bush, and was the first hit on Demon, the label set up in 1980 by Jake Riviera and Andrew Lauder.

The group, managed by Clive Banks, had materialised from Guns For Hire, and counted Elvis Costello among their celebrity admirers. They had built up a strong live reputation and when they arrived at Stiff, they put the case for "Clap Now" to be released as their next single, which was knocking 'em dead when played on stage. It was recorded by Dale Griffin and Pete Overend Watts from Mott The Hoople. But Stiff rejected it, prompting the band to wonder if it had made a huge mistake.

Guitarist Mike Herbage says: "It was always the one at gigs that everyone ended up going bonkers to – it was the obvious single. We recorded it and it came out really well. But when we came to the studio, Stiff just said, 'Well, we're not sure about that one. Great piece of art lads, but not a single'. They were immediately kind of saying, 'Well, we've signed you, we've heard all the demos, we came to see you live ten times, now we want to change you'. Why do that?"

Stiff sacked Griffin and Watts and brought in David Tickle to oversee things in the studio. The British engineer had worked on Blondie's breakthrough album *Parallel Lines*, and Stiff clearly hoped his magic touch would rub off on its new charges. With the momentum of "Is Vic There?" there to be capitalised on, the label went for "Going Left Right" as the follow-up single. This wasn't the group's choice, but given the five-figure sum Stiff had paid to prise them away from Demon, the young musicians felt they weren't in a position to argue.

"What are we going to do when they've just given us a £70,000 record contract and we're 21?" says Herbage. "At that time, Adam And The Ants got £40,000 and Culture Club got £20,000, and they were always going to sell more than us. It was a huge amount of money. It was a bit of a daft gamble really; we didn't ask for that money. We were just thinking, 'We just want to go and make a record with Pete and Dale'. We weren't even thinking about giving up our jobs, we just wanted to make a record, that's how naive we were. We just thought, 'Great, we'll make an album, fantastic, and then I can whisk back into my factory and go, "We've made a record"'. Suddenly it was, 'Right, we're going to pay you this each week, go and hand your notice in, you're going on tour with Spizz [Athletico Spizz 80]'."

The Farmyard and Strawberry Studios were used at great expense to record the single and the rest of the album. A van and other equipment was paid for as Stiff continued to pour money into the project. When the single was released in June 1981, *Melody Maker* was effusive in its praise and predicted it could be "massive". Department S were preparing for another appearance on *Top Of The Pops*, but "Going Left Right" stalled at No. 55 and managed just three weeks in the UK chart.

Stiff began losing interest in the group almost immediately, despite the huge amount it had staked on them, says Herbage. "I Want You", a song he had written with front man Vaughn Toulouse, was released as a single. In the UK, where the group did an extensive headline tour, the record did nothing. It fared better in Europe and produced a massive hit in Spain. When they returned home, however, they were called in to a meeting.

Herbage describes what happened: "Clive [Banks] got us up to his office and said, 'Right, Stiff have dropped you'. When we signed, he had said 'Stiff have signed us' – 'us' being the word. At the end, it was 'Stiff have dropped you'. I will remember that until the day I die. I thought, what happened to 'us' then? That is the way with these people. It was a bit of a shock really. He did say, 'Let's not panic, because there's another five companies willing to take us on'. But the problem was that Stiff was having financial problems. We didn't know that when they were giving little indie groups £70,000 payouts. I mean, come on, no business model is going to work that way is it? From what I can gather, Stiff wanted to try to recoup all the money they had invested. Warner Brothers or CBS were interested, but they were going, 'How much did you give them? Really? No, we're not going to give you that amount of money'. And that's why it never went anywhere."

Stiff refused to release the master tapes for less than the reported £50,000 they had cost to produce, resulting in the album being trapped in the vaults. For Department S, it was a crushing blow and halfway through 1982 they had split up. Clive Banks had designs on promoting the charismatic Toulouse as a solo artist, says Herbage. But amid the rising tide of New Romantic artists like Steve Strange, his head never appeared above the surface. Sadly, Toulouse died of an AIDS-related illness in New York in 1991, too soon to see the band recognised with the release of its entire back catalogue on the Mau-Mau label.

Their time at Stiff had been brief, but telling. That the label had paid such a vast sum of money for a relatively unknown act and then promptly dropped it is indicative of the kind of hasty – and costly – decisions it was making by the early 1980s. By hiring posh studios and bringing in a big name expensive producer, Stiff had simply amassed costs it had no realistic chance of recovering and more unsold records in its stockroom. To relieve the pressure on Madness and its finances, the label needed to snap up a group that had promise and that wouldn't cost hundreds of thousands of pounds to break. It's prayers were about to be answered.

In October 1981, Madness set out to promote 7, accompanied by an all-girl group. Not their old friends The Go Go's, then on their way to superstardom, but The Belle Stars. A brand new band, they were from North London and were familiar with Madness – some of them intimately. "Some of us were dating them at the time," says Bedders. "We knew them very well and they lived around the same area. Miranda Joyce, who I went out with for quite a long while, actually went to the school over the road from me. I had known her and her brothers, who played music, for quite a few years before. So it didn't feel like a Stiff thing as such. It was another local band with us and we went out on the road."

The Belle Stars had emerged from the ashes of The Bodysnatchers. The 2 Tone outfit had featured in the film *Dance Craze* and got to No. 22 with their cover of Dandy Livingstone's "Let's Do Rocksteady". Their last show had been supporting Madness at Camden's Music Machine in October 1980. Within a couple of months, guitarists Sarah-Jane Owen and Stella Barker, saxophonist Miranda Joyce, keyboardist Penny Leyton and drummer Judy Parsons had hooked up with new singer Jennie Matthias and bassist Lesley Shone. Matthias had never been in a band, but she was a natural.

They played their first gig on Christmas Day 1980, without even a name, and adorned the cover of *Sounds* on 14 March 1981. Stiff moved quickly to sign them. "Dave Robinson was looking for a female act that might possibly be a bit like Madness," says Matthias. "I think he got that idea because the girls were originally from a ska band. Madness were on Stiff at the time, so they poached us after they heard we were doing a gig in Dingwalls."

Stiff, in a bid to repeat a winning formula, got them in a studio with Clive Langer and Alan Winstanley, and the first result was the single "Hiawatha". The cover and picture disc had the seven girls posing in black leather jackets, boots and other casual gear. A remnant from their Bodysnatchers' days, the song certainly bore some striking similarities to Madness' early records, Joyce's sax providing the hooks over an urgent rhythm that suggested they were not abandoning their ska roots. "Hiawatha" sent out smoke signals, but nothing more, and a second single, "Slick Trick", followed suit. The Belle Stars and Stiff would have to bide their time.

In July, Madness had flown out to Nassau to Chris Blackwell's Compass Point Studios. Their accountants had advised them that if they recorded the album in another country, they would only be taxed on 80% of the proceeds. They arrived at the legendary studios just a couple of months after Ian Dury had been there making his Polydor debut *Lord Upminster* with Sly and Robbie.

On their return to the UK, "Shut Up" was released and they recorded the song for *Top Of The Pops*. On 2 October 1981, Stiff released 7 and a few days later they set off on tour with The Belle Stars on support. The women couldn't have wished for a better platform. Madness were in their pomp, "Shut Up" had made it nine consecutive hit singles and the album would climb to No.5. And given their associations with 2 Tone and ska, those turning up to see Madness would have been well disposed towards the all-girl group.

Jenny Matthias says: "Because we were label mates with Madness, it was easy for us to be on tour with them; also, one of the band members was going out with one of them. These were fun times for us. We had just come off The Clash tour and went straight on to the Madness tour: The gigs were large and the audiences really lovely, and this is where we started getting our greatest fans. Being on the road with the lads was awesome, they were funny and most of them gentlemen. This resulted in me going out with Chrissy Boy Foreman for the next seven years. He is still one of my very best friends."

Aside from Madness being Stiff's only reliable chart presence, the label was getting more than its pound of flesh from them. The lads had been on the road almost continually since their arrival. Videos had become ever more ambitious and time-consuming and their young fan-base meant they were in demand from children's TV shows like *Multi-Coloured Swap Shop* and *Tiswas*, as well as *Top Of The Pops*. Matinée shows were also put on to ensure those who weren't old enough to get into their usual gigs could see their heroes. "It was brilliant," says Foreman. "We showed films, cartoons and charged 50p to get in. Stiff liked us to be working and, in retrospect, we worked far too hard." The album was their third in two years and "Shut Up" their eighth consecutive single since their move from 2 Tone. And it had also fallen on Stiff's hardest working act to realise another of Dave Robinson's ambitions – a movie.

Seven days into the tour, Madness were driven to the Parkway Cinema in Camden in Alan Winstanley's Bentley – which they had pelted with eggs to his fury – and stepped out in tuxedos. The occasion was the premiere of *Take It Or Leave It,* a film that charted the band's rise to fame and in which they played themselves. "Here is greatness … wonder … majesty … a motion picture no human words can describe … but which every human heart can feel … and share." So read the plug for the film which filled one side of the inner sleeve of *7*.

The film – named after a track on *Absolutely* – was, in true Robinson style, an expensive gamble. Stiff had reportedly stumped up £250,000 for the project, with members of the band and their then manager Kellogs also putting up the rest of the cash. Creatively, it was a true team effort. Madness and Robinson came up with the script, with help from writer and video producer Phil McDonald. Robinson personally took charge of the filming, which took place over about two weeks.

Foreman vividly remembers the filming, which suffered setbacks from the very outset. "We did two days filming and we sent it to Switzerland and it came back bleached – it was ruined," he says. "And it was sort of a blessing in disguise, because we were insured and we'd had two days practice working with cameras, so we just carried on merrily … We were based in St Pancras Way where there was a big Post Office depot. One of the first scenes they filmed was a car chase, where we had to get from one gig to another. There was this gantry which fell over and Dave [Robinson] broke his leg right at the beginning. We got a bit of press out of it though!"

A gritty, warts 'n' all affair, shot in black and white and colour, it followed their story from their humble beginnings as the North

London Invaders to becoming a household name in pop. A mixture of documentary and drama, it ran for less than an hour and a half, and was presented by Nutty Stiff Productions. But for all Robinson's exuberance, and not to mention the vast sums that had been sunk into the project, *Take It Or Leave It* bombed. The BBC's esteemed film critic Barry Norman slammed it, Stiff experienced problems with its distribution, and many cinema screenings were practically empty.

During the *7* tour, Madness had been performing "It Must Be Love", the song with which Labi Siffre had a hit in 1971. Robinson loved it and told the band that if they released it and it didn't make No.1, he would give them the label! So, on a Sunday morning, they disappeared into a small terraced house that had a little studio and recorded it. Their glorious cover of the song was released on 5 November and came close to fulfilling Robinson's prophecy. Breathing fresh life into Siffre's sublime piece of pop, Madness' ninth single for Stiff reached No. 4 and spent three months in the chart. Videos now being requisite for any pop single, Robinson and the group started coming up with ideas. As ever, Thompson was bubbling with ideas and the challenge was to make them happen as quickly and cheaply as possible.

Foreman remembers: "Lee wanted to be underwater and I thought it was a good idea, but I thought it was going to look crap because he went and jumped in a pond, I thought, 'He's got to be underwater'. So, we found this hotel with a swimming pool who would let us film and we had this cameraman who was like a genius and he was up for anything. So, he [Lee] put all the scuba gear on and he was underwater with the camera. Dave was watching and, initially, I was standing on the edge playing. Lee jumped in and I thought, 'Maybe I should jump in'. So, I jumped in and the guitar kept floating, so Dave very kindly gave me some lead weights and I put them in them in the back pocket of my trousers to pull me down. But I tell you man, I nearly drowned. I got out and the guitar was bent and Dave got a hairdryer and we dried it out and we took it back, because we'd hired it. But then Stiff bought it and it was in a lot of Stiff videos. It's a white Stratocaster, it wasn't some cheapo guitar."

Not content with film premieres, recording singles and making videos in the middle of a major tour, Madness even squeezed in a wedding. Graham McPherson married his long-time sweetheart Anne Martin (A.K.A. Bette Bright) three days before Christmas 1981.

With 1982 only days old, Robinson had Madness being filmed on a double-decker bus going through Camden. Passers-by looked on bemused and some old ladies even climbed on board as the footage was filmed for "Cardiac Arrest". The third single to be lifted from *7* sold well, but it was the first Madness single on Stiff not to make the Top 10. Radio One was uncomfortable about such a serious subject being used by a pop group known for larking about. Kenny Everett had no such misgivings and he invited the Nutty Boys on to his then hugely popular TV show to perform it.

If there was disappointment at Stiff at the unusually sluggish performance of a Madness record, it was soon replaced with ecstasy. Before "Cardiac Arrest" had even hit the shops, they'd recorded scenes for their next video at a funfair. Robinson and the band climbed aboard the rollercoaster rides at the Norfolk resort of Great Yarmouth, where Thompson had relatives. These shots were then intermingled with footage from a chemist's shop in Camden. The record was "House Of Fun".

"Dave had got these things called zap guns – and this shows how long ago it was," says Foreman. "They were like little video cameras about four inches square with fixed legs, and they had four minutes of film. They were kind of developed in the war. You know, when you're in Spitfires and they shoot the Germans? That's what these things were, so we did some of it on that. There is a bit when it went upside down and we were all in hysterics because Robbo was filming us. As it went upside down, all these car keys fell out – everything fell out!"

"House Of Fun" didn't plummet; it sky rocketed. A tale of a boy's attempts to buy a condom on his 16th birthday, it was a stroke of genius by Barson and Thompson. Like Dury's "England's Glory" and "Billericay Dickie", it doffed its cap to Music Hall and maintained a fairground feel throughout. The everyday nature of the lyrics and sense of storytelling was also quintessentially English in its style and delivery.

The old fashioned knees-up, with one of the catchiest tunes ever to grace the label, went to No.1 in the UK chart and spent two weeks there. *Complete Madness*, the greatest hits album it came from, and released on 23 April, followed suit. A bumper collection boasting all eleven hit singles and five other tracks, it spent three weeks in the top spot and a staggering 88 weeks in the UK album chart – two weeks shy of the run enjoyed by *New Boots And Panties!!*. So strong was the record's appeal that, for the first time, Stiff took out TV adverts to promote it.

Madness were buoyant and they alone were keeping Stiff's head above water.

13

Sign Of The Times

To the casual observer, Stiff looked a model business. In just six years, it had gone from maverick to mainstream. Whatever Madness touched seemed to turn to gold and the arrival of hits from other artists suggested the label hadn't lost its ability to uncover original acts for a pop audience. Even with such commercial own goals as the Son Of Stiff Tour and *Take It Or Leave It* (most left it), Stiff had continued to notch up chart hits. The accounts, however, showed a less rosy picture. While the label's turnover had soared in 1981 to just over £5.5 million, by 1982 it had fallen to £4.6 million. Meanwhile, the financial loss of £16,259 it reported for the previous year had risen sharply to £470,000 in 1982.

Staff costs had also increased by £37,000 and Stiff had moved to larger premises for a second time, in September 1982. The Bayham Street offices in NW1 were in the heart of Madness country: close to Camden High Street and around the corner from local landmark The World's End pub. Perfect for filming Madness videos, it was more corporate looking than the ex-warehouse they had just vacated. But despite the shiny new edifice, some of its artists were beginning to feel decidedly unwelcome at Stiff; some even felt shut away. Amongst them was Lene Lovich, who turned to theatre as she reached an impasse with her label.

"We did *Mata Hari* [a musical] because problems were getting so bad with Stiff that they wouldn't let us do anything, and they'd locked us in the dungeon," explains Lovich. "I wasn't the only one in there, by the way. Jona spent a serious amount of time in the dungeon as well. So, we were in the dungeon club, but they didn't have any control over what I did live. I couldn't afford to tour, so it was just a practical way of doing something and somebody gave me that opportunity, so I thought, 'Okay', but I'm not an actress."

Lovich and her long-time partner Les Chappell had effectively reached a standoff with Robinson. The convivial relationship they had enjoyed when they first signed with the label had turned sour. Robinson wanted a hit and, to the couple's growing infuriation, kept suggesting they do a Motown cover. They wanted time to write and record their own material. And, when they did present songs they were excited about to Robinson, he either showed no interest or rejected them.

"I just didn't want to do a Motown song," says Lovich. "I could have done it for historic reasons, I could have done it for a lot of reasons. But by then I was really locked into my own creative direction, so I didn't do it. Then it became this awful stalemate. I would present new material and he wouldn't even listen to it. I had been given a song that was written by Liam Sternberg, who did a lot of writing for Rachel [Sweet]. I tried to have a meeting with Dave. Sonnie heard it and she told me straight away, 'That's a good 'un'. She had a really good ear for what was successful. I did a demo of it and I was really happy with it, but he dug his heels in." The song? "Walk Like An Egyptian", which was a monster hit for The Bangles in 1986, making No. 1 in the US and a host of other countries.

Getting Stiff to agree to Lovich going into a studio to record her album proved difficult. Keen to find a way of placating Robinson, she agreed to collaborate with his producer of the moment, Martin Rushent. Recordings for what would become *No Man's Land* got underway in 1981 and produced "Blue Hotel", the B-side for "New Toy". Lovich saw "Never Never Land" as a potential single, but this was vetoed by Robinson. Instead, Stiff reissued "Lucky Number" after it was used to advertise KP Nuts, and put "New Toy" on the flip as the song's writer, Thomas Dolby, was having hits at the time. "New Toy" was also re-released by Stiff before her third album got to see the light of day.

While she and Robinson played out their own Cold War, Lovich cast around for other ways to fulfil herself artistically. She had co-written two songs for *Flex* with Chris Judge Smith, a founder member of prog rockers Van der Graaf Generator, and with Chappell they wrote a musical about the Dutch exotic performer Mata Hari, executed by firing squad for reportedly spying for Germany during World War I. The show was staged at The Lyric in Hammersmith in October and November 1982, with Lovich in the lead role. Her dark, piercing eyes combined with her bejewelled headdress and *risqué* costumes made for a striking resemblance to the controversial figure she portrayed.

No Man's Land had been recorded before the stage show was performed and Lovich had sent the tapes to Robinson. Getting no reaction, she passed them to Epic, the label through which her records were released in the US. Epic loved the record, but wanted it to be remixed. So, amid rehearsals, she flew to New York, where the only available studio slot was the night shift. She worked through the small hours with remix engineer Bob Clearmountain and completed the record before flying back to continue preparations for *Mata Hari*. Robinson was said to have been furious that she had gone direct to Epic and, because the US label had decided to put the record out, Stiff had been left to pick up the bill for the remixing.

Lovich's indomitable spirit and belief in the record she had made was rewarded when it became her third album to make the US *Billboard* Top 200. Heavy listener requests from women prompted one radio station programme director to predict "It's You, Only You (Mein Schmerz)" could be "this year's 'Gloria'". "It's a very imaginative record," Steve Warren of WRKR-FM told *Billboard* magazine. "The synthesizers are playful, and the production grabbed me right away." British listeners were less enthusiastic. The single staggered to No. 68 and spent just a fortnight on the chart. *No Man's Land* meanwhile became her first album not to chart in the UK. Figuring it better to have no label than one that no longer supported what she was doing, Lovich parted company from Stiff.

Speaking about the breakdown in her relationship with Robinson and the label, she says: "Stiff was going around the world, or at least basically Europe and America, getting huge advances from the licensees, almost to a point where it was ridiculous. Even if every single track on the album was a hit, you could not recoup because each year the advance would get larger. But in order to keep that going, Stiff had to present the next album to Stiff Epic and they didn't want to pay for it. So, that was the situation and that was actually how we got out of our deal with Stiff. We were in a stalemate for at least two years and we managed to negotiate with Epic that we would present four or five tracks, and if they didn't like it, then they would pass. Stiff had lost confidence in us at that point.

"We went into the studio at a terrible time when the pound was worth one dollar. We worked with Mike Thorne, who is a great producer, and we produced four or five tracks to a degree where they could see where it was going, and they decided that they couldn't see it. That took all the money that Les and I had: we had no money left whatsoever. So then we couldn't do anything. We had no record deal, no money."

—

Jona Lewie was also at a crossroads with his label and finding Robinson increasingly distracted. Since "Stop The Cavalry" had become the Christmas hit of 1980, it seemed he had been mothballed along with the decorations. So drawn out was the recording of his second album, the production credits almost exceeded the track listing. Rupert Hine, who would go on to produce Howard Jones, amongst others, had overseen most of the tracks. But seven other producers were mentioned, including Lewie himself and Robinson.

Heart Skips A Beat felt more like a Greatest Hits. "I Think I'll Get My Haircut", "Stop The Cavalry", "Louise" and "Rearranging The Deckchairs On The Titanic" had all been singles, albeit only "Stop The Cavalry" had charted. Initial copies pressed by Stiff even threw in "You'll Always Find Me In The Kitchen At Parties". Released around four years after his debut *On The Other Hand There's A Fist*, it was received with the same indifference. For Lewie, as with his one-time train companion Lovich, the hits had well and truly dried up, and there was an increasing sense that Robinson had moved onto his next business.

"I remember one time, around 1982 or 1983, I had to wait all afternoon to see him," Lewie recalls. "I was in the office making myself teas and I was very much part of the furniture. He [Robinson] was spinning so many plates. There were no hard feelings and we had a very nice meeting, but you could see he was completely overwhelmed." After two albums and nine singles – only Madness had released more 45s – Lewie left the label.

While the Be Stiff era had finally drawn to a close, the label was still determined to wring something more from the sole success story of the Son Of Stiff campaign. Tenpole Tudor's second album *Let The Four Winds Blow* had produced a No. 49 hit in "Throwing The Baby Out With The Bathwater", but precious little else. Tudor Pole and the band weren't entirely happy with the record and felt Robinson, in particular, had rushed them into putting it out. "We were still within our contract and we had to have one by September or whenever," says Tudor Pole.

"We could have made a fuss and said, 'You'll jolly well have to wait until we're ready', like The Pretenders did. They waited about four years before their second album and everyone said, 'They've blown it, they've taken too long'. But they hadn't blown it, because when it did come out it was a good album and is to this day. So, wasn't it worth just spending a little bit of time? But Dave Robinson could never see the long term. It was always tomorrow – the quick buck."

By 1983, chainmail and battle flags had been discarded and the group had parted company from its looning leader – although not from Stiff. They were re-marketed as The Tudors and looked to Cajun-influenced music for their new sound. "Tied Up With Lou Cool" was released in February that year, but their solo venture sank as if swallowed up by the Bayou itself. This left Stiff banking on the singer they had jettisoned to deliver the goods. Cue the sound of fiddles and Ed in a kilt, holding sway in a medieval English village and romping in a hay barn. Robinson despatched his film-making team to Great Tew in Oxfordshire, along with members of the historical society The Sealed Knot, for the video to promote "The Hayrick Song".

But due to Robinson's "strangely puritanical streak", Tudor Pole says his bawdy antics in the hay with his then girlfriend were censored. "It was done in a lovely countryside setting, where we did the barn shots and the bit going in the horse and cart and some Morris dancing – that sort of mix," he says. "But to take the sex out of it – that was what the song was about, shagging in the country – that was a completely weird misjudgment and I can only put it down to the Irish, old fashioned, Catholic thing."

In a classic publicity stunt, a horse and cart took Tudor Pole and some staff in costume down to the BBC offices in Great Portland Street, with the view to getting up some photographs with any passing Radio 1 presenters. Bails of straw had been thrown on the back and a loudspeaker was blaring out his hoedown. What happened next was a characteristically Stiff ending. Former press officer Jamie Spencer says: "Afterwards, we all went back to work in our cowboy gear. The horse and cart goes down Regent Street, turns round in Oxford Street, and the horse falls down and dies in the middle of Oxford Street and causes traffic chaos!"

"The Hayrick Song" died too. By then, the UK chart was all about synthesisers, hair lacquer and earnest-looking artists in dry ice. Tudor Pole's knockabout theatrics were decidedly out of place and Robinson decided to call time on one of the label's entertaining and most off-the-wall characters. "I had to beg him to let me call myself Eddie Tenpole Tudor," says the singer. "He just wanted me to be Eddie Tenpole. I said, 'My name is Tudor Pole'."

The Belle Stars had attracted plenty of attention on the back of their tour with Madness and their breakthrough had finally come the following summer with the release of Stiff BUY 150. "Iko Iko", a cover of The Dixie Cups' 1965 hit, was the first record to feature Clare Hirst, who had replaced Penny Leyton on keyboards. Irritatingly, another version of the same song was released at the same time by a scantily-clothed blonde called Natasha. The Belle Stars' version peaked at No. 35; hers soared to No. 10.

Robinson had a brainwave: he called up "Watermax". An ex-DJ and A&R man, Pete Waterman had cut his teeth on the Philadelphia scene, championing acts like The Three Degrees. Returning to the UK, he had worked with CBS and then Magnet, for which he reeled in "Save Me" by Silver Convention, one of the earliest disco records. He acted as a consultant for John Travolta during *Grease* and *Saturday Night Fever* and briefly managed The Specials, who were from his native city of Coventry. Along with his friend Peter Collins, Waterman had set up a production company called Loose Ends, and the partnership yielded five Top 50 hits for retro rockers Matchbox. By 1981, he had also lent his expertise to MCA and Elton John's Rocket label, for which he produced "Poison Ivy" for Mod revivalists The Lambrettas.

Robinson had reportedly liked the production work Collins had done with Matchbox, so he phoned Waterman and told him he had something they might be interested in. At Stiff's office in Bayham Street, he played them a demo of The Belle Stars. Waterman said he'd work with them if he could involve his friend Pete Hammond, who had a studio in South London. A week later, they met up with the group. "They were nice girls, and a complete mixture of personalities in the group, but as I recollect there weren't exactly in love with each other," said Waterman [48]

Covers could generate hits, as Robinson had learned, so he stuck with the formula and struck oil. "The Clapping Song", a 1965 hit for Shirley Ellis, went to No. 11 in the UK, completing the Belle Stars' transformation from B-list ska act to A-list pop group. Inez and Charlie Foxx's "Mockingbird" quickly followed, making it three cover versions in a row, and it reached No. 51.

Bass player Lesley Shone says while the cover versions led to accusations in the music press that the group had lost their street cred, it was these records that introduced The Belle Stars to a wider audience and provided the launchpad for the success that was to come. "We weren't having much chart success with our own material, so when the suggestion of recording 'Iko Iko' came up, we were more than happy to give it a go," says Shone. "Stiff had persevered with us up until this point and now needed us to make the company some returns. Dave really pushed us to do this and he also suggested the follow-ups, 'Clapping Song' and 'Mockingbird'. At the end of the day he was right, as they zoomed up the charts, and we still receive royalties on the back of them."

For Stiff and The Belle Stars, however, the best was yet to come. Of the four songs Robinson had initially played Waterman, he'd hated them all except one. It had promise in a "Motownish way", the producer reckoned. When it came to recording it at Trident Studios, Hammond had brought along a LinnDrum machine and asked the group if he could use it. The drummer refused, so they played the drum machine under the mixing desk and if the group stopped playing and heard it, they said it was her real drumming and there was just a delay in the studio.

The finished track was played back to Robinson, who was impressed. But as was his wont – he wanted it speeded up. "He told me he had this theory that when they played a record on Radio One it automatically slowed the record down by three beats per minute," said Waterman. "Quite where he'd got this bit of advanced physics from I don't know, but he was convinced of it. Now some people have perfect pitch. I've got perfect rhythm. I know exactly the right speed for any record and to speed this up made it sound awful. We managed to dissuade him." [48]

It proved a sound decision. In January 1983, "Sign Of The Times" entered the UK chart at No.19, rocketing to No. 5 the following week. By 12 February it was at No.3. The band's eponymous debut album meanwhile spent three months on the album chart, peaking at No.15. *Top Of The Pops* and the eighties was about partying, and The Belle Stars were the perfect hostesses.

Lesley Shone looks back fondly on the making of this and other records with the production team recruited by Robinson: "Pete Collins was a fantastic producer and Pete Waterman was in the role of hanging around basically, but they did make a great team; Collins in his purple strides, toting a clipboard. Every section of song would be mapped out with a stopwatch in advance of the studio. It was like organising the D-Day landings. His mantra was, 'Give them the chorus in the first 30 seconds'. He really understood the art of making good pop music and I, for one, appreciated the experience.

"However, one unforeseen problem was that studio technology was way ahead of live performance technology and some of those productions were difficult to reproduce on stage: electronic drum machines that would suddenly speed up being a particular pain in the arse."

In Britain, electro pop was the story of the early eighties. Stiff frantically tried to elbow its way into this hip and lucrative scene and had picked up The Electric Guitars after spotting them supporting The Thompson Twins in 1982. A five-piece outfit from Bristol, they had been formed in 1979 by Neil Davenport and Richard Hall and released two singles on small local labels. For their live shows, they added two girl singers and, in another Human League parallel, Stiff teamed them up in the studio with Martin Rushent, the mastermind behind *Dare*. Fresh from winning a Brit Award for Best producer, he took charge for the single "Language Problems", mixing the electro-dance sounds for which he had been lauded, with the urgency of his earlier new wave projects. Sadly, the record disappeared beneath the radar, dismissed by *NME* as "sub-XTC".

The proposed follow-up from Stiff's great electro hope sounded like KC & The Sunshine Band's "That's The Way I Like It", re-imagined for the colourful club dance-floors of the eighties. "Beat Me Hollow" was a heady fusion of synthesisers, guitars and drum machines and its high tempo strongly suggested the hand of Robinson. But BUY 161 was never released, and their recordings were consigned to the Stiff vaults. The Electric Guitars' support slots at some of U2's early London shows, would stand as their claim to fame.

All the ingredients of an electro hit were thrown into the mix on Albania's single "Could This Be Love". The Freshies' "Fasten Your Seatbelts" was of the breezier synth-pop variety, and Brigit Novik's "The Wedding Dance" was a strange, Russian affair.

The nearest Stiff got to an electro hit was "I Love You" by Yello, a mesmerising, futuristic creation that was ahead of its time. Stiff capitalised by producing limited edition 3D picture discs with free glasses and the leftfield Devo-esque trio toyed with chart success, reaching No.41. When the subsequent "Lost Again" hit a ceiling at No.73, Stiff knew they weren't going to make it. *You Gotta Say Yes To Another Excess*, Yello's only album for the label, featured a diagonal flash across the corner and a hole-punch style logo – record store shorthand for a bargain bin release. Carlos Peron left the group, while Boris Blank and Dieter Meier carried the Yello concept on to bigger and better things.

Stiff's urgent quest for artists who would suit the video-led, MTV era led it to a singer, songwriter and multi-instrumentalist whose music and look was very much of the time. Jakko Jakszyk cited King Crimson's Robert Fripp as his inspiration for becoming a musician [he now plays with King Crimson], and he graduated through several bands before being signed by Chiswick in 1981. Three solo singles were released with no success, and the album he had been working on was still at the manufacturers when the label that had much in common with Stiff went bankrupt.

Jakszyk had played on a record released by Stiff before being signed in 1983. Dave Stewart had become a close friend through musical collaborations and he had hooked up with Jakszyk for his version of "What Becomes Of The Broken Hearted". "One day he called me up and said did I want to sing on this song he was doing, a version of 'What Becomes Of The Broken Hearted?'", says Jakszyk. "Originally he wanted Robert Wyatt to sing on that, but Robert couldn't do it, or didn't want to do it, so he got me in and I sang on it. Then later along the line he hooked up with Colin Blunstone and I got relegated to backing vocals."

Performing the song with Stewart and Blunstone on *Top Of The Pops*, Jakszyk got to meet Sonnie Rae and was impressed with what he saw as Stiff's proactive and exciting way of operating. When Stewart financed the recording of one of Jakszyk's songs and began punting it around some of the major record companies, Stewart's manager John Marshall suggested they try Stiff.

Jakszyk did just that: "We had deals on the table from CBS and MCA and then we went to see Stiff. At the time, Stiff were in Camden in Bayham Street. We went there and we sat outside by reception waiting to see Dave Robinson, and this unbelievably stunning looking bird kept coming up and down the staircase, and I was really smitten with her. John Marshall said, 'Jakko, you're not going to be really so pathetic and predictable as to want to sign to Stiff just because you fancy one of the employees?' I said, 'Give me some more credit than that, for Christ's sake. And anyway, that's my wife Amanda'. So that is why I signed to Stiff!"

Robinson was convinced he had a hit on his hands with Jakszyk's "Dangerous Dreams", as was plugger Gary Farrow. In his plush office, Robinson turned on the charm. A smaller label like Stiff, he told them, would be able to give him the kind of personal attention and support he would never get from the majors. Jakszyk, having seen what Stiff had done with Dave Stewart's records, needed no further convincing. He signed and in May 1983 "Dangerous Dreams" became BUY 183. However, he became exasperated with Stiff's hands-on boss almost immediately, as he meddled in everything – from the mixing process to the artwork and videos. From his control centre in Bayham Street, he played back demos at practically deafening volume and demanded changes. Records had to be sped up. 12-inch records had to be pressed up to boost marketing. Artists were meanwhile derided as being "ten a penny" or "pebbles on a beach".

Sitting in Robinson's office one day, nervously crossing his legs, Jakszyk knocked over a poster propped against a desk. As it fell, he noticed some graffiti scrawled into the desk. "Dave Robinson gave us a fucking hard time", it read, followed by a date. It was signed "All the members of Madness".

The conversation that followed was typical of the singer's dealings with the label boss, as Jakszyk recalls: "During the playback, Dave Robinson said, 'This is great, this is great. There's a better vocal; I love the sound of the vocal on this.' I thought, 'What's he talking about?' He said, 'This is great. Is this the same arrangement as the 7-inch?' I said, 'Yes, exactly the same arrangement.' He said, 'So the first part of this 12-inch is the same arrangement as the 7-inch?' I thought, 'What's he talking about? It is the 7-inch!' I said, 'Yeah, yeah Dave it's the same.' So he said, 'Well, I think we ought to put out the first three minutes of this mix as the 7-inch'.

"And I made the biggest mistake I could have done in my relationship. What I should have said was, 'What a great idea Dave, yes let's do that.' But I said, 'It's exactly the same – it's a copy of the 7-inch,' which made him look like a lunatic, and I had a problem with him ever since. Of course, the single wasn't a hit. It got a fair amount of airplay, but it wasn't the enormous hit that everyone thought it was going to be."

The video for "Dangerous Dreams" was a typical eighties affair, filmed at a country pile with a swimming pool into which the suited singer was thrown at the end. Jakszyk had come up with a storyboard with the help of an art director friend, which they took to show Robinson. But their ideas were not well received. "He looked at the storyboard for about ten seconds and he picked it up and he put it in the bin," Jakszyk recalls. He said, "'Don't worry about the video', and my involvement in that video and the subsequent videos I made with Robbo, was simply turning up at the allotted venue at the allotted time."

Jakszyk's arrival at Bayham Street had coincided with that of a woman who would be a godsend for Stiff during this difficult early eighties period. Tracey Ullman had made her name as a comedian in the popular TV show *Three Of A Kind,* with David Copperfield and Lenny Henry. "One day I was at my hairdresser, and Dave Robinson's wife Rosemary leant over and said, 'Do you want to make a record?'" said Ullman. "And I was like having some of these Boy George kind of dreadlock things put in and I went, 'Yeah, I want to make a record.' I would have tried anything." [12]

A TV celebrity who had never sought a record deal, Ullman seemed the antithesis of Stiff, the champion of the underdog. But without hits the label was toast, and Robinson knew it. Ullman and two backing singers shimmied in matching leather mini-skirts and sang into hairbrushes on *Top Of The Pops* to perform "Breakaway". In the official video, they were schoolgirls, bopping around in their uniforms, dreaming of pop stardom. For Ullman, that came instantly. The single went to No. 4 and spent almost three months in the chart. Sandwiched between, "Sign Of The Times" and Madness' "Tomorrow's Just Another Day", it also sealed a rare consecutive run of hits in an otherwise barren period.

The overnight success of Ullman vindicated Robinson's decision to send her over to Waterman and Collins, following their triumphs with The Belle Stars. Waterman didn't know Ullman, but he was familiar with "Breakaway" as the B-side of Irma Thomas' biggest hit, "Wish Someone Would Care". Ullman asked Waterman how they wanted her to do the song. She then proceeded to impersonate Lulu, Diana Ross and other well-known singers, leaving him falling around the studio with laughter.

A blueprint had been written. A celebrity face, classic pop songs, great producers and fun videos filmed by Robinson. So, it was simply a case of repeating the same trick – but with which song? Months went by before Waterman suggested they contact one of his favourite singers, Kirsty MacColl. As a consequence, Ullman ended up giving "They Don't Know", the song MacColl had recorded for Stiff four years earlier, a spring-clean. With Rosemary Robinson contributing to the Shangri-Las-style vocals, it was left to Waterman to apply the finishing touches in the studio in the middle of the night for about £30. In characteristic contrariness, Robinson had planned to scrap the record as it didn't "swing along" enough.

"I explained that everything didn't have to swing along and that housewives everywhere would be swinging along to it when they were doing the ironing," said Waterman. "It went on to be Tracey's biggest hit and the record that broke her in America." [48] Waterman sent Robinson a gold-painted ironing board when the song got to No. 2!

Ullman's album, *You Broke My Heart In 17 Places*, also made a very respectable No. 14 in the album chart. Kirsty MacColl had made a surprise return to Stiff that year and she befriended the woman who had made one of her compositions such a huge hit. The record contained this and three of her other songs: "You Broke My Heart In 17 Places", "Terry" and "You Caught Me Out". Stiff had also invited MacColl to produce the title track. MacColl was still wrestling with her fear of performing and Ullman supported her, taking her out for dinner and encouraging her to continue with her writing.

Rubbing shoulders with Ullman in the upper reaches of the British charts at the time was Howard Jones. The electro-pop singer appeared from nowhere in September 1983 with a mime artist performing beside him. Stiff fans wouldn't have been aware of it but, as the label had cast its net for new acts, Jones was the one that got away. "Yes, I was about to sign with Stiff Records when WEA stepped in," he revealed on Twitter in 2011. "It was a big moment!"

Davey Payne was living in Buckinghamshire at the time and would later add his saxophone to Jones' debut album. He remembers indirectly pointing the up-and-coming performer towards Stiff: "The girl in the health shop in Amersham said to me, 'What do you think

Howard should do?' and I said, 'Tell him to go to Stiff', because that was all I knew," says Payne. "He went to Stiff and Dave Robinson said, 'There's no fucking hit singles here' and Paul Conroy said, 'Well, I think there is'. He [Conroy] then left, after all those years, and took him to Warner Brothers, where he had all those hits."

Paul Conroy, one of Robinson's closest allies for six years, left Stiff in 1983 for Warner. It was because he was Jones' strongest advocate that the singer and his manager David Stopps, the promoter at Friars in Aylesbury, followed him to the major label. Like many others who did their indentures at Stiff, Conroy went on to become an influential industry figure. In 1989 he became president of Chrysalis in the UK and in 1992 he was poached by Virgin. There, he oversaw an increase in the company's revenue from £61m to £196m at the height of Spice Girls' mania.

He explains his reasons for quitting: "My decision to leave Stiff was very hard, but as a family man I cannot say that money didn't come into it. I was looking to the future, a new challenge as marketing director of such a large operation. The budgets I had dwarfed anything at Stiff and I had the chance to revamp WEA with Rob Dickins. Also perhaps, I felt some of the more recent Stiff signings prior to my leaving were not altogether my choices.

"At my leaving bash, Dave Robinson made a brilliant speech and I must say it was very moving, saying how much I had brought to the company over the years. I left the wine bar a little teary, hoping I had made the right decision. But for me and my career in showbiz, it was undoubtedly the right move."

Warner's gain was very much Stiff's loss.

If Tracey Ullman was the queen of video, Madness remained the undisputed kings – and Stiff's only dependable breadwinner. From July 1982 to June 1984, all seven singles they released made the Top 20: four reached the Top 5. Even the group knew some of the videos were now stronger than the songs. But coming up with ever more existential ideas and then trying to film them on the cheap was something the band regarded as a challenge. And when Stiff moved into Bayham Street in Camden, a large garage to the rear of the premises proved the perfect space for film shoots.

Mark Bedford remembers: "We would go into Stiff and we would sit around a table in one of the rooms there. It would be us and Dave, and we would literally fire off as many ideas as possible. Some of them were hysterical and completely un-filmable, because they would take up hundreds of thousands of pounds or would defy the laws of physics to actually film. There was one fantastic time when Chas and Chris got into talking about building a rubber street, so that when you stepped on it would move and bend. Those brainstorming meetings were absolutely fantastic for the amount of things that came out of them. From a few hours of having lists and lists of stuff, it would be then knocked into a workable, filmable sort of story, but with hardly any money!"

Health and safety was never Stiff's strong suit. A piano was dropped into a muddy field from a height in the making of "Shut Up" narrowly missing someone's foot and "It Must Be Love" had involved a devil-may-care attitude to filming under water. For "Driving In My Car", the boys wore straw boaters and were filmed driving around Camden in a white Morris Minor. The Fun Boy Three were on the pavement trying to thumb a lift to Coventry, but the "Maddiemobile" drove on. All pretty safe by Stiff standards; until it came to the last scene. "The big deal at the time was there was these Volkswagen ads where the Volkswagen fell and Dave wanted to do that," says Foreman. "We got this Morris 1000 and I mean, Christ, it was hauled to the top of this studio by just a piece of rope and poor Nigel [Dick] had to climb up this thing. I remember it to this day. He had a pole with a knife on and that is how they did it – a pole with a frigging knife on! And it just went and we filmed it in super slow motion."

Madness' eleventh Top 10 hit didn't feature on an album, but the next single did. "Our House" was one of the group's strongest songs in years and although it didn't reach the rollercoaster heights of "House Of Fun", more than three decades later it stands as their most iconic. "Our House" made No. 5 in the UK chart and the video featured on the Christmas edition of *Top Of The Pops*, the BBC long having decided not to attempt to get them all in the same room.

"Tomorrow's Just Another Day" was the second single to be taken from *The Rise And Fall,* and reached No. 8. A darker affair, like "Grey Day", the video began in a prison and in a reversal of the video for "It Must Be Love", they wore white against a black background. This time, Foreman had come up with the story idea, causing a fallout with Robinson in the process. "Before 'Tomorrow's Just Another Day', Dave had seen this advert where a car gets chucked out of a plane on a parachute and he kind of got the rights, or so he said, to this advert," Foreman explains. "We were rehearsing and he [Robinson] turned up and he was going on about this ad and I go, 'Look Dave, I've written a flipping idea for "Tomorrow's Just Another Day"'. He had this kind of hamper to reward us, or something like that, and he threw it on the floor. And I said, 'Sorry to have hampered your plans' and he was livid. But it was a great idea and everyone was coming up with good ideas."

"Wings Of A Dove" did even better and – not to be outdone – the Stiff boss got his wish. The video was shot at an airfield where Madness and an entire steel band boarded a Dan-Air plane. After take-off, they leapt about the cabin performing the song. Then at the end, both groups piled into a van, giving Robinson the chance to use the advert he'd got showing a large van being parachuted from an aircraft and hitting the ground. Another victory for style over content, "Wings Of A Dove" soared majestically to No. 2.

In reality, it wasn't a van, but a bombshell that was about to be dropped on Madness; arguably one from which it would take years to recover. Mike Barson announced he was leaving. The pianist, on whose timeless pop melodies so many of their songs were founded, had married his Dutch girlfriend and was moving to Holland with her. He had also felt under increasing pressure to come up with material for the group, but Foreman says it was a band decision that proved the final straw. "Ben Elton and Richard Curtis were writing a television series for us because they really liked us," he says. "We told Mike and that's when he said, 'I'm leaving'."

Top Of The Pops viewers didn't know it yet, but the sight of his arms growing longer and longer in the video for "The Sun And The Rain" was symbolic of his departure, which would come months later. The poignant touch was added by Lee Thompson. "Mike Barson was going to leave the band and he [Lee] wanted Mike to play the piano and his arms to get longer as he moved away from the piano," says Foreman. "Lee and Chas were going to burst out of the piano as well. So, we were in the old basement in the wee midnight hours and they got this guy, the Stiff carpenter, to build a piano out of balsa wood. And they'd given him all kinds of speed to keep him up and he'd made this piano. We start filming and the first thing that happened was that it got smashed to bits."

A Madness Christmas Party for Greenpeace on 21 December 1983 at London's Lyceum Ballroom turned out to be Barson's swansong. Ian Dury and his new group The Music Students were also on the bill, along with hippie Neil from *The Young Ones*. Barson moved permanently to Amsterdam and would not play another show with the group for nine years. As 1984 dawned, Madness were about to enter a new era. And Dave Robinson was about to make the biggest mistake of his Stiff career.

14

Boys From The County Hell

Island Records was running out of money and Chris Blackwell was so concerned, he decided to hand over the reins to the one man he believed could steer it through the industry's shark-infested waters: Dave Robinson. The spectacularly diverse label, so lovingly curated by the hippie tycoon since 1959, had achieved the seemingly impossible by housing progressive rock, glam, folk and reggae, and all genres between, under one roof. From John Martyn and Traffic to Sparks and the B52s; from Bob Marley and Burning Spear to Grace Jones and U2; all musical life could be found beneath the iconic palm tree. However, the late seventies and early eighties had been less fruitful for the label and Blackwell, who had a restive but open mind, was diversifying.

In 1983, producer Trevor Horn and journalist Paul Morley had set up ZTT under the auspices of Island. Blackwell, as well as ushering in this exciting new enterprise, had used Island to bankroll a film and production operation called Alive. Although unimaginable success lay on the horizon for ZTT and Island acts like U2 and Robert Palmer, at the tail end of 1983 the label was not in good shape. The death of reggae star Bob Marley in May 1981 had robbed it of one of its greatest ambassadors and Blackwell's venture into films was proving a financial drain. Island, like many other record labels, was also finding the market an increasingly competitive one. Sitting still wasn't an option and Blackwell knew he needed help. Over a restaurant table, he got it.

"Blackwell and Robinson met for dinner," says Nick Stewart, then working in A&R at Island. "Blackwell said, 'I need somebody to run Island' and Dave wanted somewhere to park some of his acts. So, in 1984, it was a fantastic time to be here." In January 1984, Blackwell bought a 50% stake in Stiff and installed Dave Robinson as managing director of Island. Publicly, both parties were at pains to stress the deal was not a merger and that the companies would retain their separate identities. "Island has a lot of resources we don't have," said Robinson at the time. "It's getting harder and harder to operate in the music business today. Acts get an offer from you, then go to Richard Branson at Virgin to top it. We have been unable to match the offers being made. Now we're setting up the alternative Virgin. We'll have two separate companies, which will be even better than they are now." [50]

Stiff shifted its entire staff to 22 St Peter's Square, a Grade II listed building on the borders of Chiswick and Hammersmith in West London, and Island's premises since the early seventies. For those at Stiff, it was a period of great uncertainty and Island seemed far from a natural bedfellow.

Employees at both labels could also have been forgiven for wondering how their respective owners would get along. The suave figure of Blackwell was born into wealth, the son of a major in the Jamaican army, and educated at Harrow. He was as laid-back as the Caribbean culture in which he had grown up, in contrast with the brilliant, but excitable and somewhat brash figure of Robinson. But taking risks went with the territory and both companies knew this was a massive roll of the dice.

Alan Cowderoy was at Stiff when the deal was struck. "Dave and Blackwell were close," he says. "At that point, we were in Bayham Street in Camden, and we were bumping and not doing as well as we had. We'd gone through a long period where we either had something in the charts or something on the radio; there was always some activity. I would suggest at that moment, we were in a slightly difficult position, when we probably had neither one or the other. Robbo, bless his heart, understood this, and he was out there talking to Blackwell. And Blackwell was looking for someone to run Island Records and Robbo managed to sell him the Stiff company.

"So, there was an agreement written on the back of an envelope that Island were going to buy Stiff for an amount of money, and the amount of money was spread over three years. There was an initial amount and then two subsequent amounts of money to be paid to the company. As part of the deal, we gave up our offices, moved into Island Records and Robbo was running Island. As soon as he got there, I got the impression that he'd looked at their accounts, and I remember him saying to me, 'They've got less than we have. I don't know where their payment is going to come from'."

Island's finances were in disarray and Stiff reportedly had to lend Island £1 million in order to fund the deal. Robinson must have wondered what he had got himself and Stiff into. But while the Island coffers might have been empty, from an artistic point of view, Robinson's arrival couldn't have been better timed. A single by Frankie Goes To Hollywood called "Relax" had been issued on ZTT towards the end of 1983, to a modest reception. Trevor Horn produced the record and brought in members of The Blockheads to bolster the sound, after being unconvinced by initial sessions with the group. Norman Watt-Roy made a critical contribution, coming up with its arresting bass line. Horn had then continued to hone the track in the studio until he got the throbbing, club anthem he envisaged. Only singer Holly Johnson appeared on the record.

"Relax" made a sedate progression up the UK's Top 75. But on 5 January 1984, it was performed on *Top Of The Pops* and a week later it was No. 6. Suddenly waking up to the sexually explicit nature of the song, Radio 1 banned it. By 24 January the song was No.1 and *Top Of The Pops* also refused to play it. ZTT's controversial release continued to taunt the Beeb for a further five weeks from its lofty position. It stuck it out in the Top 75 for 48 consecutive weeks and even returned in February 1985 for another four.

The Stiff template showed through in the artwork and aggressive marketing campaign. Picture discs, as well as 7 and 12-inch versions, were pressed up and, in keeping with the lyrics, the advertisements didn't hold back. "All The Nice Boys Love Sea Men" read one above a photo of band member Paul Rutherford in a black vest and a sailor's hat. "Soap it up ... rub it up ... Frankie Goes to Hollywood are coming ... making Public Image look like men of good will, making Duran Duran lick the shit off their shoes". T-shirts saying "Frankie Says Relax" in huge bold letters became the fashion accessory of the moment. Months later, the follow-up single "Two Tribes" went to No.1 and settled in for a nine week spell, confirming that ZTT's phenomenon was no flash in the pan.

However, it wasn't for these revolutionary, boundary-pushing records that Robinson's reign at Island would be remembered, but a greatest hits package by an artist who had died three years earlier. A Bob Marley fan himself, Robinson reasoned: "My theory was that Bob was not as big as people thought he was: he hadn't sold that many records." [51]

His instincts were right. Marley had enjoyed significant success in the UK and his native Jamaica. But in his lifetime, only three of his singles had reached the British Top 10, he had received little radio play, and had never made the Top 40 in the US. "I Shot The Sheriff" had been turned into a British No.1 but by Eric Clapton, not its originator. Robinson felt that most white record buyers were wary of reggae and the political nature of Marley's songs made them doubly so of him. That there was a wider market for him, Robinson had no doubt: but the approach had to be right.

Robinson's sequencing for the Island compilation was to prove masterful. *Legend: The Best of Bob Marley & The Wailers*, released 8 May 1984, became the biggest-selling reggae album of all time, with 25 million sales worldwide. It spent twelve weeks at No.1 in the UK and an extraordinary 340 weeks on the chart. If some music fans only bought one reggae record in their entire lives, it was likely to be *Legend*.

The question on many lips, especially those at St Peter's Square, was whether Dave Robinson was triumphing for Island at the expense of Stiff. Could he really run two such demanding record companies at the same time, and look after the best interests of their respective artists? Early indications suggested not. Madness' first release of the year, "Michael Caine", ran out of steam at No. 11, only their second ever Stiff single not to make the Top 10. And even a cameo appearance by the then Labour Party leader Neil Kinnock in the video for Tracey Ullman's "My Guy" couldn't propel it beyond No. 23. A twist on Madness' "My Girl", it represented a sharp fall in her chart fortunes just a matter of weeks after her revisit of Doris Day's "Move Over Darling" managed eighth spot.

All the while, other Stiff releases came and went with no return on the money and time taken up in recording, pressing, designing, plugging, marketing and other activity. The Inspirational Choir Of The Pentecostal First Born Church Of The Living God certainly set the record for the longest name of any Stiff act and had helped give Madness a whole new sound on "Wings Of A Dove". They also featured in the big-budget video at the aerodrome.

But the label's attempt to capitalise on their new public profile with their own release "Pick Me Up" didn't take off. Riotous psychobillies King Kurt had scraped into the Top 40 in 1983 with "Destination Zululand" and teamed up with Dave Edmunds for *Ooh Wallah Wallah*. But the album bombed and the subsequent singles "Mack The Knife" and "Banana Banana" stopped short of the Top 40. Passion Puppets, Personal Column, Jamie Rae and Robert Sleigh joined the ranks of the Stiff also-rans.

_____

One of the biggest millstones around Stiff's neck was its failure to have two or more major acts on its books simultaneously. In the summer of 1984, Stiff was dealt a body blow – Madness announced they were leaving.

An entry in the band's diary for 11 May 1984 is revealing: [39] "Montreux. Chris and Lee go out nightclubbing with UB40 after meeting them in the street. They attend the CBS party as Madness have all been invited and are now looking for a new record deal as relations with Stiff are deteriorating, which is partly due to Stiff being swallowed up by Island Records. Mayhem then ensues. Someone throws a chair and an amplifier from the seventh floor and breaks a glass coffee table by sitting on it and burns cigarette holes in the carpet. The last word on the party incident hasn't been spoken yet, not least because this particular suite was due to be used by Rod Stewart the next day."

Madness' relationship with Robinson continued to unravel when they returned to London. He had wanted "Victoria Gardens" to be the next single from their fifth album *Keep Moving*, but had a last minute change of heart. "One Better Day" was chosen instead but "he [Robinson] didn't want to do a video, so the band had to finance it themselves".[39] The video was shot in black and white and colour and, keeping with tradition, filmed in Camden. Mike Barson flew over from Amsterdam to take part and the opening shots featured Arlington House, then a homeless hostel which was name-checked in the song. Taking up where "Michael Caine" left off, it was indicative of a conscious change of direction and more reflective songwriting.

Barson officially left the group in June 1984 and the remaining members of Madness left Stiff. They had wanted to set up their own label, within the Stiff stable. After all, Chrysalis provided a home for 2 Tone and The Beat had had its own boutique label, Go Feet. Robinson rejected the proposal, but Virgin didn't and allowed Madness to establish Zarjazz.

However, Chris Foreman says this wasn't the only issue which ended their time at Stiff. "I don't know how well Stiff was doing financially, but there were all these rumours that Dave was going to leave," he says. "There was this thing about having a 'key man clause' – if he leaves, we can go. And what happened was, he said, 'I'm not going to go', and he went to Island Records, and even though he was MD, it just wasn't the same. And Mike, who was a very important person in the band, wasn't there, and that's where our relationship with Stiff all ground to a halt. It was sad and we went off to Virgin. We didn't really go off to Zarjazz. We just said to Virgin, 'We'll have our own label', which wasn't entirely a vanity thing, but it got us a bit more money. Then we sort of vanished a bit really."

In the BBC Four documentary, Robinson said Madness had never liked touring and that "their ambition didn't like leaving Camden Town". They had also felt they were being asked to do too much and that too many records were being released. "But they were a pop band and they wanted to be a serious music band," he said.

His remarks rankled with the group. "It was one of the few things that stuck in the band's mind," says Bedford. "Dave has said that quite a few times, but it's something the band have never got their heads around. We did nothing but tour and that rather defeats it. He made a rather crude remark like, 'Oh, they don't want to eat spaghetti Bolognese' and basically portraying us as tourists abroad who eat egg and chips, which is completely wrong. I'm not sure where that came from.

"Dave is like all those great people in the music business down the years – Alan McGee springs to mind. They are fantastic at creating their own headlines and they are fantastic at rolling their whole thing forward, and I think maybe there was a little of that going on. It was plainly wrong and we've told him that. I think we did want to be serious in the sense that creatively we wanted to push it forward. And sometimes that didn't involve doing a train, but working out what we wanted to do and write. We did think about those things and I'm not trying to intellectualise it, but I think that was one of our strengths down the years that we did think about the way we wanted to go and the things we wanted to do."

Virgin had effectively deprived Stiff of its prime source of revenue, but in August 1984 Robinson did get even with Branson by winning a lengthy legal case. The action pivoted on a deal Branson had made with Robinson which allowed Virgin to act as Stiff's sales force and in 1983 had ended up in the High Court. In short, Branson had agreed not to represent any other label without Robinson's consent, but he had then signed a separate agreement with Island. When the

Irishman found out, Branson offered him a cut-price contract, which he refused to sign. Branson then sued for £100,000 claiming breach of contract when Robinson tried to cut all ties.

In court, Branson was confidence personified. Wearing an open-neck shirt and tanned from a holiday on his private island of Necker, he produced notebooks and letters which he said backed up his case. Robinson's lawyer had none of it, telling him he was making it all up, and he turned up the pressure. The following day, Branson dressed in a more respectful suit and tie, but things got no better. "As Robinson's lawyer pressed to embarrass him further, he was halted by the judge, who said, 'I think you've made your point'," reported one paper. "The judgment was damning. The judge decided Branson's notes were unreliable. His case was rejected and he left the court visibly shaking." [52]

Back at St Peter's Square, Robinson continued to run Island, while keeping the plates spinning at Stiff. Artists wanted meetings with him, but it wasn't like the old days when he would chat to artists over a pint in the nearest boozer. Now Robinson had an office on a mezzanine floor with a large window from where he could watch everything that was going on. Beneath was an open-plan area known as the War Room.

The artist who provided Stiff with its first big hit single after its move to Island was Kirsty MacColl. Since leaving the label in 1979, mainstream success had continued to elude MacColl. She'd been on *Top Of The Pops* clad in blue denim to perform her "There's A Guy Works Down The Chip Shop Swears He's Elvis", which got to No.14. But as had been the case with "They Don't Know", she hadn't had the recognition which her songwriting and wonderful voice merited. Polydor's decision to mothball *Real*, the album she had recorded for it, had only deepened her frustration. "I can't see why Polydor signed me up really, except I may have been a tax loss," remarked MacColl. [41]

She had sung guest vocals on "I Want Out" a single by Matchbox, who had been on Chiswick Records during her spell there, and agreed to join them on stage at a show in London. MacColl gave "Chip Shop ..." an airing and accompanied them for a performance of their new record. However, even being on stage for just those two songs proved traumatic. A song called "Berlin" from her unreleased album was then re-recorded and released as a single on an obscure indie label, North of Watford, but sold only a few copies. Frank Murray, her manager, was determined to get her a deal and approached Y Records, which would sign The Slits, The Pop Group and Shriekback among others.

Then, the day before she was due to put pen to paper in 1983, he called Stiff and told Robinson she might be prepared to return for the right offer. Songwriters were something Stiff had been sadly lacking since its early days and, with the financial picture at St Peter's Square a growing concern, MacColl was as good a gamble as any. The move paid off almost instantly, Ullman turned "They Don't Know" into a hit on both sides of the Atlantic. She also included other MacColl songs on her album, which had the look and feel of *Jackie* magazine set to music.

MacColl's own love life blossomed when she began seeing Stiff press officer Andy MacDonald, who would shortly form his own independent label Go! Discs. Within a short time they were both married – but not to each other. When MacColl appeared on the BBC's *Pop Quiz* show on 1 October, MacDonald accompanied her and got chatting to Juliet de Valero Wills, manager of fellow guest Pauline Black of The Selecter. They would go on to marry and within a month MacColl had met her future husband. For years she had been a huge fan of Simple Minds and had been nagging them to let her sing on one of their records. In the studio to work on their new album *Sparkle In The Rain,* they phoned her with two requests. First, could she come and join them and sing on the record? Second, could she collect some cocaine and bring it with her? She dutifully did so and not only got to record with her idols, but met their famous producer, Steve Lillywhite, at a Big Country gig at the Glasgow Barrowland Ballroom on New Year's Eve. Lillywhite proposed. The following August they were married.

Jakko Jakszyk was a regular caller at Stiff's offices and things were not happening for him. "Who's Fooling Who?", his second single, had flopped on its release in early 1984, and Robinson told him he needed a change of image. "I remember one thing he said to me was, 'Jakko, the trouble with you is that you are unfashionably heterosexual,'" says Jakszyk. "'Can't we get you hanging out at Heaven [a fashionable gay club] for a while? You don't actually have to do anything, just be seen with the right people.'"

A prankster with an impudent sense of fun, Jakszyk was also a brilliant mimic. So, it wasn't long before he'd perfected his impression of Robinson and members of staff would egg him on to do it. Simon

Ryan from the art department was one of them and one day the phone rang while Jakszyk was there. "Go on, go on, just pick it up and pretend to be Robbo," begged Ryan. Jakszyk picked it up and put on his best Irish burr. "Hello, this is Dave Robinson in the art department. Who's this?" A brief silence at the other end was broken by the inevitable words, "It's Dave Robinson". Jakszyk didn't answer the art department phone again.

On another occasion, Jakszyk was in Robinson's office with Robinson's personal assistant Annie Pitts, and Kirsty MacColl. The latter was telling him how she had a single coming out, and her husband Steve Lillywhite was in Paris, about to produce a solo album for Abba's Agnetha Fältskog. She wanted to go and stay with him in Paris, but Robinson was saying he wanted her to be around to promote her new record. He also tactlessly told her that he thought she should lose some weight. MacColl sensed an opportunity for the singer's party-piece.

Jakszyk recalls: "Kirsty said, 'Why don't you phone up Steve and pretend to be Dave?' And I said, 'And say what?' She said, 'Oh, just make up some stuff about the fact that Dave doesn't want me to go to Paris'. So, she phoned her home number and Steve Lillywhite answered and I said, 'Hello Steve, it's Robbo'. And Steve immediately bought it and went, 'Oh, hi Dave. How are you doing?' I said, 'Listen Steve, we need to talk about Kirsty.' And Steve said, 'Oh God, not that again Dave. What is it?' 'Well we really don't want her out there, the bloody temptations in Paris are an absolute nightmare, all those cream cakes. Quite frankly Steve, she's fat enough as it is.' Annie and Kirsty are absolutely pissing themselves laughing, but Steve got absolutely fucking furious and slammed the phone down. Kirsty had to phone him back up and say, 'No, it was Jakko doing an impression of him'!"

Of the scenes he witnessed at St Peter's Square, as Robinson desperately tried to juggle his dual responsibilities, the most entertaining involved Tracey Ullman. Stiff's golden girl had scored a fourth Top 20 hit with "Sunglasses", written by US composer John D. Loudermilk. The beachside video featured fellow comic actor Adrian Edmonson. However, when "Helpless" became her first single not to make the Top 40, the formula appeared to be wearing thin. With Madness no longer on Stiff and no other hit acts on the horizon, Robinson was understandably keen to identify suitable material for one of his star acts of the eighties.

1983's "They Don't Know" had been Ullman's biggest hit and Stiff reached again for a Kirsty MacColl song. "Terry" had been released by MacColl herself a couple of months earlier, after her return to the label, and Edmonson had also appeared in the mainly black and white video. Ullman recorded the song and a video shoot had been scheduled to take place in advance of its release in December 1994. A mix-up, however, had left Ullman standing in the freezing cold waiting for the crew to arrive. Apoplectic, she headed straight to Stiff's headquarters.

"I was in the office being given a bloody hard time and in the middle of the meeting the door flung open and Tracey Ullman walked in," says Jakszyk. "Tracey had obviously had a great deal of success with Dave, but she came flying in and she was absolutely furious, screaming and swearing at him. It turned out, I found out retrospectively, that very day there had been a video shoot for her then current single, a song called 'Terry'. She had got a call to get to a location, which I think was Hackney Marshes or some unpleasant place like that at about seven o'clock in the morning. She had already had a great deal of argument with Dave because he insisted on directing her videos and she didn't need any direction – she was Tracey Ullman. Dave, for whatever reason, had decided to cancel the shoot or had to cancel the shoot and he had told everybody, apart from her.

"She turned up to Hackney Marshes at half past six in the morning and there was nobody there. So, she drove up to Stiff, at Island in St Peter's Square, and just burst into the meeting I was having, and she was effing and blinding. She said, 'I don't care. I don't care if I never make a fucking record for you ever again. You can go fuck yourself, I've had enough. Piss off!' and she slammed the door. And I kid you not, Dave Robinson, with barely a beat after the door had slammed, just picked up the phone and he said, 'Get me the video department … Hello John, yeah John, could you get hold of a Tracey Ullman look-alike to finish this video? Not for all of it, but for some of it.' Unbelievable."

"Terry" flopped and her second album for Stiff, *You Caught Me Out*, on which it appeared, was her last. Ullman went on to move to the US where her TV show launched the cartoon series The Simpsons and she became a megastar.

It is ironic that some of the finest songwriters, Elvis Costello included, have enjoyed some of their best-remembered successes with other people's songs. MacColl is a case in point. For all the sublime songs she had written, it took Tracey Ullman to imprint "They Don't Know" on the nation's consciousness. And when she finally provided Stiff with a hit at the second time of asking, no one should have been surprised that the song had come from someone else's lyrical notebook.

MacColl had started work on an album for Stiff, but Lillywhite wasn't convinced and felt it was "one-dimensional". "I think when I said that, she said, 'Well, you do better then'," said Lillywhite. "I said, 'All right', and she said, 'I've got this song that Billy Bragg wrote. It's a great song, but it sounds like a demo. I know I can make it a pop song'." [53] "A New England" featured on Billy Bragg's debut album *Life's A Riot With Spy Vs Spy*, released on Andy MacDonald's Go! Discs. MacColl approached Bragg and asked for his help.

"She suggested I came round to see her and we would re-write the lyrics," said Bragg. "But she could only do it in the morning and I'm not much of a morning person. But she said, 'Come round and I'll cook you a fried breakfast'. So, I went round to her house – she was living near Shepherd's Bush at the time – and she done a fried breakfast and I done an extra verse for her." [53]

MacColl's love for bold pop melodies and her exquisite vocals shone through on the finished record, a stark contrast from the gritty original, in which the tune was stabbed out on Bragg's electric guitar. Released in December 1984, it soared to No. 7 in the UK. The biggest hit of her stop-start career, it was overdue recognition for one of England's most underrated artists. However, it would be another three years before one of the most extraordinary groups ever signed by Stiff would help her conquer her debilitating fear of walking out on stage.

Elvis Costello fans who sauntered into college halls and other venues to see him on his autumn tour were greeted by a startling spectacle and sound. On stage was a shambolic-looking group playing traditional Irish music, but at breakneck speed. One of those lined up at the front of the stage was hitting himself over the head with a metal tray. Their drunken singer stood at the microphone, slurring his way through largely indecipherable lyrics. The spiky-haired woman on bass wore a look menacing enough to make any heckler think better of it. The merchandise stall revealed this ragtag support act already had an album on sale. It was called *Red Roses For Me*. The band was called The Pogues.

Back in the days of The Pink Fairies, The Damned and The Adverts, this motley crew would have fitted right in. But in the Stiff epoch of Tracey Ullman, The Belle Stars and Jakko, they looked like the black sheep of the family; the bastard offspring of the Sex Pistols and The Dubliners. Dave Robinson was taking a last glorious throw of the dice.

Shane MacGowan comments: "Stiff were the only people who could understand why people liked going to see us. The only people who were worth a job in the record business. There was all these A&R men going, 'The Pogues are going to be huge. But we don't understand why people are going to see them'. But Stiff got it. That's why they signed Wreckless Eric, that's why they signed Nick Lowe, that's why they signed The Damned. People thought they were mad when they signed The Damned and Richard Hell, because they thought it was just a fleeting fad. But anybody involved in it knew that punk was never going to go away again."

MacGowan had been present at the birth of punk and stood out even against its colourful array of characters. He was a pasty-faced teenager with jug ears who would wear a beret with crucifixes and rosary beads – religious symbols from his upbringing in Catholic Ireland. His hair had been matted and reached his shoulders a couple of years earlier when he'd started frequenting Rock On, the record stall in the old Soho Market.

That all changed when he wandered into The Nashville one night to watch the 101'ers and been blown sideways by the support act, the Sex Pistols. He became a face at their gigs, usually right at the front, and was inadvertently captured by rock photographers recording this cultural quake. MacGowan was far more than a spectator, however. Everyone was doing fanzines and he produced his own handwritten one, *Bondage*. He turned up in bands, firstly Hot Dogs With Everything and then The Nipple Erectors. The latter made their debut at the Roxy in the autumn of 1977 and were managed by Phil Gaston and Stan Brennan, who both worked at Rock On. MacGowan's stage sobriquet Shane O'Hooligan suited him well.

By the early eighties, MacGowan was still being managed by Brennan, although this time in a band playing traditional Irish music. The singer, like others from the Irish diaspora, was living in the dilapidated area of Kings Cross, and the group had emerged from local bars, housing projects and squats. Pogue Mahone – which was the Gaelic for "kiss my arse" – were: MacGowan, vocals and guitar; Jem Finer, banjo; James

Fearnley, accordion; Andrew Ranken, drums; Cait O'Riordan, bass, and Spider Stacy, who provided backing vocals and smashed himself over the head with a metal beer tray. "Spider played whistle and tray and did vocals," recalls MacGowan. "In the early days, if they didn't have a beer tray on the premises, we'd have to go out round the pubs in the area and borrow a couple. Traditionally it would have been a light tray, but we had to put up with what we got. On 'Waxie's Dargle' he hits himself 32 times with the tray, and they could be really hard and he would be covered in bruises, suppurating sores [*laughs*]."

MacGowan was born in Royal Tunbridge Wells in Kent, but grew up on a farm in County Tipperary and was immersed in traditional music from a young age. He listened to his family play music and sing and developed a strong affinity with Irish music. The well-read youngster had a particular respect for Seán Ó Riada, an influential composer who led a revival of Irish music in the sixties through his group, Ceoltóirí Chualann. Ó Riada was seen as a rebel in Ireland where traditional music was tightly controlled by Comhaltas Ceoltóirí Éireann, an organisation set up to promote Irish culture and language. "I saw Irish music as a living thing, a thing that was still going on," explains MacGowan. "I was brought up in a huge family and neighbourhood scene. Seán Ó Riada was a big man all over, and my uncles and aunties were all great musicians and singers."

Later, in London, MacGowan became a regular at The Favourite, a pub on the Hornsey Road, Islington. Music sessions there were legend and some were recorded and released by the traditional folk label Topic. The pub had a strong London Irish ["Lirish"] community and was run for years by the parents of MacGowan's close friend Tom McManamon. When they died close together, he was left reeling from the tragedy and running the pub single-handedly at the age of 17. McManamon, or "McAnimal" as he was nicknamed, played banjo in Dingle Spike and Irish Mist and went on to feature in MacGowan's group The Popes, before his own death in 2006 at just 45.

"'The Band Played Waltzing Matilda' was one of our big songs and he used to sing that playing the banjo with the house band Dingle Spike," recalls MacGowan. "They were a great band and that inspired us in The Pogues. Like The Pogues and The Popes are the same thing, you know what I mean? I'm the important one, yeah [*laughs*]. But there were other important ones in The Pogues and there were other important ones in The Popes. But Tommy was the most important."

Pogue Mahone was a reaction to what MacGowan saw as a dilution of traditional Irish music which was blighting people's perception of it. Christy Moore's group Moving Hearts was an abhorrence in his eyes, along with pub bodhran players who played with no passion or soul. His group would have these qualities in spades, he decided, and reclaim the music that so profoundly inspired him.

In January 1984, Pogue Mahone released a single, funded and produced by Stan Brennan and issued on Pogue Mahone Records. The band converged on Elephant Studios in Wapping and recorded "Dark Streets Of London" as the A-side, with "And The Band Played Waltzing Matilda" for the B-side. A couple of hundred of the records were pressed up as white labels and sold at a gig at the Irish Centre in Camden on the eve of St Patrick's Day.

A session for John Peel's Radio 1 show was still as good a launch-pad as ever in 1984, and in February the group were invited to record. O'Riordan knocked back so many drinks in the BBC bar that when they got to the studio, she got into an argument with the staff. She ended up being wrestled out of the building by some of her bandmates and Fearnley and Finer stepped in to play her bass parts. Meanwhile, "Boys From The County Hell", one of the four songs chosen for the radio session, was rejected by the BBC because of the lyrics.

"Dark Streets Of London" began to sell, helped by the band's appearance – along with The Shillelagh Sisters and The Boothill Foot-tappers – on *South Of Watford*, the TV show presented by comedian Ben Elton. The song was picked up by John Peel, Kid Jensen and other Radio 1 presenters. However, more trouble with the BBC lay ahead when someone phoned in to let them in on what Pogue Mahone meant, and the airplay dried up. MacGowan says the call was made by an Irish lorry driver who was amused by the name.

"He rang up John Peel when we were doing a session and he really liked us and he thought it was a great joke," says MacGowan. "He didn't realise he was getting us into trouble with the BBC. It took a week or two to reach the old farts at the top and they went, 'This is unacceptable', because they'd had the Pistols with 'God Save The Queen' and they'd had Frankie with 'Relax'. They were terrified of getting their fingers burnt again. So, they said they weren't going to ban it, they weren't going to do anything like that. But they were not going to play the record and just pretend we didn't exist unless we changed our name."

MacGowan had been on Dave Robinson's radar for several years. He had wanted to sign The Nips (a later incarnation of The Nipple Erectors), but Chiswick beat him to it. So, when he heard about Pogue Mahone, he made his way to The Pindar of Wakefield in King's Cross, where the group played regularly. He liked what he heard and saw. "I thought, 'I'll definitely sign them'," recalled Robinson. "Stan Brennan came to see me and then I met the band and we did the deal. We worked out a very cheap budget to make the first album and we, Stiff, put the money up."

On a bright morning, the group excitedly arrived at St Peter's Square to sign their first record deal. They were taken through the contemporary, open-plan office, past the white boards where the progress of current acts was constantly updated with marker pens, and out onto a sunlit patio. Robinson was waiting for them and had laid on champagne to toast the deal. He told them how fantastic they were and how well they were going to work together. But while the atmosphere was congenial, MacGowan and company left him in no doubt that they weren't about to be stitched up.

"Dark Streets Of London" became the band's first Stiff release in May 1984. Initially the deal was to have been for one single, with the option on an album and another single. But Robinson had agreed to an album straight up, on condition they drop the name Pogue Mahone. MacGowan, who had already seen The Nipple Erectors shortened to The Nips, offered no resistance. "People were already calling us The Pogues because Pogue Mahone is a bit of a mouthful," he says. "So we just changed to The Pogues and got on with it."

Robinson had been giving some thought to Stiff having an offshoot label and launching it with The Pogues, reveals Jamie Spencer. While Madness had wanted their own bespoke label to be set up within Stiff, what Robinson is believed to have had in mind was an imprint for indie artists. "I can't remember what he was going to call it, but it would have been a wing label," says Spencer. "It didn't happen, but I remember that Pogue Mahone would have been the first one for this little offshoot. In the end they signed to Stiff. I think there was such a vibe and noise about the band and maybe they were already too big for this incubator idea."

Red Roses For Me, the record that would launch The Pogues, was recorded at Elephant for £5,000 and produced by Stan Brennan. Robinson had reportedly wanted to bring in Clive Langer, who, with Alan Winstanley, had applied the golden touch to Madness. Loyalty won the day, however, the group sticking with Brennan. However, when it came to the design of their important debut album, the group had less of a say.

A photo shoot was arranged but it was beset with problems. Stiff had matching, western-style coats with black collars and cuffs for each band member. But MacGowan arrived with his foot in plaster and carrying a walking stick having broken his ankle falling down a flight of stairs. The photographer then announced he didn't have enough film and they would have to reconvene several weeks later to finish off. The Camden Irish Centre was chosen as the venue, but by the time of the shoot, Andrew Ranken had gone on holiday. The rest of the group were grouped around a portrait of John F. Kennedy during the photo session, and when the art department chose this image for the cover, Ranken's head was crassly inserted in a bottom corner. The gaudy lettering across the top of the sleeve, which Robinson had encouraged the designer to use, only made matters worse. No one liked the sleeve and, in terms of group-label relations, it wasn't the best start.

Some months earlier, The Pogues had attracted a famous fan – or at least Cait O'Riordan had. Phil Chevron, part of the band's wider scene, had encouraged Elvis Costello to see them playing at The Diorama Arts Centre in Regent's Park and, as he stood in the audience, he was spellbound by the volatile bassist. She and the group remained at the top of his mind and when he began planning an autumn tour with The Attractions, there was only one group he wanted to support him. So, from late September to the end of October 1984, The Pogues played in front of packed houses.

The tour crackled with tension. MacGowan and Costello didn't see eye to eye and tensions developed as Costello and O'Riordan smooched on the bus and backstage. He and other members of The Pogues sought out ways to wind up the headlining star. "We nearly got thrown off the tour three times," says MacGowan. "I did IRA graffiti all over the PA bus and Spider did UDA on the other side. When Costello and that lot were on stage, we used to drink their fucking booze. The guy was in love with Cait, so that's the reason we didn't get sacked off the tour – and we gave him street cred."

One backstage spat involved Gary Barnacle, the sax player who appeared on the *Goodbye Cruel World* album Costello was touring. "I had a big row with Gary Barnacle," says MacGowan. "Elvis had a roadie called Paddy, a real fun guy and he really liked us. Gary Barnacle was going out with Kim Wilde and we were just having a chat and Gary Barnacle came up and said, 'Stop chatting up my girlfriend, you asshole'. I said, 'She can talk to anybody she wants'. So he went up to Paddy O'Donnell and he [Paddy] says, 'I don't care what he does to you.'"

Red Roses For Me made No. 89 in the UK album chart and "Boys From The County Hell", released as a single to coincide with the tour, didn't register at all. While The Pogues had left an indelible mark on many of those who had seen them during the Costello tour, it hadn't translated into sales just yet and hits were becoming few and far between for the label. Comedian Billy Connolly brought in a minor Top 40 hit with "Super Gran", but another novelty single was the last thing Stiff required. Pin-up boy Jamie Rae was tried again, this time with a single called "Pretty One", to no avail.

Stiff's search for commercial success was becoming increasingly desperate and some at the label were dismayed by the Island deal. Sonnie Rae had been dubious about moving to St Peter's Square, but had gone with Robinson out of loyalty.

"It was the biggest mistake he [Robinson] ever made," she says, "and I compounded it because he desperately wanted me there and I was doing really well freelance and I said, 'I don't really want to do this'. But because I loved him so much, I thought, well maybe I should, and he said, 'You can still work on Mari Wilson'.

"I hated it. I thought it was the crappest, most appalling place to work on God's earth having had total freedom all my life really in what I did … to go somewhere that was motivated purely by office politics was vile, I can't tell you. I do believe I assaulted the head of sales in the stationery cupboard over Aswad. I was getting loads of airplay on them and he didn't want it to be a hit because he had got other plans or something. I thought, how can you work like this? Dave loathed it as well. It was so bad for him because it stifled his creativity too. I think Stiff disappeared under the weight of the politics. It kind of put me off the music business."

Robinson, in an interview in 2006, admitted the tie-up with Island was a mistake. "Island was in a bad financial state and I spent too much time worrying about his label and not enough about my own," he said. [57]

The Pogues, for the time being at least, were to save Robinson thanks to one of the most extraordinary albums ever released by Stiff – *Rum, Sodomy And The Lash*. A number of game-changing developments had taken place within the Pogues camp. Frank Murray had taken over from Stan Brennan as the group's manager, bringing with him a wealth of experience. The Dubliner had tour-managed Thin Lizzy at their peak and was a confidante of lead singer Phil Lynott. Elton John and The Specials also appeared on his tour management CV, and he and fellow "Dub" Dave Robinson went back years.

Murray had meanwhile introduced another musician to the fold. Philip Chevron had played guitar in The Radiators From Space and, along with Kirsty MacColl, was on the books of Murray's management company Hill16. Terry Woods, another acquaintance of Murray's, would later join the group to play mandolin and cittern. The Pogues' new manager and fixer also had a hand in the events that led to their second album being produced by Elvis Costello.

A rumour had spread in the camp that O'Riordan's boyfriend wanted to produce the record. Murray knew Riviera, who was still managing Costello, so he called him to investigate. Riviera seemed horrified by the idea but, to his amazement, Costello confirmed it. Robinson was equally aghast at the news. "You couldn't just *get* Elvis Costello," he said. "Getting him to do a Stiff band other than this one wouldn't have happened. The whole thing was remarkable. I thought, 'What a great thing'." [54] MacGowan was not so enamoured with the idea and looked for opportunities to wind Costello up. "Costello was making out with Cait on the settee and I was turning up the levels and conspiring against him," he laughs.

Mixing work with pleasure didn't adversely affect the finished product. *Rum, Sodomy And The Lash* – which took its title from Winston Churchill's apocryphal view of the Navy – was a masterpiece which took the traditions of Irish music and storytelling and hotwired them with the attitude of punk. The Pogues were a wild phenomenon on stage and capturing that within the confines of a studio was a tall order for any producer. But having done justice to The Specials, whose reputation was also built on their pulsating live shows, Costello had done his girlfriend and her bandmates proud. The whole glorious affair, like MacGowan himself, sounded like it had been steeped in Jack Daniels.

MacGowan's standing as one of the most original songwriters of his generation was confirmed with compositions such as "The Old Main Drag", "A Pair Of Brown Eyes" and "I'm A Man You Don't Meet Every Day"; the latter sung sublimely by O'Riordan. As for possible singles, Stiff was spoiled for choice.

First up was "A Pair Of Brown Eyes", which was coupled with "Whiskey You're The Devil" in March 1985. Alex Cox, who had just directed the movie *Repo Man*, was hired for the video, which began in a tube train and was itself fated to remain underground. The record attracted some airplay and reached No. 72 in the UK chart. "Sally MacLennane", the follow-up, was among the songs played by The Pogues when they were featured on *Whistle Test*, but still only made 51. The album itself, however, was a very different matter.

Its nautical theme had sent Stiff's publicity department into overdrive and the launch was one of the most drunken and eventful press shindigs ever. Phil Hall, who looked after The Pogues publicity at Stiff, hired HMS Belfast and Nelson-era naval uniforms for the band to wear. Around 400 members of the press were invited on board to drink free rum and so drunk was one journalist that he flung himself over the side into the Thames. Robinson hid, fearing he might be thrown overboard.

Rum, Sodomy And The Lash received some positive notices, but more importantly for Stiff's ailing accounts, sales were strong. The album achieved a position of No.13 and spent fourteen weeks on the UK chart, an excellent performance for a record that stuck out like a sore thumb in 1984. The future looked bright for The Pogues. But at the label, a pall was descending.

15

Grey Day

Many had predicted the deal would fail and, just 18 months later, they were proved right. "Stiff, Island Dissolve Their UK Partnership", *Billboard* informed readers on 24 August 1985. Stiff had "disengaged" itself from the operation and Dave Robinson was resigning as head of Island. A statement released by Island said the move had come about because Robinson wanted to devote more time to Stiff, although he was being retained as a consultant on marketing and television advertising campaigns. Stiff would go back to having its records manufactured and distributed by EMI, as it had before the Island tie-up.

Robinson made no comment, but it was suggested Island's success in 1984 had been to the detriment of Stiff. Chris Blackwell's label had doubled its UK turnover as a result of the television advertising campaigns around Bob Marley's *Legend*, U2's *The Unforgettable Fire* and the early Frankie Goes To Hollywood records on ZTT.

"Robinson recently cut short his holiday to supervise arrangements for the departure of Stiff," said the report, "which has recently gone through quiet times sales wise, but is rebuilding with such acts as The Pogues and The Untouchables. No decision has yet been made concerning who will succeed Robinson as managing director of Island.

Too many of Stiff's records were living up to the company name and stiffing. A lull had set in after Kirsty MacColl lit up the charts with "A New England". Of the thirteen singles Stiff issued in 1985, only Billy Connolly's "Super Gran" graced the Top 40, never mind the Top 10. No matter whether they were produced on shaped discs, 12-inches, coloured vinyl, it made no difference to its sales, consigning acts such as The Untouchables, The Catch, Romeo & Juliet and Phranc to history. Journalists were naturally drawn to The Pogues like moths to a flame. But, as in the very early days of the label with Elvis Costello and Ian Dury, that had not translated into hefty sales. Stiff's accounts made for pretty bleak reading.

Nick Stewart believes Blackwell and Robinson's attempt to keep their two labels separate was a fatal error and Stiff would have fared better if its most promising acts had been given the chance to transfer to Island, and the rest allowed to leave. In trying to head up two labels at the same time, Robinson had spread the jam too thinly and Stiff had suffered.

He says: "What he should have done was said to someone, 'Alan Cowderoy will run Stiff and come to me once a week and tell me what's going on, and I can give advice on anything'. But he took his eye off the ball because suddenly we had ZZT and Frankie Goes To Hollywood, *Legend* and U2's *The Unforgettable Fire*, and Island was making a lot of money."

As Island set about bolstering its artistic roster under the managing directorship of Clive Banks, Stiff moved out and set up in a former warehouse in Hoxton. Nick Stewart went with Robinson, taking a full-time role at the struggling label. Robinson is said to have had to sell the house he owned on the banks of the River Thames. Industry chatter about Stiff's financial problems was getting louder and Stiff needed a hit record from which it could build some momentum.

The Mint Juleps arrived at Stiff with quite a CV. The six girls had toured with Sister Sledge and Billy Bragg and supplied backing vocals for Bob Geldof and The Belle Stars. The a cappella group, managed by former Darts members Griff Fender and Rita Ray, was made up of four sisters, Sandra, Debbie, Lizzie and Marcia Charles and friends Julie Isaac and Debbie Longworth. All six of them had gone to the same school and loved singing, but hadn't harboured any ambitions to form a professional group.

"We were working in a theatre, some of us, and we used to sing songs after the shows," said Debbie Charles. "We just enjoyed singing; it was never a dream of ours to be singers." [42]

Their first record for Stiff was a pretty ambitious one: a cover of Neil Young's devastating "Only Love Can Break Your Heart". Far from reconstructing the timeless classic, the girls simply used their voices and harmonies to record a soulful and highly contemporary version. Sadly, however, it made only No. 62 in the UK chart and Stiff had to look to its other all-girl act to save the business.

The Belle Stars had downsized to a trio by 1986; Sarah-Jane Owen, Miranda Joyce and Lesley Shone deciding to continue following the departure of the others. Financially, things had been tight for the group, says Shone. Even when they were riding high in the charts, the girls had been earning £75 per week, and the royalties didn't start rolling in until later. Some of the girls had also had enough of the constant touring and wanted their lives back.

"Male musicians can have the wife and family at home while they're on the road. But being female, there was the question of the old 'biological ticking clock'," says Shone. "The band's mantra at the time was 'no babies in the band'. Things have moved on for women now and, in certain respects, times have certainly changed for the better. Women can 'have baby will tour' these days. Some of the girls went on to start their own families when they finally called the band a day."

The girls had flown out to New York to record a new album with the production team at 4th & Broadway, a US-based subsidiary of Island Records that specialised in hip hop. A track called "World Domination" emerged from the sessions and was released as a single, along with a textbook MTV video. In the US, the record caught on and got to No. 2 in the dance chart there. But in Britain it flopped and the album was shelved.

A beacon of hope briefly shone above the floundering operation in Hoxton. Nick Stewart had brought in Furniture, the kind of brooding indie band Stiff could have done with a few years earlier when Korova had Echo & The Bunnymen and PolyGram had The Teardrop Explodes. The group had been formed in Ealing way back in 1979 by singer Jim Irvin, guitarist Tim Whelan and drummer Hamilton Lee.

While they'd not enjoyed any commercial success, Furniture had released a string of singles and EPs on Survival Records. And on their arrival at Stiff, they offered up their strongest composition of all. "Brilliant Mind" was drenched in atmosphere and steadily grew in both sound and stature in a way that was as compulsive as Irvin's imploring vocals. The four-note guitar riff that prefaced the chorus capped an indie classic.

"Brilliant Mind" and another song "I Miss You" were performed by the group after they appeared on The Tube in March 1986. It took off on release and by July it was a No. 21 hit. But Furniture's timing couldn't have been worse and any thoughts that it would finally ignite things for them were snuffed out almost immediately. Stiff Records was going to fold. Things were about to get dirty.

That Stiff had been sailing close to the wind for some time in financial terms was an open secret. But the scale of the debt was shocking.

At an electrically charged creditors' meeting held at the Connaught Rooms in Great Queen Street, Covent Garden, on 18 August 1986, the truth was laid bare, as reported in *Billboard*.

Those who packed into the specially convened session heard how Elcotgrange Ltd, Stiff's parent company, had debts of more than £3.5 million. Quite a revelation given Robinson's very recent public assurances there was "nothing to worry about" and the letter Stiff's accountants had sent to creditors just weeks before inviting them to submit details of debts and promising a rosy future for the company. The last paragraph had advised them against taking legal action against Elcotgrange, because litigation could result in Stiff's main assets – its artists' contracts – reverting to the artists and managements "so that nobody will get anything".

There were almost 300 names on the list of creditors, with *Billboard* reporting that Island was owed $1.1 million and The Mechanical Copyright Protection Society (MCPS) around $330,000. It was reported elsewhere that Robinson stunned Stiff creditors by placing a personal claim against his own company for more than £191,000. In a 2006 interview, Robinson claimed he had been Stiff's biggest creditor, but insisted Stiff's debts were more modest, "more like £1.4 million". [47]

Robinson was photographed leaving the meeting with a sheaf of documents under one arm and giving the victory salute. He refused to answer any questions and hurried off up the street. "Robinson's Jam" read the *NME* headline on the short piece run on 30 August, and he was certainly in one.

Coincidentally, the exact same headline had been run about three weeks earlier in another publication and whose sudden interest in Stiff's affairs would alarm Robinson. *Private Eye* hadn't been known for its reporting on the music trade industry, but it had a fearsome reputation. Disturbingly for Robinson, it decided to poke its investigative snout into his and Stiff's affairs.

"I remember all that," says Paul Conroy. "I'd gone by then, but it was still very important to me. There was a big thing about where it was all coming from. Someone had a bit of a vendetta. It's like the whole thing with phone hacking now, we played the media game for a long time and things like not letting people have front pages or not giving exclusives to someone, those things can come back and bite you on the bum."

Company records show that Stiff Records Ltd, originally named Claspstick Ltd, had been incorporated on 18 June 1986. According to *Billboard*, the transfer of assets from Elcotgrange to the new company had taken place in July and "hurried through to allow the Stiff logo to continue".

In the Connaught Rooms, Robinson and his team of accountants had pleaded with creditors to stick with this new company and not to continue pushing for liquidation. Stiff Records Ltd had been set up to keep the record operation running, they said. The group Dr. Feelgood had signed with the new company and "Don't Wait Up", their first single in two years, was then being released.

—

Winding up proceedings began and, in September 1986, Stiff Records Ltd was sold for £305,000. The buyer was the late Jill Sinclair, chairman of the Sarm Group of companies and ZZT, and the wife of the producer Trevor Horn. Sinclair had set up a company called Cashmere specifically for the purchase in order to keep the deal separate from her other business operations. The proceeds from the sale would go to Elcotgrange's creditors, who could expect payments of 10p in the pound. What remained of the company was to be liquidated by the receivers.

Stiff would continue to trade, its staff having already been reduced to eleven, and Dave Robinson would continue at the helm. Sinclair said: "Dave Robinson is a great marketing man, but not so good at administration. I plan to look after the running of the business and leave him free for the artist side. Stiff already has some excellent acts on its books, and there will be no changes in that sector. But we won't initially be looking to sign new bands." She added tellingly: "Selling Stiff had a bittersweet element for Dave Robinson, because he no longer owns the company, but he explored all other possibilities before agreeing. Now he seems quite relieved." [55]

Those still aboard the good ship Stiff at the time of its sinking included Furniture, The Belle Stars, The Untouchables and The Mint Juleps. The label had also been joined by Andy Fairweather Low, one of the founders of sixties hit-makers Amen Corner, although his single "Bossa Nova" had disappeared when it was released as Stiff went into meltdown the previous summer.

Dr. Feelgood were still managed by Chris Fenwick and fronted by Lee Brilleaux when they joined Stiff in 1986, shortly before it went into liquidation. However, this time they couldn't help Stiff and their singles, "Don't Wait Up" and "See You Later Alligator" were swallowed amid the gloom engulfing the company.

Stiff had become almost a complete stranger to the UK chart. In 1985 it mustered just three singles in the all-important Top 40 and just two in 1986, courtesy of Furniture and The Pogues. The "Poguetry In Motion" EP had made No. 29 on its release in February that year and if there was on act on its books that stood any chance of fulfilling Sinclair's prophecy that she and Robinson would "make a dent in the next ten years", it was them. More than a year after giving Stiff its last hit, The Pogues coalesced with The Dubliners, some of the musicians who had first inspired them, to record their next single. "The Irish Rover" was a traditional and hugely popular Irish folk song which told the story of a ship that met an unfortunate end. A more appropriate theme they couldn't have found.

Released in May 1987, "The Irish Rover" proved its timeless appeal by sailing into the chart. The Dubliners returned to *Top Of The Pops* studios twenty years after they performed their biggest hit "Seven Drunken Nights", while The Pogues made their debut. Both bands clearly enjoyed the occasion as they played amid an array of flashing lights and MacGowan and Ronnie Drew made for one of the most memorable duos ever seen on the show. The song climbed up the chart, peaking at No.7 and delivering the new Stiff double-act of Sinclair and Robinson their first hit.

Unbeknown to Robinson, rehearsals for their third album had already got under way at Abbey Road Studios and a plot hatched to leave the label. "In order to circumvent our contract with Stiff Records – from legal necessity or not, I didn't care – Frank enjoined us to let no one know, going so far as to pretend we were assisting Terry [Woods] with a solo project," said James Fearnley. [56]

Robinson, in an increasingly desperate state, had rung alarm bells in the group as to Stiff's perilous position. They had been rehearsing for their Christmas tour of 1985 when they were interrupted by the Irishman, who looked tired and unshaven. Sitting on a flight case with his hands in his coat pockets, he had pulled no punches about the state the label was in and begged them to stay.

Frank Murray suggested the group finance the record themselves and they managed to set up their own label, Pogue Mahone Records, under Warner Music Ltd. Steve Lillywhite was recruited to produce it thanks to Murray's acquaintance with his wife Kirsty MacColl. The band, having extricated themselves from their obligations to Stiff, adjourned to RAK Studios to record what would be *If I Should Fall From Grace With God*. In a cruel twist, one of the songs that would appear on the record might well have been Stiff's saviour had it come sooner. But it was too late.

"Fairytale Of New York", a MacGowan/Finer composition, had been recorded as part of the sessions for *Rum, Sodomy And The Lash* with MacGowan and Cait O'Riordan singing the duet and producer Elvis Costello accompanying them on the piano. However, it wasn't included on the album and Costello had decided against its release as a single.

MacGowan explains: "We had left Stiff by the time we did that. But we were touring with it before we left Stiff, so we had got a better sound and we didn't have to deal with Elvis Costello! I don't know why Elvis Costello decided not to put it out as a single, but as a producer that was his shout. Cait did a great version of it."

Two years later, with the Christmas song being dusted down and Lillywhite in the producer's chair, it was decided that MacColl sing the female parts of the drunken ballad. MacGowan says MacColl "went off and did her bit on her own; she produced herself". Still favouring a studio over a stage, the self-conscious singer had continued to be apprehensive about performing in public. "Fairytale Of New York" not only gave her a share in a huge hit record, but playing with The Pogues bolstered her confidence.

MacGowan says: "She didn't like playing live, so Frank put her on a tour of Ireland, which is about the fucking worst thing you can do to somebody with stage fright, you know what I mean? You have to get used to it and she got used to it. She was very comfortable by the time she was working with us. We'd known her for a while. She was really confident; she used to smack me round the place, 'You're out of it again, aren't you? It's disgusting'."

"Fairytale Of New York" reached No. 2 in the UK in December 1987 and stayed on the chart for nine weeks. But for the label that had launched them, there would be no merry Christmas or happy ending. Time was about to be called on Stiff Records.

Dr. Feelgood's third single "Hunting Shooting Fishing" had done nothing on its release earlier in the year and their second Stiff album *Classic*, produced by Will Birch and Kevin Morris, was shelved. As Stiff tried to stave off the inevitable, it put its remaining chips on The Mint Juleps.

Trevor Horn himself came in to produce their single "Girl To The Power Of 6", their first original release. He sent the group in a completely different direction, rapping Salt-n-Peppa-style over a drum machine rhythm, and introducing the concept of "Girl Power" many years before The Spice Girls. But the record (BUY 263) made even less of an impression than the previous two and became the last Stiff record, its proposed follow-up "Docklands" being dropped.

Stiff was wound up and its catalogue and, later – its name – were bought by Sinclair and Horn. Almost twelve years after it had exploded into life along with punk, it fizzled out amid eighties yuppiedom. Stiff Records was over.

A combination of factors attributed to its demise. The move to Island Records had certainly been detrimental, preventing Robinson from giving Stiff his full attention, and the departure of Madness was a bitter blow. The label had also sunk large sums of money into certain acts and their recording projects as it pursued the commercial success its spiralling operational costs necessitated. In a Catch-22, it didn't have the money it would have needed to break a group on the scale achieved by U2 or Simple Minds. And – when the hits dried up – it couldn't pay the bills.

Paul Conroy cites the lack of songwriters at Stiff as one of the reasons for that. While Elvis Costello, Ian Dury, Madness and other acts from its golden era supplied a rich seam of original material, too many of its artists didn't, making hit songs even harder to come by.

"A lot of the artists just weren't writers," says Conroy. "That's the long and short of it. When you look at Squeeze and some of the other acts that were floating around like Joe Jackson, we lacked that. We didn't have an in-house writing team and that was the difference with a label like Motown, which had Marvin Gaye and Holland-Dozier-Holland. They had writing teams. I remember we tried Sylvia & The Sapphires, and that's the closest we ever got to a Motown thing."

Andy Murray points out that while Island enjoyed healthy sales in the US, Stiff never had that luxury. Also, once success had arrived Stiff found itself in a vicious circle. "You've got to be bigger or you are such a genius like Clive Calder, that you keep your roster so tight and you've got somebody like Mutt Lange tucked up your sleeve, who is a hit machine on his own," says Murray.

"Then, when you decide to sell up, your catalogue is worth something and you can sell for a lot of money. But mostly that doesn't happen.

Mostly what happens is you are Magnet. You do quite well at the lower level, you make the mistake of having hits with Chris Rea, which means that you then have to give Chris Rea proper advances, and then his manager comes in and he wants to have bigger royalties. At which point, you can get better money, but your distributors start saying, 'Well, Magnet, where's the next Darts album? That Darts album didn't do as well as the previous one'. 'Oh, don't worry, We'll get Chris Rea to do a greatest hits album'. So, then you've actually got to sign a further two Chris Reas to pay the bills that you've created by having Chris Rea and eventually you have to sell up because you can't keep it going."

—

Stiff achieved what Riviera and Robinson had set out to do. It had taken industry rejects and no-hopers and proved there was a mainstream audience for them. It flouted every industry taboo, promoting other label's artists on its record sleeves while using self-deprecating slogans to draw attention to its own. From a marketing standpoint, it had completely rewritten the rulebook, making its products visually appealing and collectable, and complementing them with everything from badges and sew-on patches to handkerchiefs and combs.

Stiff made artists signed to other labels demand more and better promotion and their complacent labels to try harder, as Robinson explained: "Marketing meetings used to happen on Tuesdays and you wouldn't get anyone in the majors from 10am to 3pm. All they were talking about was, 'What are Stiff doing this week? What are they up to? I mean, you can't do this, it's ridiculous. How can you spend this money?'

"Every week we were doing something. We were saying, 'Give up smoking, give us your money!' We were saying, 'Fuck you' really, and the groups were asking why they couldn't have advertising like that and picture bags on their singles, so everybody was irritated." [5]

Nigel Dick contends, however, that while Stiff became renowned for its marketing, its success was not owed to its full-page music press adverts and extravagant promotional campaigns, but its uniquely talented artists.

"On some level we had great success with it, but by and large the success came down to the quality of the records," says Dick. "Everybody marvelled at Stiff's marketing, but off the top of my head,

I can't think of one act which had real long-term success as a result of the marketing. I mean the train tour is a very good example of a fantastic marketing campaign, which Andy Murray put together with Paul Conroy, and it was all over the papers, and it resulted in one top five single for Lene, which arguably would have happened with the most mundane tour out of the back of a transit van."

Nevertheless, not only did Stiff succeed in creating a buzz around its acts but also around the label itself. Most record buyers took little notice of what labels their favourite acts were signed to and cared even less. But through its distinctive marketing, quirky collectables and the personal rapport it built up with those buying its records, Stiff created a unique brand.

Much of that was down to the talented people it employed. People like Paul Conroy and Andy MacDonald took their experience from Stiff and used it to further their careers at Warner and Virgin, and Go! Discs, respectively. Nigel Dick, the one-time office boy and press officer, picked up tips on video-making while helping out Madness. He went on to produce the Live Aid video for Phonogram before moving to LA. He has worked with Guns N' Roses, Oasis and Britney Spears among others, and directed feature films. Stiff's legacy lives on, not only through the amazing music of its artists, but its enduring influence on how pop music is sold and collected.

Whatever else it was, Stiff was never grey. For almost twelve years it blazed a trail across the industry, always doing things its way and proving beyond any doubt ..."If It Ain't Stiff, It Ain't Worth A Fuck".

Epilogue

Yesterday's Hits – Today!

Stiff Records specialised in resurrections. So, it was fitting that twenty years after it was wound up, the label returned from the dead.

On 16 October 2006, Stiff released BUY 265, The Enemy's double A-sided single "Dancing All Night/40 Days and 40 Nights". The 1,000 copies of the record by the young Coventry group were hand-numbered and issued on vinyl only. They sold overnight. On the same day, five albums were reissued, all digitally re-mastered and featuring singles, B-sides, label memorabilia and extensive sleeve notes. The records exhumed for the occasion were: Rachel Sweet *Fool Around;* Wreckless Eric *Big Smash!;* Dirty Looks *Dirty Looks/Turn It Up;* Any Trouble *Where Are All The Nice Girls,* and Desmond Dekker *Compass Point.*

Jill Sinclair and Trevor Horn had acquired the Stiff catalogue when it folded in 1986, although not all the rights, as some of the artists had ended up getting theirs back. The couple had also acquired the Stiff name from the receivers. Pete Gardiner, a longtime fan of the label, began working with them in 1998, recalls: "When I started working for Jill and Trevor, they didn't have a copy of anything," says Gardiner. "All the master tapes had gone missing, I think because someone dumped them when the company went under. I bought tapes off German licensees for a couple of thousand Euros. These were all production masters and I found some other tapes. I drove down to Taunton one day and bought the first 100 singles from someone who was selling their collection."

Stiff was run as a catalogue concern only at this point, the label hooking up with reissue specialist Union Square Music. Releases tended to be compilations of individual artists. Wreckless Eric, Kirsty MacColl and Tenpole Tudor all got the "Best Of" treatment in 2001 and Jona Lewie and Tracey Ullman collections followed in 2002. Stiff was about nostalgia and showcasing its past, not its future.

But it was through a similar trawl through the Stiff archives by the BBC that the real re-energising of the label came about. Gardiner had pitched the idea of BBC Four shining a torch into Stiff's dusty recesses with a view to getting the catalogue some profile. Clearly bosses of the channel felt its audience and the Stiff demographic was a good fit: a full-length documentary was produced and broadcast on 11 May 2007.

By the time it aired, the first new Stiff records for two decades had been released, using an approach that harked back to its earliest days. "My particular influence for re-starting the label as a cottage industry was the OFF Stiff imprint, which released singles by The Members, Ernie Graham, The Subs and The Realists in 1978," says Gardiner. "These cheap, one-off singles were intended to give the bands a leg-up and help secure a deal elsewhere, while at the same time giving Stiff some exposure. All of the acts we released owned their own rights and we just secured short-term licences to release and promote the singles. We were really just looking to cover our costs and have some fun."

The Enemy's debut was followed up by further singles "It's Not OK" and "Away From Here". Revitalised after two decades away, Stiff began adding an eclectic assortment of acts to its BUY catalogue, from UK techno rock group Eskimo Disco and Canadian power pop outfit The Tranzmitors to star-studded collective The Producers. Trevor Horn himself featured in the line-up of studio veterans led by Lol Creme of 10cc and Godley & Creme fame. Chris Braide, Stephen Lipson and Ash Soan completed the group which released the one-off "Barking Up The Right Tree" in the summer of 2007.

All of the 1,000 limited edition, hand-numbered, single pressings sold out quickly, the fastest selling release was the "Happy Birthday You" CD EP by Jay Jay Pistolet. Every copy of the record was accounted for in pre-sales and a launch gig at the Dublin Castle was packed out. Not long after, he reappeared under his real name Justin Hayward-Young as the lead singer in The Vaccines.

Following the resurgence of interest in Stiff generated by the documentary and single releases, Union Square Music issued *The Big Stiff Box Set* in 2007, a 4CD set covering the history of the label from 1976 to the present, from Nick Lowe to The Producers and all points in-between. As of August 2014, the set has sold in excess of 60,000 copies.

Vicky Ball worked alongside Gardiner on the re-launch and, like so many others before her, got her introduction to the music industry thanks to Stiff. "I'd always been aware of Stiff, but really getting to know the catalogue inside out was great," she says. "The letters Stiff wrote and the way the label was run seemed cheeky and rebellious. It was exciting being involved with reissuing the likes of Tracey Ullman, Tenpole Tudor and Rachel Sweet records, and I always got excited when the finished product came in – unwrapping the CDs and praying everything looked like we'd hoped!

"During the re-launch it was a pleasure working with the likes of Wreckless Eric and Amy Rigby, Chris Difford and Jay Jay Pistolet. I got hands-on, organising the mastering, artwork and manufacturing, as well as hand writing every single digit on the limited edition numbered singles and selling vinyl at gigs around the country."

Stiff's fresh burst of activity also saw it reconnect with some of those who had been on the label first time around. Any Trouble's album *Life In Reverse* felt like just that, bringing them back together with Stiff and their original producer, John Wood. To complete the circle, the video for their digital download single "That Sound" was shot by Nigel Dick.

Wreckless Eric returned to the fold along with his wife and songwriting partner Amy Rigby. The duo released a download single "Here Comes My Ship" and their first album together on Stiff in 2008. Henry Priestman, formerly of Yachts, then joined the reunion the same year with his debut collection, *The Chronicles Of Modern Life.* Chris Difford from Squeeze meanwhile made his first appearance on Stiff with his solo album *The Last Temptation Of Chris,* the sleeve of which featured him mimicking the comic Tony Hancock.

It was a brand new act, however, that sent Stiff to No.1 for the first time since Madness with "House Of Fun" in 1982. Sam And The Womp's Balkan-influenced floor-filler "Bom Bom" was picked up by Radio 1 when it was released as a download in August 2012 and went to the top of the UK chart, selling almost 500,000 copies in the UK alone. The video on You Tube has been watched over 25 million times! One of the hit-making trio is Trevor Horn's son Aaron.

A new catalogue distribution deal for Stiff in the US and Canada was announced in 2013 via Razor & Tie, North America's largest privately owned independent label. Ally Horn, managing director of the SPZ Group and Trevor's daughter, pointed to Stiff's colourful American past with Devo, The Plasmatics and the Akron compilation, and said a return to American shores was "long overdue". Razor & Tie was a label that "embodies the independence of Stiff, the futurism of ZTT and the spirit of adventure of both," added Horn.

Back in the UK, Stiff unveiled Razorlight frontman Johnny Borrell as its latest signing. His debut single "Pan-European Supermodel Song (Oh! Gina)" was given a digital release in June, with his debut album *Borrell 1* following a month later. The songs had originally been captured on a four-track recorder by the singer and a group of musicians including Razorlight bassist Freddie Stitz. After road-testing them live, Borrell went into a London studio to record them with Trevor Horn.

"It's an album that was born in the spirit of a party," said the singer, trumpeting his first studio album for five years. But the record's sales were no cause for streamers and champagne. In its first week, it sold just 594 copies, prompting the label to respond with the previous regime's self-deprecating style of humour.

"First week sales of 594 makes *Borrell 1* the 15,678th bestselling album of the year to date," said a Stiff spokesperson. "So far we've achieved 0.00015% sales of Adele's *21* – and 0.03% sales of this week's No. 1 album from Jahmene Douglas – so we feel like it's all to play for as we move into the all-important week two. We might even break the Top 100."

Whether Riviera and Robinson would have shouted quite so loudly about such a flop is debatable. It's more likely such a "stiff" would have been quietly forgotten about and the unsold copies given away later with another release. However, the tongue-in-cheek statement, which signed off with the slogan "If they're dead we'll sign 'em", demonstrated a commitment to keep not just the name, but the spirit of the label alive.

A limited box-set of seven-inch singles, entitled *Ten Big Stiffs,* was released for Record Store Day in North America in November 2013, packaging classics such as Jona Lewie's "You'll Always Find Me In The Kitchen At Parties" and Tenpole Tudor's "Swords Of A Thousand Men" in their original sleeves, with The Mint Juleps' never released "Docklands". A series of short videos telling the stories behind the artists and the records was produced by Nigel Dick and made available on YouTube.

Meanwhile, back in Ladbroke Grove. not far from where Stiff Records first opened for business in 1976, the "world's most flexible record label" lives on ... and Union Square Music is planning a new Stiff box-set in the near future. You have been warned.

Discography

—~—

This comprehensive discography has been compiled by Tony Judge from the Be Stiff website (www.bestiff.co.uk)
Please note: it does not include the following:
* Odd 10" & 12" releases extended plays of standard 7" vinyl
* Enigma Records (mainly imported)
* Blue Bird Records (linked to Stiff and an offshoot connection)
* DB Records (mainly imported)

Plus some oddments licensed in but too obscure and tenuous to be worth a mention. It won't please everybody, but, as Tony says, the listings could be a book in their own right.

Stiff Discography

BUY Singles

BUY 1   Nick Lowe: So It Goes/Heart Of The City
BUY 2   The Pink Fairies: Between The Lines/Spoiling For A Fight
BUY 3   Roogalator: All Aboard/Cincinatti Fat Back
BUY 4   Tyla Gang: Styrofoam/Texas Chainsaw Massacre Boogie
BUY 5   Lew Lewis & His Band: Boogie On The Street/Caravan Man
BUY 6   The Damned: New Rose/Help!
BUY 7   Richard Hell: Another World/Blank Generation/You Gotta Lose
BUY 8   Plummet Airlines: Silver Shirt/This Is The World
BUY 9   Motörhead: Leavin' Here/White Line Fever (only released in Stiff Black Box)
BUY 10   The Damned: Neat Neat Neat/Stab Your Back/Singalongascabies
BUY 11   Elvis Costello: Less Than Zero/Radio Sweetheart
BUY 12   Max Wall: England's Glory/Dream Tobacco
BUY 13   The Adverts: One Chord Wonders/Quick Step
BUY 14   Elvis Costello: Alison/Welcome To The Working Week
BUY 15   Elvis Costello: Red Shoes/Mystery Dance
BUY 16   Wreckless Eric: Whole Wide World/Semaphore Signals
BUY 17   Ian Dury: Sex & Drugs & Rock & Roll/Razzle In My Pocket
BUY 18   The Damned: Problem Child/You Take My Money

BUY 19 The Yachts: Suffice To Say/Freedom (Is A Heady Wine)
BUY 20 Elvis Costello: Watching The Detectives/Blame It On Cain/Mystery
       Dance
BUY 21 Nick Lowe: Halfway To Paradise/I Don't Want The Night to End
BUY 22 Larry Wallis: Police Car/On Parole
BUY 23 Ian Dury & The Blockheads: Sweet Gene Vincent/You're More
       Than Fair
BUY 24 The Damned: Don't Cry Wolf/One Way Love
BUY 25 Wreckless Eric: Reconnez Cherie/Rags And Tatters
BUY 26 Jane Aire & The Belvederes: Yankee Wheels/Nasty Nice
BUY 27 Ian Dury & The Blockheads: What A Waste/Wake Up
BUY 28 The Box Tops: Cry Like A Baby/The Letter
BUY 29 Humphrey Ocean: Whoops-a-Daisy/Davy Crockett
BUY 30 Jona Lewie: The Baby She's Still On The Street/Denny Laine's Valet
BUY 31 Just Water: Singin' In The Rain/Witness To The Crime
BUY 32 Lene Lovich: I Think We're Alone Now/Lucky Number
BUY 33 Wazmo Nariz: Tele-Tele-phone/Wacker Drive
BUY 34 Wreckless Eric: Take The Cash/Girlfriend
BUY 35 Lene Lovich: never issued but was to have been Home/Lucky
       Number
BUY 36 Mickey Jupp: Old Rock 'n' Roller/SPY
BUY 37 Jona Lewie: never issued but was to have been Hallelujah Europa
BUY 38 Ian Dury & The Blockheads: Hit Me With Your Rhythm Stick/
       There Ain't Half Been Some Clever Bastards
BUY 39 Rachel Sweet: B-A-B-Y/Suspended Animation
BUY 40 Wreckless Eric: Crying, Hoping, Waiting/I Wish It Would Rain
BUY 41 Binky Baker & The Pit Orchestra: Toe-Knee-Black-Burn/Rainy Day
       In Brighton
BUY 42 Lene Lovich: Lucky Number/Home
BUY 43 The Rumour: Frozen Years/All Fall Down
BUY 44 Rachel Sweet: I Go To Pieces/Who Does Lisa Like
BUY 45 The Rumour: Emotional Traffic/Hard Enough To Show
BUY 46 Lene Lovich: Say When/One Lonely Heart
BUY 47 Kirsty MacColl: They Don't Know/Turn My Motor On
BUY 48 Lew Lewis Reformer: Win or Lose/Photo Finish
BUY 49 Wreckless Eric: Hit And Miss Judy/Let's Go To The Pictures
BUY 50 Ian Dury & The Blockheads: Reasons To Be Cheerful/Common As
       Muck
BUY 51 Angie: Peppermint Lump/Breakfast In Naples
BUY 52 The 45s: Couldn't Believe A Word/Lonesome Lane
BUY 53 Lene Lovich: Birdsong/Trixi
BUY 54 The Duplicates: I Want To Make You Very Happy/Call Of The Faithful

BUY 55 Rachel Sweet: Baby Let's Play House/Wildwood Salon
BUY 56 Madness: One Step Beyond/Mistakes
BUY 57 Kirsty MacColl: You Caught Me Out / Boys (never released)
BUY 58 Michael O'Brien: Made In Germany/The Queen Likes Pop
BUY 59 The Pointed Sticks: Out of Luck/What Do You Want Me To Do?
BUY 60 The GTs: Boys Have Feelings Too/Be Careful
BUY 61 Jona Lewie: God Bless Whoever Made You/Feeling Stupid
BUY 62 Madness: My Girl/Stepping Into Line
BUY 63 Lene Lovich: Angels/The Fly
BUY 64 Wreckless Eric: A Popsong/Reconnez Cherie
BUY 65 The Feelies: Everybody's Got Something To Hide / Original Love
BUY 66 Dirty Looks: Lie To Me/Rosario's Ashes
BUY 67 Rachel Sweet: Fool's Gold/I've Got A Reason
BUY 68 Lew Lewis: 1-30, 2-30, 3-35/The Mood I'm In
BUY 69 Lene Lovich: What Will I Do Without You/Joan
BUY 70 Desmond Dekker: Israelites/Why Fight
BUY 71 Madness: Nightboat To Cairo/The Young And The Old/Don't Quote
        Me On That
BUY 72 Graham Parker: Stupefaction/Women In Charge
BUY 73 Jona Lewie: You'll Always Find Me In The Kitchen At Parties /
        Bureaucrats
BUY 74 Any Trouble: Yesterday's Girls/Nice Love
BUY 75 Wreckless Eric: Broken Doll/I Need A Situation
BUY 76 The Plasmatics: Butcher Baby/Tight Black Pants
BUY 77 Dirty Looks: Let Go/Accept Me
BUY 78 Go-Go's: We Got The Beat/How Much More
BUY 79 Any Trouble: Second Choice/Name Of The Game
BUY 80 Rachel Sweet: Spellbound/Lover's Lane
BUY 81 The Rumour: My Little Red Book/Name And Number
BUY 82 Graham Parker: Love Without Greed/Mercury Poisoning
BUY 83 Otis Watkins: You Talk Too Much/If You're Ready To Rock
BUY 84 Madness: Baggy Trousers/The Business
BUY 85 Jona Lewie: Big Shot/I'll Get By In Pittsburgh
BUY 86 The Stiffs: Goodbye My Love/Magic Roundabout
BUY 87 Desmond Dekker: Please Don't Bend/Workout
BUY 88 Joe "King" Carrasco And The Crowns: Buena/Tuff Enuff
BUY 89 Dirty Looks: Tailin' You/Automatic Pilot
BUY 90 Ian Dury & The Blockheads: I Want To Be Straight/That's Not All
BUY 91 The Plasmatics: Monkeysuit/Squirm (live)
BUY 92 The Rumour: I Don't Want The Night To End/Pyramids
BUY 93 The Mexicano: Trial By Television/Jamaican Child
BUY 94 Any Trouble: Girls Are Always Right/No Idea

BUY 95 The Equators: Baby Come Back/George

BUY 96 Never released

BUY 97 Lene Lovich: New Toy/Cat's Away

BUY 98 Tenpole Tudor: 3 Bells In A Row/Fashion/Rock 'n' Roll Music

BUY 99 Elmo And Patsy: Santa Got Run Over By A Reindeer/Christmas

BUY 100 Ian Dury & The Blockheads: Sueperman's Big Sister/You'll See
        Glimpses

BUY 101 John Otway: Green Green Grass Of Home/Wednesday Club

BUY 102 Madness: Embarrassment/Crying Shame

BUY 103 Nigel Dixon: Thunderbird/Someone's On The Loose

BUY 104 Jona Lewie: Stop The Cavalry/Laughing Tonight

BUY 105 Desmond Dekker: Many Rivers To Cross/Pickney Gal

BUY 106 London Cast Of Oklahoma: Oklahoma/Oh, What A Beautiful
        Morning

BUY 107 Never released

BUY 108 Madness: Return Of The Los Palmas 7/That's The Way To Do It

BUY 109 Tenpole Tudor: Swords Of A Thousand Men/Love And Food

BUY 110 Jona Lewie: Louise (We Get it Right)/It Will Never Go Wrong

BUY 111 Lonesome Tone: Mum, Dad, Love, Hate And Elvis/Ghost Town
        (never released) 7" Promo only

BUY 112 Madness: Grey Day/Memories

BUY 113 The Equators: If You Need Me/So What's New?

BUY 114 Bubba Lou & The Highballs: Love All Over The Place/Over You
        (never released) 7" Promo only

BUY 115 John Otway: The Turning Point/Too Much Air, Not Enough Oxygen

BUY 116 Desmond Dekker: We Can And We Shall (not issued)

BUY 117 The Belle Stars: Hiawatha/Big Blonde

BUY 118 Department S: Going Left Right/She's Expecting You

BUY 119 Any Trouble: Trouble With Love/She'll Belong To Me

BUY 120 Tenpole Tudor: Wunderbar/Tenpole 45

BUY 121 Sprout Head Rising: Throw Some Water In/Nothing To Sing (Part 2)

BUY 122 Jona Lewie: Shaggy Raggy/Shaggy Raggied

BUY 123 The Belle Stars: Slick Trick/Take Another Look

BUY 124 Alvin Stardust: Pretend/Goose Bumps

BUY 125 Billy Bremner: Loud Music In Cars/The Price Is Right

BUY 126 Madness: Shut Up/A Town With No Name

BUY 127 Any Trouble: Dimming The Day/Another Heartache (never released)

BUY 128 Department S: I Want/Monte Carlo Or Bust

BUY 129 Tenpole Tudor: Throwing The Baby Out With The Bath Water/
        Conga Tribe

BUY 130 The Belle Stars: Another Latin Love Song/Miss World/Stop Now/
        Having A Good Time

BUY 131 Jona Lewie: Re-arranging The Deckchairs On The Titanic/I'll Be Here
BUY 132 Alvin Stardust: A Wonderful Time Up There/Love You So Much
BUY 133 The Cory Band With Gwalia Singers: Stop The Cavalry/The Longest Day
BUY 134 Madness: It Must Be Love/Shadow On The House
BUY 135 Ian Dury: What A Waste, Wake Up And Make Love With Me
BUY 136 The Dancing Did: The Lost Platoon/The Human Chicken
BUY 137 Tenpole Tudor: Let The Four Winds Blow/Sea Of Thunder
BUY 138 Pookiesnackenburger: Just One Cornetto/Turkish Bath
BUY 139 Jona Lewie: I Think I'll Get My Haircut/What Have I Done
BUY 140 Madness: Cardiac Arrest/In The City
BUY 141 Not issued
BUY 142 Alvin Stardust: Weekend/Butterflies
BUY 143 Billy Bremner: Laughter Turns To Tears/Tired And Emotional (And Probably Drunk)
BUY 144 Desmond Dekker: Book Of Rules/Allamanna
BUY 145 The Astronauts: I'm Your Astronaut/Commander Incredible
BUY 146 Madness: House Of Fun/Don't Look Back
BUY 147 Jane Aire & The Belvederes: I Close My Eyes And Count To Ten/Heat Of The City
BUY 148 The Electric Guitars: Language Problems/Night Bears
BUY 149 Lene Lovich: Lucky Number/New Toy
BUY 150 The Belle Stars: Iko Iko/The Reason
BUY 151 Brigit Novik & M: Danube/Neutron
BUY 152 Alvin Stardust: I Just Want You Back In My Life Again/I Just Want To Make Love To You
BUY 153 Madness: Driving In My Car/Animal Farm
BUY 154 Sylvia & The Sapphires: Shopping Around/Street Of Love
BUY 155 The Belle Stars: The Clapping Song/Blame
BUY 156 Albania: Could This Be Love/Little Baby
BUY 157 Viva Vagabond: Who Likes Jazz?/Jazz
BUY 158 The Freshies: Fasten Your Seatbelts/Best We Can Do
BUY 159 The Belle Stars: Mockingbird/Turn Back The Clock
BUY 160 Alvin Stardust: A Picture Of You/Hold Tight
BUY 161 The Electric Guitars: Beat Me Hollow/Ghengis Khan (7" Promo Only)
BUY 162 Sylvia & The Sapphires: Baby, I'm A Fool For You/Only Wish Tonight Could Last Forever
BUY 163 Madness: Our House/Walking With Mr Wheeze
BUY 164 Lene Lovich: It's You, Only You (Mein Schmerz)/Blue
BUY 165 Never released
BUY 166 Brigit Novik: The Wedding Dance/Abracadabra

BUY 167 The Belle Stars: Sign Of The Times/Madness
BUY 168 Tracey Ullman; Breakaway/Dancing In The Dark
BUY 169 Madness: Tomorrow's Just Another Day/Madness (Is All In The Mind)
BUY 170 Jona Lewie: Love Detonator/The Baby She's On The Street
BUY 171 Lene Lovich: Maria/Savages (never released)
BUY 172 The Tudors: Tied Up With Lou Cool/Cry Baby Cry
BUY 173 Evrol Campbell: Nearest To My Heart/Nearest To My Heart (instrumental)
BUY 174 The Belle Stars: Sweet Memory/April Fool
BUY 175 Language: We're Celebrating/Deaf Version
BUY 176 Yello: I Love You/Rubber West
BUY 177 Eddie Tenpole Tudor: The Hayrick Song/Take You To The Dance
BUY 178 Passion Puppets: Like Dust/House Of Love
BUY 179 The Sapphires: My Baby Must Be A Magician/Whenever You Want My Love
BUY 180 Tracey Ullman: They Don't Know/The B-side
BUY 181 Madness: Wings Of A Dove/Behind The 8-Ball
BUY 182 Alvin Stardust: Walk Away Renee/Victim of Romance
BUY 183 Jakko: Dangerous Dreams/Opening Doors
BUY 184 Gibson Brothers: My Heart's Beating Wild (Tic Tac Tic Tac)/Come Alive And Dance
BUY 185 The Belle Stars: Indian Summer/Sun Sun Sun
BUY 186 Desmond Dekker: Hot City/Moving On
BUY 187 The Belle Stars: The Entertainer/The Spider
BUY 188 Passion Puppets: Voices/Powder Monkeys
BUY 189 King Kurt: Destination Zululand/She's As Hairy
BUY 190 Kirsty MacColl: Terry/Quietly Alone
BUY 191 Yello: Lost Again/Base For Alec/Let Me Cry/She's Got A Gun
BUY 192 Madness: The Sun And The Rain/Fireball XL5
BUY 193 The Inspirational Choir Of The Pentecostal First Born Church Of The Living God: Pick Me Up/Do Not Pass Me By
BUY 194 Robert Sleigh: First Snow/Snow Bike
BUY 195 Tracey Ullman: Move Over Darling/You Broke My Heart In 17 Places
BUY 196 Madness: Michael Caine/If You Think There's Something
BUY 197 Tracey Ullman: My Guy's Mad At Me/Thinking Of Running Away
BUY 198 Jakko: Who's Fooling Who/A Grown Man Immersed In Tin Tin
BUY 199 King Kurt: Mack The Knife/Wreck-A-Party Rock
BUY 200 The Belle Stars: 80s Romance/It's Me
BUY 201 Madness: One Better Day/Guns
BUY 202 Personal Column: Strictly Confidential/Here's Looking At You
BUY 203 Passion Puppets: Beyond The Pale/Overland

BUY 204 Jamie Rae: She's The One/Sad Song
BUY 205 Tracey Ullman: Sunglasses/Candy
BUY 206 King Kurt: Banana Banana/Bo Diddley Goes East
BUY 207 The Pogues: Dark Streets Of London/And The Band Played
        Waltzing Matilda
BUY 208 Jakko: I Can't Stand This Pressure/Living On The Edge
BUY 209 The Catch: 25 Years/The End Of The Day
BUY 210 The Belle Stars: Crime Of Passion/Is This The Night? (never released)
BUY 211 Tracey Ullman: Helpless/Falling In And Out Of Love
BUY 212 The Pogues: The Boys From The County Hell/Repeal Of The
        Licensing Laws
BUY 213 Never released
BUY 214 Ian Dury & The Blockheads: Hit Me With Your Rhythm Stick/Sex
        & Drugs & Rock & Roll
BUY 215 Never released
BUY 216 Kirsty MacColl: New England/Patrick
BUY 217 Tracey Ullman: Terry/I Don't Want Our Loving To Die
BUY 218 Billy Connolly: Super Gran/Yootha's Song (with Ralph McTell)
BUY 219 Jamie Rae: Pretty One/Fairy Tales
BUY 220 The Pogues: A Pair Of Brown Eyes/Whiskey, You're The Devil
BUY 221 The Untouchables: Free Yourself/Lebanon
BUY 222 The Catch: Find The Love/Across The Great Divide
BUY 223 King Kurt: Billy/Back On The Dole
BUY 224 The Pogues: Sally MacLennane/The Wild Rover
BUY 225 Kirsty MacColl: He's On The Beach/Please Go To Sleep
BUY 226 Never released
BUY 227 The Untouchables: I Spy For The FBI/Whiplash
BUY 228 Never released
BUY 229 The Pogues: Dirty Old Town/A Pistol For Paddy Garcia
BUY 230 King Kurt: Road To Rack And Ruin/Poppa Wobbler
BUY 231 Bob Andrews: Love Theme From Romeo & Juliet/Bahamian Rhapsody
BUY 232 Tracey Ullman: Shattered/Alone (never released)
BUY 233 Phranc: Amazons/El Salvador
BUY 234 Andy White: Religious Persuasion/Rembrandt Hat
BUY 235 King Kurt: Slammers/Ape Hour
BUY 236 Never released
BUY 237 Theatre Of Hate: The Hop/Westworld (never released)
BUY 238 The Damned: New Rose/Neat Neat Neat (7" Promo Only / issued as
        12" BuyIT238)
BUY 239 Elvis Costello: Less Than Zero/Alison (never released)
BUY 240 The Untouchables: What's Gone Wrong?/The Lonely Bull
BUY 241 The Mint Juleps: Only Love Can Break Your Heart/Move In Closer

BUY 242 Bobby Tench: Still In Love With You/Heart Out Of Love

BUY 243 The Pogue: Poguetry In Motion EP: London Girl/A Rainy Night In Soho/The Body Of An American/Planxty Noel Hill

BUY 244 Never released

BUY 245 The Belle Stars: World Domination/Just A Minute

BUY 246 Dermot Morgan: Thank You Very Much Mr Eastwood (The Barry McGuigan Song)/Version

BUY 247 Phranc: The Lonesome Death Of Hattie Carroll/El Salvador

BUY 248 Fire Next Time: Beneath The Hammers/Chains

BUY 249 Rita Wolf: My Beautiful Launderette/Take One Look (never released)

BUY 250 Never released

BUY 251 Furniture: Brilliant Mind/To Gus

BUY 252 Andy Fairweather Low: Bossa Nova/House Of Blue Light

BUY 253 Dr. Feelgood: Don't Wait Up/Just A Minute

BUY 254 Furniture: Love Your Shoes/Turnupspeed

BUY 255 Dr. Feelgood: See You Later Alligator/I Love You So You're Mine

BUY 256 Tommy Chase: Killer Joe/Double Secret

BUY 257 Mint Juleps: Every Kinda People/Ain't Seen Nothing Yet

BUY 258 The Pogues & The Dubliners: The Irish Rover/The Rare Ould Mountain Dew

BUY 259 Dr. Feelgood: Hunting, Shooting, Fishing/Big Enough

BUY 260 Never released

BUY 261 Never released

BUY 262 Never released

BUY 263 The Mint Juleps: Girl To The Power Of Six/Set Me Free

BUY 264 The Mint Juleps: Docklands/ Docklands Extended Version (Released in 2013 as part of Buy 289) Under Pressure would have been B side in '86

BUY 265 The Enemy: 40 Days & 40 Nights/Dancing All Night

BUY 266 The Enemy: It's Not OK/Waste Your Life Away

BUY 267 The Enemy: Away From Here/A Message To You, Rudy (live)

BUY 268 Eskimo Disco: What Is Woman/What Is Woman (Fred Falke Man Enough Remix)

BUY 269 The Displacements: Frontline Hearts/You Don't Know Who Your Friends Are

BUY 270 The Producers: Barking Up The Right Tree/Freeway

BUY 271 Any Trouble: That Sound (digital download only)

BUY 272 Jona Lewie: Stop The Cavalry (digital download only) The Cory Band: Stop The Cavalry (digital download only)

BUY 273 The Displacements: Lazy Bones/Amie

BUY 274 F Lunaire: Quantum Physics In The Sink/Whites & Augustes/The System Of Objects/Tarantella (For Your Tarantism)

BUY 275 Chris Difford: Fat As A Fiddle (digital download only)
BUY 276 The Displacements: Down & Out/Pirates/Lady Loss
BUY 277 Wreckless Eric & Amy Rigby: Here Comes My Ship (digital download)
BUY 278 Henry Priestman: Don't You Love Me No More (digital download only)
BUY 279 Tenpole Tudor: Swords Of A Thousand Men (digital download only)
BUY 280 Jay Jay Pistolet: Happy Birthday You/Bags Of Gold/Hooked Up On Us/I Am Always On My Way Back Home
BUY 281 Henry Priestman: Grey Is The New Blonde (digital download only)
BUY 282 Ou Est Le Swimming Pool: Dance The Way I Feel (Young And Lost Mix) (digital download only)
BUY 283 Ou Est Le Swimming Pool: Dance The Way I Feel/Outside
BUY 284 Ou Est Le Swimming Pool: Dance The Way I Feel (Digital bundle, 4 mixes) (digital download only)
BUY 285 Tenpole Tudor: Swords Of A Thousand Men (digital download only)
BUY 286 Sam & The Womp!:
      Bom Bom (Wez Clarke Radio Edit) (digital download only)
      Bom Bom (Fear of Tigers Radio Edit) (digital download only)
      Bom Bom (Fear of Tigers Remix) (digital download only)
      Bom Bom (Wez Clarke Radio Instrumental) (digital download only)
BUY 287 Kirsty MacColl: A New England / I'm Going Out With An Eighty Year Old Millionaire (Record Store Day 7" Blue Vinyl)
BUY 288 Sam & The Womp!: Riva (digital download only)
BUY 289 Ten Big Stiffs Box Set (Record Store Day)
BUY 290 Tenpole Tudor: Swords Of A Thousand Men / Love And Food (7" Picture Disc) You could call it BUY 290

NON BUY Singles (in order of release)
SPE4504 The Rolling Stones: Cocksucker Blues pt.1 / Cocksucker Blues pt.1 (Xmas Promo Joke Trade Release)
LAST1 Nick Lowe: BOWI EP: Born A Woman / Shake The Rat / Mary Provost / Endless Sleep
LAST2 Alberto Y Lost Trios Paranoias: SNUFF ROCK EP: Kill / Gobbing On Life /Snuffin' Like That / Snuffin' In A Babylon
LAST3 Wreckless Eric: PICCADILLY MENIAL EP: Excuse Me, Personal Hygiene, Rags & Tatters, Piccadilly Menial (never released)
LAST4 Mick Farren & The Deviants: SCREWED UP EP: Outrageous Contageous / Let's Loot The Supermarket Like We Did Last Summer / Screwed Up / Shock Horror Probe Looming

Freeb2 Various Stiff Artists,

Excerpts From Stiffs Greatest Hits Freebie

A Side:

Track 1: One Chord Wonders - The Adverts

Track 2: Alison - Elvis Costello

Track 3: Red Shoes - Elvis Costello

Track 4: Whole wide world - Wreckless Eric

Track 5: Sex & Drugs & Rock & Roll - Ian Dury

Track 6 Problem Child - The Damned

Track 7: Suffice To Say - Yachts

B Side:

Track 1: Watching The Detectives - Elvis Costello

Track 2: Halfway To Paradise - Nick Lowe

Track 3: Police Car - Larry Wallis

Track 4: Sweet Gene Vincent - Ian Dury

Track 5: Don't Cry Wolf - The Damned

DEV1 Devo: Jocko Homo / Mongoloid

BOY1 Devo: (I Can't Get No) Satisfaction / Sloopy (I Saw My Baby Getting)

BOY2 Devo: Be Stiff / Social Fools

LEW1 Lew Lewis: Lucky Seven / Night Talk

LOT1 Johnnie Allen: Promised Land / Pete Fowler, One Heart One Song

OFF1 Subs: Gimme Your Heart / Party Clothes

OFF2 Ernie Graham: Romeo / Only Time Will Tell

OFF3 The Members: Solitary Confinement / Rat Up A Drainpipe

OFF4 The Realists: I've Got A Heart / Living In The City

UPP1 Mickey Jupp With Legend: My Typewriter / Nature's Radio

RUM1 The Rumour: Frozen Years / All Fall Down (Promo only)

             Listens To The Radio? / Step By Step / So Obvious / Suspicious Mind

BLO1 Wilko Johnson: Oh Lonesome Me / Beauty

HORN1 Davey Payne: Saxophone Man / Foggy Day In London Town

DEA/SUK1 Wayne Kramer: Ramblin' Rose / Get Some

RUM1 The Rumour: Frozen Years / All Fall Down (Promo Copy Only)

FEELIES FLEXI The Feelies,

A Side: Extracts from Crazy Rhythms *album*

Track 1: Fa Cé-La

Track 2: Raised Eyebrows

Track 3: Everybody's Got Something to Hide ...

           (Single sided flexi disc)

CLAP1 The Thunderbolts: Dust On Me Needle / Something Else

MAX1 Various Stiff Artists & Staff:

A Side: A souvenir to commemorate the wedding of Dave and Rosemary

           (part 1)

B Side: A souvenir to commemorate the wedding of Dave and Rosemary
(part 2)
BROKEN1 Dave Stewart: What Becomes Of The Broken Hearted / There Is
No Reward
PACK1 The Pack: Brand New Soldiers / Heathen
SSH1 Janet Armstrong: Two Hearts In Pain / Exploitation
SSH2 Tex Rubinowitz: Hot Rod Man / Ain't It Wrong
SSH3 Bubba Lou & The Highballs: Love All Over The Place, Over You
SSH4 Motor Boys Motor: Drive Friendly / Fast N' Bulbous
SSH5 Lonesome Tone: Mum, Dad, Love, Hate And Elvis / Ghost Town
LYN8680 Madness: *Patches* brings you a few minutes of madness (flexi disc)
Patches Magazine
DREAD1 Mickey Dread: Break Down The Walls / Wall Street Rock / The
Jumping Master / Master Mind
MIK1 Mickey Dread: Rockers Delight / African Map
MIK2 Mickey Dread: Break Down The Walls / Master Mind
SS3 Theatre Of Hate: Original Sin / Legion
BROKEN2 Dave Sterwart & Barbara Gaskin: It's My party / Waiting In The
wings
GRAB1 Madness: 6 Vinyl Grab Pack
One Step Beyond ... / Mistakes
My Girl / Stepping Into Line
Work Rest And Play E.P.
Baggy Trousers / The Business
Embarrassment / Crying Shame
The Return Of The Los Palmas 7 / That's The Way To Do It
GRAB2 The Damned: 4 Vinyl Grab Pack
New Rose / Help!
Neat Neat Neat / Singalonga Scabies
Problem Child / You Take My Money
Don't Cry Wolf / One Way Love
GRAB3 Elvis Costello: 4 Vinyl Grab Pack
Less Than Zero / Radio Sweetheart
Alison / Welcome To The Working Week
Red Shoes / Mystery Dance
Watching The Detectives / Blame It On Cain / Mystery Dance
EXP1 Explainer: Lorraine / Leave mih man
ODB1 The Snowmen: Hokey-cokey / Don't go short
SAVE 1 The Save The Children Fun Choir: The Finchley Childrens' Music
Group, Little Star / A Map Of Africa
WED1 Hon. Nick Jones & Ian Macrae: The Ballad Of Lady Di / 3 Minutes
Silence

GFR1 Mickey Jupp: Don't Talk To Me / Junk In My Trunk
LISP2006 Ben Gunn: Viva Scotland! / Scotland's Greatest (Spain '82)
LISP2007 Ian "Sludge" Lees: Viva England! / The Young Footballer (Spain '82)
LISP2008 Gene Fitzpatrick: Viva Ireland! / Bingham's back again (Spain '82)
WIN1 The Ensemble: Viva Scotland, Ireland, England! (Sensible Edit) / Viva
     Scotland, Ireland, England! (Silly Edit) (Spain '82)
BROKEN3 Dave Stewart & Barbara Gaskin: Johnny Rocco / The Hamburger
     Song
HID1 The Firm: Arthur Daley ('e's' alright) / Arthur Daley ('e's' alright) (posh
     version)
RAW1 The Chaps: Rawhide: Ghost Riders In The Sky / I Belong To Glasgow /
     Ghost Riders In The Sky
LYN11546 Madness: My Girl (Ballad) Mono / My Girl (Ballad) Stereo
BRR1 Theatre Of Hate: Rebel Without A Brain / My Own Invention
BRR2 Theatre Of Hate: Do You believe In The Westworld / Propaganda
BRR3 Theatre Of Hate: The Hop / Conquistador
LOT2 Woodhead Munroe: Identify / The Good Life
LOT3 Woodhead Munroe: Mumbo Jumbo / B Side
SOL1 The Children Of 7: Solidarity / Solid dub
FAT1 Plum: Too Much Ain't Enough (Fat Is Back) / Enough
HID3 The Firm: Long Live The National / London Is The Biz
LAD1 Sinfonia of London – Peter Auty: Walking In The Air / Dance Of The
     Snowmen
OLD1 The Veterans: There Ain't No Age For Rock 'n Roll / Logical Doggerel
GAR1 Maximum Joy: Why Can't We Live Together / Man Of Tribes
Pres1 Yes Let's: Carried Away / Closer To The Ground
LYN15222 Yes Let's: Carried Away
Pres2 Yes Let's: Unashamedly lovestruck / Trouble With You (No known
     collectors have this, it may not have been released)
BROKEN7 Dave Stewart & Barbra Gaskin: I'm In A Different World / Henry
     & James
DBS1 Zeitgeist: Freight train rain / Hill Country Theme
DAWN1 Dawn Chorus & The Bluetits: Teenage Kicks / Dream Lover
DAWN2 Dawn Chorus & The Bluetits: I'm Going Down / What's Wrong With
     Me?
CRAZY1 Crazy Albert: Yippeei-ay! / Trigger Happy
GOBS1 Snakes of Shake: Southern cross / You walk
PRES3 Rin Tin Tin: Shake It! / Brandy
STRY1 Stryper: Winter Wonderland / Reason For The Season
OE2 The Orson Family: The Sweetest Embrace / Subterranean Homesick
     Blues
7-The-1 Spectrum: All Or Nothing / All Or Nothing

KAT1 Ruefrex: The Wild Colonial Boy (Part 1) / The Wild Colonial Boy (Part 2)
KAS2 Ruefrex: The Wild Colonial Boy / Even In The Dark Hours
KAS3 Ruefrex: In The Traps / Lenders Of The Last Resort
WINTER1 The Winterbabies: Bossanova Suicide / Tidal Moves
VAIN1 Makin' Time: Here Is My Number / Nothing Else
VAIN1 Makin' Time: Feels Like It's love / Honey
GAZ1 Potato Five: Western Special / Big City
VAIN3 The Kick: Can't Let Go / Armchair Politician
VAIN4 The Prisoners: Whenever I'm Gone / Promised Land
VAIN5 Makin' Time: Pump It Up / Walk A Thin Line
BROKEN8 Dave Stewart & Barbara Gaskin: The Locomotion / Make Me
    Promises
GLIT1 Gary Glitter: Rock And Roll Part 3 / Rock And Roll Part 4
NY7 The Pogues featuring Kirsty MacColl: Fairytale Of New York / The
    Battle Of March Medley
FG1 The Pogues: If I Should Fall From Grace with God / Sally MacLennane
    (live)
FG2 The Pogues: Fiesta / Sketches Of Spain
HELL BLOOD 1 The Pogues: The Good, The Bad & The Ugly / Unknown (No
    known collectors have this, it may not have been released)

SEEZ Albums (in order of release)

Stiff Discography
SEEZ Albums
SEEZ 1, The Damned: *Damned Damned Damned*
SEEZ 2, Various Stiffs: *A Bunch Of Stiffs*
SEEZ 3, Elvis Costello: *My Aim Is True*
SEEZ 4, Ian Dury: *New Boots And Panties!!*
SEEZ 5, The Damned: *Music For Pleasure*
SEEZ 6, Wreckless Eric: *Wreckless Eric*
SEEZ 7, Lene Lovich: *Stateless*
SEEZ 8, Jona Lewie: *On The Other Hand Is A Fist*
SEEZ 9, Wreckless Eric: *The Wonderful World Of Wreckless Eric*
SEEZ 10, Mickey Jupp: *Juppanese*
SEEZ 11, Jane Aire & The Belvederes: *Jane Aire & The Belvederes* – Never
    released
SEEZ 12, Rachel Sweet: *Fool Around*
SEEZ 13, The Rumour: *Frogs Sprouts Clogs And Krauts*
SEEZ 14, Ian Dury & The Blockheads: *Do It Yourself*
SEEZ 15, The Sports,: *The Sports* – Never Released
SEEZ 16, Lew Lewis Reformer: Save the Wail
SEEZ 17, Madness: *One Step Beyond ...*

SEEZ 18, Rachel Sweet: *Protect the Innocent*
SEEZ 19, Lene Lovich: *Flex*
SEEZ 20, The Feelies: *Crazy Rhythm*
SEEZ 21, Wreckless Eric: *Big Smash*
SEEZ 22, Dirty Looks: *Dirty Looks*
SEEZ 23, Graham Parker & The Rumour: *The Up Escalator*
SEEZ 24, The Plasmatics: *New Hope For The Wretched*
SEEZ 25, Any Trouble: *Where Are All The Nice Girls*
SEEZ 26, Desmond Dekker: *Black & Dekker*
SEEZ 27, The Rumour: *Purity Of Essence*
SEEZ 28, Joe "King" Carrasco & The Crowns: *Joe King "Carrasco" & The
      Crowns*
SEEZ 29, Madness: *Absolutely*
SEEZ 30, Ian Dury & The Blockheads: *Laughter*
SEEZ 31, Tenpole Tudor: *Eddie, Old Bob, Dick & Gary*
SEEZ 32, Larry Wallis: *Leather Foreve*r – Never Released
SEEZ 33, Various: *Son Of Stiff* – Cancelled And Released As SON1
SEEZ 34, Lene Lovich: Cancelled And Released As SEEZ 44
SEEZ 35, The Equators: *Hot*
SEEZ 36, Desmond Dekker: *Compass Point*
SEEZ 37, Any Trouble: *Wheels in Motion*
SEEZ 38, Dirty Looks: *Turn It Up*
SEEZ 39, Madness: *7*
SEEZ 40, Jona Lewie: *Heart Skips Beat*
SEEZ 41, Ian Dury: *Juke Box Dury*
SEEZ 42, Tenpole Tudor*: Let The Four Winds Blow*
SEEZ 43, Never Released
SEEZ 44, Lene Lovich: *No Man's Land*
SEEZ 45, The Belle Stars: *The Belle Stars*
SEEZ 46, Madness: *Madness Presents The Rise And Fall*
SEEZ 47, Never Released
SEEZ 48, Yello: *You Gotta Say Yes To Another Excess*
SEEZ 49, Never Released
SEEZ 50, Never Released
SEEZ 51, Tracey Ullman: *You Broke My Heart In 17 Places*
SEEZ 52, King Kurt: *Ohh Wallah Wallah*
SEEZ 53, Madness: *Keep Moving*
SEEZ 54, Passion Puppets: *Beyond The Pale*
SEEZ 55, The Pogues: *Red Roses For Me*
SEEZ 56, Tracey Ullman: *You Caught Me Out*
SEEZ 57, The Untouchables: *Wild Child*
SEEZ 58, The Pogues: *Rum Sodomy And The Lash*

SEEZ 59, Tracey Ullman: *Forever (The Best Of)*
SEEZ 60, Phranc: *Folksinger*
SEEZ 61, The Roys: *Kicked Off The Train*
SEEZ 62, King Kurt: *Second Album*
SEEZ 63, Never Released
SEEZ 64, Furniture: The Wrong People
SEEZ 65, Dr Feelgood: *Brilleaux*
SEEZ 66, Tommy Chase: *Groove Merchant*
SEEZCD 67, Dr. Feelgood: *Classic* – UK CD Only
SEEZLCD 68, Tranzmitors: *Tranzmitors*
SEEZCD 69, Any Trouble: *Life In Reverse*
SEEZCD 70, The Producers: *The Producers* – Never Released
DSEEZ 71, Chris Difford: *I Didn't Get Where I Am* – Digital Release Only
SEEZCD 72, Chris Difford: *The Last Temptation Of Chris*
SEEZCD 73, Wreckless Eric & Amy Rigby: *Wreckless Eric & Amy Rigby*
SEEZCD 74, Henry Priestman: *The Chronicles Of Modern Life*

NON SEEZ Albums
FIST 1, Various Stiffs: *Hits Greatest Stiffs*
Get 1, Various Stiffs: *Live Stiffs Live*
Get 2, Mickey Jupp: *Legend*
Get 3, Various Stiffs: *Akron Compilation*
SOUNDS 3, Various Stiffs: Stiff Sounds Can't Start Dancin'
ODD 1, Devo: *Devo*
DEAL 1, Various Stiffs: *You're Extremely Lucky To Get This - You Probably Don't Deserve It* (Promo)
ODD 2, Various Stiffs: *Be Stiff Tour*
GOMM 1, Ian Gomm: *Ian Gomm "Talks"* (Export Only)
LENE 1, Lene Lovich: Lene Lovich *"Speaks"* (Export Only)
ABRA 1, Ronald Reagan: *The Wit And Wisdom Of Ronald Reagan*
SMUT 1, Dirty Looks: *Dirty Looks* (Promo Taster)
ERIC 1, Wreckless Eric: *Big Smash* (Promo Taster)
MAIL 1, U.K. Subs: *Live Kicks*
TRUBZ 1, Any Trouble: Live At The Venue
TNT 1, Mickey Dread: World War III
OAK 1, London Cast Of: *Oklahoma*
YANK 2, Various: *Declaration Of Independents*
FREEB 3, Various Stiffs: *Wonderful Time Out There*
TOH 1, Theatre Of Hate: *Westworld*
HITTV 1, Madness: *Complete Madness*
MAIL 2, The Damned: *Damned Damned / Music For Pleasure* (2LP)
Down 1, Makin' Time: *Rhythm And Soul*

JULP 1, Mint Juleps: *One Time*
KATLP 1, Ruefrex: *Flowers For Occasions*
DREW 1, Various; *The Countdown Compilation 54321 Go*
DREW 2, Various; *Countdownunder The Party At Hanging Rock*
DOWN 2, The Prisoners: In From The Cold
PETE 1, Blood On The Saddle: *Poisoned Love*
PROM 1, Various Stiffs: *I Gave Birth To An 18lb Rhino* (Promo)
GET 4, The Damned: *The Captains Birthday Party Live At The Roundhouse*
DIABLO 1, Various: *Straight To Hell*
NYR 1, The Pogues: *If I Should Fall From Grace With God*
(LP 3745107 / CD 3743894) Johnny Borrell, *Borrell 1*

Official Stiff Re-issue CD's (2007)
CDSEEZ 8, Jona Lewie: *On The Other Hand There's A Fist*
CDSEEZ 12, Rachel Sweet: *Fool Around*
CDSEEZ 13, Frogs: *Sprouts, Clogs And Krauts / Purity Of Essence*
CDSEEZ 21, Wreckless Eric: *Big Smash*
CDSEEZ 22, Dirty Looks: *Dirty Looks / Turn It Up*
CDSEEZ 25, Any Trouble: *Where Area All The Nice Girls?*
CDSEEZ 31, Tenpole Tudor: *Eddie, Old Bob, Dick & Gary / Let The Four Winds Blow*
CDSEEZ 51, Tracey Ullman: *You Broke My Heart In 17 Places*
CDSEEZ 57, The Untouchables: *Wild Child*

The Stiff Tours

1977 – Stiffs Greatest Stiffs
Elvis Costello, Nick Lowe, Ian Dury, Wreckless Eric, Larry Wallis

October
3 High Wycombe Town Hall
4 Aberystwyth University
6 Bristol University
7 Bath University
8 Loughborough University
9 Middlesbrough Town Hall
11 Liverpool Empire
13 Glasgow Apollo
14 Sheffield Polytechnic
15 Leeds University
16 Croydon, Fairfield Halls
17 Norwich, University of East Anglia
19 Brighton Top Rank
21 Salford University
22 Leicester University
24 Rochdale, Champness Hall
25 Birmingham Town Hall
26 Cardiff Top Rank
27 Wolverhampton Civic Hall
28 London, Lyceum Ballroom
31 Guildford Civic Hall

November
2 Friars, Aylesbury
3 Essex University
4 Newcastle Polytechnic
5 Lancaster University

1978 – Be Stiff Route 78
Wreckless Eric, Lene Lovich, Rachel Sweet, Jona Lewie, Mickey Jupp

October
10 Bristol University
11 Liverpool University
13 Birmingham, Aston University
14 Plymouth Polytechnic
16 Manchester UMIST
17 Lancaster University
19 Glasgow, Strathclyde University
20 Dingwall, Strathpeffer Spa Pavilion
21 Wick Assembly Hall
23 Aberdeen, Ruffles
24 Dundee University
25 Edinburgh, Clouds
26 Stirling University
28 Portrush, Chesters
29 Belfast, Queens University
30 Dublin, The Stardust

November
1 Hemel Hempstead Pavilion
2 Hull University
3 Huddersfield Polytechnic
4 Leeds University
5 Sheffield, Top Rank Suite
6 Salford University
7 Newcastle University
9 Warwick University
10 Loughborough University
11 Nottingham University
12 Blackburn, King George's Hall
13 Cardiff, Sophia Gardens
15 Bournemouth, Village Bowl
16 Oxford Polytechnic
17 Canterbury Odeon
18 Guildford, Surrey University
19 London, Lyceum Ballroom

December
17–20 The Bottom Line, New York

1980 – The Son Of Stiff Tour
Any Trouble, Tenpole Tudor, The Equators, Dirty Looks,
Joe "King" Carrasco And The Crowns

London, The Marquee (£1.50 per show or £4 for all five)

September
24 Any Trouble
25 Tenpole Tudor
26 The Equators
27 Dirty Looks
28 Jo "King" Carrasco And The Crowns

October
1 Leeds University
2 Cleethorpes, Winter Gardens
3 Norwich, University of East Anglia
4 Nottingham University
6 Bournemouth, Stateside
8 Birmingham, Romeo & Juliets
9 Bath University
10 Sheffield Polytechnic
11 Loughborough University
12 Liverpool, Rotters
15 Dublin, Trinity College
16 Belfast, Ulster Hall
17 Glasgow University
18 Newcastle University
19 Ayr Pavilion
20 Edinburgh, Tiffany's
22 Keele University
23 Coventry Poly
24 Manchester University
25 Bradford University
27 Plymouth, Fiesta
28 Exeter University
29 Southampton University
30 Guildford, Civic
31 London City University

November
1 London, Chelsea College
3 London, Queen Elizabeth College
4 London, Music Machine

Notes & Sources

1. Joe Boyd, *White Bicycles*
2. John Blaney, *A Howlin' Wind: Pub Rock And The Birth Of New Wave*
3. Pete Frame, *Zigzag Number 17, Despite It All: The Brinsley Schwarz Aftermath*
4. *Let it Rock,* April 1974
5. Interview with the author for *Hot Press* magazine article, The Greatest Record Company Stiff Ever! In The World ...16 December 1996
6. Interview with the author for *Sex & Drugs & Rock 'n' Roll: The Life Of Ian Dury*
7. BBC Four documentary, *Graham Parker: Don't Ask Me Questions*, 2013
8. Elvis Costello interview with Greil Marcus, *Rolling Stone*, 2 September 1982
9. Chilli Willi & The Red Hot Peppers CD booklet
10. Cal Worthington, *ZigZag,* June 1976
11. www.classicrockrevisited.com interview with Greg Kihn
12. BBC Four documentary *If It Ain't Stiff*, May 2007
13. Chas De Whalley, Stiff: a label for hard-up heroes, *Sounds*, August 1976
14. Geoff Brown, Stiff upper lip, *Melody Maker,* 14 August, 1976
15. Ten Big Stiffs video, *World's Most Flexible Label*, Stiff Records, October 2103
16. Sean Tyla, *Jumpin' In The Fire*
17. Jon Savage, *The England's Dreaming Tapes*
18. Martin Ashton, *Q*, December 1995
19. Johnny Black, Destination Nowhere, *Mojo,* December 1996
20. Fran Burgess, Who Says? www.npland.co.uk
21. Elvis Costello liner notes for Rhino's 2001 re-release of *My Aim Is True*
22. Elvis Costello interview with Stuart Maconie, *Q* in June 2006
23. Elvis Costello, *My Aim Is True* CD sleeve notes (1993 issue)
24. Interview with Elvis Costello by Dave Schulps, *Trouser Press*, December 1977
25. Elvis Costello interview with Allan Jones, *Melody Maker* 25 June 1977
26. BBC Radio One documentary, 29 February 1991
27. Elvis Costello tribute to John Ciambiotti, www.elviscostello.com, March 2010

28. Stiff Steps Back Into The Future, *Sounds*, 25 June 1977.
29. Allan Jones, A Day In The Life Of A Bunch Of Stiffs, *Melody Maker*, 6 August 1977
30. Elvis Costello interview, *NME*, 25 March 1978
31. Carol Clerk, *The Book Of The Damned: The Light At The End Of The Tunnel*
32. Sleeve notes to *Reasons To Be Cheerful* compilation CD released in 1996, written by Chris Welch.
33. *Lewiston Daily Sun*, 12 September 1979
34. Bert Muirhead, *Stiff: The Story Of A Record Label.*
35. Max Bell, *NME* 28 October 1978
36. Jade Dellinger and David Giffels, *We Are DEVO!*
37. Ian Peel, *The Big Stiff Box Set*
38. *Record Business*, date unknown
39. The Ascent of Madness - www.madness.co.uk
40. Stiff Breezes On, *Radio and Record News*, date unknown
41. Karen O'Brien, *Kirsty MacColl: The One And Only*
42. Promotional video for US-only Ten Big Stiffs box-set released in 2013
43. Interview with Harlan Frey www.celebrityaccess.com
44. Belinda Carlisle, *Lips Unsealed*
45. Ian Peel, *The Big Stiff Book*
46. David Hepworth, *The Face*, Issue 7, November 1980
47. Pierre Perrone, *The Independent*, 15 September 2006
48. Pete Waterman, *I Wish I Was Me*
49. Suggs, *That Close*
50. *Billboard*, 13 September 1986
51. *Billboard*, 4 September 1993
52. *Daily Mail*,19 September 2000
53. Kirsty – The Life And Songs Of Kirsty MacColl, BBC 2 documentary
54. Carol Clerk, *The Story Of The Pogues*
55. *Billboard*, 27 September 1986
56. James Fearnley, *Here Comes Everybody: The Story Of The Pogues*

Other books
Will Birch, *No Sleep Til Canvey Island*
David Cooper, *Stiff Records - A Comprehensive Guide To Collecting The Label*
George Gimarc, Pu*nk Diary 1970-1979*
Paul Gorman, *Reasons To Be Cheerful: The Life And Work Of Barney Bubbles*
Eric Goulden, *A Dysfunctional Success*
Guinness British Hit Singles, 12th edition
Mark J. Prendergast, *Irish Rock: Roots, Personalities, Directions*

Mick St. Michael, *Elvis Costello*
*Graeme Thomson: Complicated Shadows: The Life And Music Of Elvis
    Costello*
The Q Book Of Punk Legends
Keep On Running, The Story of Island Records

Online and other sources
davebarb.demon.co.uk
be stiff.co.uk
buythehour.se/stiff
eannabrophy.blogspot.co.uk
stiffallstars.com
irishrock.org
irishshowbands.net
elviscostello.com
elviscostello.info/
alice bag.com
furious.com
officialcharts.com/archive-chart
ltmrecordings.com

When Albums Ruled The World, *BBC Four*, first broadcast 8 February, 2013
Stiff's Greatest Stiffs, article by Will Birch, *Mojo* October 1997

Index

—

7 (album) 259–263

Absolutely 232, 234, 261
Advancedale Ltd 33, 80, 83, 90, 110, 117
Adverts, The 71–75, 291
Aire, Jane 153, 155, 160, 178, 180, 206
Akron Compilation, The 154, 155, 157, 311
Alexander Street offices 34, 35, 37, 38, 41, 48, 56, 76, 78, 79, 80, 83, 84, 86, 91, 95, 98, 100–103, 111, 115–118, 120, 121, 141, 142, 158, 163, 189, 195, 200, 215, 241, 244
"Alison" 84, 87, 95
Anarchy Tour 59, 60, 74
Any Trouble 216, 221–224, 228, 255, 256, 309, 311
Armstrong, Roger 37, 61, 65, 66

"B-A-B-Y" 158, 170, 172, 202, 203, 217
Backstage Pass 69, 70, 71, 100, 129, 212
"Baggy Trousers" 231–233, 235
Barker, Edward 43, 44
Bayham Street offices 264, 269, 273, 274, 276, 281
"Be Stiff" 149, 152
Be Stiff Route 78 Tour 165–169, 171, 172, 175, 177, 191, 202, 203
Bedford, Mark (Bedders) 192, 196, 197, 277, 285

Belle Stars, The 259, 260, 269–271, 291, 300, 301, 303
Beserkley Records 29, 30, 86, 120
Birch, Will 114, 158, 167, 254, 305
"Bird Song" 200, 204
Blackhill Enterprises 35, 124, 175, 184, 186, 241
Blackwell, Chris 85, 141, 149, 189, 254, 260, 280, 281, 299, 300
"Blank Generation" 58, 59, 61, 62
"Bom Bom" 311
Branson, Richard 119, 150, 151, 281, 286
Bright, Bette 212, 262
Brilleaux, Lee 27, 30, 33, 48, 108, 303
Brinsley Schwarz 6–16,18, 19, 20–23, 26, 29, 32, 40, 45, 80, 83, 104, 119, 127, 158, 181, 182
Brown, Dez 87, 131–133
Bubbles, Barney 21, 23, 24, 62, 63, 72, 93, 95, 100, 101, 111, 119, 124, 135, 139, 174, 175, 185
Bunch Of Stiffs, A 110, 111
"Butcher Baby" 209, 210

"Cardiac Arrest" 263
Carrasco, Joe 'King' 217, 220, 224
Carroll, Ted 37, 65, 191
Casale, Jerry 146, 147, 149, 152
CBS/Columbia Records 23, 24, 26, 65, 94, 96, 118, 119, 180, 181, 200, 205, 207, 216, 284
Chappell, Les 159–161, 177, 204, 265, 267

Chilli Willi 16, 20–26, 36, 41, 43, 47, 88, 89, 98

Chiswick Records 37, 38, 40, 51, 66, 111, 191, 220, 286, 294

Clash, The 51, 53, 59, 61, 84, 91, 99, 140, 214, 260

Clover 9, 80–82, 90-92, 99, 123

Colson, Glen 25, 67, 86, 87, 92, 97, 119, 121–123

Conroy, Paul 98–100, 114, 116-118, 127, 138, 140, 141, 152, 154, 163, 166–177, 178, 192, 221, 243, 250, 252, 276, 302, 306, 308

Costello, Elvis 5, 10, 15, 17–19, 48, 60, 71, 76–98, 101, 102, 106, 107, 110, 114, 115, 117–123, 125–131, 135, 136, 138, 141, 142, 145, 160, 162, 164, 169, 170, 174, 184, 190, 192, 193, 196, 207, 213, 214, 241, 255, 257, 289, 290, 295–297, 300, 305, 306

Cowderoy, Alan 99–101, 113, 117, 141, 168, 177, 190, 192, 250, 281, 300

Crippen, Dick 219, 224, 225

Damned Damned Damned 57, 61, 63, 64, 67, 74, 85, 118

Damned, The 48, 50–57, 59–74, 80, 86, 88, 98, 100, 101, 103, 106–108, 117–119, 136–142, 179, 199, 203, 291

Davis, Clive 142, 143, 148, 214

Dekker, Desmond 199, 200, 216, 254, 255, 309

Department S 257–259

Devo 51, 146-154

Dick, Nigel 145, 155, 177, 186, 191, 199, 208, 210, 211, 221, 243, 245, 253, 277, 307, 311, 312

Dirty Looks 211, 217, 223, 255, 309

Do It Yourself 181, 184–187

Dr Feelgood 16, 23–27, 29, 33, 40, 41, 42, 49, 58, 67, 69, 71, 88, 164, 165, 303, 305

Ducks Deluxe 16, 26, 25, 46, 47, 53, 104

Dury, Ian 13–16, 19, 25, 31, 34, 35, 60, 104, 105, 108–113, 115–128, 131, 136, 142–145, 166, 169, 170, 173–175, 180, 181, 184–187, 190, 193, 196, 201, 204, 216, 217, 227, 238–242, 253, 260, 263, 279, 300, 306

Eddie & The Hot Rods 40, 48, 52, 64, 85, 108, 132, 133

Edmunds, Dave 41, 75, 79, 80, 102, 108, 110, 121, 126, 127, 130–134, 137, 283

Eggs Over Easy 9, 10, 36, 45

Eire Apparent 4, 5, 11

Elcotgrange Ltd 34, 201, 302, 303

"Embarrassment" 206, 232, 234

Equators, The 217, 220, 222, 255

Farmer, Barry (Bazza) 39, 63, 80, 82, 106

Flex 204, 205, 265

Flip City 18, 19, 32, 77, 88

Fool Around 158, 166, 167, 181, 203, 309

Foreman, Chris (Chrissy Boy) 192, 193, 194, 195, 197, 198, 231, 233, 260, 261, 262, 263, 277, 278, 284

Frankie Goes To Hollywood 282, 293

Frey, Allen 207, 208

Fulcher, Colin *see* Barney Bubbles

Gabrin, Chris 95, 123, 185

Gardiner, Pete 309–311

Gaskin, Barbara 249–254

Geller, Greg 93–94

Gillett, Charlie 12–14, 16, 40, 77, 78, 160, 161, 163, 173, 213
Go-Go's, The 69, 212, 232, 359
Gomm, Ian 9, 29, 80, 181, 182, 216, 222
Goulden, Eric *see* Wreckless Eric
Grainger, Fred 14, 15, 17
Gregson, Clive 221, 222, 223, 255, 256

Hart, Fay 129
"Heart Of The City" 36, 37, 39, 41, 42, 48, 104
Hell, Richard 53, 58, 59, 61, 62, 69, 291
Hendrix, Jimi 4, 5, 31, 44
Herbage, Mike 257–258
"Hit Me With Your Rhythm Stick" 173–175, 181, 184, 186, 201, 227, 239, 240
Hits Greatest Stiffs 111, 132
"Hokey Cokey" 253
Hope & Anchor, The 14–17, 19, 31, 32, 39, 46, 56, 78, 79, 183, 194, 197
Horn, Trevor 280, 282, 309, 310, 311, 312, 313
"House Of Fun" 263, 277, 311
Hynde, Chrissie 51, 92, 133, 219, 245

Invaders 262, 194, 262
Island Records 40, 48, 57, 58, 63, 64, 71, 84–87, 101, 102, 118, 141, 149, 189, 190, 205, 207, 280–283, 285, 286, 296, 299, 300, 306
"Israelites" 199, 200, 254
"It Must Be Love" 262, 277
"It's My Party" 249, 251

Jakszyk, Jakko 7, 272–274, 287–289, 291

James, Brian 51–55, 63–65, 68, 70, 72, 136–138, 140
Jankel, Chaz 109, 123, 124, 142, 186, 187, 238
Jenner, Peter 35, 98, 99, 122, 124, 127, 185, 241
"Jocko Homo" 148–150, 152, 154
Johnson, Wilko 26, 27, 33, 44, 238
Jupp, Mickey 164, 165, 170–172
Juppanese 165, 167

Kaufman, Matthew 30, 86
Kihn, Greg 30
Kilburn & The High Roads 13, 14, 26, 34, 43, 104, 109, 111, 123, 174, 193
King, Andrew 35, 98, 122, 124, 127, 142, 143, 184–186, 238, 240, 241
Kirkland, Bruce 216
Kokomo 23–25
Knowles, "Knocker" 86, 190

Lauder, Andrew 24, 40, 47, 57, 66, 117, 141, 257
Laughter 238–240
"Less Than Zero" 82, 83, 95, 110, 111
Lewie, Jona 162–165, 167, 172, 181, 216, 227–230, 247, 251, 264, 267, 309, 312
Lewis, Bob 146–148, 150–153
Lewis, Huey 80, 82, 103
Lewis, Lew 48, 49, 57, 108, 165, 232
London Invaders *see* Invaders
Lovich, Lene 44, 158–162, 165, 169, 171, 172, 176, 177, 180, 181, 183, 191, 200, 201, 204, 216, 217, 227, 228, 232, 235, 236, 251, 264–267, 308, 310
Lowe, Nick 6, 7, 10–13, 15–20, 28–31, 33, 36, 39–41, 44, 45, 47, 48, 53, 54, 57, 63, 64, 79, 80, 94, 102-108, 110, 117–120, 122, 126–128,

130, 132–136, 138, 141, 142, 145, 160, 163–165, 169, 174, 183, 184, 190, 193, 241, 257, 291
"Lucky Number" 160, 171, 176, 177, 183, 200, 205, 265

MacColl, Kirsty 38, 178–180, 205, 227, 229, 275, 286–290, 297, 299, 304, 305, 309
MacGowan, Shane 291–295, 297, 304–305
Madness 192–201, 206, 212, 217, 220, 227, 231, 234, 235, 248, 249, 253, 254, 259–264, 267, 273, 274, 276–279, 283, 284, 288, 294, 306, 311
Marley, Bob 85, 280, 282, 283
Martin, Anne see Bright, Bette
Matthias, Jenny 260
McCartney, Paul 10–12, 36, 45
McDonald, Andy 287, 290, 308
McLaren, Malcolm 50–52, 55, 59–61, 140, 218, 247
McPherson, Graham (Suggs) 194, 196, 212, 232, 233, 234, 249, 262
Morley, Paul 211, 212, 280
Morris, Keith 33, 95
Morton, Chris 62, 101, 154, 155, 175, 245, 246
Motörhead 42, 43, 61
Murray, Andy 167–170, 177, 182, 188, 191, 238, 241, 306, 308
Music For Pleasure 137, 139, 140
My Aim Is True 81, 84, 87, 92, 94–97, 100, 101, 112, 123, 141, 142, 200, 216
"My Girl" 192, 197, 206, 219, 235, 283

Naughty Rhythms Tour 15, 23–26, 98, 115
"Neat Neat Neat" 58, 61, 63

Nelki, Gordon 14, 160
New Boots And Panties!! 113, 122–125, 134, 141, 142, 144, 145, 184–187, 229, 240, 263
New Hope For The Wretched 209, 210
"New Rose" 54, 55, 57, 59, 61, 65, 199, 203
Nieve, Steve 89, 114, 129, 135
"Night Boat To Cairo" 206, 231, 232, 235

O'Riordan, Cait 292, 293, 305
"One Better Day" 284
On The Other Hand There's A Fist 167, 267
"One Chord Wonders" 72, 73
One Step Beyond (album) 198, 231, 234
"One Step Beyond" (track) 198, 199, 201

Parker, Graham 10, 15–17, 19, 31–33, 47, 56, 67, 75, 77, 78, 80, 83, 84, 89, 90, 93, 99, 108, 110, 120, 144, 157, 162, 182, 183, 190, 192, 203, 207, 213–16, 235, 245
Pathway Studio 38, 39, 59, 80, 81, 90, 106, 114, 132, 133, 138
Payne, Davey 115, 124, 126, 157, 172, 239, 240, 275
Peckham, Porky 37, 63, 83, 111, 135, 155
Peel, John 44, 49, 74, 98, 112, 177, 221, 227, 293
Pink Fairies 21, 42, 43, 53, 57, 127, 131, 132, 291
Pitts, Annie 179, 245, 288,
Plasmatics, The 208–211, 216, 311
Plummet Airlines 61
Pogues, The 38, 61, 290–299, 304, 305

"Police Car" 132, 133
Priestman, Henry 113, 114, 311
Protect The Innocent 202, 203

Radar Records 117, 120, 122, 128,
   141, 142, 174, 191, 197
Rae, Sonnie 223, 227, 228, 230, 233,
   253, 265, 296
"Reasons To Be Cheerful (Part 3)"
   187, 188, 201, 239
Records, The 166, 167
"Red Shoes (The Angels Wanna
   Wear My)" 90, 93, 102
Reed, Lou 142, 143
Richman, Jonathan 27, 29, 30, 111
Riviera, Jake
 – Pre-Stiff 1, 15, 19-33
 – Partnership 34–38, 39–45, 47–51,
   53, 56–58, 61, 62, 64–72, 78–80,
   82, 83, 85, 86, 88, 90, 92, 95–101,
   103–108, 110, 115, 116
 – Post Stiff 117–120, 127–137, 139–
   141, 160, 162, 163, 166, 174, 175,
   180, 188, 190, 192, 257, 307, 312
Robinson, Dave
 – Pre-Stiff 1–17, 19, 21, 22, 29,
   31–33
 – Partnership 34–37, 39, 43, 46–49,
   51, 56, 57, 64, 65, 67, 71, 72, 74,
   77–80, 83, 90, 97–101, 105, 106,
   108, 110, 113, 115, 116
 – Sole Ownership 117–120, 124,
   127, 128, 135, 136, 139–141, 143,
   148, 149, 152, 155, 157, 160,
   161, 163–166, 168–173, 175, 176,
   179–186, 188–193, 195–199, 205–
   207, 211–217, 219–222, 224, 226,
   227, 229–233, 237, 241, 242, 244,
   246, 248, 250–256, 259, 261–263,
   265–271, 273, 279
 – Island Involvement 280–289,
   294–300, 302–304, 307, 312

Roogalator 43–45, 53, 57, 114, 204
Rowe, Fred 108–110, 115, 116, 128,
   143, 174, 175, 185
Roudette, Denise 108–110, 115, 126,
   238
Rough Trade 113, 250, 252
Roxy, The 71, 72, 291

Sam And The Womp 311
St Peter's Square 281, 283, 286–289,
   294, 296
"Satisfaction" 149, 151, 152
Scabies, Rat 50–52, 54, 56, 57, 63,
   65–70, 137–140
Scot, Jock 189, 190
Sensible, Captain 53, 54, 63, 70, 91,
   137, 140
"Sex & Drugs & Rock & Roll" 112,
   113, 126, 134, 136, 144
Sex Pistols 50, 51, 53, 55, 59–61, 84,
   91, 109, 140, 200, 213, 218, 291,
   293
Shone, Lesley 259, 270, 271, 300,
   301
"Sign Of The Times" 270, 274
Sinclair, Jill 303, 303, 306, 309
Sire Records 59, 162, 196, 198, 216
"So It Goes" 36, 37, 39–41, 100
Son Of Stiff Tour 216–218, 220–225,
   235, 247, 255, 264, 267
Snowmen, The 253
Spiro, Suzanne 80, 106
Stateless 161, 167, 171, 176, 177,
   181, 204, 205
Sternberg, Liam 143, 144, 153–155,
   157, 158, 167, 178, 179, 191, 203
Stewart, Dave 244, 249–254, 272,
   273
Stiff's Greatest Stiffs Tour 115,
   121–123, 125, 136, 141, 165, 169,
   189
Stone, Martin 20, 21, 110, 162

"Stop The Cavalry" 229, 230, 267
Suggs *see* McPherson, Graham
Sweet, Rachel 156-158, 165,
    168–171, 178, 180, 181, 190, 192,
    201–204, 217, 228, 309, 311
"Swords Of A Thousand Men" 246,
    248, 312

Take It Or Leave It (movie) 261, 262,
    264
Tally Ho, The 10, 13, 14, 20, 193
"They Don't Know" 178, 275, 286,
    287, 289, 290
Thomas, Bruce 80, 89, 91, 102, 126,
    129, 130, 189
Thomas, Pete 22, 23, 25, 70, 88–91,
    100, 120, 126, 129–134, 136
Thomas, Philippa 8, 100, 101, 120,
    121, 152, 166, 171
Toulouse, Vaughn 258–259
Travis, Dave Lee 144, 174, 229, 250
Travis, Geoff 250
Tudor Pole, Edward 217–220,
    223–225, 246–248, 267–269, 309,
    311, 312
Two Tone Records 194–199, 206,
    220, 254, 259, 260, 284
Tyla, Sean 45–48, 53, 56, 57, 61, 79,
    108, 110, 120, 133, 165

UA Records 40, 47, 48, 57, 66, 120
Ullman, Tracey 274, 276, 283,
    287–291, 309, 311
Up Escalator, The 215, 235

Vanian, Dave 52, 54, 67, 70, 101,
    138

Vinyl, Kosmo 87, 122, 127, 130, 131,
    142–144, 166, 184, 185, 188

Wall, Max 111, 164, 202, 231
Wallis, Larry 42, 43, 53, 72, 110,
    115, 117, 122, 126, 127, 130–133,
    241
"Watching The Detectives" 135
Waterman, Pete 269–271, 274, 275
"What A Waste" 144
"Where Are All The Nice Girls?" 222,
    223, 309
"Whole Wide World" 103, 105, 107,
    110, 112, 134, 169, 236, 237
"Wings Of A Dove" 278, 283
Williams, Wendy O 208–211
Wingate, Dick 94, 181
*Wit And Wisdom Of Ronald Reagan,
    The* 225
*Wonderful World Of Wreckless Eric,
    The* 167, 171
Woodfield Road offices 201, 244, 245
Wreckless Eric 102–113, 115, 117–
    120, 122, 125–127, 131, 145, 165,
    169–171, 181, 191, 201, 202, 204,
    208, 217, 226, 227, 232, 236–238,
    241, 291, 309, 311
"Wünderbar" 247, 248

Yachts, The 113, 114, 118, 119, 311
Yello 272
Yentikoff, Walter 94
"You'll Always Find Me In The
    Kitchen At Parties" 228, 229, 235,
    267, 312

ZTT 280, 282, 299, 312

About The Author

Richard Balls was a news journalist for 20 years and now works in communications. At 14 years old, he went to his first gig – Madness supported by The Belle Stars – an event that sparked a lifelong love of Stiff Records. His acclaimed first book, *Sex & Drugs & Rock 'N' Roll: The Life Of Ian Dury*, was published in 2000 by Omnibus Press. He spent three years researching and writing *Be Stiff*, interviewing more than 50 people along the way. Richard lives in Norwich with his wife Anne, daughters Katherine and Jessie, two cats and a dog.

Also Published By Soundcheck Books

A Howlin' Wind: Pub Rock And The Birth Of New Wave
by John Blaney
Paperback: ISBN: 9780956642042 £14.99
Kindle: ISBN: 9780957570092   £6.11

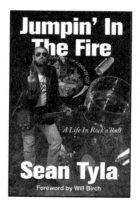

Jumpin' in The Fire: A Life In Rock 'n' Roll
by Sean Tyla
Paperback:ISBN: 9780956642004   £14.99
Kindle: ISBN: 9780957144217   £6.60

www.soundcheckbooks.co.uk